Boundaries of Belonging

EARLY AMERICAN STUDIES

Series editors: Kathleen M. Brown, Roquinaldo Ferreira, Emma Hart, and Daniel K. Richter

Exploring neglected aspects of our colonial, revolutionary, and early national history and culture, Early American Studies reinterprets familiar themes and events in fresh ways. Interdisciplinary in character, and with a special emphasis on the period from about 1600 to 1850, the series is published in partnership with the McNeil Center for Early American Studies.

A complete list of books in the series is available from the publisher.

Boundaries of Belonging

English Jamaica and the Spanish Caribbean, 1655–1715

April Lee Hatfield

PENN

UNIVERSITY OF PENNSYLVANIA PRESS

PHILADELPHIA

Published by
University of Pennsylvania Press
Philadelphia, Pennsylvania 19104-4112
www.upenn.edu/pennpress

Printed in the United States of America on acid-free paper
10 9 8 7 6 5 4 3 2 1

Hardcover ISBN: 978-1-5128-2401-8
eBook ISBN: 978-1-5128-2402-5

A catalogue record for this book is available from the Library of Congress.

For my parents, Craig Bond Hatfield
and Nancy Lee Clark Hatfield

CONTENTS

MAPS

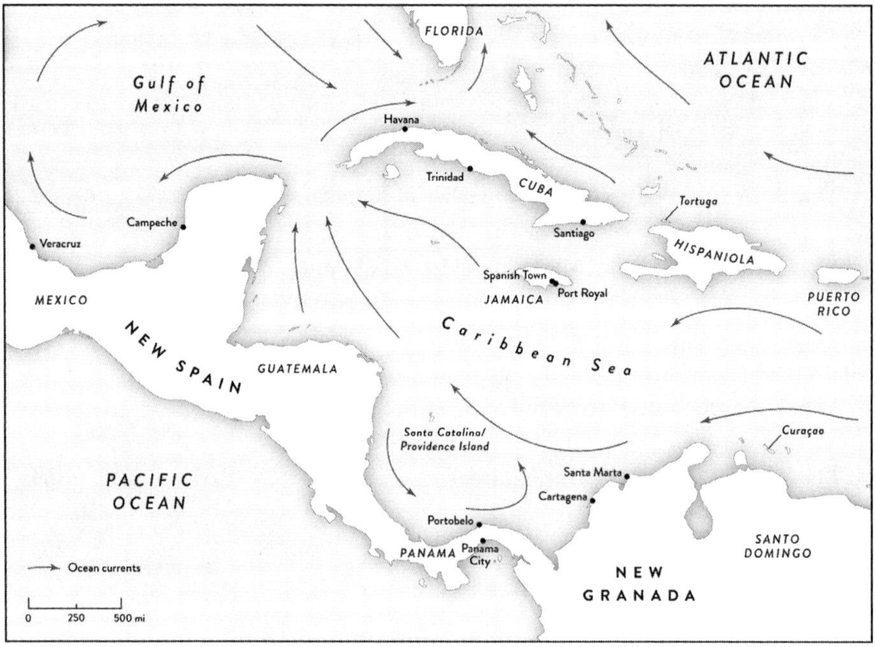

Map 1. *The Western Caribbean*. Drawn by Erin Greb.

Introduction

"In the Midst of the Spaniards"

When English forces conquered Spanish Jamaica in 1655, they acquired an island in the midst of the Spanish Caribbean. From Jamaica they could access the official imperial ports of Cartagena, Portobelo, Vera Cruz, and Havana as well as many other coastal towns, such as Santa Marta, Trinidad, Santiago de Cuba, and Campeche. The English understood well that Jamaica's location would aid further predation on the Spanish, but they also quickly realized that the island provided access to Spanish wealth via commerce. As the "navell (as the Spanyards call it) of the Indies," according to Jamaica governor Thomas Modyford, Jamaica could serve as a base for trading enslaved Africans and English textiles to Spanish colonists in exchange for silver. Jamaica would be a magnet, drawing the commerce of the Spaniards and other traders in the vicinity, who would "finde themselves to[o] strongly held" to resist the pull of "that noble Center."[1] This belief that Jamaica's value rested on its proximity to Spanish America persisted beyond the island's initial conquest. In 1672 the cartographer Richard Blome observed that its importance to King Charles derived from its being "seated in the heart of the Spaniards American Territories."[2] And in 1681, Jamaica's deputy governor recommended currying favor with local Spanish officials by offering naval convoys to protect Spanish American slave traders. Jamaica's situation "in the very centre of the American seas" would facilitate the project.[3] Its proximity to the Isthmus of Panama was especially important. There, enslaved Africans crossed from the Caribbean to the Pacific, and the silver they mined returned, to be shipped to Europe.

Proximity to so many Spanish American port towns and coastal settlements reflected a more general Caribbean reality: over one hundred habitable

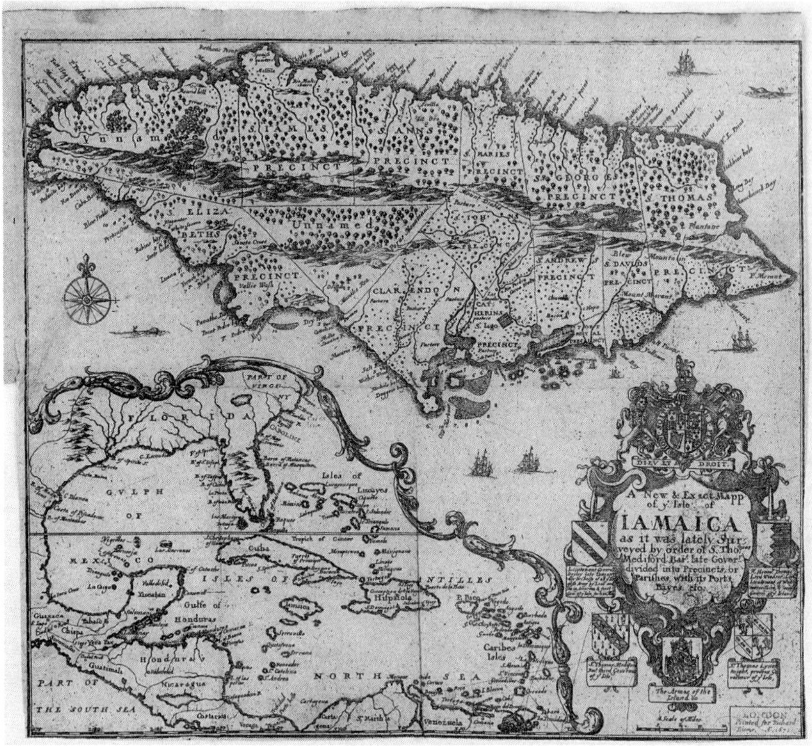

Map 2. *A New & Exact Mapp of ye Isle of Iamaca* underscores Jamaica's location in the center of the Spanish Caribbean. Printed for Richard Blome, 1671. Courtesy of the John Carter Brown Library.

islands lie close to one another and to the surrounding mainlands. By the second half of the seventeenth century, Spanish, English, Dutch, French, Carib, Tule, Maroon, Scottish, and Danish jurisdictional claims ran up against and sometimes overlay one another, with disputed or common maritime space between islands. A great variety of people journeyed among these islands and the surrounding mainlands, some by choice, some under duress, and some with no choice at all. Traveling sometimes only very short distances, they crossed political, linguistic, and cultural borders. In the process, many tried to redefine themselves or found themselves redefined by others, because different Caribbean societies construed political belonging—and related rights and privileges—in different ways. When the people of the region strove to define categories of belonging, they knew that other possibilities lay just over the mountains or within a day's canoe trip. This archipelago of overlapping and entangled borders, together with its multinational, multilingual, multireligious, and mobile populations, led people in the Caribbean to declare their inclusion within particular communities and to challenge beliefs about where people belonged and why.

The people who lived and sojourned at the Caribbean borders of English and Spanish empire between 1655 and 1715 understood themselves to live within multiple circles of inclusion, with the result that they possessed expansive and flexible definitions of belonging. They claimed membership in groups that ranged from local to global: they identified themselves by place of birth or residency (from household to town to nation), by religious adherence, by race, by loyalty to or acceptance within a polity such as an empire, by nonstate affiliation (such as pirate crews), by membership in a trading company, or by a universal humanity that placed them under the oversight and protection of the law of nature or of nations. Local, religious, and other corporate memberships mattered deeply to many individuals, and individuals made clear that they recognized multiple sources of identity. Each of those sources of belonging helped constitute or disqualify membership in a colonial body politic attached to a European empire. While some people rejected the specific empire or empires that claimed them, or rejected imperial conceits altogether, colonialism ultimately shaped the region, and its denizens understood that. Their birth towns and religious adherence meant something in part because they signaled imperial subjecthood. Border crossings and efforts to police such crossings mattered because imperial officials sought to exercise authority over both territory and people. This book's central question—how imperial definitions of who belonged to the body politic evolved—is grounded in this ongoing tension between local and imperial definitions of belonging.

As a result, the voices of local officials as well as Caribbean denizens loom large in this book.[4] In both the English and Spanish Atlantic empires, colonial governors played a key role in translating imperial goals to colonial settings and communicating colonial realities to metropolitan administrators. Caribbean officials tried to reconcile European-derived definitions of political belonging with colonial societies that included new levels of human diversity and mobility and a profoundly international context. The decisions they made remain important because we continue to live with the influence of early modern imperial definitions of belonging and boundary marking that emerged so visibly in the Caribbean.[5]

The majority of people who crossed borders in the colonial Caribbean did so against their wills, as African and Indigenous captives sold by Portuguese, Dutch, English, Genoese, French, or Native slave traders to purchasers throughout the region. To many of them, with slight chance of escape, it likely mattered little how religion or race fit into competing Caribbean expressions of imperial bodies politic. They figured in all colonial bodies politic, whatever the empire, as unfree laborers under the control of the masters who legally owned them. In imperial reckoning, enslaved men and women were property, not people with legal identities or souls but producers of wealth and commodities themselves. Caribbean plantation labor was brutal for the enslaved, no matter the enslavers or their laws and theories.

But it was precisely that shared plantation political economy that spurred the development of a competitive regional slave trade, which in turn created conditions for frequent border crossing. And such border crossing allowed the widespread dissemination of information and impressions about how Caribbean colonies, despite their shared commitment to slave-based economies, might also offer different people membership using distinct criteria for belonging.[6] Caribbean denizens recognized these sometimes inchoate definitions of belonging and seized on them to stake claims to membership in the bodies politic that seemed most likely to include them. In the process of making those claims, they often provided the first full articulation of criteria for belonging, which imperial officials later confirmed or even turned into policy.

Other denizens of the Caribbean intentionally moved across the jurisdictional borders of empires seeking refuge or opportunity, and they too gave meaning to those borders—insisting, for example, that on the other side, religious identities would figure differently in the definition of who belonged in the body politic, or that ideas about racial difference or universal humanity would influence membership in that body in particular ways. Individuals made claims to belong to locales, to particular sovereigns, to political bodies, and to legal, commercial, and religious communities. Local rulers and administrators weighed those claims using a variety of criteria, including perceived race, linguistic ability, religious knowledge, willingness to take oaths, property ownership, and previous behavior. European officials who inscribed imperial definitions onto terrestrial and maritime space in the Caribbean necessarily responded to the movements and arguments of the region's mobile residents, and so individuals' choices, combined with the official responses they provoked, together created Caribbean bodies politic.[7]

Caribbean border crossers sparked diplomatic disputes about what it meant to belong to one or another locale or empire, and over who could move where and who had authority to decide. These moments of interpolity negotiation occurred in port towns or at sea, at borders or in zones of interaction where multiple jurisdictions converged and overlapped. There, people arguing about the status of specific individuals articulated competing definitions of Caribbean and imperial bodies politic, pressing for varied and often incompatible criteria for belonging.

The individuals who traveled between distinct Caribbean spaces perceived, substantiated, and sometimes invented differences between the polities taking shape in the early modern Caribbean. For example, sailors who wished to make a living on private men-of-war tried to insist on lasting hostilities—a region of "no peace" that would preserve their place as agents of militant empire—even as officials and merchants strove for interimperial peace and trade.[8] Servants and slaves sought escape from their bondage and, in some cases, the chance to live in accordance with the religion they professed. They, too, emphasized religious distinctions as meaningful boundaries between empires. Merchants and traders, on the other hand, hoped to relax borders between empires to expand cooperative legal trade across jurisdictional boundaries while maintaining their political ties to their sovereign. They worked to uncouple loyal subjecthood from exclusive commercial policies that defined border-crossing trade as smuggling. Those various men and women, with their disparate and sometimes irreconcilable goals, helped determine the definitions of Caribbean borders for all the people who lived alongside them as well as for those who viewed them from afar.

Because the Caribbean Sea contained spaces claimed by so many political communities (imperial, Indigenous, Maroon, rogue), Jamaica's coastlines and the maritime space surrounding the island did not form a single unitary border that might distinguish it from nearby islands or mainlands. Instead, shipping lanes, coastlines, and port towns provided the opportunity for interactions across myriad competing jurisdictions, involving people who lived as subjects of various European empires and Indigenous polities as well as stateless people fleeing or seeking a political attachment and sometimes even free agents pursuing autonomy. Nonetheless, Jamaica's geographic location—in the middle of the Spanish Caribbean—and English merchants' and officials' determination to profit from that location, made Anglo-Spanish relations central to the island's early economic and political development. As a result, Jamaicans' entanglements with the surrounding Spanish Caribbean frame this study.[9]

When people who crossed borders strove to make a place for themselves in a new locale, they articulated their claims to political belonging in relation to nearby alternatives, usually the one they had just left. Their actions and words reveal to us how they saw Jamaican colonial society relative to the surrounding Spanish Caribbean. Differences that came to distinguish English and Spanish (and Dutch, French, Portuguese, and Danish) bodies politic drew on long-term distinctions between economic, religious, or political policies in Europe. But they gained clear expression when actual people, crossing Caribbean jurisdictional borders, claimed specific protections or privileges, and when imperial officials responded by enacting policies to govern inclusion, flight, and commerce in colonial and imperial societies.

I follow these Caribbean residents and sojourners in comparing how different colonial societies incorporated or excluded the diverse people living in the Caribbean, as cross-border confrontation required that officials determine who belonged where and why. But what interests me most is the relational process that both revealed and produced distinctions: distinctions that were sometimes real, sometimes exaggerated, and occasionally imagined. The historian Frank Tannenbaum set the terms for an extensive literature comparing British and Iberian (or more broadly Protestant and Catholic) colonial American societies with his 1946 *Slave and Citizen*. There, he argued that in Spanish and Portuguese America, "the law accepted the doctrine of the moral personality of the slave," which made freedom possible. In contrast, British American law denied the "spiritual equality of all men" and rendered enslaved people as "incapable of freedom."[10] He linked these legal histories to mid-twentieth-century race relations, arguing that as a result of differences in legal heritage, people of African descent faced far more discrimination in English than in Iberian America.

While Tannenbaum's work influenced much subsequent scholarship, it has also been criticized on many fronts, including its lack of regional specificity and its overly benign picture of slavery and modern racism in Latin America.[11] Like another familiar comparison—of relative religious tolerance in English America and religious intolerance in Spanish America—it sometimes settled into unhelpful stereotypes.[12] Thus we need to be careful; on the one hand, the people living in European imperial spaces drew from a common well of understandings of the body politic that flowed from churches, officials, local communities, networks of merchants, and treaties. And the colonies of different empires in the Caribbean shared many characteristics: a commitment to developing plantation economies, a growing population of enslaved people to run those economies, a dependence on the sea, a greater proximity to nearby rivals than to faraway metropolitan oversight and aid, and a firm commitment to stratified colonial society.[13]

Nonetheless, when we consider how people behaved at and across imperial borders in the Caribbean, we can see two realities. First, peoples' perceived racial identities and religious affiliations often afforded them different treatment in neighboring jurisdictions, revealing that distinctions in law and political theory mattered. Borders encouraged the expression of differences even as those same borders assured borrowing and shared contexts.[14] Second, even at the time, the distinctions that were being created and revealed sometimes led people to exaggerate the differences that distinguished how race and religion affected belonging in the Spanish and English Caribbean.

Early modern Europeans used the human body to represent polities, with the sovereign as head, the subjects as various body parts, and political or economic instruments such as shipping and money as the ligaments that tied it together and the blood that nourished all the parts.[15] This metaphor presumed inequality among subjects: some parts of the body performed more exalted tasks than others and enjoyed higher status within the body politic. But the model also assumed interdependence: the body functioned because all of its parts worked together.[16]

Many early modern Europeans presumed the body politic to align with other corporate bodies, most notably that of an official church. Indeed, the metaphor in part derived from Paul's description of the body of Christ in 1 Corinthians 12. Medieval political theorists also held that a body politic should map onto a nation (a people sharing common descent, language, and culture, and often a common territory, reflected in the word *nation*'s derivation from French and Latin words for birth). However, the body politic could not align with both church and nation in a colonizing, evangelizing empire. Because Christianity instructed its adherents to convert non-Christians, and because Europeans used this religious obligation to justify their colonial expansion, colonization laid bare a tension inherent within European political theory. Europeans who believed they must spread Christianity as they colonized, and who thereby incorporated these new Christians of foreign nations into the body politic (by means of their inclusion in the body of Christ), could not also continue to limit the body politic to the nation. Colonizing empires would have to give up on the mandate to evangelize, the alignment of body politic and body of Christ, or the alignment of body politic with ethnic nation.

In the Caribbean, Europeans' responses to this conundrum were varied and changed over time. But by and large, the Spanish let go of the alignment of body politic and ethnic nation. They forced Africans and Indians to convert to Catholicism and incorporated them into the body politic as unequal members. The universalist ideal of Catholicism and its consequent emphasis on evangelizing colonialism encouraged such incorporation, because ideally every person in the world could (and should) be (made) Catholic. By the seventeenth century, Spanish political identity was synonymous with Catholicism, and Spain saw itself as uniquely responsible for colonial enterprise as a means to spread orthodox religion to the people it colonized. Despite lingering distrust of converted Christians and their descendants, inclusion of all Catholics as members of the Spanish body politic followed logically from Spanish theory and practice.[17] Enslaved Catholics' status as vassals of the crown was tenuous in Spanish America, and some officials even denied it.[18] But in border regions such as the western Caribbean, enslaved and free people of color defended the Spanish crown and the Catholic Church against Protestant incursions, bolstering their claims to political membership and encouraging Spanish officials to formalize practices of inclusion into explicit policy.[19] Officials who extended protection to enslaved men and women in the international realm exhibited a hallmark obligation of sovereigns (and their proxies) toward subjects.

In the English Atlantic, despite crown efforts to impose one unified church on the nation, Protestantism's original breaks from Catholicism launched further splits, and by the 1660s English subjects adhered to multiple Christianities. Aligning the body politic with one church, as did Spain, became increasingly difficult, and religious requirements for membership in the body politic weakened.[20] (The 1689 Toleration Act confirmed the dissociation that had been developing for decades.)[21] In the English Caribbean, escalating fears of an enslaved majority overwhelmed the evangelizing efforts of a small number of missionaries working to convert Africans and Indians.[22] Even if those fears had not stymied conversion efforts, in the absence of a body politic synonymous with a body of Christ, newly converted Africans' or Indians' Christianity would not have guaranteed legal identity or crown protection.[23]

Paying attention to people's movements and interactions across borders shows us that English Jamaicans were loath to accept people of color into the body politic. When enslaved and sometimes even free people of color were caught between empires, English Jamaican officials denied them the protections due subjects and treated them as goods. In contrast, they admitted (if uneasily) a variety of European Christians and Jews as *unequal* members. Scots, for example, who had chafed at their commercial exclusion from English Atlantic trade, could exploit English Caribbean desires to bolster White colonial populations as English officials broadened their Atlantic world into a British one.[24] Thus, while the Spanish in a colonial context reaffirmed the significance of church membership to political belonging, partly in response to English challenges, the English instead developed the nonreligious category of whiteness as the primary basis of political belonging and incorporated into colonial bodies politic other members of a trading world.[25]

Because Anglo-Spanish relations across Caribbean borders reveal so much about the borders of belonging, this study begins with English merchants' concerted efforts to obtain Spanish American silver via Jamaica-based slave trading, and ends with the British South Sea Company's acquisition of the asiento, granting them a monopoly to trade enslaved people from Africa to Spanish America. During those years, English Jamaica's place in the center of Spanish America immersed it in a world of overlapping borders and movement and created the chance, over and over again, for people to claim belonging and for officials to uphold, quash, or negotiate those claims. Jamaica's central location drew people, willingly and unwillingly, from throughout the Atlantic world, so the conversations involved Tule, Scottish, Maroon, Jewish, Brandenburger, Danish, Portuguese, and French in addition to English, Spanish, African, and Indigenous people.

English and Spanish subjects in the Caribbean had long regarded one another as enemies, whether their crowns were at war or not, and they often expressed their geopolitical relationship in religious terms: the Spanish attempted to repulse the incursions of English heretics, while the English hoped their conquests, plundering, and colonizing would weaken Spanish papists.[26] Both sides believed that the silver the Spanish extracted from its colonies strengthened the government and the church of the European kingdom that eventually acquired it, in addition to lining the pockets of all the individuals through whose hands it passed. Thus silver (like gold, which Spanish America produced in lesser amounts) possessed economic, diplomatic, and potentially cosmic power.

Many imperial officials believed that an empire ought to be closed to foreign commercial penetration and economically self-sufficient. While such theories never reflected reality, they nonetheless shaped the ideal of a loyal subject and the laws that governed subjects' behavior.[27] Through the mid-seventeenth century, individuals and their rulers expected political allegiance, religious affiliation, and economic behavior to coincide. However, the increasing efforts of European traders to access Spanish American markets and silver (either as bullion in bars or minted into coins, usually pieces of eight) drove merchants, officials, and consumers to question whether inter-imperial trade necessarily threatened religious identity or political allegiance.

Most Spanish American silver bound for Europe flowed through the Caribbean, coming overland from the mines of Peru or Mexico to the Caribbean ports of Portobelo and Vera Cruz, and amassing at Havana before being shipped on to Seville. The flow of silver explains why the region became the central site of rivalry for all who challenged Spain's claims to monopoly on American lands, people, water, and minerals. Those rivals focused particular attention on the Isthmus of Panama, the main Spanish transport route moving silver from Andean mines to ships bound for Spain.[28]

Other Europeans seeking Spanish American silver, gold, or jewels pirated it beginning in the sixteenth century. But Spain's failure to supply its colonists with the European manufactured goods or enslaved Africans they desired gave rival Europeans a second means of acquiring Spanish American silver: through commerce, which also began in the sixteenth century but expanded dramatically over the course of the seventeenth century, as the transatlantic slave trade grew and as Spain's manufacturing capacity failed to keep up with that of other Europeans.[29] The origins of Spain's foreign-licensed slave trade stretched back to the 1494 Treaty of Tordesillas between Spain and Portugal, which drew a north-south line in the Atlantic and granted all discoveries west of it to Castile and everything east of it to Portugal. Thus, when Spaniards in Europe or the Americas wanted to purchase enslaved Africans, they initially turned to Portuguese traders to do so. But while Spain was obliged to respect the treaty that gave it the right to most of the Americas, other Europeans challenged Portugal's monopoly on African colonization and trade as they did Spain's monopoly on America. Spain never developed a transatlantic slave trade sufficient to meet its colonists' demands for enslaved African laborers and over time came to rely on Genoese, English, Dutch, and French traders, in addition to Portuguese.

Beginning in 1595, the Spanish crown issued a licensed contract (*asiento de negros*), often to a foreign merchant company, to import enslaved Africans. By the seventeenth century, the holders of those asientos commonly subcontracted a portion of the trafficking to multiple other traders, widening the number and diversity of foreigners engaged in the trade of enslaved Africans to Spanish America. Foreign merchants avidly sought asiento subcontracts because they provided access to silver, both directly and via the smuggling of European manufactured goods that accompanied the legal trade in slaves.[30] The slave trade to Spanish America was always international, despite Spain's goal of closed empire.

The widespread European desire for Spanish American wealth, combined with English anti-Catholicism, provided the context for England's conquest of Jamaica. Oliver Cromwell's militant Protestantism and providentialism led him to imagine English forces gaining a toehold in the Caribbean and conquering all of Spanish America. Instead, in 1655 the seven thousand–man Western Design force (recruited in England, Barbados, and the Leeward Islands) suffered an embarrassing defeat on its first target, the island of Hispaniola. There, as would be the case in Jamaica, the conflict between English and Spanish forces aroused English anxiety over the composition of Caribbean colonies. Already during the Western Design, the English began to consider what kind of society they would and could create if they succeeded in conquering any Spanish holding. They had eastern Caribbean models in Barbados and the English Leeward Islands. But the Spanish presence that drew them to the larger, colonized islands also provided people and precedents, some of which challenged English assumptions about the composition of the body politic. For example, while scholars have noted the prevalence of Black Legend justifications (purporting Spaniards' intrinsic cruelty) for the Western Design, the invasion also evidenced another trope, one that would recur in Anglo-Spanish relations. The English saw indeterminate racial borders in Spanish America as a sign of degeneracy. One English observer noted in horror that "a few despicable Mongrel-Spaniards, Shepherds and Blacks" defeated Cromwell's forces at Hispaniola.[31]

The English forces that survived the disastrous attack on Hispaniola then managed to seize the capital city of more sparsely populated Jamaica. While the Spanish governor signed a capitulation and accepted transport from Jamaica soon after the English assault, the majority of Jamaicans, of both Spanish and African descent, remained to try to drive out the invaders. They were reinforced by Indigenous militias from Spain's mainland colonies and supplies from Cartagena. Some Black Jamaicans remained with Spanish defenders, but others split from all colonizers to establish separate, independent settlements. The English then waged a multipronged war aiming to defeat both Spanish and Black resistance, which succeeded only after five years of protracted combat. In gaining Jamaica, the English acquired far less than the expeditions' planners had envisioned but nonetheless met the Western Design's goal of establishing an English presence in "the very heart [of] the Spaniard."[32]

Even before the conquest was complete, some anticipated that an English takeover would transform the boundaries of political community, changing the meaning of religion and race for the island's inhabitants. When the Spanish governor agreed to surrender the island, the Western Design's commanders did not follow Cromwell's instructions to offer Spanish Jamaica's "persons" the usual option of transferring allegiance. They instead insisted on the departure of most Spaniards, and promised enslaved "Negroes and others" "some favourable concessions . . . touching their liberty." But despite lip service to the idea that their arrival would save Africans and Indians from Spanish tyranny, the actions of the English suggested that they resisted seeing non-Europeans as subjects with rights. In 1656 the English army council decreed that any English soldier who captured a "negro or mulatto" would receive three years of that captive's labor. The decree made no distinction between captives who had been free vassals or soldiers in Spanish Jamaica and those who had been enslaved.[33]

But early Black Jamaicans had lived with Spanish colonizers who accepted free Black communities as an unavoidable if undesirable corollary to slavery, and they used their experience to negotiate with invaders who desperately needed their alliance.[34] When the English discovered the African-led town of Juan de Bola, they threatened its destruction to force an alliance against the Spanish and other independent Black towns. De Bola and his followers insisted that in return for their "friendship," "fidelity," and "faithfulness," the English must promise to respect their freedom and land and recognize them as a self-governing polity.[35] James Robertson notes that the terms were similar to those the Spanish had earlier offered de Bola.[36] Whether the initiative came from the Spanish or de Bola, his experience with colonizers willing (if not happy) to acknowledge free Black settlements created the context within which he negotiated with the English, who recognized the town's freedom in part by adopting the Spanish term *palenque*.

Restoration officials attempted to undo this situation, trying in 1663 to reduce de Bola from "governor" of his "*pelinco*" to "Colonel of the Black Regiment." Although de Bola's followers would possess "the same state and freedom as the English enjoy," English administrators wished to end their corporate status, instead dividing them into heads of household, each to receive thirty acres "in such places as shall be thought fit by the Governor

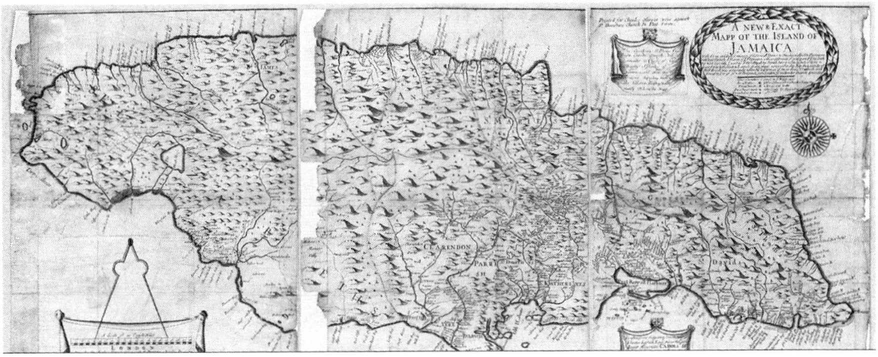

Map 3. *A New & Exact Mapp of the Island of Jamaica*. By Charles Bochart and Humphrey Knollis, 1682. Courtesy of the Library of Congress.

and Council to them and their heirs forever." Both plans reflect early English readiness, perhaps of necessity, to incorporate Africans into colonial society, and evidence exists for both a continued palenque and for greater integration into English Jamaica as colonial householders.[37] However, despite their utter dependence on de Bola's alliance, the English played down the participation of people of color in chronicling their continuing conquest of the island. As Carla Pestana has noted, de Bola appears "hidden within [an] enumeration" of 2,500 Jamaica militiamen in 1664 militia records, as commander of a 150-man company, with no other reference in English records. English efforts to silence Black participation stood in sharp contrast to Spanish officials, who readily acknowledged and even celebrated the contributions of African and Indigenous military forces to Spanish colonial efforts.[38]

Indeed, the unique threats English invaders posed to people of color led Spanish officials to underscore their contributions and the protections they were owed. After the last Spanish-led forces surrendered in 1660, the English again attempted to separate them by race, and offered transportation off the island for "only the Spaniards." The Spanish commander resolved "to die sooner than abandon" (to likely English enslavement) "the greater part of the soldiers of the force [who] were Indians, Negroes, and Mulattoes." He rejected the English offers of transport and instead built two canoes rigged with sails, large enough to transport to Cuba 76 of the 112 people who remained.[39] But some of the soldiers of color defending Spanish Jamaica nevertheless ended up enslaved by the invaders. English commanders indicated that they turned over captured Indigenous militiamen to Jamaican planters.[40]

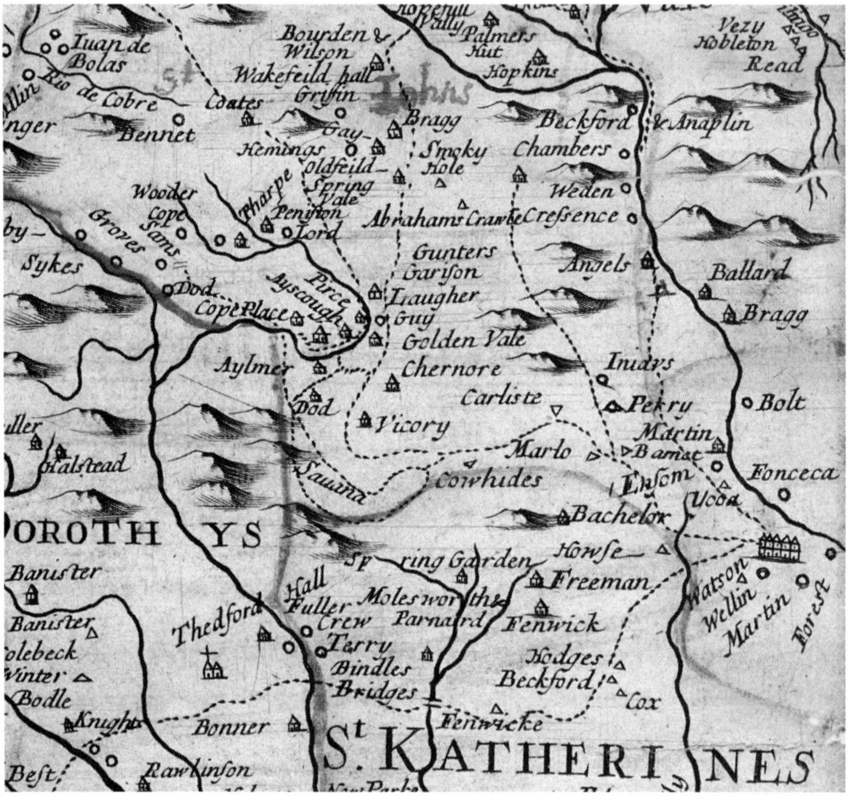

Map 4. Detail of Map 3 showing Juan de Bola's town northwest of Spanish Town, situated among English plantations. The key identifies the town as a provision plantation. The map also notes a "negro Palink" and an "Old Palink" to the northwest in St. James Parish. Courtesy of the Library of Congress.

While the English conquest of Jamaica boded ill for most people of color on the island, it offered hope to Jews unable to live openly under Spanish rule. Prior to the English conquest, Spanish Jamaica likely contained a higher proportion of *conversos*—forced converts (and their descendants) from Judaism to Catholicism—and crypto-Jews (those secretly practicing Judaism) than did other regions of Spanish America.[41] During an English raid on the island ten years before the Western Design, "divers Portugals" (almost certainly Sephardic Jews) had offered aid to the invaders.[42] In 1655, at least one provided intelligence to the English forces.[43] English leaders, recognizing that Jews and conversos would likely welcome their conquest of the island, distinguished between Portuguese prisoners, whom they "hope[d] to make good subjects of" and Spaniards, whom they planned "to remove."[44]

England's conquest of Jamaica coincided with a period in which a number of English officials (including Cromwell) and European Jews advocated English acceptance of Jewish immigration.[45] The Amsterdam-born Jewish merchant Simon de Caceres outlined for Cromwell the supplies needed to keep possession of Jamaica. He explicitly connected Cromwell's expansive goals to conquer Spanish America with Jewish inclusion in the English body politic. In proposing a further venture to Chile, Caceres offered to recruit and lead "some young men of my owne nation" as long as he be named a commander and that "those of my nation" go "*as Englishmen*."[46]

Caceres's offer came just as the Amsterdam rabbi Menasseh ben Israel traveled to London and began his (ultimately successful) two-year effort to encourage Cromwell to readmit Jews to England. Cromwell's favorable stance toward the open practice of Judaism in England and its colonies signaled to Atlantic world Jews their welcome in Jamaica, just when many sought a place to settle.[47] During the Western Design, then, its leaders and residents of the Atlantic world anticipated that new colonial rulers would mean a redefined body politic. Race, religion, and nation would all figure differently in English Jamaica than they did in the surrounding Spanish Caribbean. Those initial distinctions added cultural meaning to new geopolitical borders, providing a basis for further elaboration in the next half century, as Caribbean residents and officials tangled over membership in colonial societies.

Charles II's restoration to the English, Scottish, and Irish thrones in 1660 made possible a formal end to the hostilities between England and Spain. English efforts at peace came in part from merchants' and investors' hopes to further penetrate Spanish American markets, especially for enslaved Africans.[48] After Spain and Britain established peace in the 1667 and 1670 Treaties of Madrid, Caribbean denizens and European officials spent the next half century working out what that would mean. These processes involved multiple polities, corporate bodies, and individuals. *Boundaries of Belonging* follows the great variety of people who navigated the intersections of Spanish, English, and other claims to the region, from efforts at Anglo-Spanish peace beginning in the 1660s to the end of the War of the Spanish Succession and the award of the asiento to the British South Sea Company in the 1710s.

The English merchants who sought the asiento challenged other residents of the region who opposed their vision of Jamaica as a slave-trading entrepôt. They competed with other European merchants (Scottish, French, Dutch, Genoese, and Danish) for Spanish American markets. They argued with other English Jamaicans (planters, privateers, and those officials who supported them) over whether developing the interimperial slave trade benefited the island or the English empire.[49] The captive men and women brought to the island as slaves contested their status. Neighboring Indigenous polities entered the shifting geopolitical fray. All of these people moved across porous and uncertain jurisdictional borders to pursue their goals—for wealth or freedom, or to escape religious or political persecution.

In the six decades following England's conquest of Jamaica, the island became the slave-trading entrepôt that early planners had envisioned and at the same time developed a sugar-producing plantation economy. Recent scholarship has rightly emphasized the violence inherent in settler colonialism and the racism that plantation economies fomented.[50] Plantation logic permeated the Caribbean. Racism, inequality, exploitation, and violence underlay colonial bodies politic in the colonies of all Europeans, including the Spanish. But the Spanish Caribbean shows us that such plantation logic did not necessarily lead to a race-based theory of membership in the body politic.[51] Everyone theoretically belonged to the body politic, though unequally, as Catholics and as vassals of the crown. English Jamaicans, in contrast, created a racially demarcated body politic, with whiteness as a basis for belonging, because in addition to the plantation logic they shared with other Caribbean societies, they also hewed to a slave trading logic. Interimperial slave trading, which provided the primary justification for loosening exclusive commercial policies, demanded a distinction between people who could be sold and people (of the trading world) who bought and sold them.

The logic of human trafficking led its agents to commodify people in a way that even plantation labor did not. The people who were enslaved in Caribbean colonial societies had to be severed from their African and Native American networks of political belonging. But when they became capital that traders could move across imperial and other political borders, it followed that for slave-trading empires, those women and men also be kept from joining new imperial bodies politic. Selling away subjects violated a sovereign's responsibilities to provide protection in an international arena. Purchasing them did not.

Spanish Americans, as purchasers, were complicit in this process of commodification, which we can see in their adoption of the Portuguese term *peças/piezas de India* to refer to captive men and women. But because they did not systematically trade enslaved people away to other empires, and because they both insisted on evangelizing and equated Christianity with political belonging, they did not follow slave-trading logic to its exclusionary conclusion. The French and Portuguese, who held (as the Spanish did) that Catholicism demanded legal personhood, but who also committed to international slave trading, maintained a tension over the place of people of color that defied the logic pursued by either the Spanish or the English. Jamaica and its Spanish American environs represented only one part of centuries-long multi-imperial processes defining political belonging in the Atlantic world. By examining the ways that various people in the western Caribbean noted the distinctions between English and Spanish space, we see how these two empires, both dependent on the unfree labor of people of African and Indigenous American descent, created colonial bodies politic that both borrowed and diverged from one another. Doing so lets us listen in on multiple conversations about the criteria for political belonging among the variety of people who inhabited and traversed through the western Caribbean.

English, Spanish, African, Tule, French, Maroon, Portuguese, Scottish, Dutch, Brandenburger, Genoese, Jewish, and creole individuals people this book. They lived and interacted at the intersections of English, Spanish, and rival imperial, Indigenous, and Maroon spaces in the Caribbean, and in the contested maritime commons, in a western Caribbean where Spanish and English officials tried to create the common ground necessary for commerce but also encountered and created numerous and complicated reasons for conflict.[52] The diverse people living under or at the edges of English and Spanish jurisdiction articulated varied and conflicting foundations for incorporation into rival bodies politic, which I describe in chapters both thematic and roughly chronological. In the first two chapters, I consider English Jamaica's efforts to establish neighborly communication with surrounding Spanish colonies to trade slaves. I trace English officials' efforts to suppress peacetime privateering and piracy because they threatened slave trading. In doing so, Jamaican officials distanced themselves from the militant Protestantism that such maritime predators often deployed. But I also examine how pirates and privateers treated all people of color as sellable. When they seized people of African, Indigenous, and mixed descent, many of them free, from Spanish America and sold them in Jamaica or elsewhere, they gave planters and officials a stake in denying the legitimacy of those captives' Spanish vassalage. In their denials, we can also see the beginnings of English denigration of Spanish Americans not merely for their Catholicism but for the (resultant) integration of African and Native people into the body politic. English colonists invested in creating a racially bounded, White body politic began to label Spanish Americans "mongrels" with tenuous standing in the international arena. Spaniards could not employ their own exclusionary basis for belonging—Catholicism—to the same effect, given the growing international political and military power that accompanied Protestant nations' commercial ascendance.

Chapters 3, 4, and 5 deal with border crossers. Chapter 3 follows pirates' captives when they managed to escape slavery in English Jamaica and reclaim or gain their freedom in Spanish America. They used both their Catholicism and their immersion in local communities to establish claims to imperial belonging, and they pointed to the piracy and heresy of their English enslavers to make the case that in protecting them, the Spanish crown defended its own interests as well. Spanish American officials' acceptance of those claims, and the crown's confirmation of them, paved the way for a broader sanctuary policy to evolve in the Spanish Atlantic. At the same time, as I show in Chapter 4, Jews fleeing persecution in Iberian America sought belonging in English and Dutch colonies, and at times found Jamaican officials eager to welcome them as additions to the island's free population. English officials and Jews themselves were inconsistent about how much integration into Jamaican society they desired, and uncertainty persisted about Jewish Jamaicans' relationship to colonial taxation, militia service, property ownership, and naturalization status. Their movement between jurisdictions repeatedly raised diplomatic questions about the relationship between national identity and imperial subjecthood. Chapter 5 addresses merchants' claims to cross-border belonging by considering in detail the efforts of one particular slave trader, Santiago del Castillo. Castillo worked to smooth political and commercial conflicts across Anglo-Spanish political, legal, religious, and linguistic borders in the Caribbean, and in doing so provides us with an arresting example of the "sinew populations"—outside the plantation complex but crucial to imperial projects—that Jesse Cromwell has identified as crucial to the colonial Caribbean.[53]

Chapters 6 and 7 examine how people's personal and corporate border crossings both contributed to and help us better discern developments in economic and legal theories. Chapter 6 describes Scots' emphasis on their membership within "the trading world" as they attempted to establish a slave-trading colony on the Isthmus of Panama. In the process, they allied with Indigenous Tule polities and invoked natural law arguments to justify their invasion of Spanish-claimed territory. While their colony failed, it prompted English and Spanish officials to consider how fuller incorporation of wayward subjects might prevent similar independent action in the future. Chapter 7 illustrates how the War of the Grand Alliance and the War of the Spanish Succession raised questions about whether subjects' allegiance and belonging were "natural" (inborn) or chosen. At the same time, wartime disruptions led English Jamaicans to reaffirm their willingness to naturalize European foreigners and reassert their exclusion of Maroons from the body politic, while Spanish American officials confirmed their reliance on Indigenous and African-descended vassals to defend crown holdings from enemies.

The conclusion reflects on the ways that, throughout the book, actors made explicit and implicit appeals to law, especially to common legal understandings (or practices that they believed ought to be shared), which they sometimes referred to as the law of nations. Britain's emergence from the War of the Spanish Succession as the Atlantic's ascendant commercial power predicted its ability, over the next century, to begin imposing an emergent English view of people (as White or not White) and nations (trading or not) beyond the British empire. Britons conflated those categories, creating a world made up of two kinds of polities. Trading nations' commercial activities provided the grounds for their asserting the lead role in the international realm, and their (theoretically White) subjects traveled through the world with the privileges and protections that sovereigns provided to their subjects. Nontrading nations, made up of nonwhite peoples, could be excluded from the international legal arena as both polities and individuals. Between 1655 and 1715 Jamaica was at the center of a region where Europeans competed to move captive people, whom they tried to make into commodities, to colonial spaces where they could produce export crops and mine precious metals. Jamaica's importance to this story, during years crucial for the definition of an English Atlantic body politic, allows us to see how England's role in international slave trading generated whiteness and fastened it to commerce as foundations for political belonging and access to international law. Considering Jamaica and its Spanish American surrounds within a multinational Caribbean lets us see how English colonists and officials chose to reject Christianity's universalist demands in the process.

A Note on Translating the Vocabularies of Belonging

Early modern Europeans used the Latin *subdito* in treaties and treatises to denote individuals who owed allegiance to a recognized sovereign and had legal standing as members of political states. In English translations the word became *subject*, and in Spanish it remained *subdito*.[54] However, people who lived in Spanish dominions and accepted the sovereignty of the Spanish crown far more commonly described themselves as *vasallos*, a term that also implied loyalty to the crown and membership in the body politic. In the Spanish Atlantic, *subdito* was frequently left to diplomats. In English, the word *vassal* conveyed greater subjection than did *subject*, which signaled an individual's rights (for example, to the sovereign's protection). *Nation* and *nación*, derived from the Latin word for birth, referred to a community of descent that usually shared language and place of origin, similar to modern *ethnicity*, though also often tied in European thinking to a political kingdom. Contemporary Spaniards also used *gente* (a people) where English speakers might use *nation*.

Local categories of belonging existed alongside imperial allegiance and national identity. The Spanish term *vecino*, entailing citizenship and often property ownership in a town, had no exact English equivalent.[55] *Freeholder*, a local status that provided property owners with rights to political representation, comes closest, but the term does not appear in diplomatic correspondence between empires. English colonial governors or assemblies could grant *denizen* status to foreigners, allowing them property rights (although not always the right to pass that property on to heirs), but denizen status often applied only within a particular jurisdictional location such as a colony. In all three instances in which property ownership helped to determine an individual's status (*denizen*, *vecino*, and *freeholder*), the context was local, whereas a subject's or vassal's relationship with his or her sovereign—an identity that individuals carried with themselves as they moved across borders—rested on markers of belonging other than property ownership. However, local ties mattered even when they were not tied to property ownership and in ways that related directly to national or imperial belonging. Birth in a specific locale made someone a *criollo* or *natural* in the Spanish Atlantic, and a creole or natural-born Englishman in the English Atlantic. Corporate identities retained relevance—especially visible in Indigenous communities, among Jews, and among Catholics of African or mixed-race descent. Spanish Americans further pointed to their local networks of employment and patronage, and sometimes even their ownership by another member of a local community, as constituent elements of their ties to the crown and therefore their membership in the body politic. Peoples' efforts to determine individuals' political affiliations during interimperial negotiations were further complicated by the fact that these categories were contested and unstable within each imperial context. For example, English law distinguished between temporary and local denizenation (the prerogative of the crown and its delegates, such as colonial governors) and permanent empire-wide naturalization (theoretically reserved for Parliament). In practice, officials often ignored the distinction and issued naturalization papers more generously than English law allowed. As a result, when treaty law or early law of nations treatises refer to the obligations, rights, and privileges of subjects, what might appear clear on paper was anything but. Many of the contests described in this book entailed conflict over the definitions and translations of these terms. Those disagreements occurred across borders as part of interimperial diplomacy. But they also occurred within jurisdictions in the archipelagic western Caribbean jurisdictions, because all parties understood that close, overlapping, and shifting borders destabilized the categories of belonging, and required and allowed the articulation of explicit criteria to replace often implicit assumptions that might have functioned in Europe but in the Caribbean no longer held.

CHAPTER 1

"The Lawless Motions of Privateers"

Beginning in the middle of the sixteenth century, English privateers played a central role as agents of empire in the Caribbean. Those independent mariners held officials' commissions to conduct maritime military expeditions against enemy shipping and territory during times of war. Published accounts celebrated private men of war as vanguards of Protestantism and of state expansion.[1] They were supposed to enact a clear line of accountability from the sovereign to an official authorized to issue commissions under specific circumstances and to the holder of such a commission. In reality, officials issued illegal commissions, and mariners violated the commissions they held.

Spanish and English imperial officials had long adhered to a formula that linked geographical jurisdiction, political allegiance, religious adherence, and national origin. Since the sixteenth century, militant Protestantism had provided justification for English mariners' violent attacks on Spanish American shipping and settlements, and equally militant Catholicism had provided justification for Spanish violence against English shipping and settlement in the region. As long as that model prevailed, privateers reaped both plunder and pride of place, enjoying membership in religious and political community.

English predation on the Spanish Caribbean embraced a Protestant nationalistic anti-Catholic narrative. The Spanish viewed English arrival as an invasion of foreign heretics who not only challenged the crown's sovereignty in the region but also threatened its subjects' souls. Much of the violence that ensued from these attitudes depended on the crewmembers who sailed private men-of-war. Spanish *corsarios* (including *guardacostas*), like English privateers, possessed official license to attack, arrest, or seize as prize any ships breaking their licensing sovereign's regulatory laws or sailing on behalf of that sovereign's enemies. While they clearly sought plunder, English privateers portrayed themselves as advancing Protestantism against popery, and

Spanish corsarios claimed to defend the church while protecting the crown and its subjects. Europeans in the Caribbean maintained these hostile postures even when peace prevailed in Europe, as suggested by the phrase "no peace beyond the line," which belligerents periodically invoked. The phrase drew on the concept—expressed in the 1559 Treaty of Cateau-Cambrésis between France and Spain—that "lines of amity" restricted peace agreements to Europe while allowing continued warfare in the Caribbean.[2] The most obvious regional example was the Puritan effort in the 1630s to establish a colony on Providence Island, attractive because it stood, like Jamaica, "in the heart of the Indies & the mouth of the Spaniards." Confidence in God's favor encouraged a project that in retrospect seemed certain to fall to Spanish reconquest, as it did in 1641.[3]

Although by mid-century hostilities diminished, as Spain unofficially resigned itself to the growing number of European colonies in the small islands of the eastern Caribbean, Cromwell's Western Design reignited religiously framed warfare. Cromwell cited an obligation to save residents of Spanish America from "the Miserable Thraldome and Bondage, bothe Spiritual and Civill," that the Spanish crown imposed on them "by meanes of the Popish and cruell Inquisition and otherwise."[4] Many, though not all, of the participants likewise shared the sense that they were combining patriotic duty with obligation to God, making sure to desecrate Catholic buildings and statues. Spanish defenders responded in kind, understanding their defense of their homes and king as a defense of their church and its saints, against heretics bent on the destruction of all.[5]

After the conquest of Jamaica, when English merchants and officials sought to use the island's central location to access Spanish silver through slave trading and textile smuggling, privateers' role in the Atlantic became increasingly problematic.[6] At the English crown's restoration in 1660, the Stuart royal family fostered England's participation in the transatlantic slave trade, chartering the Company of Royal Adventurers Trading to Africa (precursor to the Royal African Company) the same year, partly in anticipation of a reexport trade from Jamaica and Barbados to Spanish America. As the company's name suggested, the Stuarts tied their fortunes to slave trading, with Charles II an investor and his brother James, Duke of York, the company's governor and largest shareholder.[7] These merchant and crown efforts to increase England's human trafficking dovetailed with other investors' attempts to establish a plantation economy on Jamaica, where enslaved people would produce agricultural products for export. However, English slave traders and planters disagreed about whether reexporting captive people to Spanish America should play a dominant role in Jamaica's economy. Jamaican planters believed that English slave traders ought to meet English demands before supplying foreigners. The merchants who used the island as a slave trading entrepôt countered that the Spanish paid more and in bullion or coin, requiring no credit, all of which benefited not just the merchants but the entire island and England itself. The combined Spanish and English demand for captive laborers created an expansive market for enslaved men and women of African and Indigenous descent, which encouraged transatlantic and regional slave traders to build their commerce in the Caribbean.[8]

English merchants' efforts to develop international commerce with Spanish Americans, their historical enemies, foretold the end for privateers as representatives of English empire in the region. While officials continued to depend on them during periods of hostility and found suppressing them difficult, privateers nonetheless lost their central place as the English vision of empire became increasingly commercial. This chapter traces English officials' and merchants' efforts—in conversation with their Spanish counterparts—to impose this new colonial strategy on the region during the 1660s. They attempted to build a shared Anglo-Spanish commitment to a regional political economy based on cooperative international slave trading.

Cultivating voluntary trade demanded that the English and Spanish relinquish their postures of hostility in the region. The commerce English merchants envisioned required historical belligerents to interact as neighbors in the region—rivals, but no longer enemies. But privateers and many officials could not move beyond the Anglo/Spanish Protestant/Catholic enmities that had so long shaped their views of themselves and of one another.

In the first dozen years following England's 1655 conquest of Jamaica, when Spanish officials in Europe and the Caribbean regarded England's hold on the island as illegal, Cuban officials backed numerous attempts by corsarios to retake Jamaica, and Jamaican officials responded by licensing private men-of-war. Theoretically, they were to defend the island and its shipping, but they regularly exceeded their commissions, attacking Spanish settlements.[9] Jamaica's economy came to depend on the plunder they brought in, plunder that included not only silver and consumer goods but also captives whom they sold in Jamaica as slaves.[10]

As Jamaica-based English merchants tried to foster consensual trade with nearby Spanish Americans, they sought ways to rein in privateers and mitigate the damage they inflicted on Anglo-Spanish commerce. The pursuit of voluntary trade suggested an alternative Caribbean geopolitics, one in which English Protestants and Spanish Catholics would move beyond religious and nationalist hostilities to engage in a trade that would benefit both English and Spanish participants.[11] Spain would receive captive Africans to work in mines, agricultural production, and service economies and would also acquire illegal textiles at lower prices than those offered legally by Spanish merchants. The English would receive an injection of silver into their specie-poor economy.

Even though this trade rested on the shared acceptance of human trafficking, efforts to establish trade (and Jamaican officials' concurrent efforts to control the damage privateers did to that trade) also revealed significant tensions among the English in Jamaica about whether people of African, Indigenous, and mixed descent possessed political identities or even legal personhood in English plantation societies. At several periods during the 1660s and early 1670s, English officials entertained the possibility that—as in Spanish America—people of color could live as unequal subjects of the crown, with that identity perhaps tied to Christian conversion. Ultimately, Jamaican officials largely rejected such a model in favor of a formula that denied legal personhood to people of color and excluded from the body politic anyone who fell outside of the newly emerging category of White. In official records, they often subsumed distinctions between people of African, Indigenous, and mixed descent (much less national distinctions *among* Natives or Africans) in favor of the legal category of "slave." As later chapters will show, the English articulated these developments during moments of conflict with their Spanish (or French or Dutch) neighbors, and in response to their rivals' insistence on racially capacious political subjecthood.

Privateers played an important role in this process. As they tried to retain their role as agents of empire, they repeatedly treated people of African, Indigenous, or mixed descent—whether free or enslaved—as plunder, to be severed from local social and religious networks that gave meaning to their political identity as vassals, and sold as slaves in Jamaica. Even those English officials seeking to disempower privateers in order to promote Anglo-Spanish slave trading resisted recognizing such captives' political identities, instead allowing privateers to define people of color in the region as "slaves" as soon as they entered English jurisdiction. When English record keepers did assign these captives a racial identity as "negroes" (or, more rarely, "Indians" or "mulattoes"), they nonetheless erased the particularities of birthplace and of African, Indigenous, and European descent that in a Spanish American context might embed them in networks of kin and community.[12]

English officials initially failed to recognize how much privateers would interfere with Anglo-Spanish trade in the region. When London officials appointed Sir Thomas Modyford governor of English Jamaica in 1664, they signaled both their commitment to using the island as a slave-trading base and their reliance on long-term residents of the Caribbean to do so. Modyford had managed the Royal African Company's interests in Barbados prior to his appointment as governor of Jamaica, in part by carrying on an extensive correspondence with his brother, RAC shareholder and factor James Modyford. Thomas Modyford had sold captives to Spanish slave traders in Barbados and had sent his own ships, laden with enslaved men and women, from Barbados to Cartagena.[13]

In 1662, two years before his appointment, Modyford had written several letters from Barbados attesting to the profitability and the feasibility of a Caribbean Anglo-Spanish slave trade. He described Spanish "overtures" in which Spanish merchants confirmed the Cartagena governor's interest in promoting the trade. They assured English merchants that in Peru, where the captives would eventually labor, "their Markett" price was one thousand pieces of eight per person, many times their sale price in Barbados. The Cartagena merchants promised they would bring five million pieces of eight to Barbados every year, and would pay ten percent customs for any goods or people they purchased, if English merchants could supply them. Modyford recommended that Charles II license the trade, which he promised would deliver £100,000 per year to the king, money that would otherwise go to the Spanish and Dutch treasuries.[14]

Two months later Modyford wrote that a Spanish ship had "filled our island w[i]th money," paying 125 to 140 pieces of eight per person. Having purchased four hundred Africans, the Spanish captain remained in Barbados awaiting the arrival of four hundred more captives. Modyford hoped to meet some of that additional demand himself and said that if "his negro ship" had not yet arrived in Barbados before the Spanish merchant departed, he would send it on to Cartagena. Later that summer, he reported that English merchants had sold an additional hundred individuals to Spanish merchants (also bound for Cartagena) for 220 pieces of eight per person.[15] Another Spanish ship arrived with silver, jewels, and indigo but was denied trade, and Modyford hoped that his brother had "done something" to help secure a license for a Barbados-based trade in captive people, which if "well managed" would yield "unexpressable" gain, so much that "wee need thinke of noe other way to gett wealth" than by trading slaves to the Spanish.[16]

Perhaps angling for Jamaica's governorship, Modyford wrote proposals for realizing the recently conquered island's potential to benefit Charles II and his subjects, emphasizing the need to attract colonists and the gains to be had by trading with Spanish Americans. His previous experiences in Barbados prepared him to understand that Jamaica's location offered easier passage to and from Spanish ports and thus presented English merchants with the opportunity to increase this trade. Consequently, he created detailed plans for how best to strengthen England's new Caribbean colony to build internal and external markets for captive laborers.[17] Those plans, which he and his close associates shared with crown officials, returned to him in the royal instructions he received when he indeed became Jamaica's governor. He recommended that colonists be allowed to depart England's Leeward Island colonies without restraint, that they receive free passage and one hundred acres of land, and that they be assured the same "liberties" that subjects in England and Barbados enjoyed.[18] After learning that Modyford would receive the governorship, his brother-in-law and business partner Thomas Kendall proposed on Modyford's behalf that to attract colonists, the new governor be given the power "to grant liberty of conscience," to lure immigrants with land grants, and to declare Jamaica custom free for twenty-one years. To promote trade, specifically with Spanish Americans, Modyford should be instructed "to call in all private men-of-war; to proceed against those who refuse and continue pirates or take commissions from other princes; to settle an Admiralty there; [and] to give assurances to Spanish subjects of free trade at Jamaica."[19]

The king's instructions for Modyford demonstrate the influence of his Caribbean experience, because they echoed back to the new governor his own advice. He was to do everything he could to promote the RAC's slave trade and, more broadly, Jamaica's commerce "with all neighbouring planta[tio]ns Colonies & Countries." He was to invite "as many Planters as you can" from such places and provide ships to transport them to Jamaica.[20] Attracting merchants and planters who might add to the island's and the crown's prosperity took precedence over any desire to make the colony religiously or politically homogeneous. Modyford was "to give all possible encouragement to p[er]sons of all opinions & parties" to transport themselves to the island. To convince potential migrants that they would be welcome, the governor was to ensure that no man be disturbed "in the exercise of his Religion," and he was to "dispense with the taking the Oathes of Allegiance & Supremacy to those who beare any part in the Government" and instead find "some other way" to secure himself "of their allegiance to Us & Our Government there."[21] Charles thus accepted that men whose opinions, religion, and party diverged from his own might yet serve him as loyal subjects. He aimed not merely to co-opt former opponents of the crown but to entice foreigners as well.[22] "Strangers" who moved to Jamaica could strengthen England's hold on the island as long as they were "mingled" with "our owne Subjects" and not permitted to live in settlements "apart by themselves." Instead, Jamaica's English colonists would absorb the newcomers, who could then contribute to Jamaica's economic development without threatening the island's security or its Englishness.[23]

Crown officials understood from their Caribbean informants that the close proximity of islands claimed by multiple nations, and the need to attract settlers who would establish dominion by cultivating land and providing defense, put them in competition with rival colonies for potential immigrants. While officials believed that natural identities and allegiances derived from birth nations, they also recognized that individuals' loyalties might follow their opportunities for landownership and independence. Thus, in confirming Kendall's suggestion for a twenty-one-year custom-free period, London officials noted that without such a concession, "freemen will rather goe to ye Dutch & French plantations then to Jamaico, by which his Majesty will loose his subjects."[24]

As for trade, Modyford was especially to court "the Spanish Dominions," offering to furnish them with anything they desired that he could provide, and emphasizing Charles II's amity with "the Catholicke King." Private merchants could conduct this trade, as long as Modyford made sure that they did not, in "greedinesse," trade away to the Spanish things that Jamaica needed.[25] To build the Anglo-Spanish trust that such plans would require, Governor Modyford sent delegates to negotiate with the governors of Santo Domingo and Puerto Rico, to propose that the Spanish and English governors maintain "a good correspondence" with one another and to test Spaniards' interest in conducting more regular trade.[26]

To foster such international trade in Jamaica, officials tried to situate the English island as a commercial center within an international Caribbean context. Rather than as a base for violent colonial rivalry, Jamaica would serve as part of a regional interimperial project to transform the Caribbean from a center of plunder to a center of commerce and production, by the massive importation of enslaved African and Indigenous men, women, and children.[27] English colonizers competed with other Europeans in the region, particularly the Dutch and the French, to profit from both Spanish American trade and from plantation agriculture. The asiento became the driver of interimperial trade that inspired efforts at peace and spurred changes in regulation, leading merchants to propose that loyal colonial subjects need not limit their economic exchanges to their countrymen.

Thus, less than a decade after England's religiously framed military conquest of Jamaica, Jamaica and London merchants and officials envisioned a Caribbean world no longer "beyond the line" but one where English Protestants and Spanish Catholics would coexist as neighbors, trading across political and confessional borders. English promoters argued that such trade would benefit Spanish and English colonists alike (though not Spain itself), by providing Spanish buyers with captive laborers and manufactured goods they otherwise could not acquire.

Ultimately, these English planners sought willing trade to drain Spain of bullion, a goal consistent with Protestant nationalism. But the means of achieving that goal—through collaboration—necessarily mitigated the exercise of anti-Catholicism or anti-Spanish sentiment on the ground or at sea in the Caribbean. The English could thus see their project in terms of "peace," despite all the violence inherent in the slave trading and plantation societies at its core. Modyford aligned human trafficking with peace when he instructed messengers to emphasize to officials at Santo Domingo "his Ma[jes]ties great love of Peace and good Neighbourhood, . . . Perticulerly wth the Spanish Nation." They were to stress that "it behooves us to Imitate our Princes to bee Peaceably minded and good Neighbours to each other." After thus assuring the Spanish of their peaceful intentions, they were to "treate wth them for a Trade at Jamaica especially for Blackes."[28]

Foreign policy in the region could no longer be trusted to private military contractors whose Protestant nationalism might interfere with their Protestant nation's geopolitical goals. (Privateers' Protestant nationalism had perhaps been in part instrumental, but they held on to it, insisting on its continued relevance in the region.) So to change course and encourage trade, Charles in his 1664 instructions to Modyford followed the governor's advice and prohibited the governor from granting commissions to privateers for predation against Spanish shipping or settlements. Rather than molesting "their neighbours," Jamaicans should "live with . . . Friendship & good Correspondence." Modyford was to restrain any of Charles's subjects from taking commissions from foreign princes "upon what pretence soever," and punish violators by confiscating their goods and ships.[29]

Although scholars often (and contemporaries occasionally) linked smugglers and pirates in one breath, interimperial merchants (smugglers from the Spanish perspective) and maritime thieves worked at cross-purposes. It is true that some English officials on both sides of the Atlantic briefly considered forcing trade in 1662 and 1663, hoping that a show of military strength would compel Spanish officials to accept trade. But such a route required the English to admit to treaty violations and risk the reverse—a complete shutting down of the openings peace provided. For example, the Jamaica Council declared "that the letters from the Governors of Porto Rico and San Domingo are an absolute denial of trade," and that under such circumstances, the governor's instructions permitted "a trade by force or otherwise."[30] But slave traders and English officials rejected the plans, instead seeking conflict-free commerce in the region, which would necessarily downplay the religious division that had long loomed large in defining Anglo-Spanish relations. In a 1663 draft letter to Jamaica's governor, Charles II seemed to approve of anti-Spanish violence and forced trade, but he quickly reversed course and in the clean copy "emphasized caution."[31] Would-be privateers, in contrast, clung to the old enmity to justify their depredations and confirm their continued place in the geopolitical arena.

Modyford faced two difficulties in executing his plans for willing trade. First, his Spanish counterparts, while agreeing to regular communication, had no authority to approve foreign trade. By and large they refused to discuss it, even if they tacitly condoned smuggling. The archival record of English and Spanish efforts is therefore uneven, because English Caribbean officials shared a desire for international Caribbean trade with their London superiors and could write about their efforts to promote it. Indeed, several lobbied for policy changes that would encourage the trade. In contrast, late seventeenth-century Spanish metropolitan officials opposed the legalization of foreign trade with English America. These differences in European officials' attitudes toward interimperial trade lay in the nature of the goods traded and their perceived relationship to national economic and political strength. Metropolitan officials from both European nations saw the trade as benefiting England at the expense of Spain because Spanish American colonists purchased enslaved Africans and European-manufactured goods from English merchants, usually paying in coin; England gained specie, markets for manufactured goods in Africa and Spanish America, and increased employment in England. Spain lost silver to its rival and lost the potential to increase its manufacturing capacity.[32]

Thus, while Jamaican governors were forthright in reporting their efforts to increase trade with their Spanish American neighbors, the governors of Cartagena de Indias and Santiago de Cuba were not. Our evidence that they condoned or even engaged in Anglo-Spanish trade comes from English accounts, from their political enemies' accusations, or from official investigations into their conduct rather than from their own writings.[33] As a result, we lack Spanish officials' explicitly expressed views of a regional political economy based on Caribbean colonial perspectives and instead must extrapolate from their actions.[34] Nonetheless, economic historians estimate that by the second half of the seventeenth century, foreign smugglers carried the majority of imports into Spanish America, a situation that could only have developed with cooperation from local Spanish officials.[35]

Even though all parties believed this trade benefited England at the expense of Spain, in the Caribbean, Spanish officials and merchants had the upper hand over their English counterparts. Because silver possessed such value, and because the English competed with Genoese, French, Dutch, and Portuguese merchants to obtain it via Spanish American trade, English officials and merchants had to assume the role of petitioners in their relationship with Spanish officials.[36] Moreover, what was bad for Spain might be good for Spanish American colonists and for the officials who condoned their illicit trade. Despite the risks to their careers, Spanish Caribbean governors who participated in contraband understood that local economic prosperity depended on increasing both the enslaved labor force and colonists' ability to purchase the people and the consumer items they desired at competitive prices—prices lowered by interimperial competition. They just could not say so to their superiors.

In addition to taciturn Spanish American officials, Jamaica governor Modyford faced a second challenge in fostering Anglo-Spanish trade: his initial zeal in decommissioning Jamaica's privateers turned them into his enemies. Against Charles's orders, they acquired French commissions in Tortuga and Hispaniola, where they joined forces with their French counterparts. They continued to assault Spanish prizes and towns, bringing Spanish anger and reprisal down on English merchants, but now their plunder would line French pockets and enrich French treasuries instead of English. Moreover, Modyford lost his ability to demand security (a bond) for good behavior in exchange for a commission, and the Tortuga-based Anglo-French privateers might use their French commissions to attack English as well as Spanish targets. Without enough naval ships at his command, Modyford was powerless to confiscate their goods and vessels. Even if they did not directly threaten Jamaican trade or plantations, when they were out on foreign commissions, they were unavailable to defend Jamaica should the governor need their services. And their attacks on Spanish shipping and ports undercut his attempts to convince Spanish officials and merchants that the English had changed course in the region.[37]

From the early 1660s to the early 1680s, then, two incompatible English plans (both potentially consistent with the developing plantation economy) for acquiring Spanish American silver and gold vied for ascendancy among English planners.[38] These two visions attached to two strikingly different imaginings of how political loyalty, religious adherence, and economic activity aligned. Merchants eyeing lucrative Spanish markets saw their own self-interest and broader English interests best served by removing restrictions on interimperial trade, especially with Catholic Spaniards. To trade across political and confessional borders, merchants and their supporters relinquished the idea that political allegiance or religious adherence should delimit economic activity. A community of merchants could transcend bodies politic or confessional loyalties.

Privateers, on the other hand, presumed alignment of political, religious, and economic categories. When they disobeyed superiors to attack possible Spanish trading partners (an act of piracy), sometimes under foreign commission, they could nonetheless see themselves as loyal English subjects because they held to an older version of Englishness that required hostility toward Catholic Spaniards.[39] This viewpoint retained enough sway that even their opponents sometimes continued to call those with commissions privateers, decades after many of them ceased to follow their sovereigns' orders. While these competing visions may not have originated in the Caribbean, its close and contested jurisdictions both widened and revealed the split. Purported privateers, operating in a new context of Anglo-Spanish peace and in a region of overlapping jurisdictions, forced officials over a quarter century to clarify what private military action mariners could perform and still retain their status as loyal subjects.

English officials willingly participated in the fiction of peacetime privateering during the 1660s and 1670s, most obviously by continuing to use the term *privateer* to refer to the maritime predators who targeted civilians with whom they were not at war. Some scholars have simply dismissed the seemingly messy contemporary English terminology as disingenuous and replaced the word *privateer* with *pirate* or *buccaneer*.[40] They have painted officials such as Modyford as uninterested in legal niceties and seeking only to acquire silver by all possible means. But in neglecting contemporaries' language we miss their struggle to place mariners within the appropriate legal categories in the rapidly changing and difficult-to-read geopolitical world of the Caribbean. When even officials endeavoring to define privateering narrowly continued to use the term expansively, some seemed to believe that calling pirates privateers could render the men obedient and loyal. Their use of the word *privateer* to describe men acting as pirates reflected that persistent hope, but also the difficulty everyone had in reframing their Caribbean worldview so dramatically and so quickly. Whether their slippage was unconscious or disingenuous, it nonetheless shows us moments of uncertainty among the English about which vision for the Caribbean would prevail.[41]

Many people in the Caribbean had been raised to see enmity between Spanish and English subjects and between Catholics and Protestants as both natural and necessary. For them, eschewing conflict required overcoming lifelong prejudices. More importantly, lasting amity depended on English and Spanish officials' ability and desire to change the course of privateers whose livelihoods depended on mutual depredation. Officials commonly received a share of the prize goods from privateers whom they had commissioned, and such officials hesitated to give up these supplements to their salaries. They also faced pressure from the elite investors who supplied privateers with ships and provisions. Thus, many people in the Caribbean, from governors to common seamen, drew income from prize taking and resisted a truce that would end such activities. As a result, English officials who promoted trade found their authority circumscribed by their inability to police the region.

In these circumstances, privateers possessed complicated identities vis-à-vis the polities they allegedly served. While "English privateer" might conjure a natural-born Englishman holding a commission from an officer of the English crown, the term could also refer to a natural-born Englishman holding a foreign commission or to a privateer of any nation who held an English commission. The notion that the normative subject was "natural-born" lumped together a sovereign's jurisdiction over territory and his jurisdiction over his mobile subjects: people born within his territory were "naturally" his subjects. In the seventeenth century, the term *natural* in English retained the meaning natal or native, making it a cognate to the Spanish *natural* (a usage that survived in the English *naturalization*). But it had also begun to acquire its meaning of "intrinsic," adding a new layer of meaning to the connection between natural subjects and their sovereign.

Charles II's prohibition against his subjects' taking foreign commissions sought to keep allegiance and jurisdiction tightly yoked, forbidding a "natural" subject to divide his loyalties. Otherwise, when English-born privateers whose commissions derived from non-English channels of authority attacked, their victims could hold English officials, and ultimately the crown, accountable for their depredations. Mercenaries, including privateers, fought and sailed for foreign crowns in Europe. But because in the Caribbean many rival colonies lay so near one another, mariners there could and did shift commissioning authority rapidly. And because colonial officials representing the privateers' natal sovereign were also likely close at hand, victims, in this case Spanish, could hold both the natural sovereign and the commissioning officer (and his sovereign) accountable when privateers overstepped their licenses or violated treaty agreements. In other words, a privateer whose commission and natal identity derived from different sovereigns operated under two separate jurisdictions simultaneously—a situation that proved especially combustible in the Caribbean, where mariners could cross multiple imperial borders in a day. Charles II's prohibition also recognized the reality that many English privateers, despite their displays of Protestant patriotism, were willing to sell their services to foreign and even Catholic officials.

And yet, the scarcity of naval ships meant that Caribbean officials depended on privateers to enforce both treaty law and the laws of particular empires and colonies. The Spanish, like the French, English, and Dutch challenging their dominance in the region, depended on such private men-of-war, a reality often lost in the differing terminology. They used the term *guardacostas* (coast guard), which emphasized their defensive role, but they functioned much like the private men-of-war their rivals employed. The captains and crews of Spanish guardacostas also commonly operated as independent contractors sailing under the license of colonial officials. And despite Spain's reputation as a more closed empire, its officials, too, relied on foreign mariners to sail and even command those ships.[42]

Spanish Americans' view of their privateers as defensive rested on their precedence in the region: they possessed the mines that produced American treasure, most of the region's coastline, its largest islands, and its longest-settled colonial cities and towns. Moreover, they had long claimed exclusive jurisdiction over Caribbean waters. Thus, the Spanish saw guardacostas as private defense contractors whose job it was to protect what was legitimately

Spain's by attacking foreign invaders. Until the conquest of Jamaica, the English might have understood their own presence in the western Caribbean as invasive, but after 1655, they believed they held legitimate right to the island and its shipping lanes. When Spanish forces attempted to retake the island or targeted merchant ships sailing to and from Jamaica, the English began to describe their own privateering in defensive terms as well.[43]

Because Governor Modyford lacked royal ships to defend the island or to confiscate the goods and vessels of English subjects taking foreign commissions, he resumed issuing commissions himself to lure English privateers back from Tortuga. As soon as he received news of the Second Anglo-Dutch War in early 1665, he granted Edward Mansfield (Mansvelt) a letter against the Dutch as a means of employing the privateers he hoped to control. Had they targeted Curaçao as their instructions directed, they could have weakened Jamaica-based merchants' primary competitor for Anglo-Spanish trade. But some of them (likely including Mansfield) were Dutch themselves and all preferred more lucrative Spanish targets, so instead of obeying Modyford's commission, they joined with French mariners who held a commission from the Tortuga governor, and together the French, English, and Dutch "privateers" attacked the Spanish island of Santa Catalina (Providence Island to the English), forcing its surrender.

Despite his Tortuga commission against Spanish targets, Mansfield proffered his accomplishment to Jamaica governor Modyford as a prize for the English (bringing with him one hundred plundered captives, some of them free in the Spanish colonies, to sell as slaves in the English island). He suffered no repercussions for violating his English commission, which had permitted action only against the Dutch.[44] Governor Modyford defended his decision to condone Mansfield's offense. Noting that he had "reproved" Mansfield for taking the Spanish island "w[i]thout order," he claimed that he had had no choice but to "accept ye tender of it in his Ma[jes]tie's behalfe." To do otherwise would have exhibited "manifest imprudence," considering Santa Catalina's location just off the Central American coast—perfect "for ye favouring any designe his Ma[jes]ty may have on that rich maine."[45] Charles II's ostensible "designs" on Spanish America at that moment involved commerce rather than conquest. These were plans that Modyford shared, but the governor revealed that even he, a slave trader nurturing his own Spanish American commercial network, had trouble letting go of English dreams that they might conquer large swaths of Spanish America. Therefore, although Mansfield had violated his commission and the king's new policy, Modyford regarded it his "duty" to send a commander and reinforcements to hold the island for Charles II.[46]

Modyford alleged that Mansfield and his men retained their identity as privateers, despite lacking an English commission to attack the Spanish.[47] Calling them privateers rested instead on a historical presumption of Anglo-Spanish enmity and on the traditional practice—now outlawed for Charles's subjects—in which mariners freely took commissions from the designees of any legitimate sovereign. The term *privateer* afforded the men a continuing claim to act as representatives of England, even as regulations began to deny them a role as legitimate geopolitical actors.

Indeed, although the Spanish quickly retook the island, Mansfield also succeeded, in the short term, in defining Charles II's interests in the region. His unauthorized assault on a Spanish settlement generated further English investment in the project. Despite English interest in trade, militant Protestant conquest persisted in the actions of the men who would call themselves privateers, and in the officials, who saw no choice but to let them continue their violence. The apparent ease with which French Catholics and English Protestants joined forces on this expedition neither erased religious differences nor reflected religious disinterest. The English reported that their French Catholic partners had foiled their attempt to plunder and destroy a church on Santa Catalina and had guarded its priest from harm. The Frenchmen did so perhaps to protect the sacred space of their coreligionists, or perhaps from a belief that they had a better claim to its plunder: one observer reported that the French pirates planned to take a bible back to furnish their own church in Tortuga.[48]

Mansfield's disobedience illustrates how the Caribbean's geopolitical situation—with rival jurisdictions so near one another, and officials so far from their superiors—gave privateers leverage over their commissioning officers and other officials in the region, and therefore slowed and complicated the efforts of merchants and colonial administrators trying to create a region dependent on more open trade. When Modyford revoked commissions, Tortuga governors Jeremie Deschamps and Bertrand d'Ogeron granted them. If Modyford had refused Mansfield's offer of Santa Catalina/Providence, d'Ogeron might have accepted it, if not for France then (perhaps worse) for himself.

The mariners did not, however, hold all the power. Even as they flouted specific laws and their own commissions and forced the hands of their supposed superiors, they depended on the colonial administration of internationally recognized law because the very category of privateer rested on shared law. Privateers needed commissions—paper affirmations of their legality that they could present to any European official—to avoid hanging as pirates.[49] Moreover, many English privateers sought to maintain their natural-born national (and religious) identities even as they took foreign commissions and joined multinational coalitions to act against Charles II's orders. Mansfield's "gift" of Santa Catalina/Providence and his claim to act on Charles II's behalf, rather than Tortuga governor d'Ogeron's, may have reflected the Protestantism that at least some of his men had exhibited as well as an effort to retain or regain Jamaican support.

Modyford, squeezed by the privateers who used d'Ogeron to resist the English governor's authority, and rebuffed by Spanish officials who rejected or ignored his trade overtures, requested and received permission from London officials "to graunt, or not to graunt Commissions against the [Spaniards], as to [him] should seeme most advantagious for his Majestie's service." They thus freed him from his original instructions. His fear of alienating the pirates derived in part from his concern about French expansion in the region. If the English could trust that the current peace with France would prove "immortall," or if they could believe that "that warr like Prince had noe designe this way," then Modyford "should be little concerned at the lawlesse motions of these Privateers." However, given the geopolitical realities—that Louis XIV indeed planned Caribbean expansion and that peace was surely temporary—Modyford thought it crucial to harness the mariners' collective power rather than allow the French to do so.[50] So in February 1666, Modyford and his council retreated from their earlier commitment to "good correspondence and commerce" with Spanish America and declared that letters of marque against the Spanish would foster "the strengthening, preservation, enriching and advancing the settlement of this island."[51] The experiment of an unaggressive Jamaica within a Caribbean region characterized by "good neighbourhood" thus foundered in the short run, justified in part by arguments of "no peace beyond the line," even as the vision of expanding slave trading persisted among English and Spanish Caribbean merchants and some Caribbean and London officials.[52]

When the English tried to establish their own jurisdiction over Santa Catalina/Providence Island, they confirmed the disparity between their own and Spanish beliefs about how race might determine a person's capacity for political allegiance. Mansfield offered those residents whom he perceived as Europeans the option of transferring their allegiance and staying to live under English rule. But he seized as slaves all he deemed "negroes." Mansfield thus divided Santa Catalina's residents into two categories that he believed he could recognize on sight. Each encompassed both a legal and a racial category—free and Spanish or slave and Negro—despite the racial complexity of Santa Catalina's population and the fact that many of its residents of African, Indigenous, and mixed descent were free and loyal vassals. He presumed that those whom he saw as White possessed the capacity for allegiance they could offer to a sovereign, while those he perceived as "negroes" did not.[53]

English opinions about the place of African- and Indigenous-descended people varied and changed. Nonetheless, Mansfield (of Dutch descent but operating on behalf of and within an English sphere) foresaw an English Caribbean without free Black subjects and without recognition of Indigenous or mixed-race categories that carried meaning for individuals and for officials in Spanish America. English privateering commissions, which commonly gave private men-of-war no pay beyond what they could plunder, encouraged them to take whatever they could sell, including human beings. English, Dutch, and French reliance on privateers during the seventeenth century therefore increased the likelihood of a more thorough commodification of people of color than the Spanish practiced in the region.

Given the important place that free people of color held in the Spanish Caribbean, it is not surprising that several of the people Mansfield seized were free. Some were soldiers and at least one a military officer, positions that attested their loyalty to the crown.[54] Indeed, the Spanish retook the island with a force that included 29 Mulatto and 12 Indigenous men (of a total of about 350) from Portobelo, who were joined by 126 soldiers from Cartagena, half of them Mulatto. Perhaps ironically, they sailed in a fleet led by an asiento ship that the governor had found in Portobelo. Because the vessel was "well provided with munitions of war," he chartered it for the recapture effort. When the ships reached Santa Catalina, they were met by three Black men who swam out to let them know that only seventy-two pirates held the fort and "that they were under a great consternation, seeing such considerable Forces come against them." This intelligence convinced the Spanish to land, and they easily overwhelmed the outnumbered English. The three swimmers, after forty-five days of English rule, conveyed their preference for Spanish control by risking their lives to help the Spanish retake the island.[55]

While privateers hindered interimperial slave trading, they fostered the commodification of Caribbean people of color. In their raids, they seized Spanish American vassals of African and Indigenous descent, both free and enslaved, as plunder they could seize and sell to English, Dutch, or French buyers, rather than as subjects and prisoners of war who might be held for ransom or forced to labor on public works, but not sold into slavery. The privateers and smugglers associated with English colonization (and the officials who supported each), although often at odds with one another, both created an English Caribbean political economy that rested on the racialized exclusion of people of color from the body politic.

In 1666, English and Spanish diplomats in Europe negotiated for peace, and English hopes ran high that Spanish American ports would open to them. Governor Modyford received reports from London that "freedome of trade will be had, for our People in America, or a Peace will not bee."[56] The resulting 1667 Treaty of Madrid, *Articles of Peace, Commerce, and Alliance, between the Crowns of Great Britain and Spain*, indeed promoted trade but limited it to places "where hitherto Trade and Commerce hath been accustomed." That vague qualification permitted competing interpretations, although those close to the negotiations understood it to prohibit Anglo-Spanish commerce in the greater Caribbean.[57]

The language of the 1667 Treaty of Madrid clearly forbade violence between subjects of the Spanish and British crowns, pledging the "subjects, people, and inhabitants . . . of what degree or condition soever" of both crowns to observe "amity, confederation, and peace" with one another and to "serve each other well by mutual help, aid, kindnes, and all manner of friendship." The treaty applied "by land as by sea and fresh-waters" and "between the lands, countries, kingdoms, dominions, and territories, belonging unto, or under the obedience of either of the said kings."[58]

When news reached the Caribbean of the treaty, English and Spanish officials tried at first to comply. Although mutual mistrust and uncontrolled mariners defeated the attempt, Caribbean officials' initial efforts to police the region and create enough cooperation to foster trade belie the image of condoned anarchy suggested by the phrase "no peace beyond the line." Indeed, there was little consensus among seventeenth-century actors that "the line" legally affected peace or war beyond the specifics of Cateau-Cambrésis. In the Anglo-Spanish case, belligerents who used the notion of "no peace beyond the line" to defend violence after 1667 did so without legal sanction. Both the stipulation of peace between people and the declaration of peace between territories applied to subjects and lands throughout the world, including the Caribbean. The 1667 treaty clearly applied to both crowns' subjects everywhere. Thus, the violence between 1667 and 1670 resulted from willful disregard for the treaty rather than any ambiguity in it.

Although the treaty promised peace, it did little to weaken privateers' power in the Caribbean. Instead, an increasing French presence expanded privateers' leverage. Jamaica-based privateers continued to resist any suggestion that the region's future should rest on open interimperial commerce, pushing instead to perpetuate a confrontational model in which national and religious identities aligned and together delimited both economic commerce and neighborly correspondence. The Caribbean of "no peace beyond the line" gave them purpose, preserved their national identities as they understood them, and rested on Catholic-Protestant enmity as a given. They used their strength to insist on retaining their legality as privateers and their national identities as Englishmen, even when they threatened violence to force officials' hands, disobeyed their superiors, violated the English commissions they did receive, and illegally took foreign commissions—behaviors that should have discredited them as pirates. Even when they acted as members of joint Anglo-French forces, they claimed (and were often granted) continued political identity as English subjects.

The most notorious of the privateers who disrupted Anglo-Spanish peace efforts after 1667 was the Jamaica-based Welshman Henry Morgan. In June 1668 he led combined French and English forces of 422 men and took Portobelo, capturing "300 negroes," despite a commission against Spanish shipping permitting him to take only a small number of prisoners from shore for intelligence purposes. Governor Pérez de Guzmán ransomed the captives along with the town. Morgan and his fellow captains viewed the exchange as a purchase of property rather than as a ransom, claiming that they "condiscended to" accept the one hundred thousand pieces of eight proffered, "though [it] was far short to the Vallue of [the] Negroes."[59]

One French commander wrote home that had they gone with twice as many men—a mere eight hundred—they could have taken the city of Panama and controlled the primary conduit for Peruvian silver and for the African captives who mined it. When Spanish officials intercepted the French commander's letter, the Spanish ambassador, the Count of Molina, protested to Charles II that in commissioning Morgan, Governor Modyford had behaved "unjust[ly] and contrary to the faith of the general peace." London officials' responses seemed to Molina "soe different from what has been promised" in the treaty that he demanded written explanation. Molina was careful twice to identify the culprits as "his Majesty's subjects of Jamaica," echoing the 1667 treaty language that obligated the subjects of both princes to preserve the peace.[60]

Molina was correct to suspect London officials of bad faith; as the 1667 treaty was finalized, they told Governor Modyford that he could commission privateers against Spanish shipping if necessary, to avoid "loos[ing] them from his Ma[jes]t[y]'s service." James Modyford wrote to his brother that as soon as he heard that the treaty had "at last" been signed, he asked London officials whether the treaty addressed Caribbean trade, hoping to hear that Spain had agreed to allow English merchants into its American ports. Instead he was told "that trade would never be admitted, so [tha]t nothing was done, but all left as formerly." When James then asked whether the privateers might "go on or not, in takeing of Spaniards, as formerly," he was told "yes, you might permitt them to do it."[61] Thus, frustrated at the failure to obtain permission to trade, London officials chose to violate the treaty they had just signed.

Not surprisingly, Spanish American governors objected and then retaliated, issuing their own commissions to private guardacostas.[62] As the situation escalated locally, Spain's queen regent Maria protested to Charles II and held the British sovereign accountable for French depredations undertaken in consort with the English. She later claimed that when she alerted him to these violations of "the peace celebrated in 1667," he "answered that his subjects had no peace in the Indies." In response, she issued a decree on April 20, 1669, commanding the Santiago de Cuba governor Pedro Bayona de Villanueva to publish a declaration of war against the English and "to execute all the hostilities which are permitted in war," taking all "ships, islands, places, and ports" the English had in the Caribbean.[63] Jamaican officials, to justify their own further violence, then collected evidence that Spanish Caribbean officials violated Englishmen's rights in the region.[64]

Clearly, despite a short-lived effort by slave traders and some Caribbean officials, the 1667 peace had failed in the Caribbean. Privateers ignored it, and London officials backed their violence. Raiding the Spanish remained so important to Jamaica's economy that in 1669, resident John Style wrote that the island's trade "now consists principally in plate, money, jewels, and other things brought in by the privateers," purchased by Jamaica merchants, and then traded to New England for food or to Madeira for wine. He estimated that Jamaica had eight hundred privateers (which would have equaled about a fourth of the White male population).[65]

Despite privateers' patriotic posture, Style doubted their attachment to the island. He believed that loyalty derived primarily from a person's "interest," and interest came from owning land within the colony's jurisdiction. Oaths and nativity mattered little compared to holding a personal stake in a sovereign's landed dominion. Because so few privateers owned land in Jamaica, they could not value the colony or, by extension, England, even though they boasted of their necessity to the island's defense and performed a belligerent anti-Catholic patriotism. Ultimately, however, they had no reason to come to Jamaica's aid should it need defending, because "gold and gain is the only god they worship," and French commissions were easy to come by. Style failed to see that an "interest" in land, which he believed could reform men, also arose from desire for "gain," which he criticized. Oblivious to the contradiction, he recommended that England send planters rather than merchants to bolster the island's population.[66]

Style did stress that planters sent to Jamaica ought to be Christian. In invoking religion, he suggested a second source of loyalty to the crown and the island, less tangible than landed interest but nonetheless real and, in his view, linked to civil behavior. In an inversion of the Black Legend, he described in graphic detail how privateers tortured Portobelo's civilians in 1668 to extract information about the wealth they imagined hidden everywhere. He contrasted the "evil and wickedness of those privateers who call themselves Christians" with the helpless innocence of Spanish women and men, asserting that the "privateers" outdid even "the most savage heathens" and "the Jews that crucified our Saviour" in their capacity for "cruelty and oppression." His argument for a general Christianity rather than the militant Protestantism of the privateers was consistent with his assertion that English officials ought to care about how men holding English commissions treated Catholic Spanish civilians.

Style argued that privateers' unchristian incivility endangered English as well as Spanish colonists in the region. Because privateers brought back to Jamaica the violence they had honed on innocent Spanish vassals, their value to the island was dubious—residents had reason to fear the same ruthlessness that made them formidable "protectors" of Jamaica. They returned to the island spewing "horrid oaths, blasphemies, abuse of Scriptures" and committing "rapes, whoredoms, and adulteries." The island's authorities not only tolerated such behavior but even "made . . . jest of" it. Style thus rejected privateers' claims that they occupied a still valid role as defenders of Protestant England, in part because they owned no land, but in part because they were not the Christians they purported to be.

Having linked privateers' failed Christianity with a dystopian colonial society, he further linked Christianity with allegiance by suggesting it could trump race. Style believed that when landowners assigned "negroes" (he did not specify free or enslaved) to manage their estates, they "destroy[ed] the Christian interest." However, the problem lay not in African ancestry but in English Jamaicans' negligence in converting enslaved people to Christianity. He believed that "bringing up negro children in the Christian religion" would promote the island's success. If Africans accepted Christianity as a source of shared identity with colonizers, "they might prove as good, if not better subjects than many of their masters" and develop a loyalty to colonial Jamaica that could overcome their patent lack of "interest" in the island's developing plantation society.[67]

Style thus imagined an English colonial body politic that incorporated African-descended people on the basis of their conversion to the religion of empire. For Style, as for the Spanish, Christianity provided a unifying corporate identity that would allow unfree people a political identity, albeit one that (as in Spanish America) would not challenge their captivity and would require their assimilation to their colonial masters' culture and religion. Placing such speculations about enslaved Africans' potential as "good . . . subjects" immediately after his condemnation of privateers "who call themselves Christians," Style also foreshadowed peacetime privateers' eventual loss of place as agents of empire and even as subjects. Although he called the men privateers and indicated that many Jamaican officials dismissed their misdeeds as unimportant, his critique of them as unfit for inclusion in the body politic predicted the coming rejection of peacetime privateering as piracy. He saw the men as native-born subjects who, through their landless, mobile, and unchristian behavior, had forfeited membership in all legitimate sovereigns' bodies of subjects, and had placed themselves outside the bounds of humanity and natural law. For Style, then, meaningful ties to a sovereign's landed jurisdiction, along with Christian education and behavior that he believed followed from it, formed the basis for good colonial subjecthood.

Governor Modyford, in contrast, ignored religious adherence as a potential component of political loyalty. He ultimately blamed French officials for providing the commissions that encouraged mariners' disloyalty, a formulation that assumed the tenuous nature of privateers' allegiance: it could be bought and sold. He, like Style, tied allegiance to interest, but for Modyford that interest might be both transitory and transferable. Nonetheless, he saw privateers as an unavoidable force in the region, whose alliance (if not allegiance) would benefit whatever official could harness it. The distinction between alliance, or even just contractual obligation, and allegiance blurred in Caribbean officials' portrayals of mariners. In attaching national or local place-based jurisdictional identities to the designation of privateer (calling them "our," "Jamaica," or "English" privateers), Modyford suggested that ideally the men would exhibit loyalty, even while he acknowledged that they rarely did so.

In June 1669, perhaps responding to Spanish complaints about Morgan's 1668 attack on Panama, Modyford wrote directly to Spanish ambassador Molina in London. He asserted a shared Anglo-Spanish interest in preventing French expansion in the Caribbean and emphasized his own efforts to pursue those common goals. Molina must know that the "whole nation" of Spaniards "in these parts" had praised Modyford's "justice and civility to them" when he arrived in Jamaica, a course he would have continued had he been able to control the privateers. But the international context and his lack of naval forces left him powerless to prevent English privateers from joining with "mine and your master's enemies" the French, except to issue them commissions. Withholding any deference we might expect from a colonial official writing to a metropolitan ambassador, Modyford stressed Spanish weakness in the region, due to sparse settlement, a lack "of hearts, Arms, and knowledge in warre," and the "doubtful obedience" of Indigenous vassals, asserting that the English could take any Spanish town they wanted "this side of the line." While (according to Modyford), England's Charles II harbored no such wishes for conquest, France's Louis XIV did, and if the French king controlled the combined privateering forces available in the Caribbean, he could take what Spanish territory he desired. Thus, Modyford advised Molina, even though Modyford's decision to issue anti-Spanish commissions had exposed the Spanish to English pillaging, he had actually *saved* the Spanish from a more devastating French attack.

But even after admitting his own impotence to rein in these unruly English subjects, Modyford suggested that Molina invite them into the Spanish ambit. The privateers could "be brought to serve your Master," making up for the lack of Spanish forces in the region. He insisted that the privateers would readily "put themselves under any imployement" and that they would as willingly serve the Spanish as attack them, if doing so provided legal standing and a source of income.[68] Modyford acknowledged no tension between his claims on these men as "our Privatiers" and his recognition that they would follow employment wherever it led them, or between his own inability to control them and his suggestion that the Spanish (despite lacking "hearts, Arms, and knowledge in warre") might somehow be able to keep them in check. In the same year, in a narrative designed for his superiors, Modyford deplored "the lawless motions of these privateers," throwing doubt on his contention that their obedience could be safely bought.[69] Not surprisingly, if Molina read Modyford's proposal, he made no response to the governor. When English officials could not control these (largely English) mariners, why should any expect Spanish officials' authority to sway them?

In late 1669, Modyford claimed that English privateering had stalled, though he acknowledged that this new development depended partly on international circumstances beyond his control: French officials in Tortuga had been forbidden to grant commissions, a situation that might change at any moment. In the meantime, a few of the wealthiest men who had formerly held Jamaican commissions had bought plantations, encouraged perhaps by having captured Indigenous, African, and mixed-race people in their attacks on Spanish and Indian towns and coastal settlements. Their human plunder comprised a ready-made labor force of people already fully aware of their new masters' capacity for violence. Others of the former privateers hunted hogs and cattle in sparsely settled parts of Cuba, which Modyford mentioned as evidence of privateer reform, ignoring its illegality. "Most," however, were trading with Natives or themselves processing hides, tallow, turtle shell, and logwood on the Miskito Coast, Campeche, and the Darién region of Panama.[70] Modyford neglected to mention what he certainly knew—that in addition to dealing in logwood and animal products, these men bought or seized Indigenous captives to sell as slaves in Jamaica and other English colonies.[71] Earlier, in writing to the Spanish ambassador, Modyford had pointed to the "questionable loyalty" of Spain's Indigenous subjects who collaborated with Spain's rivals, adopting a Spanish colonial worldview that saw Miskito and Tule who cooperated with English invaders as rebels against the Spanish colonial order that defined them as vassals of Carlos II. Here, he implied instead that they were independent and sovereign, and that English commerce with them therefore fell within the bounds of European law. He could thus describe the privateers as having "turned merchant," despite their incursions into Spanish-claimed territory. The governor also acknowledged that some privateers continued to take Spanish ships, landing their plunder in remote Jamaican harbors beyond officials' reach, but he dismissed them as "knaves" and alleged that they represented a small minority of the former privateers.[72] He insisted that the tide had turned.

In the spirit of such purported conciliation, in January 1670 Modyford sent the former privateer Captain Bernard Claesen Speirdyck to Cuba to deliver four Spanish prisoners and letters to the governor of Cuba "signifying peace between the two nations." This local gesture of peace, before metropolitan officials renegotiated a stronger peace treaty later in the year, included an invitation to engage in contraband trade. Instead of going to Havana, where he could find the governor but where smuggling would prove more difficult, Speirdyck sailed for the sparsely populated Manzanillo Bay on the southern coast and contacted the mayor of the inland town of Bayamo. The mayor sent his lieutenant aboard Speirdyck's ship.[73] After receiving the prisoners and searching the ship three times for evidence of privateering, the lieutenant agreed to buy Speirdyck's entire cargo (its contents unspecified). The Dutch captain Speirdyck had served English Jamaica as a privateer in the past and so had already accepted the equivocal allegiance inherent to privateers who identified as subjects of one sovereign while acting under another's commission. Modyford's decision to entrust this foreigner to affirm Anglo-Spanish peace in the region shows an even greater flexibility for individuals in the Caribbean to acquire new political roles. As Speirdyck and his crew left Cuba to return to Port Royal, Manoel Ribeiro Pardal (Manuel de Rivero in Spanish and sometimes English sources), a Portuguese privateer fitted from (and with a commission from the Spanish governor of) Cartagena, attacked Speirdyck, saying he had letters of reprisal against the English, as revenge for the Jamaica-based privateers' 1668 taking of Portobelo.

We do not know whether the eighteen crew members aboard Speirdyck's ship were English or Dutch-born, or something else. But the purser Cornelius Carsten, Dutch like his captain, referred to the men lost in battle between the Dutch- and Portuguese-commanded ships as "the English" and "the Spaniards." Modyford and another English writer referred to Bernard Claesen Speirdyck by the moniker Captain Bart and never identified him by nationality, thus stressing his ties to Jamaica and his service to its English governor rather than his Dutch origins.[74] Indeed, in Modyford's first report of the incident, he identifies Speirdyck only as an unnamed "merchantman," a former privateer who had done just as English officials had asked, reformed his ways, and turned to commerce. From Modyford's perspective, the "merchantman's" voyage represented precisely the sort of shift he hoped would follow his revocation of privateering commissions. He complained to his superiors that these reforms, combined with the fact that the Cubans had "admitted [Speirdyck] to a trade," ought to have saved the captain from attack. But while Modyford asserted that the cooperative nature of the trade justified it, the commerce violated Spanish American law and the 1667 Treaty of Madrid, and therefore Ribeiro's commission likely condoned taking Speirdyck as prize.[75]

Ribeiro's attack on the smugglers and his killing of Speirdyck "so incensed the whole body of privateers" (who regarded Speirdyck as one of their own, despite his "reform") that they planned "a general rendezvous" at the Cayman Islands the following month to plot their revenge. Modyford planned to send an envoy "to diver[t] them or moderate their councils," recognizing their functional autonomy but hoping nonetheless that he could influence them.[76] Both the English and Spanish worlds thus contained individuals acting at cross-purposes. Modyford, Speirdyck, and the mayor, merchants, and lieutenant of Bayamo pursued interimperial trade. Such trade violated the 1667 Treaty of Madrid and Spain's colonial regulation, but it also reflected their local efforts to assert the peace that the treaty demanded of them. The governor of Cartagena and his privateer Ribeiro aimed to enforce Spain's economic regulations and the articles of the treaty prohibiting trade, but in so doing violated the peace that the treaty required. The group of privateers whose favor Modyford curried preferred predation on Spanish shipping to less combative pursuits, although some, such as Speirdyck, were willing to turn in their commissions to try their hand at smuggling and even diplomatic missions.

Local officials' disagreement about whether Anglo-Spanish peace should entail trade, along with privateers' refusal to abide by new regulations, raised concerns that establishing Anglo-Spanish amity might be impossible. One Jamaican wrote that the Spanish at Cartagena had declared war against the English, and that they "tell us plainly" of their plans to "ruin" Jamaica, "obstructing [its] commerce" by taking the island's ships. Ignoring the English role in rejecting the 1667 treaty, he suggested that the English had been duped by the Spanish and had made "a blind peace" that the Spanish never had intended to respect.[77]

In April, Modyford wrote to London requesting permission to retaliate against the Spanish, not only for Ribeiro's attack on Speirdyck, but also in response to widespread rumors that the Spanish had declared war on Jamaica. As evidence, he sent along the deposition of a prisoner captured from a Cartagena-based man-of-war in the Bay of Campeche. This prisoner was "an Englishman . . . who had revolted from his allegiance and lived with the Spaniards at Cartagena," and who informed Modyford that "there was war proclaimed in Cartagena by beat of drum against Jamaica."[78] Modyford heard similar news from an English gentleman who had been in Curaçao the previous November, where he had met an English pilot of a Spanish ship from Portobelo. This pilot reported that in Portobelo, too, the Spanish had vowed "they would never have peace with the Englishmen."[79]

Modyford had other evidence of Spanish hostility toward Jamaica, notably the words and deeds of local Spaniards. (Jamaicans' regular access to dire news from Spanish Americans revealed that even among escalating conflict, communication channels never broke down.) Yet the governor went out of his way to send to London the reports of two men born English but patently disloyal to England, suggesting his greater willingness to trust information from a born Englishman—even one "who had revolted against his allegiance." Men such as these used the close borders in the Caribbean to cross boundaries of nation, language, and loyalty. But Modyford's regard for them as "Englishmen" reveals how difficult it was for observers committed to stable political identities to accept such mutability—a mutability that existed in border and port towns around the world but that defined the Caribbean, which consisted so overwhelmingly of port towns, unpoliced coastlines, and contested maritime spaces. Officials in London and Madrid were left with little choice but to renegotiate the 1667 Treaty of Madrid. They clarified their expectation that Anglo-Spanish peace should prevail in the Caribbean. Leaving no room for misinterpretation about whether lines of amity persisted, they put the word *America* into the title of the 1670 Treaty of Madrid.[80]

Nevertheless, the escalation of hostilities in the western Caribbean proved difficult to stem. Even in June 1670, as rumors of the new Treaty of Madrid began to reach the Caribbean, Jamaica governor Thomas Modyford's councilors recommended that he grant a commission to Henry Morgan to attack Santiago de Cuba.[81] The new treaty required that Spanish subjects recognize current English possessions in the Americas, and therefore Jamaicans with coastal plantations, who had been suffering Spanish strikes, had much to gain. But rather than push toward peace, the governor's council defended continued maritime marauding, by recounting Governor Bayona's misdeeds the previous year. Citing Spanish attacks to justify their own, they recommended that Modyford issue Morgan a commission to command all the warships, officers, and seamen "belonging to" Port Royal and permit him to engage in "all manner of Exployts" that would protect Jamaica, "his Ma[jes]t[y']s chief Interest in the Indies," from the Spanish, whom they referred to as "the Enemy" in "this Warr," undeclared by their sovereign.[82] Accordingly, Modyford granted

Morgan a commission to attack Santiago de Cuba "or any place else where there are stores and kill all officers soldiers and seamen."[83] Modyford extended Morgan's charge to protect Jamaica and its shipping to include also any merchant ships passing near the island, thereby asserting that Jamaica's security depended not only on the safety of the island's inhabitants but also on the more general flow of commerce in the region.

Modyford gave Morgan a set of additional instructions that outlined the privateer's powers: he operated as a semiautonomous agent of English empire. European privateers had long maneuvered with such freedom, but the Caribbean context in the late seventeenth century allowed such independent actors to wreak considerable diplomatic havoc. Representatives of multiple imperial and Indigenous polities with rival jurisdictional claims gave privateers the authority and the incentive to make war. Distant from the sovereign, political agency devolved onto colonial officials, who further distributed it to privateers. Furthermore, Modyford authorized Morgan to issue additional privateering licenses to any ship captains he wished, English or foreign. When Modyford specified that the men who joined Morgan's expedition would work on the "old pleasing account of no purchase no pay," with all plunder divided "according to the accustomed Rules," he explicitly acknowledged the privateers' place in an "old" order, one that the trade overtures of the 1660s and treaties of 1667 and 1670 suggested was obsolete. But here, despite the governor's own role in that trade, he expressed nostalgia for the "pleasing" arrangement that instead encouraged assault against Jamaica's neighbors in Spanish America.[84]

Morgan recruited both English and French captains to join him. When those French captains attacked Spanish settlements with an English Jamaican commission, as when Mansfield took Santa Catalina/Providence Island under Tortuga commission, or when Spanish governors commissioned Portuguese or Irish mariners to seize English interlopers, they operated under a set of geopolitical assumptions at odds with the emerging plantation political economy of the region, which depended on safe passage for the ships transporting enslaved Africans and the products they mined and grew.[85] Officials may have believed they issued privateering commissions in their sovereign's interest. But when they issued licenses to foreigners or when they allowed privateers to put together multinational fleets and crews, they helped create a population of men who saw their personal interests as dependent on ongoing warfare and divorced from that of any one sovereign, severing the men's identities from their "natural-born" subjecthood. They thus weakened any link between mariners' places of birth and subject loyalty, and any hope that either could be used to mark the boundaries separating European empires from one another in the Caribbean.

Modyford also gave Morgan a plan for establishing English jurisdiction in Santiago de Cuba. Modyford, like Mansfield two years earlier in Santa Catalina/Providence Island, proved open to acquiring new English subjects from among Spanish colonists, here imagining that individuals might transfer their allegiance (despite his earlier reluctance to accept that Englishmen might ever cease to be Englishmen).[86] While Mansfield dismissed Santa Catalina's African-descended residents as impossible potential subjects, Modyford seemed willing to consider a colonial future for Jamaica that resembled its Spanish neighbors, where people of African descent lived as both free property-holding subjects who formed part of the body politic *and* as enslaved laborers constituting property. If Morgan succeeded in capturing the city, he was to "proclayme mercy and Enjoyment of Estates and liberty of Conscience to all the Spaniards that will submitt & give Assurance of their Loyalty to his Ma[jes]ty." He was also to grant "liberty to all the slaves that will come in," and if any aided the English invasion, Morgan was to divide among them their former masters' plantations "as reward." Aware of the danger of capture and enslavement that free Black people faced in the Caribbean, Modyford commanded Morgan to "make them sufficient Grants in Writing both for their Libertys and Estates," reserving one fourth of each estate's yearly produce to help maintain military defenses for the region. If he could, Morgan was to preserve houses, sugar works, and cane in the field. The former Barbadian recognized the growing importance of sugar to Cuba and its potential to shape an English future in the western Caribbean.

Modyford's willingness to consider that such a future might include free Blacks, like John Style's similar recommendations the same year, run counter to our understandings of how Englishmen believed Africans fit into their colonial plans. Their proposals reveal an English recognition—in 1670—that populations of African descent not only possessed strategic power in the region but also that they did so as potential subjects who could, through their political allegiance, strengthen Europeans' colonial claims over territory. But at the same time, the governor revealed his underlying doubt that enslaved Cubans might espouse loyalty to a European sovereign or value membership in a colonial community. In defending his decision to commission Morgan against the Spanish, Modyford explained that the seeming risks of a small new colony making war on a huge empire masked a very different colonial reality. While the "Spanish possessions [were] very large, . . . the possessors [were] very few," and moreover, most of the inhabitants of the Spanish territories were "Indians, negroes and other slaves, to whom," he believed, "it is indifferent who is their master."[87] Even while contemplating an offer of freedom, Modyford revealed his assumption (in the case of Cuba incorrect) that people of African and Indigenous descent were by default slaves.

In case he was wrong about enslaved people's allegiances, Modyford outlined yet another possibility, more in keeping with the historical belligerence of the region and with English merchants' increasing role as slave traders: if "the Spaniards and slaves are deaf to your Proposalls," Morgan was to destroy and burn all habitations "and leave it as a Wilderness putting men slaves to the sword" and imprisoning women, who would be brought to Jamaica and sold, with the proceeds added to the plunder that Morgan's men would share.

All these proposals applied only to Spanish-speaking slaves. Modyford assumed that unlike enslaved creoles born or long resident in Spanish America, newly arrived Africans would lack the cultural and political understanding of colonial Caribbean societies to choose English or Spanish allegiance. They thus were enslavable but not capable either of becoming English subjects or of dying as loyal Spanish vassals. Enslaved men who had arrived from Africa recently enough that they spoke no Spanish were, like women and children, to be sold in Jamaica or, if merchant ships were in the vicinity, to buyers who would take them to New England or Virginia.[88] Modyford's confidence in Morgan's ability to exploit North American slave markets accorded with his order that Morgan protect merchant shipping "around" Jamaica. That regional commerce increasingly included not just the sale of captive Africans but also the redistribution of people of color throughout the region.

Morgan and his fleet never attempted Santiago de Cuba. He claimed to learn, both from Englishmen recently imprisoned there and from captured Spanish mariners, that he could not take the city without risking his entire fleet. But he may have manufactured the excuse in order to pursue greater plunder than Santiago offered. One captive testified that Panama president Juan Pérez de Guzmán had given Spaniards "great Incouragement" to attack Jamaica, having issued commissions to multiple ship captains who had since captured several Englishmen. Moreover, a fleet from Spain was coming to join the effort. So when Morgan demanded of his thirty-seven captains "what Place was fittest to attacque" to preserve "his Ma[jes]t[y']s honor," to protect Jamaica, and to best "curb . . . the Insolencys of the Enemy," they unanimously agreed on the City of Panama on the Pacific coast. Divulging their material rather than imperial goals, Morgan identified it as "the greatest Mart for silver and gold in the whole world." The attack succeeded. The multinational raiders occupied the city for twenty-eight days, took nearly three thousand prisoners, and divided among themselves a plunder that Morgan believed worth about thirty thousand pounds.[89]

Panama president Pérez de Guzmán prepared for Morgan's approach in ways that stressed the overlap of church and state in the inclusion of African and Indigenous men, free and enslaved, among the crown's loyal vassals. Contradicting Modyford's suggestion that enslaved people were "indifferent" to distinctions between imperial and colonial powers, Pérez de Guzmán believed them both obligated and motivated to defend Panama.[90] He equated Catholic adherence with Spanish allegiance; Panamanians of all backgrounds would defend crown and church together from English heretics.

Pérez de Guzmán and Morgan's privateers shared a belief that Anglo-Spanish enmity, based on fundamental differences, was immutable: to Pérez de Guzmán, the English represented a threat not only to Spanish jurisdictional claims but to Roman Catholicism and therefore to orthodox religion. Thus the president's first preparation for military defense was to visit "the great Church" in Panama City, where he received communion "before our Blessed Lady of Immaculate Conception, with great Devotion." He then announced "that all those, who were True Catholicks, Defenders of the Faith, and Devoto's of our Lady of Pure and Immaculate Conception," should follow him into battle. Suggesting that the Virgin Mary witnessed his and his soldiers' fealty, he framed the struggle as a religious war in which the arms-bearing men of the city and the region would understand their obligation as "true Catholicks" to defend Panama from heretic invaders. Then, in the presence of the Virgin Mary at the church, he and his men prayed for her help in battle and vowed to die in her defense. Pérez de Guzmán gave to Mary and the church a diamond ring worth forty thousand pieces of eight, all the rest of his jewels, and the relics he had collected in an earlier religious pilgrimage.[91]

Free and enslaved Black soldiers indeed remained loyal to Pérez de Guzmán as he led the defense of the isthmus. He identified "one Negro and one Servant" as his last supporters, remaining after Spanish soldiers had fled. Most remarkably, among his twelve hundred soldiers were "three hundred *Negroes*, that were Vassalls, and Slaves of the *Assentistaes*." Because *asentistas* represented the merchant firm holding the crown license to trade African captives to Spanish America, the enslaved soldiers who belonged to them would almost certainly have included men born in Africa.[92] In their defense of Panamá, they disproved Thomas Modyford's contention that recent African arrivals could not understand political loyalties or the obligations of subjecthood.

To Pérez de Guzmán, such loyalty (like that of one hundred Tule men of Darién who also came to his aid) depended on conversion to Christianity, which Spanish law required.[93] Their choice to fight for Pérez de Guzmán instead of joining Morgan's mixed fleet of northern Europeans may also have derived from their experiences of the transatlantic crossing at the hands of Dutch or English slave traders, and their resale in an entrepôt such as Curaçao or Port Royal. Some would have remembered Morgan's previous invasion two years earlier, in which he had seized one hundred people of color as captives, whom Pérez de Guzmán had paid to free. Perhaps some had been among those ransomed captives. For others, allegiance to the Spaniards may have developed on the spot, as they sized up Morgan and his fellow pirates, who indeed came away from Panama with five hundred enslaved and free people to sell as plunder in Jamaica.

In contrast to Pérez de Guzmán's portrayal of the region's African and Indigenous people as Christians and loyal vassals who chose to defend the crown and the church, and to Modyford's depiction of creole men of African descent as potential political actors and subjects, Morgan and his men saw everyone of African, Indigenous, or mixed descent as enslavable, to be seized if possible and sold in Jamaica or kept as laborers.[94] This behavior was the logical result of commissions that encouraged (via "no purchase, no pay") the commodification of every sellable thing, including human beings. Some scholars have emphasized pirates' and privateers' willingness to incorporate African and Indigenous mariners into their crews as evidence of their resistance to racialized slavery or even empathy with fellow sufferers at the hands of the merchant capitalism coming to define the Atlantic.[95] Such examples may reveal that mariners harbored little intellectual commitment to the racial hierarchies underpinning slavery. But their practice of selling captives of African and Indigenous descent (because they could) nonetheless contributed to the hardening of those hierarchies and to the articulation in Jamaica of a racial binary that effaced distinctions between Native, Black, and mixed-race people. Caribbean privateering practices defined people as goods to be valued for their labor potential rather than political beings who could contribute their allegiance to town, colony, or empire, much less souls whose inherent value gave them admission into the body politic.

CHAPTER 2

"A Mungrel Breed of Spaniards"

The 1670 Treaty of Madrid, in establishing peace explicitly for the Americas, also specified that unlicensed trade should cease. Ever optimistic, merchants persisted in interpreting peace as license to trade, and English and Spanish officials frequently disagreed about how openly to disregard the treaty's trade restrictions. English merchants and officials (in England and in the Caribbean) hoped Spanish Caribbean officials would condone open trade, despite treaty prohibitions, but Spanish officials approached the problem warily. They knew that their own careers depended on a careful balancing of local demands (for goods that only foreign merchants provided) and imperial policy (that prohibited trade with those merchants).

Moreover, English and Spanish officials in the archipelagic Caribbean had to work out their own relationships in an international region filled not only with English and Spanish subjects but also with people under other sovereigns, European and Indigenous. Most of those people had no interest in or obligation to uphold an Anglo-Spanish treaty. They competed with the English for Spanish American trade or facilitated privateers' continued attacks on Spanish targets and interimperial commerce. Outlaw mariners justified their depredations in court and in the written word. The genre of pirate narratives that proliferated in the final quarter of the seventeenth century perpetuated the Black Legend, allowing the writers to celebrate their own violence rather than denying it. Though English pirates threw in their lot with multinational crews and took commissions from any willing officials, they deployed the same anti-Spanish tropes that had undergirded the Western Design as an excuse to violate the Anglo-Spanish peace their sovereign's treaties obligated them to uphold. In particular, they suggested that their thievery served to support the struggles of Natives resisting unjust subjugation at the hands of the Spanish.

But this old English critique of Spanish America joined with a newer trope. When Spanish American administrators balked at illegal trade, or when smuggling, piracy, or prize disputes drew English and Spanish officials into discord, English Caribbean officials adopted postures that were alternately supplicating, patronizing, and surly. On the one hand, they acknowledged Spanish Americans' advantage in possessing silver and having multiple European merchants competing for their favor. They admired the trappings of European civility that Spaniards displayed in their American cities. But the English were also confident in their own superiority, and chafed at what they saw as excessive legalism and commitment to administrative hierarchy in the Spanish empire, growing frustrated and outright angry when local Caribbean officials referred them to Madrid. They saw this administrative excess as evidence of Spanish stagnation and an inflexibility that stymied Spanish commercial potential. Indeed, they justified their smuggling on the grounds that the Spanish had failed to make good on the commercial potential their American mineral wealth afforded them.

They also zeroed in on Spanish American incorporation of Catholic people of color into the body politic as a marker of difference between the rival colonial societies, and they used that difference to paint Spanish Caribbean society as degenerate. This denigration existed alongside incompatible Black Legend imagery. Catholicism made Spanish society inferior both because it fostered tyranny and abuse of Indigenous Americans and because it inspired Spanish Americans to incorporate Africans and Natives into their colonial worlds.

In 1671 the new Jamaica governor Sir Thomas Lynch sent slave traders William Beeston and [John] Reid to Cartagena "to Adjust the Peace that had been made in Madrid for the West-Indies" and to work out details such as prisoner exchanges.[1] Jamaica merchants and officials, like many of their counterparts and superiors in London, hoped the local adjustment would include an expansive interpretation of the treaty's terms to permit more open trade between Port Royal and Cartagena. Lynch's arrival as governor signaled renewed English commitment to peace following the 1670 treaty; he came to replace Thomas Modyford, who had been recalled to London to answer for Henry Morgan's post-treaty sack of Panama.[2]

Governor Lynch's choice of two slave traders to serve as local diplomats was no accident. They and the "half a dozen Gentlemen" who joined them sought connections with merchants in Cartagena who purchased captive

Africans and sold them locally or arranged for their overland transport to Peru. But disagreements about race and slavery soured the negotiations. Henry Morgan's treatment of people of color the previous year created the most tension between the Spanish and English negotiators. When Beeston asked the Spanish to hand over any English prisoners being held in the city, Cartagena officials delivered thirty-three and in turn demanded that the English release the people of African and Indigenous descent whom Morgan and others had seized from Cartagena and Panama and sold as slaves in Jamaica. Beeston balked.

The Cartagena governor, Pedro de Rivadeneira, no doubt understood that English planters in Jamaica saw little reason to recognize the people of color they had purchased as vassals of the Spanish crown and constituent members of local Spanish American communities. Beeston, by his own account, resisted the governor's demand for the captives' return on the grounds that people of African and Indigenous descent were not equivalent to Europeans in prisoner-of-war exchanges. He ultimately agreed to facilitate their return only in order "to pacifie in some measure" Spanish officials who remained angry about Morgan's illegal attack on Panama. Captives who could prove they had been free in Spanish America would be released and returned. (Those who had been slaves in Spanish America when Morgan seized them would depend on their Spanish masters, who could come to Jamaica and pay eighteen or twenty pounds to retrieve each individual they had formerly owned, an unlikely scenario.)[3] Beeston understood the Spanish umbrage at the timing of the attack and yielded to the Spanish demand in the interest of hoped-for future commerce. But when he nonetheless resisted returning even those now-enslaved captives who had been free when seized, he indicated that he shared Morgan's view that seizing and selling people of color was acceptable. Beeston and Rivadeneira operated from fundamentally different assumptions about Africans' and Indians' place within colonial societies.

A year earlier Thomas Modyford's instructions to Morgan to offer some enslaved Cubans membership in an English order, like John Style's proposals to convert and incorporate Africans, had indicated an English Caribbean capacity to consider African Americans as potential subjects who could choose their own political allegiance. Lynch's decision to send slave traders to Cartagena reflected Jamaica's commitment to more thorough commodification of people of African descent. Beeston and Reid refused to regard free Black Spanish vassals as political beings eligible for participation in a prisoner exchange. In Rivadeneira's view, if they were Christians and Spanish vassals, their personhood was fundamental to their status in the international arena. To Beeston, their African or Indigenous descent reduced them to property, subject to seizure and sale and without legal standing as political persons whose sovereign could protect them.

Despite Beeston's capitulation to Spanish demands, many of the captives surely never returned to Spanish America. The resolution regarding people who had been enslaved might at first glance seem an English victory: Spanish former owners would have to repurchase (at near-market prices) enslaved people whom Morgan and his men had seized as plunder. But if the English view of slaves as property had prevailed, even the option of repurchase would have been shut down. Neither the treaty nor the local adjustment made any provision for the return of property.[4]

The English party operated at a disadvantage not only because of Morgan's crime but also because of the general asymmetry of Anglo-Spanish relations in the region. The English, who competed with Dutch, Genoese, and French merchants for access to Spanish American trade and silver, approached the Spanish as petitioners. Although Spanish American demands for laborers and manufactured goods exceeded what Spanish and legally licensed foreign merchants could supply, Spanish buyers held the upper hand in their relationship with English Jamaicans because so many European merchants competed to trade captive men and women for their silver. Beeston's awe at Cartagena's refinement reflected the asymmetry. He emphasized Spanish officials' capacity to host banquets and stage diplomatic ceremonies rivaling European courts and far exceeding anything in English America.[5]

At the same time, however, Beeston criticized the composition of Cartagena's local population. Although he thought Cartagena well built and beautiful, he saw weak defenses, poorly armed soldiers, and too few people. The city's inhabitants consisted of "Church Men," "Creolians who are half Spaniard and half Indian," and "many Molatto's and Negroes," all categories Beeston believed useless for defense.[6] Beeston acknowledged no contradiction in praising the city's beauty and civility—singling out the churches in particular for praise—while at the same time assessing its population as defective due in part to its plethora of clergy.

Although Beeston may not have made the connection himself, the Catholic Church's central place in Spanish Atlantic society led directly to Spain's inclusion of African, Indian, and mixed-race people as members of the body politic. Because the Spanish regarded membership in the church as constitutive of the polity, all people, by virtue of their Catholicism, could claim a place as legal persons within the community, even when conversion (of conquered Indians, captive Africans, or conversos) had been forced through threats and violence. Whether or not he understood those connections, Beeston saw Cartagena's free people of color, racial mixing, and church-centered society as defects that made the city weak, implicitly contrasting the city to a colonial ideal that rendered people of color as laborers outside the boundaries of colonial society and the church as an auxiliary.

Officials and residents in Cartagena warily welcomed Anglo-Spanish peace, but overcoming the fear born of years of hostility did not come easily, especially not for the free Blacks and Natives who knew themselves to be targets for enslavement. When the English visitors tried to meet with the "Eminent Factor" "Francisco Hermans, the Cartagena elite prevented it. Hermans represented Domingo Grillo's Genoese merchant firm, which had held the asiento contract from 1662 to 1669 and continued to trade enslaved Africans to Spanish America thereafter.[7] Beeston and his companions sought out Hermans to plan future Jamaica-Cartagena trafficking, should Cartagena officials allow it. Even though elite Cartageneros stood to gain from an increased supply of captive laborers, they blocked the meeting because they "were so suspicious of" their guests. According to Beeston, the Spanish feared that the English might even "sell the *Negroes* which waited on us" during their time in Cartagena.[8] Cartagena elites, slave owners and traders themselves, objected to the English attitude that increasingly equated African descent with commodification. Spanish Americans readily bought recently captured African men and women and accepted their lifelong and hereditary enslavement. They nonetheless resisted selling away people who were part of the community fabric, perhaps especially creoles born in the city or even in their households. William Beeston, in freely reporting the Spaniards' concern, tacitly acknowledged a greater English willingness to commodify known individuals, even as he and the Spanish alike pursued a Caribbean future more and more dependent on enslaved Africans and their descendants.

At the conclusion of their negotiations, despite feting, feasting, salutes, and "all other expressions of their Joy for the Peace," Beeston detected among the Spaniards suspicion that the English intended to breach the peace. The mistrust seemed justified when news arrived that two privateers had anchored five leagues from Cartagena. The Spaniards told Beeston and his men that they could hardly expect a lasting peace if privateers arrived even while local diplomats sat at the negotiating table. Beeston assured them that Lynch had called in all commissions "and that he was confident we had not one Privateer abroad." Rather, they must be French privateers or hold commissions from Tortuga, where Governor d'Ogeron continued to defy the authority of his French superiors and issue privateering commissions to multinational buccaneers.[9] Those privateers disrupted Anglo-Spanish slave trading directly by preying on ships, and indirectly when their indeterminate allegiances inflamed Spanish fears of continued English predation.

As the English sailed back to Jamaica, they met with one of Domingo Grillo's asiento ships, also leaving Cartagena, and headed for Curaçao. The English Jamaicans were reminded of what was at stake when they learned that Grillo's ship carried 120,000 pieces of eight headed to Dutch slave traders.[10] If the English were to tap into that trade, not only would they have to police the region to prevent privateers (of whatever national origins or commissioning port) from disrupting commerce, but they would also have to overcome Spanish distrust. That distrust rested partly on the halfhearted nature of English crackdowns on privateering. But it also stemmed from English disregard for the political construction of Spanish American societies. Spaniards could see that disregard most clearly among privateers, but it was also visible among the English planters and traders who purchased privateers' human plunder, and the diplomats who denied that those individuals possessed political personhood in the international arena.

Not surprisingly, when Beeston returned to Jamaica with the details of the settlement, English planters who had purchased Henry Morgan's human plunder resisted giving up their new captives. Governor Lynch, "troubled about the negroes and mulattoes freedom and other differences that happened in [Beeston's] wretched voyage," planned to "free them cautiously that the people may not be too much exasperated."[11] The Jamaica Council, anxious to facilitate commerce as their king had commanded, ordered "that all persons give account of all Spanish negroes they have and of what age, sex, and country they are, on pain of being sent prisoners to the Council for contempt." Furthermore, the councilors and Governor Lynch argued that the Spanish prisoners were "useless and dangerous persons." People who had previously lived as free vassals or even as enslaved persons in a more urban Spanish colonial society would resist their new situation in ways both large and small, and might coordinate their efforts. Jamaican planters would be better off returning them to Cartagena and replacing them with Africans purchased of "our own merchants."

Had Jamaican slave owners agreed that the Spanish prisoners were useless, they would have returned them willingly. Instead, they resisted the order, and as a result, an "abundance of suits and disputes [arose] about freeing Indians, negroes and mulattos" who had arrived captive in Morgan's ships. The council assured those who had purchased Spanish vassals that they would be paid within two months for captives "commanded out of their hands." They noted that Charles II had "strictly commanded the Governor to release all prisoners," a requirement of the 1670 treaty, and that Beeston and Reid had extracted from Cartagena governor Rivadeneira the promise of eighty pieces of eight per person over age twelve and half that for kidnapped children.[12] Undeterred by the challenges of his Cartagena trip, Beeston set out for Cuba shortly after his return, again to seek trade in human captives. This time he took enslaved people with him to tempt Cuban buyers. Although "the people" of Trinidad and the governor disagreed over whether to trade with the English, ultimately Beeston succeeded in exchanging his captives for cattle.[13]

Over the course of the 1670s, legal and illegal trade between Port Royal and Spanish American ports grew, and although privateers continued to overstep their commissions, Jamaican officials made a show of prosecuting them. Governor Lynch labeled them pirates, and took "pains to provoke" them, in hopes of "oblig[ing] the Spaniard by it." William Beeston had captured a party of French and English privateers who, holding an English commission, had burnt Villa de los Cayos on Cuba. Lynch wrote in 1672 that "the Spaniards seem highly satisfied of his Majesty's care to preserve the peace."[14]

While a crackdown on privateers might not be surprising coming from slave traders like Beeston and Lynch, even Henry Morgan seemed briefly to change his tune to endorse willing trade over predation as the best source of Spanish money. After his arrest and a two-year stint in the Tower of London, Morgan returned to Jamaica in 1675 as lieutenant governor, to the alarm of Spanish Caribbean officials.[15] Spanish suspicions proved correct. Despite instructions to maintain peace with Spaniards and a royal proclamation forbidding privateers from accepting foreign commissions, Morgan pursued maritime predation surreptitiously. No longer leading expeditions himself, he arranged to receive a tenth share when privateers holding commissions from the new Tortuga governor Jean-Baptiste du Casse brought their plunder into Port Royal. As lieutenant governor, a member of Governor Vaughan's council, admiralty court judge, and Port Royal's militia captain, Morgan possessed the power (along with a significant local following) to get away with such lawbreaking. To Governor Vaughan's frustration, Morgan insisted that any mariner holding a commission from a recognized sovereign's officer was a legal privateer.[16]

Charles II seemingly sided with Morgan, recalling Vaughan and replacing him with Charles Howard, the Earl of Carlisle, who gave Morgan free rein. This turn of events emboldened the pirates, who saw even greater opportunity in 1680, when Carlisle's return to England put Morgan in charge as acting governor. Even though Morgan's new position required lip service to improving Anglo-Spanish relations and promoting Anglo-Spanish trade, a group of English and French mariners, many of them from Jamaica and claiming to be privateers, took their cue from his new position and assembled in the western Caribbean to pillage their way across the Isthmus of Panama. They entered an alliance with the Indigenous Tule of the Darién region of Panama, agreeing to fight together against the Spanish. After attacking Spanish settlements on the isthmus, some of the mariners retraced their steps while others continued down the western coast of South America, returning to the Caribbean via the Strait of Magellan in 1682.

These men, who began under the leadership of John Coxon and completed their voyage in 1682 under Bartholomew Sharpe, secured commissions from various sources in an attempt to retain their legitimacy and to maintain a place within one or more European bodies politic. In the defenses that several of the English participants later offered in court and in print, they called themselves privateers and defined Caribbean geopolitics in pre-1670 terms that presumed Catholic-Protestant and Anglo-Spanish hostility. They thus shared Henry Morgan's insistence that holding any commission distinguished a privateer from a pirate.[17]

When the mariners who had continued their pillaging around South America approached English Barbados in January 1682, they initially expected a friendly reception, inviting aboard men from a royal navy frigate, to learn "how affairs stood since our Maritime Pilgrimage." But because the navy sailors refused the invitation, the privateers feared being taken prize, so they fled for English Antigua. There they sent a letter to the island's governor, along with jewels for his wife, but the governor returned the bribe and refused to let them "publickly" come ashore for fresh food and water. So the outlaws split up, each to shift for himself, giving the ship to seven men who had "played away all their Money." The broke men intended to sail to Tortuga but made it only as far as Danish St. Thomas, where Governor Nicolai Esmit gave them amnesty.[18] Despite the change in English posture, the proximity of competing jurisdictions allowed many of the marauders to escape punishment.[19]

Four of the mariners went to Jamaica, perhaps anticipating that Port Royal would welcome them as it had numerous "privateers" during the previous decade. But Henry Morgan, the most famous of those privateers, had learned that he risked losing his position. Two of his opponents, supporters of the asiento, had gone to London to lobby for his removal (and Lynch's return). So despite his normal respect for legally dubious commissions, he brought the four men to trial for piracy; three were condemned to hang.[20]

Those who went to London faced arrest "by his Majesties Order" and trial at a Court of Admiralty, with the Spanish ambassador Ronquillo as prosecutor.[21] The indictment of Sharpe and nine others focused not on the accumulated crimes of two years but on the men's final assault, against the Spanish ship *Rosario*, perhaps because that was the crime with the strongest available evidence. The indictment emphasized the breaking of the peace as a crime against the English king Charles II and that the attack occurred "within the jurisdiction of the Admiral of England," as much as it did the crimes committed against the murdered captain Juan Lopez, the *Rosario*'s crew and owners, or Spanish jurisdictional claims. The transcript mentions five times in two pages that the crimes occurred under England's admiralty jurisdiction and five times that Lopez, the seamen, and the ship were "in treaty and friendship of the said lord our present King." The goods stolen belonged to persons who, as subjects of Carlos II, lived "then and there in the treaty and friendship of our lord the King." The ship likewise belonged to "subjects [of] the most Serene King of Spain now in the treaty and friendship of our present King." Thus, when Sharpe and his men took the *Rosario* "and with malice aforethought killed and murdered the said John Lopez," they not only assaulted men "in the treaty and friendship of our said lord the King" but acted "against the peace of our lord the present King, his Crown and dignity" and against the very "peace of God."[22] Nonetheless, the court acquitted all ten men, recording neither their defense nor a reason for the acquittal, and released them upon payment of the nominal fee of eight shillings fourpence apiece.[23]

Not satisfied with their acquittal, the mariners who took part in the 1680–1682 invasion continued to defend their legitimacy in a rapidly changing Caribbean. The raids generated at least five English narratives, three of them published. These contributed to a genre of pirate narratives that gained popularity during the 1680s by romanticizing the violent criminals whose lives were characterized by greed, deprivation, and desperation. In celebrating unbridled avarice and predation on Spanish Catholics, English audiences perhaps came to terms with their discomfort at abandoning anti-Spanish rivalry to adopt merchants' goals as the goals of the nation. The narratives wavered between boasting about transgressions and insisting on the legality and justice of their pillaging. Within an archipelagic colonial and Indigenous Caribbean, they cast about for legal standing. Their disjointed efforts provide evidence that the contested jurisdictions of the region complicated categories of political belonging and allegiance. The structure and tone of the Coxon/Sharpe narratives, and their virtual erasure of French participation, suggest the persistent strength of a nationalist confessional view of Caribbean geopolitics.[24] The authors wrote as Englishmen and Protestants engaged in a patriotic militant confrontation with Spanish Catholics, who constituted their nation's natural enemies. They necessarily omitted their French allies, some of whom were Catholic, from a story that tried to recast their international crime ring as a vanguard of Protestant English expansion.

Sharpe and his cohorts returned to English jurisdiction at a moment of change. In contrast to the conflicting messages that had emanated from London over the previous two decades, English officials seemed ready to join slave traders to pursue commerce with Spanish America. They revoked Morgan's commission in July 1681, news that would soon reach the Caribbean, and the governor and Council of Jamaica offered a pardon to all men serving under foreign commissions "who would 'return' to their allegiance" by September 1.[25] In 1681, the Jamaica Assembly also had passed its first Act for Restraining and Punishing Privateers and Pirates, notable for its restraint of privateers as well as pirates. After London officials confirmed it in 1683, Parliament used it as a basis for its own Jamaica Act, and the Lords of Trade and Plantations recommended it to other colonies as a model for their anti-piracy laws. It reaffirmed Charles II's proclamation prohibiting foreign commissions, permitted the trial and execution of pirates in Jamaica without need for London's approval, established punishment for those who harbored or traded with pirates *or* privateers, and finally ordered militia officers to arrest and jail "any Privateers, Pirates, or other Persons suspected to be upon any unlawful Design," authorizing them to kill as felons any who resisted.[26]

While Caribbean officials would continue to rely on privateers during periods of warfare in the Caribbean, the 1683 law's assumption that privateers, like pirates, were likely engaged in "unlawful designs" reflected a new rejection of the idea that privateers could act as legitimate peacetime geopolitical actors in the Caribbean. The act represents a turning point in the English identification of privateers with piracy, aligning with the Spanish view. In using the term *privateer*, with the word's meaning muddied to include criminals, lawmakers bowed to common usage. Those with foreign commissions, and those who took commissions against one enemy and targeted another, retained the label but became criminals. It was in this context of growing but contested intolerance for lawbreaking privateers that Henry Morgan sued the English publishers of Exquemelin's *Buccaneers* for libel. He objected to being labeled a buccaneer, insisting that he had never acted without a commission.[27] His suit sought not only to protect his own reputation but also to revive the old definition of privateers as legal and even laudable in their autonomy.

In contrast, the authors of the Coxon and Sharpe narratives readily referred to themselves as buccaneers, eschewing the legally meaningful terms *pirate* and *privateer*.[28] However, several of the accounts took care to lay the basis for a claim to legal privateering. While the mariners held no prize-taking license from any English official, the narratives offer three possible sources for their claim to act as legitimate agents of a sovereign power. First, one author took care to emphasize in his account's title that he and his companions had received "letpasses to goe into the bay of Hundorus, to cutt Logwood, [from] his Maj[es]ties Ro[y]all Subject the Earl of Carlisle." Although the narratives did not highlight logging, the author may have meant to justify their claims to privateering status with this reference to logwood letpasses. His identification of Jamaica's former governor Carlisle as a subject of Charles II rather than as governor highlighted the licensing official's relation to his sovereign rather than his jurisdiction over Jamaica, thus underscoring the pirates' English identity and implying that they acted for Charles II, even as they broke his international treaty obligations.[29]

The second possible basis for the claim to privateering status appeared in their agreement to fight against the Spanish on behalf of the Tule leader Andreas. That "Emperour" "gladly listened to our Propositions and accepted us into his Service." Together they resolved to recover some of the Natives' lands from the Spaniards.[30] The invaders took encouragement from "the Company of our Emperour, under whose Commission we fought."[31] An agreement to fight under the authority of a sovereign but with their own weapons and ammunition, and in exchange not for pay but for the right to acquire plunder, fit clearly within the European legal definition of a privateer, but only if the buccaneers established that Andreas and not Carlos II was the sovereign of the Tule people and held dominion over the Darién region of the Isthmus of Panama.[32]

If the narrators could establish Andreas as the legitimate sovereign of the region, natural law could provide a basis for the European invaders to claim legal status as privateers. A series of Spanish *reducciones* had produced a population of about 1,400 baptized Tule, many of whom retained ties to the roughly 18,500 Tule who had resisted or ignored Spanish efforts to unite and resettle them into Spanish-administered towns comprising loyal Christian vassals.[33] Those with whom the pirates allied had accepted Catholicism and taken oaths of loyalty to the Spanish crown. The English editor of the voyages' published narratives claimed that Andreas and his followers had relinquished that loyalty and political identity, an impossibility under Spanish political theory. Because political and religious conversion intertwined for the Spanish, such defection constituted heresy in addition to disloyalty.

Because Protestants rejected Catholicism's claims to orthodoxy, and because natural law recognized sovereign peoples' right to jurisdiction over their own territory, the English authors constructed their narratives to emphasize that their Tule allies acted as independent agents who had never been subjects of the Spanish crown. Moreover, their use of natural law arguments to legitimate their violation of treaty law fit into a Black Legend tradition that would play well among English readers. As Ignacio Gallup-Diaz has shown, the narratives presented Darién as a unified polity, with Andreas as sovereign "emperor" who could enlist the English invaders as subjects, engage them as privateers, or treat with them as allies. Such portrayals of the Tule as constituting the Empire of Darién masked a reality less suited to the narrators' purposes: the Indigenous people of the region in fact lived in small polities loosely tied to one another, some Spanish vassals but most not.[34]

Perhaps English observers' ability to see an empire within a loose affiliation of smaller polities does not look consciously dishonest if placed alongside European Caribbean realities. English residents and sojourners in the Caribbean did not doubt the reality of Charles II's sovereignty. Nor did they doubt that English subjects' presence and English jurisdictional claims in the region represented a larger English nation, even when they failed to act in concert with one another. This English nation and empire were real to them, even as they debated exactly how that king's sovereignty operated and where or over whom it extended. Indeed, the mariners' very ability to claim English identity as they broke English law reflected the loose nature of English empire.[35] These English outlaws violated Charles II's treaty obligations and claimed legal status as privateers based on foreign, even non-European commissions, without either renouncing their Englishness or challenging the existence of an English polity.[36] Should their (or our) standards for Indigenous empire be different? Spanish officials recognized the complexity of their own claims to sovereignty over the Indigenous population of the isthmus, but they denied that continued Tule efforts to resist subjugation challenged the legitimacy of such claims. Rather, they identified Andreas and his Indigenous followers as "rebellious," an accusation that made more sense given that other Tule joined with the Spanish to defend the isthmus against the mariners.[37]

The marauders' third possible claim to privateering status did not appear in the published narratives but may have loomed large in diplomatic responses to the voyage. It comes to us from the same anonymous author who pointed to Carlisle's logwood-cutting let-passes for legitimacy. At the end of this narrative, he referred to the French settlement of Petit-Goâve, on Hispaniola, as the mariners' "commission port."[38] Despite interimperial resistance to French claims over Saint-Domingue, the mariners had reason to believe that such a commission would provide them with their best legal defense in European courts.

The circumstances surrounding the original leader John Coxon's return to Jamaica suggest that he, too, thought the Tortuga commission pertinent: he abandoned the voyage to take advantage of Governor Henry Morgan's offer to pardon any privateers who returned to Jamaica and surrendered their commissions.[39] Even one Spanish source refers to these invaders as English and French *corsarios* (privateers), while identifying most other foreign invaders of the era as *piratas*, and also acknowledged the joint Anglo-French nature of the venture.[40] Although the Jamaica Council and the Spanish ambassador had requested in 1680 that Charles II reissue his prohibition against his subjects' taking foreign commissions, he only did so in the wake of the Sharpe acquittal and ensuing Spanish outrage.[41] Given their need to justify their voyage, the first published narrators' silence regarding a possible French commission seems intentional, along with their choice to downplay the presence of their French comrades. Those who published their accounts had the opportunity to consider both popular and official opinion before deciding to emphasize Andreas's role over the French governor's commission. Unlike the French Tortuga commission, Andreas's alliance allowed them to maintain their posture as agents of English Protestant empire. Indeed, it played to a key historical element of that trope, that the English were saviors who would help persecuted Indigenous victims throw off Spanish tyranny.

In addition to their efforts to claim natural law justifications for their predations, the men who narrated Sharpe's voyages also admitted that simple greed drove them. The mariner who authored the first published account began by owning desire for wealth as the impetus for the journey: "Gold was the bait that tempted" them. He connected this desire to a more general truth: that a "sacred hunger of Gold" spurred men to undertake "the most difficult Adventures." What others might see as avarice became sacred, the means by which humankind accomplished great deeds. The author overturned the Christian teaching that pursuit of material gain as its own end was sinful. At the level of the most basic moral code, he acknowledged the men's lawlessness. However, in the same sentence, he also offered evidence for the natural law justification for their depredations on the Spanish: the nearly three hundred men, "being all Souldiers of Fortune" rather than of a sovereign or of a higher cause, "lift[ed] our selves in the Service of one of the Rich West Indian Monarchs, the Emperour of Darien." He defined himself and his crewmates as mercenaries fighting for money and possibly fame rather than principle or loyalty.[42]

Nonetheless, the narrator framed the English mariners' agreement with Andreas as one that carried with it expectations of mutual fidelity. When the party split into two to take separate routes across the isthmus, they did not meet up as planned. The mariners initially suspected the Tule of dividing them, "the better to execute some treachery, by the assistance of the Spaniard." But they eventually reunited, proving their suspicions wrong and affirming instead the former "good opinion we had of the Indians['] fidelity."[43] Despite his earlier assurances that the Spaniards and the Darién Indians were "Enemies" of one another, engaged in "continual Wars," the mariners' fears of double dealing reflect their awareness that they did not fully understand the region's geopolitics and that many Indians might indeed ally themselves with Spanish colonial power in the region.

The privateers took their relationship with Andreas seriously enough that when, in a "mutiny," seventy-five of the mariners pulled out to return the way they had come, they "deliver[ed] up their Commissions to the Emperour."[44] Later, those who remained raided their way south along the Pacific coast until they had both "got the Booty we expected, and weakened the Spaniards as much as we could, as our Emperor had obliged us to do."[45] In one sentence he linked the mariners' acquisitive goals to their claims to serve Andreas, even beyond the Isthmus of Panama and into the Pacific. Yet in describing themselves as subjects of Andreas, the English narrators of Sharpe's voyage never suggested that giving him their allegiance precluded either their Englishness or their Protestant opposition to Spanish Catholics.[46]

Instead, one author invoked Black Legend imagery when he described "the poor Natives" serving as "Drudges," gathering gold dust for the Spaniards.[47] Justifying their violence against Spanish towns and ships in this way let him frame the mariners' predations using the religious language of "pilgrimage." While his emphasis on Spanish cruelty toward Indians hearkened back to a Protestant worldview that demanded saving Indians from inhumane Spaniards, he also pointed forward to an emerging ideal that saw the pursuit of wealth as a positive good, the source of human ingenuity and progress. When that ideal did gain acceptance, it would stipulate that wealth should accumulate via commerce and production rather than plunder.[48] Although it would depend on the theft of African labor and Indigenous land, (Northern) Europeans were able to define such production and commerce as not plunder because, as chapters below emphasize, they had excluded African and Indigenous people from colonial bodies politic.

The desperate effort to claim an increasingly outdated religious motive is apparent in another narrator's reference to Francis Drake's voyage in the region a century earlier. He reminded readers of England's long-standing religiously based challenge to Spanish claims over the region when he described their arrival at what they called Drake's Bay, where the Elizabethan pirate had reportedly watered. There, the author claimed, "to this day is standing a church which . . . Drakes causd to be Built" to commemorate his exploits in the South Sea.[49] Even if they were wrong about the origin of the chapel they saw, the persistence of the story—that Drake had taken the time to construct a visible symbol of Protestantism in South America, that such a symbol had survived for almost a century, and that the bay continued to carry his name—suggests how a religious rivalry that Jamaica and London merchants were working to overcome shaped these pirates' perception of their peacetime hostilities. Moreover, the author expected such rivalries to resonate with his readers.

The author reported that the Spanish kept Indians in such subjection that they could no longer reproduce, and relayed an incident in which the Spanish had bludgeoned wounded pirates and killed a member of Sharpe's crew. This murdered mariner, a man of African descent, had been a slave in Jamaica until the pirates had freed him. After having his leg shot off, he refused quarter when the Spanish offered. He managed to kill four or five Spaniards before they shot him dead.[50] This story evoked century-old depictions in which the English presented themselves as especially humane to victims of Spanish cruelty, earning the sufferers' loyalty.

At the same time, however, the author denigrated Spain's American subjects as "Creolians"—"a mungrel breed of Spaniards and Indians mixt," whose ancestry and "Copper colour'd Complexion" explained their cruelty.

These were "Men that never give" "quarter" to captured enemies. As race became increasingly important in the English Atlantic, English observers in the Caribbean used racializing as much as Catholicism to define Spanish Americans as less civil than themselves and less enmeshed in norms of law that dictated humane treatment of prisoners. This might seem an ironic stance for violent outlaws, and it contradicted the Black Legend that they also employed, but delegitimizing the Spanish victims they assaulted as deserving to be punished for behavior attributed to their race helped the narrator assert his status as a privateer rather than a pirate.[51]

A further story, that at first glance suggests the author's capacity to revise his prejudices against Spanish American "creolians," ends with a commitment to racial boundary formation. When the mariners seized some Spanish carpenters to do ship repairs, they took a liking to them and decided that they should no longer enslave Spaniards to do manual labor. Instead, they "resolve[d] to keep no more but Negroes to do our drudgery."[52] In the same breath, the author reduced Africans, who in the previous anecdote appear as potential full participants, to drudges whose enslavement demanded no explanation and whose freedom, instead, bore noting.

While the Coxon/Sharpe men were in the midst of their pillaging in 1681, a Spanish ship arrived in Jamaica with a Spanish license to trade "in the American seas" for two years. Its captain, "the Spaniard" Juan Ignacio Croquer (John Crocker in English sources), and his one hundred crew members awaited the arrival of Royal African Company ships so they could buy enslaved Africans to sell in Cartagena. They hoped to purchase captives and depart the following week. Henry Morgan, newly appointed deputy governor of Jamaica and now ostensibly supporting English plans to build conflict-free Anglo-Spanish commerce, approved the venture because he saw "no question but that Jamaica will gain much by this trade with the Spaniard."[53]

While Croquer was in port, four privateers arrived with three Spanish prizes and letters of reprisal against the Spanish. The privateers, although "belonging to the Duke [Elector] of Brandenburg," were not his subjects but instead "Flushingers" from Vlissingen in the Netherlands. They asked to enter Port Royal harbor to refit their own ship and sell the three Spanish vessels. They maintained that the Elector of Brandenburg's alliance with Charles II gave them permission to sell their prizes to obtain money they could then use to purchase provisions. When Morgan learned that they wished to spend

£800 in Jamaica, he allowed them to sell the seized ships. The privateers purchased stores and left Port Royal to "search the coast of Hispaniola first and then the [Spanish] Main" for more Spanish victims.

Not surprisingly, Croquer feared that the privateers would take him when he left Jamaica. Morgan believed "they would certainly have done so (the temptation being so high)" had he not intervened, requesting "protection" for Croquer, which the privateers "graciously granted."[54] Within a few days Croquer purchased the enslaved women and men he had come for and left for Cartagena. Morgan sent a frigate to convoy the slave trader in his return trip, safeguarding him against attack from the privateers Jamaica had just supplied.[55] The English protection proved a doubtful advantage for Croquer. While he arrived safely in Cartagena, he faced charges of having illegally brought in an English sloop loaded with enslaved Africans. Because his own ship seems to have been licensed, the charge suggests that Morgan or the captain he employed took advantage of the voyage to engage in smuggling human cargo.[56]

Morgan admitted to misgivings at having let the privateers sell Spanish vessels and goods. He purportedly was striving to foster Anglo-Spanish slave trade and working to convince Spanish officials and merchants in the region that Jamaicans deplored attacks on Spanish targets, even as Sharpe and his fellow pirates plundered their way down Spanish America's Pacific coast. Morgan "beg[ged] for instructions" from London about how to behave toward other sovereigns' privateers, and requested copies of the treaties with all of England's allies. Without them, he alleged, he was "at a loss how to guide his conduct." He needed Charles II's treaty with the Elector of Brandenburg in order to judge whether the elector's Dutch privateers were correct that the English governor of Jamaica must supply them. Morgan did not doubt the privateers' legal status to operate in the region's waters, but he did not know how far his own obligation to them reached or what their status was in an English port. When faced with a conflict between the subjects of two different sovereigns, both at peace with his own but at war with one another, he wanted guidance, but in the meantime tried to have it both ways, not surprising given his own history of abetting privateers.

Charles II may not have anticipated the degree to which his respective agreements with Spain's Carlos II and the Elector of Brandenburg might conflict with one another in the unsettled jurisdictional context of the western Caribbean. There, ships and mariners from all over appeared in port routinely, virtually ensuring such questions would arise. Officials dealt with them on the spot, as in Morgan's case, creating Caribbean practices even as they requested (and influenced) new metropolitan policies to deal with Caribbean realities.

Morgan claimed surprise that the "Spanish interest . . . all around us" was "strangely shocked" by "the whole matter." For the previous decade, while the English had courted Spanish merchants, English officials repeatedly denied that they condoned privateering against Spanish targets, so the sale of three Spanish prizes, with a Spanish merchant in port as witness, could only seem to prove English deceit. Upon reflecting after the fact on his conflicting responsibilities, Morgan came down on the side of the Spanish. He suggested to his superiors that Jamaica regain Spanish trust by offering regular English protection for Spanish commerce, which Jamaica's situation "in the very centre of the American seas" would facilitate.[57] That central location all but ensured that Jamaica would confront increasing numbers of mariners with uncertain loyalties. As the presence of the Brandenburg/Vlissingen privateers attests, numerous European rulers aimed to access Spanish American wealth, layering complexity on complexity.

Foreign commissions muddled membership within a particular body politic and within an international maritime world bound by a common code of conduct, increasingly understood to help constitute a law of nations. Morgan called the ship captains "Brandenburgers," suggesting that their employment superseded their political and cultural identity. But he also called them "Flushingers," emphasizing their ties to a locale—Vlissingen—where they were born or lived or registered their ship. He notably did not identify them as Dutch, perhaps because doing so would have emphasized a political identity rather than a cultural one, and the political identity that mattered here was the Brandenburg commission and the Duke's agreements with Charles II.[58]

Morgan's collusion with the Brandenburg privateers, coinciding as it did with the Coxon/Sharpe invasion, provoked Spanish retaliation. They seized eight vessels of Jamaica logwood cutters, imprisoning all "their people." Spanish officials frequently ignored English logwood cutters in the Yucatán and Central America, even though their activity violated the Treaty of Madrid. That tacit permission meant that a population of Englishmen lay vulnerable to seizure should the Spanish wish to make use of them for reprisal, as in this instance. The imprisoned logwood cutters wrote to Jamaica governor Morgan, attesting to their mistreatment and asking for help.[59]

London officials hoped to repair the damage done to Anglo-Spanish relations during Henry Morgan's stint in office by sending Thomas Lynch to Jamaica for a third term as governor. The slave trader Lynch immediately set out to reestablish correspondence with Spanish governors in the region.[60] Although his efforts against privateers in the 1670s had ultimately failed, he had stronger law on his side and more support from London this time. He moved quickly to rein in Robert Clarke, the captain-general of the Bahamas, who threatened to ruin the Anglo-Spanish peace by issuing illegal privateering commissions.[61]

As part of the new English drive to disempower privateers, Lynch pressured Spanish officials to better regulate their guardacostas privateers and to cooperate with Jamaica officials to police Caribbean waters for pirates. Lynch argued to Spanish officials that doing so would be to their mutual benefit. It would also change the nature of Caribbean maritime space. Spanish officials had continued to claim it first and foremost as their own jurisdiction. Lynch proposed that they, too, would reap the benefits of a Caribbean order friendly to commerce, if they could instead regard the region as a regulated international space, jointly controlled.[62]

The new legal clarity provided to English subjects by the Jamaica Act did not convince English mariners to give up predation while privateering commissions remained available elsewhere, and some guardacostas captains continued to behave as though the entire region belonged wholly to Spain. Spanish and English governors clashed several times during the 1680s over these issues. In August 1683 Lynch wrote to Governor Fernandez Córdoba in Havana demanding to know whether "divers pirates in *barcos luengos* and piraguas" who "rob[bed] and murder[ed]" English subjects in the Caribbean did so under the governor's orders. Lynch demanded action: if the marauders were Fernandez Córdoba's privateers, the governor should stop issuing commissions (and thereby relinquish peacetime privateering as Lynch was trying to do). If they acted without commission, Fernandez Córdoba should control his king's subjects who had turned pirate. Either way, Lynch tried to impose on Fernandez Córdoba the same pressure he himself faced to make the region safer for trade.

Despite Lynch's high-handed tone, his posture toward the Spanish governors testifies to English weakness in the region relative to the Spaniards. The English so desired to trade in Spanish American ports that they were willing to disable their own privateers in order to sway their potential commercial partners. But they could not make local Spanish officials do the same, and they took umbrage at the refusal, alternating between chafing at an administrative apparatus that they saw as overly bureaucratic and—contrarily—calling the Spanish uncivilized.[63] When Lynch sent an English man-of-war to Santo Domingo to demand Dutch pirate Nikolaas van Hoorn "as a rebel and a pirate," the president of Santo Domingo "thought fit to protect him, and afterwards released him" for a bribe of twenty thousand pieces of eight. When Lynch tried to alert Cuban officials that van Hoorn planned a major attack on Vera Cruz, the Cubans refused to receive the ship he had sent with a messenger and letters.

Lynch then tried to help a Spanish official who had come to Jamaica from Santo Domingo seeking assistance against van Hoorn. Lynch found a sloop for him to hire to warn officials in New Spain, but when it arrived at Campeche a Spanish "armadilla" "barbarously fired on" the envoy, forcing him to flee into the woods where he was "lost and like to have perished." The Spanish armadilla kept the sloop's crewmen in irons for twenty-six days and seized £800 worth of goods (evidence that the sloop was not just on an alarm-sounding mission but that it planned also to engage in illicit trade). Lynch informed his Cuban counterpart that in refusing English overtures, the Spanish "owe that calamity"—the sack of Vera Cruz—"to the Dutch and to yourselves."[64]

Lynch alleged that the English king's men-of-war always protected "merchants of your nation" and treated them humanely. He claimed to have "freed several from pirates and transported them to their homes," "chased out of these Indies all the pirates that prey on us or on your nation" at his own charge, and, in short, "done all in my power to serve the Spanish nation." Such service included helping to protect the Spanish from the French, who intended to get revenge for an attack they had suffered at the hands of the notorious Juan Corso "by your commission." Lynch told Fernandez Córdoba that he believed it crucial to "the whole Indies, both ours and yours," that the French not acquire the cities of Santo Domingo or Santiago de Cuba, as he feared they intended. Lynch believed the English deserved thanks, civility, and favor for helping "protect" the Spanish from the French; instead, Spanish ships continued to "try to take and plunder all our ships they meet with."

Lynch complained that Spanish officials in the Caribbean clung to a formal hierarchy of administration that prevented them from addressing inter-imperial problems quickly, with "not one Governor" giving "satisfaction even for the most notorious injury," instead referring English complaints to Spain. His list of specific grievances made clear the degree to which commissions continued to shape the character of the Caribbean. Lynch both complained about Spanish use of commissions and threatened to issue them himself if he could not receive satisfaction for complaints via other means. He began with his threat: that ten years before, two of "your King's" longboats took a ketch of Lynch's with one hundred enslaved Africans aboard and "gave it" to Spanish asiento factors, for which, Lynch claimed, Carlos II owed him thirty-six thousand pieces of eight. If he did not receive repayment, he hoped "our King will grant me letters of marque." In a second case, Lynch sent a frigate to Santiago de Cuba to demand an English ketch that French privateers had seized under Fernandez Córdoba's commission and brought in to Santiago, imprisoning its English mariners with insufficient food, then sending them away starving, "naked and without their ketch." The seizure was "contrary to treaty," as the English had committed no crime.

At the same time, Lynch demanded the return of people who had escaped their Jamaican enslavement for Cuba. In contrast to Panama president Pérez de Guzmán's ransoming of people of color as prisoners of war, Lynch demanded captives as stolen property. He accused the Santiago governor of keeping them in his house, perhaps implying that Spanish officials profited from their harboring of sanctuary seekers.

But, according to Lynch, what reflected most poorly on "the justice of his Catholic Majesty" was Spanish officials' issue of commissions to "such pirates and thieves as Juan Corso."[65] The Spanish guardacostas captain Juan Corso represented all that the English governor feared in privateers generally and in Spain's private men-of-war more specifically. First, he did not appear to the English to be a natural-born Spaniard. Corso may have been an alias referring to possible Corsican origin, and "Corsicans" was one of the epithets Lynch used to tar Spanish guardacostas as illegitimate outsiders. Lynch complained that the holders of Spanish commissions "committed barbarous crueltyes & Injustyces, & better cannot be expected, for they are Corses, Slavonians, Greeks, Mulatos, a Mongrel parcel of Theyves & Rogues that rob & murther al that comes into theyr Power wthout ye least respect to humanytie, or comon justyce."[66]

Moreover, "strong desperate rogues" such as Corso posed a danger because they possessed "no houses, friends, or relations." They had nothing to offer as security that they would obey the terms of their commissions and no one who would do it for them. They therefore risked nothing to "rob and murder all they can master."[67] Someone (like Corso) of indeterminate nationality who was not rooted in a local community, was not tied to a residence and a network of family and friends, and held no landed interest could not, Lynch argued, be trusted as an agent of empire or enforcer of legal order. A legitimate role in the international arena depended on the local belonging that qualified people for membership in a body politic and, in turn, in the international order.

Corso had acted outside the bounds of the law, taking ships on the high seas "contrary to treaty" and seizing English vessels carrying "*frutas de las Indias*" (American-grown produce). If the English vessels had carried smuggled produce from Spanish American sources, they would indeed have been liable to seizure, but by 1683 the English grew an "abundance of the produce of the Indies" and could also buy it from Dutch Curaçao, so commissioned guardacostas such as Corso could no longer seize English ships in the Caribbean on the presumption that locally grown produce indicated illegal trade with Spaniards.[68]

Cooperation against maritime crime would require a new and more open diplomatic protocol: Lynch wrote, "If I could send, or you could receive, anybody at Havana, I could much strengthen my case against Juan Corso." In the future, Lynch promised to "take it as a public violation of the peace and a tacit declaration of war" if "honest" English traders were seized on the high seas or fishing at uninhabited cays, if they were murdered or tortured, if "bearers of despatches" were seized or robbed while delivering messages, or "if you give Rogues orders to seize our vessels that carry produce of the Indies, for all our ships are laden with it."[69]

Lynch worked to convince other Spanish governors to coordinate their efforts to reduce maritime predation. In 1684 he wrote to Cartagena governor Juan de Pando y Estrada, acknowledging that there were "som desperate Rascals" from Jamaica who had "turn[ed] Pyrats" (renouncing both their ties to their sovereign and their place within the community of humanity) "by themselves" (without any support from English officials). Lynch noted that they might "serve undr the french," but he insisted that they were rebels not under his command, and that they could not return to Jamaica. Spanish officials were welcome to proceed against them as pirates if they could catch them.[70] Lynch thus invited the Spanish into shared regional policing that would permit Spanish authorities to seize natural-born Englishmen turned pirate, rogue, and rascal. But in protesting against Spanish privateers' seizure of English vessels likely trading with the Spanish, Lynch also pressed Spanish governors to encourage international commerce, whether legal or not, and to distinguish between pirates, whom they should seize, and merchants (including smugglers), whom they should allow to carry on.

While Lynch did not vow to chase down English pirates, he promised that "if they fall into my hands" he would prosecute them as pirates, noting that he had recently hanged several English pirates, armed a longboat to protect the island's shipping (which included Spanish asiento ships), "& in every Curcumstance kept ye Peace." Lynch vowed to Governor Pando that for the English, the era of sanctioned peacetime privateering had ended. He insisted that "all those of ye English Nacon that rob or injure yours are theyves & Pyrats, & such as never com under my power." As pirates, they had renounced the protections due subjects. But, he complained, Spanish officials continued to condone violence: "those that murther, & Rob us ar ye K[in]g of Spaynes ships."

Lynch stopped short of calling the pirates Spaniards, identifying them rather as "Greeks, Mulatos & Vagabonds, & desperate Rogues," thus giving the Cartagena governor an opening to place the pirates outside Spanish subjecthood.[71] Lynch objected to the continued Spanish practice of using private men-of-war for defense. Lynch's letter to Pando reveals tentative efforts to distinguish between subjects of England or Spain and pirates outside of state protection. At the same time, his characterization of Spanish privateering crews as racially inferior vagabonds and rogues represented a recognition and critique of expansive Spanish definitions of subjecthood and an invitation to Spanish officials to follow England's lead.

The project of outlawing peacetime privateering for the English was bound up with the project of restricting subject identity to individuals who could be defined as White and loyal to the king and his laws. These two projects intertwined in part because both served to foster conditions under which English and Spanish merchants could increase their exchange of textiles and captive people for silver. This goal of bringing tens of thousands of enslaved Africans into the region threatened to confuse racial hierarchies through racial mixing in a region of porous boundaries, even as it fueled manufacturing and agricultural productivity and brought pieces of eight into Jamaica and the rest of the English Atlantic. Lynch's letter to Pando reveals his desire to impose a regional order that would permit slavery to grow without racial mixing or a racially expansive subject identity. It also shows his inclination, if they refused to cooperate, not only to see the Spanish as violators of "common justice" but as outsiders themselves, beyond the racial and cultural boundaries the English wished to create in the Atlantic. The holders of Spanish commissions "committed barbarous cruelties and injustices," but rather than doing so because their Catholicism led them to tyranny (as the Black Legend would have it), their behavior derived from the universalist requirements of Spanish Americans' religion, which permitted them to mix with peoples from Africa, the Americas, and the Mediterranean. The English placed Spanish Americans, even though they were slave traders and co-creators of plantation political economies, not alongside themselves, but instead among "Corsicans, Slavonians, Greeks, [and] mulattoes." As "a mongrel parcel of thieves and rogues," they were a people from whom "humanity" "cannot be expected."[72]

CHAPTER 3

“Free Negroes Must Not Be Sold”

When privateers and pirates abducted Native, Black, and mixed-race people from Spanish and Portuguese America and sold them as slaves in Jamaica, they rejected their captives’ political personhood as vassals of the Spanish and Portuguese crowns. Instead, they regarded those women and men, including many who had been free, as material plunder. At the same time, during the frequent wars of the late seventeenth and early eighteenth centuries, combatants in the Caribbean took prisoners who included free and enslaved soldiers and civilians. All Europeans in the Caribbean took prisoners of war and seized slaves as wartime plunder, but English captors made little effort to determine the status of captives they did not see as White. Instead, they equated their African or Native ancestry with slavery and denied captives of color the rights normally accorded to subjects in the international arena.

In the aftermath of those wars, when Spanish and French officials demanded the return of free and enslaved prisoners from new English masters, they and English officials argued over captives’ legal standing. English officials questioned their claims to prewar freedom and insisted that non-European captives should figure as property in postwar negotiations. Spanish and French officials argued that people of color who had been free when captured were prisoners of war just as were any other captured subjects, and that they should be returned to the jurisdiction of their sovereign. Spanish and French officials sometimes also recognized seized slaves as individuals who warranted attention from their church and crown (as Cartagena governor Rivadeneira had done in his 1671 negotiations with William Beeston). More commonly using language of religious than political belonging, they argued that enslaved women and men, like free people, possessed rights by virtue of their Christianity, and called for their repatriation to a society that recognized their membership in a community that would allow them to live as Catholics.

Captives noted such distinctions and took matters into their own hands when they could, risking their lives to get back to Spanish or French territory if opportunities arose. Their persistent flights spurred the Spanish crown to enact a formal sanctuary policy that awarded freedom not just to captured vassals returning but to any individuals who escaped enslavement at the hands of Protestant captors and affirmed their desire to live as Catholics.[1]

The individuals who escaped testified to Spanish officials about their captivity, and officials wrote to one another about such seizures, flights, and restitutions. The resulting documents reveal fundamental incompatibilities between English, French, and Spanish views on the ideal composition of a colonial body politic. Most importantly, they show disagreement about the qualities that determined who held membership in political community. How important were religious and racial categories in constructing each colony and empire? Could a person who was owned by another still be loyal to a sovereign? Or did enslaved individuals, regarded as property in the colonial law of all Atlantic empires, necessarily live outside the body politic? The answers to these questions determined whether captives fell under the protection of a European sovereign, and whether that protection extended into the arena of interimperial relations governed by treaty law and the laws of war.[2]

Officials *and* captives weighed in on these questions. Their actions and words reveal how, in the Caribbean, the ideas underpinning criteria for political belonging diverged, even as a not-yet-formalized law of nations wrongly assumed shared understandings of the body politic.[3] Treaties bound sovereigns' subjects to particular behaviors and granted them certain protections but did not specify who fit into the category of "subject." The greater Caribbean, with its close and overlapping jurisdictions, reliance on multinational privateers, frequent border crossing, and ethnic, linguistic, racial, and religious diversity, lets us see—more easily, perhaps, than in Europe—the trouble that arose from a law of nations that assumed that everyone could recognize who was a subject of what sovereign and what characteristics made people subjects. Captives and religious refugees in the Caribbean show us that the law of nations rested on a flawed belief that the languages and concepts of political identity translated across political borders.

The (mostly) people of color who escaped English captivity and who asserted their subjecthood by claiming a place within the Spanish or French bodies politic did so in a world where a growing commerce in human beings increased the enslaved populations in all Caribbean colonies. In the second half of the seventeenth century, Spanish, Portuguese, English, French,

Dutch, and Danish colonies in the region shared expanding plantation agriculture, increased reliance on slavery, and growing Black populations. As in the colonies of all Europeans, enslaved people in the Spanish and French Caribbean faced brutal labor regimes, especially if they toiled on sugar plantations. Europeans in Catholic and Protestant colonies alike deployed race to construct social and legal hierarchies. Rights and privileges accompanied whiteness, and people of African and Indigenous descent endured discrimination and abuse. Spanish, Portuguese and French colonists, like the English, Danish and Dutch, often resisted incorporating Black and Native people into their communities.

In Spanish and French colonies, however, crown officials intervened. Catholics' commitment to their religion's universalist ideals led the Spanish, French, and Portuguese crowns to require conversion of all conquered peoples. Indeed, in the late seventeenth century, Spanish officials remained highly aware that incorporation of heathens into Christianity had served to justify their entire colonial venture.[4] Partly on religious grounds, then, Catholic metropolitan officials established legal protections promising enslaved people sufficient food, clothing, and shelter, the ability to live religious lives (if Catholic), recognition of family bonds, recourse against abuse, and the possibility of gaining freedom. Such laws had limited reach in faraway colonies, and it is crucial to acknowledge that the individuals described in this chapter fled one violent colonial regime for another. Nonetheless we need to take seriously that those who could do so repeatedly chose Catholic over Protestant colonies.

It was largely within contexts of geopolitical rivalry that Spanish and French officials accepted these freedom seekers' claims to belonging. Spanish officials' clearest insistence that enslaved women and men were members of the body politic, deserving crown protection, came during wartime and postwar negotiations. Prisoner exchanges precipitated by wars exposed and helped crystallize distinctions in subject identities that derived from other sources of belonging such as religion. When people of color fled English for Spanish or French jurisdiction, they also gave rise to moments of geopolitical contest. Scholars have noted that people of color influenced the comparative trajectories of Spanish, French, and English law regarding race, freedom, and enslavement by seeing openings for themselves and by acting on them, thereby making theoretical potentialities meaningful.[5] Less recognized is the degree to which colonial officials in these emergent empires worked out questions of race, religion, and subject identity in debate with one another. In trying to understand, and often in arguing against what they did understand about these processes in rival empires, officials articulated their own evolving views.

When they were engaged in conflict with the English, both the Spanish and the French found it useful to explicitly affirm a body politic that included Black and Native people, for two reasons. First, it boosted the number of loyal inhabitants in border regions. Second, in resting their diplomatic arguments for inclusion on Catholicism, the Spanish and French painted themselves as better Christians and kinder slaveholders than their Protestant rivals. Spanish and French officials, recognizing the intertwining of geopolitics and religion in determining free Blacks' identities as crown subjects, could thus portray themselves as moral superiors in their negotiations with the English. While the argument served strategic demographic purposes, in articulating it, Spanish and French officials strengthened in their own minds and in those of residents a sense that their colonial societies incorporated—fundamentally though not equally—all Catholics.

Women and men enslaved in the Spanish and French Caribbean could attest to slave owners who were both cruel masters and indifferent or hypocritical Christians. But for Spanish and French officials and clergy facing moments of geopolitical entanglement involving enslaved people—of which there were many in the frontier region of the Caribbean—the story of their own inclusivity mattered. It thus provided real opportunity to the enslaved who could cross those borders. Nonetheless, because it was a self-image built on comparison with English Protestants, we need to be careful before assuming that it mattered more broadly within Spanish American jurisdiction, beyond these moments of contest or these zones of contact.

At the same time that enslaved people of African and Indigenous descent fled English for Spanish and French spaces, Jews fled the Spanish, Portuguese, and (after 1685) French Caribbean for English and Dutch jurisdictions. Upon arrival, they laid claim to belonging, naturalizing themselves and their children, buying property, and establishing schools and synagogues. Like people of color in Spanish or French America, Jews were incorporated into English or Dutch Caribbean bodies politic was as unequal members, their otherness marked in a variety of ways. English officials in Jamaica, for example, even when granting denizenship or naturalization to Sephardic arrivals, referred to them as belonging to the Hebrew "nation" and taxed them corporately and at higher rates than non-Jewish Jamaicans.[6]

Sephardic Jews in the Caribbean were thus excluded from full membership in Protestant Caribbean colonial societies. But they also found themselves pawns in geopolitical contests between Spanish, English, and Dutch officials who were all loath to let them depart for rival jurisdictions. Because of their vested interest in staying in the region, they contributed community stability and arrived with commercial contacts in far-flung international familial networks that included Jews and conversos.[7] Mirroring Catholic officials' moral posturing regarding Black and Native sanctuary seekers, English officials decried Spanish mistreatment of Jews and boasted of their own comparative humanity.

Two migratory movements—of enslaved people of color from English and Dutch to Spanish and French colonies, and of Jews from Spanish, Portuguese, and French to English and Dutch colonies—reveal the divergent evolution of bases for belonging in Catholic and Protestant spaces in the Caribbean. Those differences stemmed partly from distinct European histories but also arose from the particular world of the late seventeenth-century Caribbean. After outlining the most germane differences between English and Spanish theories and structures of Caribbean governance, this chapter considers several cases of enslaved people fleeing Jamaica for surrounding Spanish jurisdictions and examines a conflict between English and French officials in the Eastern Caribbean over the status of Black war captives. Chapter 4 then turns to the stories of Jewish immigrants who sought to establish lives in English Jamaica. Their collective experiences reveal that in the Spanish and French Caribbean, officials and sanctuary seekers alike understood Catholicism as the foundational grounds for inclusion within the political community. Membership within that political community was hierarchical: non-Catholics were excluded, but among Catholics, Europeans enjoyed more rights and privileges than did Natives, Africans, or others. In contrast, English officials made whiteness the essential basis for membership in the body politic. Englishness and Protestantism mattered, but they were not indispensable to inclusion. Instead, English Protestants placed themselves at the top of a hierarchy of belonging mostly confined to White people but incorporating those who were foreign, Catholic, dissenting Protestant, and Jewish as lesser constituents.

After Spain forced conversion or expelled resident Jews and Muslims by the early sixteenth century, it aimed not only to bar anyone who was not Catholic (or a candidate for conversion) from some privileges of subjecthood, but to keep them geographically outside the bounds of Spanish dominion. They extended this policy to Spanish America, along with massive efforts to convert colonized Indigenous peoples to their religion. As in French and Portuguese Catholic colonies, royal and local officials required planters to facilitate the conversion of enslaved people to Catholicism and their incorporation into the church. Therefore, with few exceptions, every person living within the bounds of Spanish territory was nominally part of the religious, political, and social order. That inclusivity, however, was sometimes segregated and always hierarchical. Indigenous and Spanish towns maintained parallel structures of governance, sometimes described as representing two societies, a *república de indios* and a *república de españoles*. Despite theoretical separation, however, in reality the worlds of Indigenous and Spanish Americans were always entangled.[8] The república de españoles included African and mixed-race people as well as Europeans, and inequalities were obvious not just in the enslavement responsible for bringing large portions of the Black population to Spanish America but also in free Black peoples' exclusion from various occupations and offices.

Part of the professed rationale behind the theoretical separation of Indigenous and Spanish colonial society was an attempt to protect vulnerable new Indian converts (neophytes) from corrupting influences. To further that effort, Spanish colonizers sought to limit voluntary immigration to "pure" Christians. In the Americas as on the Iberian peninsula, those who could prove unsullied Christian lineage were regarded as having pure blood (*limpieza de sangre*) and enjoyed significant political privileges over those whose ancestry included known converts from Judaism or Islam. To further ensure conformity, the Inquisition used torture to enforce orthodoxy for people of European, African, and mixed descent. A separate investigative body did the same for Natives. Spanish officials took the ideal of Catholic universalism seriously, which meant that residents of Spanish America had little choice but to outwardly comply. In exchange, they gained (ranked) membership in the social and political order, with access to law.

Spanish policies of separation never worked to keep populations of Europeans, Natives, and Africans apart from one another. By the late seventeenth century, Spanish officials' zeal for maintaining two separate republics weakened as they recognized the reality of mixing. Even as officials' commitment to the system of two republics waned, however, support persisted among some Spanish, Indigenous, and African residents. African and Native peoples recognized that segregation conveyed some benefits. Jane Landers has shown that in Mexico at the end of the century, the free Black community of San Miguel de Soyaltepeque, in requesting "the respect due to governors and alcaldes," explicitly called their town a *república de negros*.[9] For Indigenous communities as well, the influence of separate republics persisted. Native towns continued to operate under their own town councils, and legal, religious, and military institutions operated separately or differently according to race.[10]

The mixing that foretold an end to separate republics gained expression in the *sistema de castas* that developed in Spanish (and Portuguese) America in the eighteenth century. It was an effort to understand and categorize—culturally and visually—the children of unions between Spanish, Indian, and African men and women, and then the children of those mixtures. It reveals Spanish colonists' obsession with hierarchy but also their willingness to acknowledge the failure of segregation and the fiction that colonial populations could be divided into three racial categories. The word *casta* is often translated as English *caste*, but Spaniards also used it as the English used *nation*: an ethnically defined polity. For example, casta was the category that included *Zambo*, a child of Indigenous and African parents, but the Spanish also referred to a person from Calabar (in southeastern Nigeria) as *casta Caravali*.[11]

In addition to royal regulations that decreed conversion and inclusion, local law and custom allowed officials and elite colonists in the Spanish and French Caribbean to shape their societies. As in English America, they tried to impose slave regimes that allowed owners to maximize profit and control and to minimize church or state protections for enslaved people. But because everyone was regarded as part of the same church, because the body of the church constituted the political body, and because this mattered to the crown, the racial difference that undergirded slavery was not bolstered by religious rejection and could not become the basis for excluding enslaved people from legal or religious protection. Although Iberian ideas about religious purity placing converts below those of unbroken Christian descent relegated African and Indigenous people into an inferior category lacking limpieza de sangre, there was no religious basis (there or in Portuguese or French America) for race to develop into a binary separating the included from the excluded, because everyone in colonial society was admitted or forced into the church. Church-influenced laws protected enslaved people's right to become free, so blackness could not be inexorably tied to enslavement. Therefore, while slavery in the Catholic Caribbean derived from the ongoing transatlantic slave trade and brutalized those caught in it, Catholic colonial societies could not equate blackness (or indigeneity) with slavery or whiteness with freedom, nor could they deny the legal personhood of enslaved men and women.

As its name suggests, the Church of England did not aspire to universality (in contrast to the Catholic Church, whose name advertised its aspirations to encompass everyone). In the English Caribbean, slave owners worked to exclude Africans and Natives from conversion to Christianity. The religious otherness of enslaved people then provided colonizers with a rationale to deny political rights. It also facilitated the emergence of race as a binary category and whiteness as the fundamental marker of belonging. Although the English in the Caribbean recognized multiple racial categories (White, Negro, Indian, Mestizo, Mulatto), they often elided complexity into "white" and "negro," a simplification that ignored racial mixing and obscured the extent to which the English enslaved Native Americans. Both results served the project of using race to exclude enslaved people from religious, social, and political community.

Several factors contributed to creating race-based belonging in the English Atlantic. First, the English royal family's decision to invest directly in human trafficking (for its own benefit, aside from that of the nation) created a crown-captive relationship that emphasized ownership of property rather than sovereignty over subjects.[12] Second, English clergy showed less interest in the religious standing or human suffering of enslaved captives than did Spanish clergy, and the relative weakness of church influence on the crown and church participation in colonization discouraged even sympathetic English clergy from intervening to insist that masters and colonial officials recognize slaves' humanity. Third, the legislative assemblies in English America, elected by and made up of local slaveholders, possessed greater autonomy to define the status of African laborers in their midst than did Spanish or French colonial administrators. Those assemblies, which some English officials believed were the envy of Spanish American elites, produced definitions of race that made it increasingly difficult for people of color to profess political standing as subjects of the English crown or even to become free.[13] Furthermore, planter control of Anglican vestries hamstrung clergy who may have wished to intervene but depended on slave owners for their salaries.[14] Fourth, the English lacked a concept of imperial vassalage, which in the Spanish Atlantic recognized mutual obligations between sovereign and subject even as it downplayed subjects' freedoms. Vassalage gave exploited, subservient people in Spanish America grounds for claiming limited political belonging and legal personhood. Finally, the English invented their colonial body politic at the same time as the concept of "trading nations" gained ascendance as a fundamental building block of the international order, creating further justification for excluding traded people. None of these factors was unique to the English, but in the English Atlantic they combined in such a way (and chronologically at a key moment of definition) as to promote the production of a racial binary that divided people, whatever their national and ethnic backgrounds or mixed heritage, into two categories that yoked legal status and race. Regardless of a persistent, complex reality, English colonies increasingly operated under the legal fiction that people were either free and White or enslaved and Black. The imperial employment of that binary then determined who could be a political subject. To promulgate such a race-based political order, the English explicitly rejected Christianity as a sufficient (and in Jamaica even as a necessary) basis for inclusion.

While English political theory did not couple denominational religious adherence and political subjecthood to the degree that Spanish and French did, Christianity was a central marker of humanity to all seventeenth-century European Christians. Thus, even after they enacted laws ensuring that they could enslave Christians, English Caribbean colonial legislators discouraged efforts to convert enslaved Africans or Indians to Christianity. As Edward Rugemer has noted, "slavery was . . . fundamentally at war with the humanity of the people enslaved."[15] Catholic officials, knowing both that slavery made human beings into legal property and that Christianity demanded that its adherents regard one another as members of the same community, opted to create societies that tried to contain the tension of Christian slavery. Protestant officials knew that withholding Christianity facilitated the denial of enslaved peoples' personhood, even when legal codes ensured the enslaveability of Christians.[16] As the Anglican clergyman Francis Le Jau observed, English Caribbean planters opposed conversion efforts not because they feared it would challenge enslavement, but because if slaves converted, masters "would be obliged to look upon [them] as Christian Brethren, & use 'em with humanity." And, crucially, he noted that when English slave owners opted to withhold Christian instruction and baptism from enslaved people in their own jurisdictions, they did so because they perceived that in neighboring Spanish and French colonies, shared Christianity curbed masters' brutality.[17] We need not accept Le Jau's claims uncritically—Spanish American slaveholders used violence to keep men and women enslaved and productive. But his perception—that Christianity mitigated that violence and that

English slaveholders both saw its ameliorative effects and sought to avoid them—is instructive.

When London officials in the 1680s and 1690s called for the conversion of enslaved people, English Caribbean elites responded with various objections that made clear their resistance to including enslaved people within the colonial body politic. English lawmakers understood that spreading Christianity to enslaved people would limit slaveholders' access to violence as a tool of subjection. They therefore rejected their religion's injunction to proselytize. Barbados elites in London protested that conversion would require English language instruction. If enslaved people all spoke the same language, they could more easily coordinate resistance, but withholding English instruction also clearly signaled slaveholders' desire to exclude enslaved men and women from colonial society.[18] Barbados governor Richard Dutton's 1681 speech to the Assembly made clear his belief that shared Christianity might limit planters' use of violence. He instructed them to pass a bill that paired "restrain[ing] bad masters and overseers from cruelty to their Christian servants" with finding "an expedient for the conversion of negroes to the Christian faith." Thus faced with language that explicitly linked shared Christianity with limits on the brutality that sustained slavery, the Barbados Assembly passed the first part of the bill but deemed the latter impossible.[19]

Pirates' and privateers' narratives mention their capture of people as plunder. They also note that African-descended and mixed-race men participated in Spanish defenses against their depredations. But they fail to admit to enslaving people they encountered as free. Indeed, some took care to distinguish their captives as either "prisoners" or "slaves," with prisoners to be ransomed and slaves to be kept or sold. When, for example, Henry Morgan found himself trapped in Lake Maracaibo (between Caracas and Cartagena) by a Spanish man-of-war, he offered to release all of his Spanish prisoners and "give up half of the slaves" he had captured as plunder, not acknowledging that he certainly had on his ship captives who, by Spanish reckoning, fit neither category.[20] Pirates made their decisions based on physical appearance ("Negroes and Mulatos") rather than legal status.[21] Generally, these narratives neglect to describe what happened to "slaves" after their capture, leaving readers to assume that they were sold (along with other plunder) in Jamaica or other locales whose residents would participate in the fiction that the people they bought were legally sellable. Other English records likewise fail to identify such individuals by their former status in Spanish America. Indeed, when

English governors noted that pirates had sold plunder in Jamaica, they rarely even mentioned that such plunder included human captives, although they certainly knew it.

Despite their own diverse makeup, the outlaw mariners who captured free vassals of the Spanish king and sold them as slaves—like the English officials who failed to question the captives' identities—imposed an emergent, albeit contested, English definition of race onto the international geopolitical stage. That definition treated all people of color as slaves. Spanish and French officials resisted that imposition when they insisted that African, Indigenous, and mixed-descent people be included in prisoner-of-war exchanges, and when they offered sanctuary to runaways. Spanish officials, even when protecting the interests of Spanish slave owners, preserved the words of people of color and, in moments of international rivalry, accepted them as Catholic members of their local communities. Officials considered such people's racial makeup within a complicated framework that acknowledged multiple categories of mixing and took seriously the question of their pre-capture legal status. Sanctuary records rarely use the words *subject* or *vassal*, instead emphasizing local belonging and religious identity, but they treat petitioners as subjects who could expect mercy from their sovereign. Those seeking sanctuary emphasized the Caribbean context of geopolitical rivalry by referring to imperial boundaries and religious differences, and whether they sought sanctuary during a time of war or peace.

Thus the testimonies in these cases underscore a fundamental distinction between English and Spanish sources that stems from diverging attitudes toward race and subject identity. The asymmetrical development of Spanish and English ideas about race and political identity in the region also led to fundamental differences between English and Spanish record keeping. Those differences show up clearly in the archives surrounding sanctuary seekers. In sanctuary cases, Spanish officials accepted the testimonies of captives, reflecting their belief that free or enslaved people of African and Indigenous descent, if Catholic, might embody political identity as Spanish subjects. A person of color who crossed between Spanish and English Caribbean jurisdictions during the late seventeenth century was likely to appear as an individual with a name, a religious identity, political belonging, a hometown, a personal history, and a family in Spanish but not in English records. English sources usually failed to recognize individuals of Indigenous or especially African descent as potential subjects, not only of their own crown but of any other polity. English elites and officials increasingly, though not universally, foreclosed the theoretical possibility that people of color would help compose the body politic. Thus, English records rarely record the voices of African, Indigenous, and mixed-race individuals in their Caribbean colonies. Indeed, we often cannot even detect the presence of enslaved Indians, who are lumped together with Africans and creoles as "negroes and other slaves" in many English records, leaving their audiences to assume African descent. If privateers and pirates captured significant numbers of free Spanish vassals to sell to Jamaican slave owners, then English officials and planters, like mariners, had geopolitical as well as economic reason to elide those captives' backgrounds.[22]

Spanish officials and clerks, however, did not hold to such fixed racial categories, nor did they link racial identifications irrevocably to free or unfree status. Instead, they were prepared to recognize and accept how dynamic race might be in the multi-imperial Caribbean environment. Spanish sources not only describe racial complexities and uncertainties but permit individuals to describe themselves, even when their self-identification differed from a clerk's own perceptions. This chapter therefore includes many details from these testimonies—information we can glean from Spanish sources but rarely from English—because they permit individuals who were enslaved on English plantations to describe themselves and their experiences. In doing so, they show us aspects of seventeenth-century Jamaican slavery and seventeenth-century English and French piracy that depart from our usual understandings of both.[23]

In addition to the multiship fleets of privateers and pirates whose attacks on major Spanish American towns were widely reported, small bands of maritime marauders also made a practice of capturing people of African and Indigenous descent from Spanish and Portuguese coasts and vessels and selling them as slaves in Jamaica and other parts of the Caribbean. These raids, far less spectacular than those of Henry Morgan or Nikolaas van Hoorn, rarely appear in English sources. Evidence for them comes from records of people who were captured in those raids and who later escaped back to Spanish jurisdiction.

In 1667, for example, twelve people paddled a canoe from Jamaica to the southern coast of Cuba.[24] One was a Cuban mariner of Spanish descent. The others were all of African or mixed descent, described in Spanish records as "Negros" or "Mulatos." They included five men, four women, a twelve-year-old girl, and a two-year-old child. With the likely exception of the toddler, who had probably been born in Jamaica, each of these people, including the Spanish mariner, had been seized by pirates from Spanish or Portuguese jurisdiction and sold in Jamaica. The mariner, forty-year-old Simón Rodriguez, had been turtling with several companions in the Florida Keys when an English ship seized him and took him to "Siguatei" (Eleuthera) in the Bahamas. After he spent a month imprisoned there, his captors took him to Jamaica, where they tried to sell him as an indentured servant for six years of plantation labor. But Rodriguez petitioned the governor, who, apparently recognizing him as a Spaniard, ordered him released. Before he could return to Cuba, however, he came down with a fever and was nursed back to health by Ignacio Hernandes, a thirty-year-old *moreno* (brown, or perhaps of mixed African, Native, and European descent) man born in Cartagena. The two men became friends.

Hernandes was one of four men of African or mixed descent in the traveling group. Before his capture he had been the slave of Father Luis de Paternina. In about 1662, he was working at the priest's residence in Cartagena when an English pirate seized him and his companion Juan Patacón, took them to Jamaica, and sold them to different masters. After five years of Jamaican enslavement, Hernandes fled his English master's power, risking death in order "to be a Christian Catholic" and to obtain his liberty.

Gregorio Rodriguez was a free *negro* in his fifties, also a *natural* (native) of Cartagena. In 1665 he had been "seeking a living" for himself and his wife by selling small items in Riohacha (east of Cartagena), when English pirates arrived in two large boats and sacked the town. They captured Rodriguez and two other Black men, killing one and taking Rodriguez and the other to Jamaica, where they sold them into slavery. Rodriguez later complained to Cuban officials that the English made him work day and night constructing defensive fortifications, more like a prisoner than a slave.

In comparing his situation to that of a prisoner, Gregorio Rodriguez implied that a man living as a slave should expect better treatment than a prisoner. Prior to his capture, he had lived as a free man. But he knew from his time in urban Cartagena, in the small city of Riohacha, and perhaps in rural areas in between, that the enslaved in Spanish America faced violence and abuse. He also knew that the law and the church sometimes offered protections and in theory recognized enslaved people as humans with souls and vassalage that tied them to the king. While he objected to the treatment he received in Jamaica, particularly that he worked without rest, he also objected to the nature of the work; constructing fortifications in Spanish America was frequently reserved for criminals and prisoners of war. Gregorio Rodriguez, then, believed the status of slaves preferable to that of prisoners, whose condition reflected punishment for their own crimes or their nation's enemy status. In contrast, slaves lacked freedom through no fault of their own.

Several of Gregorio Rodriguez's fellow petitioners in Havana had likewise worked on fort construction in Jamaica.[25] Salvador Francisco was a free *negro* from the island of Santa Catalina (English Providence) off the coast of Nicaragua. He had been born free to a free mother, Lusia, who had obtained her liberty after having been a slave of Captain Salvador de la Pena. When "the enemy" (led by Edward Mansfield) sacked Santa Catalina, they seized Salvador Francisco, took him to Jamaica, and sold him. He, too, worked constructing the forts and fled the "power of heretics" in order to be a Catholic Christian.

Leonel was a young man who also identified himself as a freeborn creole of Santa Catalina, the son of Cristina, who was likewise free. He, like Salvador Francisco, had been seized in the sack of Santa Catalina and taken to Jamaica. Juan Catalan was a free soldier who seemed to the clerk to be *mulato*. He was a native of Cartagena, the son of master woodturner Matheo Catalan. He testified that he had gone to Santa Catalina to serve his Majesty in the presidio there, when the English pirates attacked the island, seized him, and took him to Jamaica. He, like the rest, had been put to work constructing forts. Of the four men working on the Jamaican forts, Gregorio Rodriguez was the only one who complained that the labor or his status was inappropriate. The other three had been taken in Mansfield's seizure of Santa Catalina and therefore could have regarded themselves as prisoners of war, who in the Spanish colonial world could more legitimately be required to perform such labor.

However, although the other three may have accepted the nature of the work they performed, they nonetheless challenged the validity of English religion, English law, and even English presence in the region. When Juan Catalan testified that he had "fled to the land of Christians and left the captivity of those pirates," in addition to expressing his desire to practice Catholicism, he denied that English Jamaica fell within Christendom and extended the category of pirates to encompass all the English, including the officials for whom he toiled as well as the maritime predators who had captured and sold him. Although merchants (especially slave traders) and the Caribbean officials who supported them downplayed religious antagonisms in the interest of mutual commercial gain, in sanctuary cases we can see that Spanish officials and sanctuary seekers themselves continued to invoke religion as a boundary marker. Welcoming runaway slaves under the guise of protecting Catholics also destabilized their English neighbors, and the Spanish crown continued to confirm such local decisions.[26]

When Gregorio Rodriguez complained that the English treated him more like a prisoner than a slave, he reversed the complaints of English prisoners of war in Spanish America who complained that they were used more like slaves than like prisoners. In 1668, for example, an English shipmaster listed the many Spanish abuses he had witnessed in the Caribbean, such as the killing of an English ship captain in Havana merely for having requested water. Among the instances of illegitimate behavior he described, he noted that when in 1666 the Spanish retook Santa Catalina, they "made slaves" of about fourteen "prisoners" they had taken in the island, and in Cartagena they "made slaves alsoe" of about thirteen more.[27]

Eight years later, two English mariners testified that they had been kept prisoners in Havana for fifteen months "like slaves" before escaping. One of the mariners had witnessed two Jamaica vessels taken as prizes "and the men made slaves."[28] This trope continued into the eighteenth century, when one English prisoner, writing on behalf of ninety others, complained that the Spanish kept them in stocks and irons, whipped them, and made them work in the mines and mints and building "their forts, castles or churches," and only feeding them "what they work for like slaves."[29] Unlike the free Black Spanish subject Gregorio Rodriguez, these free White English subjects believed enslavement worse than imprisonment. They too objected to fort building but, coming from an English context, identified such work with the degradation of slavery rather than a prisoner-of-war status, which they thought should include certain protections. They associated slavery with more onerous work and a status below that of prisoners. Although none of the men connected either condition (enslavement or imprisonment) with race in their testimonies, all the men had observed both the shared context of racialized slavery in the Caribbean and the diverging contexts that tied race more inexorably to enslavement in English Caribbean jurisdictions than in Spanish.

The women in the group also described their identities before their capture and sale. Unlike most of the men, they named Jamaican owners but did not specify what work they performed. Juana de Quesada was about thirty years old, a *natural del Bayamo* in southeastern Cuba, born a slave and owned by Luis de Quesada. She told the court officials that about six years earlier she had fled her master and gone into the forest in the company of a *mulato*, Luis, also a slave but of a different master. One day Juana and Luis went to the beach and saw some vessels at sea, which Luis recognized as enemies. While Juana hid in the woods, Luis signaled the men to land, and two canoes of Englishmen came to meet him. Juana told the officials that she had never intended to go with them, but Luis apparently betrayed and sold her. He brought the Englishmen to her hiding spot in the woods, and they threatened to kill her if she did not cooperate with her captors. They took her to Jamaica and sold her to an Englishman named Churi. Juana, like the others, placed herself within the orthodox Christian world of the Spanish Atlantic, in opposition to Jamaica where she had lived captive; having the chance to escape, she had "fled from the power of heretics and come to live among Roman Catholics and to save herself."[30]

Justa y Eufina was a twenty-year-old *negro* woman who in Santa Catalina had been enslaved to Benito Martin, a soldier of the presidio at Santa Catalina. When the English enemy sacked the island, they seized her and took her to Jamaica, where they sold her to a French silversmith called Pingar. She was likely from Cartagena originally, as she verified that Juan Catalan's father was a free woodturner there.[31]

Catalina seemed to the officials to be a *negra*, and she identified herself as a creole of Santa Marta, about twenty years old. In Santa Marta she had worked as the slave of Graciana de Medina, the widow of Andres Hernandes. Six years earlier she had been with her mistress in her *trapiche* (sugar mill) near Santa Marta when an English pirate entered the river by night and took Catalina and ten or eleven other slaves. (They allowed the mistress, likely not sellable, to flee into the woods.) The pirates took them all to Jamaica and sold them to different owners.[32]

Madalena, in her late twenties, and her twelve-year-old daughter Dominga (*negrita*) were free creoles of the port of Inácio in Pernambuco, Brazil. They had been traveling north along the coast to the port of Itamaracá, in a bark carrying a cargo of wood, when a French ship seized them and took them to French Tortuga. They spent two years there before being taken to Jamaica, where they were sold to a Frenchman named Jacome Martin. Perhaps Martin was a French Protestant, because Madalena testified that, after seven years in Jamaica, she had joined the others for Havana to reach "a land of Roman Catholic Christians" and to leave "the power of heretics" and achieve her liberty.[33]

The petitioners' stated desire to live as Catholics and their ability to make the sign of the cross correctly, probably together with their fluency in Spanish or Portuguese, provided Spanish American officials with sufficient evidence to free them. The petitioners knew what to say to acquire their freedom. Whatever the state of their Catholicism prior to their English captivity, their experiences as slaves in Protestant Jamaica had strengthened their attachment

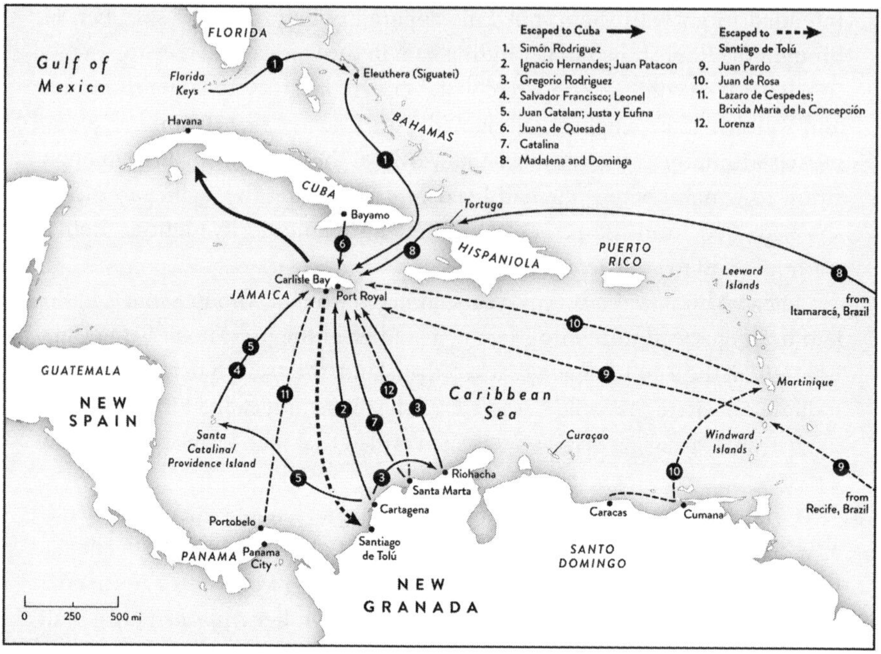

Map 5. *Routes of Captives and Sanctuary Seekers*. Drawn by Erin Greb.

to the Roman Catholic Church.[34] They embedded themselves in particular local communities as part of their claims to religious and imperial belonging. As several scholars have noted, local belonging was a crucial component of membership in the Spanish Atlantic that afforded vassals some protections from crown and church.[35] Several of the petitioners even used their enslavement to particular named individuals—the Cartagena priest Father Luis de Paternina, the Santa Catalina soldier Benito Martin, and the Santa Marta widow Graciana de Medina—to situate themselves within social networks of belonging. The governor of Havana freed all the petitioners except for Juana, the Cuban woman who had fled her master. He put her in the public jail and sent for her owner.

In addition to stressing their own former liberty and community networks, these petitioners' appeals for freedom rested on the fact that they had been seized by pirates. The petitioners used those seizures, together with Protestant heresy, to delegitimize English Jamaica itself as well as their own enslavement there. This, among the earliest sanctuary cases, illustrates that because people constituted such an important portion of pirates' and privateers' plunder in the Caribbean, pirates created a crucial opportunity for enslaved men and women to see and act on the distinctions between English and Spanish jurisdiction. The geopolitical context, including the illegitimacy of pirates' seizures and sales, made it easier for Spanish officials to respond by developing a practice of sanctuary that they later articulated as policy.[36]

These twelve escapees' testimonies illustrate that by 1667, the year of the initial Treaty of Madrid, Spanish subjects in the Caribbean had begun to perceive and reinforce a distinction between a Spanish Caribbean world that recognized the political and religious personhood of free and enslaved people of color, and an English Caribbean that increasingly foreclosed that possibility. Three years later, when Jamaica governor Thomas Modyford gave Henry Morgan instructions to offer enslaved Cubans the option of transferring allegiance (discussed in Chapter 1), he indicated that he could still envision people of color as potential members of the colonial body politic. And his decision to limit that option to Spanish-speaking "negroes" suggests that he had an easier time doing so with individuals who were already Christian and subject to a European crown. He, like Spanish American officials, understood that in border regions such as the western Caribbean, granting some people of color freedom and political rights might serve strategic ends.

Modyford failed to recognize the extent to which Spanish Americans, including those of African and Indigenous descent, having witnessed pirates' repeated seizures, saw English Protestants as committed to dehumanizing persons of color and linking enslavement inexorably to blackness. That very year, some Black creoles, who had lived in Spanish Jamaica before the English conquest and remained for over a decade, appraised the English Jamaica that was emerging in 1670 and decided to flee, according to a report that "42 Spanish negroes from Jamaica have got safe to Cuba."[37] Morgan's behavior, in contrast to the instructions he carried, reinforced that Spanish American awareness. In taking people of color as plunder to be sold rather than prisoners to be ransomed, he and his men provided further justification for Spanish officials to expand their practice of offering sanctuary and formalize it as policy.

Ten years after Morgan's 1670 sack of Panama, at least some of the free people of color that Morgan and his crew had captured remained enslaved (in English terms) or imprisoned (in their own or Spanish officials' words) in Jamaica. In 1680 a sloop arrived in Santiago de Tolú, about sixty miles southwest of Cartagena de Indias, with seven people aboard—three men, two women, an adolescent girl, and a six-year-old boy.[38] They had escaped from a Jamaican plantation near Carlisle Bay, west of Port Royal. Juan Pardo was a free man of mixed race, as his name (*pardo*/brown) implies, and a native (*natural*) of Recife, Brazil, where he had been a fisherman. Twelve years earlier Flemish pirates had abducted him from the coast of Brazil and sold him in the Windward Islands. From there, he had been taken to Jamaica and sold again. The two children, Isabel (*zamba*, or of Indigenous and African descent) and Juan, were his, both born in Jamaica and, as he told Cartagena officials, baptized there in the English manner.[39]

Juan de Rosa was an Indigenous mariner in his late twenties, from the city of Caracas. He had been sailing from Caracas east to Cumana carrying letters when French pirates seized him and took him to the French island of Martinique. He escaped, was caught again, and was sold in Jamaica, where his owners there put him to work on a plantation. (The word in the documents in *plantaje*, not a Spanish word but a Hispanicization of the English *plantation* or Dutch *plantage* without explanation. It was perhaps used regionally in Spanish America to describe English methods of staple crop production and their growing association with especially brutal forms of slavery.) There he came to know the companions with whom he later escaped. Lazaro de Cespedes, a twenty-four-year-old free *zambo* from Panama City, had been traveling by canoe from Portobelo to Chagre when the English seized him and took him to Jamaica. Lorenza, an Indian woman from Santa Marta, did not give testimony.

Brixida Maria de la Concepción was a twenty-year-old woman taken prisoner during Morgan's sack of Panama. In Jamaica she was a midwife. Spanish officials identified her variously as *mulata*, *parda libre*, and (as she appeared at first to officials), *muger ladino* (Spanish-speaking, of mixed descent) *español*, and *natural de* Panama City. Officials' uncertainty about her race, their concern to identify her correctly, and their willingness to note her self-identification (*parda libre*) illustrate their awareness of the indeterminate nature of race (and Spanish American anxieties about categorizing individuals by race).[40] This contrasts with English records, which often dispensed with such concerns and simply labeled all persons of color "negroes," as did Jamaica governor Lynch when he wrote to the governor of Cartagena requesting the refugees' return. Although he identified Pardo ("Juan Brown") as "mulato," he grouped the rest together as nameless "negros."[41]

Isabel's and Juan's Jamaican baptisms let us reimagine an enslaved father's responses to his children's situations. Whether Juan Pardo regarded his children's' baptisms merely as a ritual conferring a degree of political belonging and potential protection or also as a sacrament commanding his son and daughter to a Christian god and a Christian community, he seems both to have thought it critical and worried about its efficacy if performed by English Protestants.[42] In a slave society in which record keepers rarely noted the names and ages of enslaved individuals, much less rites of passage, testimonies such as Juan Pardo's work against any tendency to follow the lead of the sources and envision the enslaved people who lived on such estates mainly in the aggregate, as nameless and ageless. Imperial rivalries and borders generated records that give us one small window into the experiences of a few men, women, and children, which make it easier to understand that each of the individuals trapped in Caribbean enslavement lived his or her own singular life.[43]

As these Spanish prisoners lived and worked together on an English plantation, likely surrounded by African and Jamaican-born slaves, they created community with one another out of their similar histories, language, and perhaps shared religion, developing bonds strong enough to trust one another with their lives. One day, a small French sloop came to trade with the plantation's English owner. The fourteen or fifteen French smugglers loaded a small cargo of brown sugar, cotton, and indigo onto their sloop, and then left it moored while they and the Englishmen got drunk, giving the Spanish and Portuguese vassals the chance to slip on board, cut the sloop's moorings, and sail away, aiming for Portobelo. The sugar, cotton, and indigo were the only supplies on the boat, along with some fresh water. So they ate nothing but sugar for eleven days while they sailed, looking for a Spanish port. The French smugglers and English planters, who were too drunk to notice the ship's disappearance, clearly had underestimated the laborers on the plantation. The English owner perhaps did not even know that among his slaves were a fisherman, a sailor, and a canoe man, who would know what to do when presented with a sloop. While the group did not reach their destination of Portobelo, they navigated the craft to safety.

When officials in Tolú and Cartagena took testimony from the adult escapees (except the Indigenous woman Lorenza), each testified to being a Christian, and the clerk recorded their ability to make the sign of the cross correctly (as in the 1667 Cuban case). The officials referred to the escapees only as prisoners of the English, never as slaves, and accepted that each was legitimately free in the Iberian world. When they fled their captivity, they expressed confidence that in risking their lives they would find affirmation of their personhood. As in the earlier case, they declared themselves to belong to (*natural de* or *criollo de*) specific places in Spanish or Portuguese America. They described their human relations in those places, situating themselves within local communities to establish their belonging in a larger Spanish world. They passed judgement on the English as enemies, pirates, and heretics, further claiming membership in the Spanish body politic and marking boundaries that defined the English, Flemish, and French mariners who seized them as outside the law and the heretics who imprisoned them as outside the true faith. They framed a Caribbean world in which distinctions between orthodox Catholics and heretics, and between legitimate denizens of the region and pirates, overwhelmed race as the most important markers of belonging.

Their testimonies, from Spanish archives, also contribute to our growing awareness of the complexity of English Jamaican plantations. English planters, pirates, and officials did not advertise their enslavement of free Spanish vassals. Scholars have for several years been reimagining Caribbean slavery in general, and Jamaican slavery in particular, as they have tried to understand what it meant for individuals from varied locales in West Africa to labor and live together, and as they recognize that the word *slave* that we so often read in records as African or Afro-Caribbean included Indigenous people from Carolina, the Yucatán, New England, Brazil, and elsewhere.[44] The sanctuary cases from Havana and Cartagena demand that we also imagine freeborn Spanish vassals as part of enslaved plantation populations in Jamaica.[45] Their coordinated escapes reveal that they formed ties of trust in Jamaica based on shared language, experience, and perhaps religion and political loyalty. Even if these communities survived no longer than one generation, they mattered to those who formed them, and they allow us to see that Catholicism and Spanish vassalage were among the multiple sources of identity on which enslaved people of color in the international Caribbean might draw.

The documents demand that we think seriously about how many Spanish (and Portuguese) vassals English and other pirates seized and sold as slaves in the Caribbean during the labor-scarce decades at the end of the seventeenth century. When Morgan and his men left Panama in 1671 with five hundred to six hundred captives to sell in Jamaica, they participated in what seems, from sanctuary testimonies, to have been the regular practice for privateers and pirates who preyed on Spanish American settlements. The experiences of individuals such as the Spanish fisherman Simón Rodriguez, the *mulato* soldier Juan Catalan, the Indigenous mariner Juan de Rosa, and the *parda* midwife Brixida Maria de la Concepción suggest that anyone living or working on or near the water was vulnerable. The few who managed to escape and tell their stories to Spanish officials surely represent only a small portion of the people seized and sold. The same developing plantation political economy of the region, which created competition among transatlantic slave traders, put all people of color (and even some individuals of European descent, as Simón Rodriguez's case indicates), free or enslaved, at risk.

Finally, in the details of these testimonies we see a significant French presence in English Jamaica. French smugglers and English planters caroused together in addition to trading. Two of the people who bought human plunder were Frenchmen living in the English colony. French and Flemish pirates took Brazilian captives first to the French colonies Martinique and Tortuga, and when the captives were later resold in Jamaica, at least one of the French traders did business with his countryman, selling Madalena and Dominga to a French Jamaican master rather than to one of the more numerous English Jamaicans.[46]

By the end of the century, knowledge of Spain's sanctuary policy was widespread. The practice, which had begun by 1665 with crown approval, became imperial policy by 1693.[47] Captives with no obvious Spanish or Portuguese history began fleeing Jamaica and other Protestant colonies for Spanish jurisdiction in the hope of gaining their freedom. In 1699, when England and Spain were at peace, William Beeston, by then governor of Jamaica, complained to the English Board of Trade that the Spanish "secure all our negroes that run from us to Cuba, and set them free." Recently, "about 20" had escaped to Trinidad on Cuba's southern coast. When their English owners sent an envoy to secure their return, a Spanish official replied that because the Africans had fled to Cuba "for protection," Cuban authorities "could not in justice" return them. He promised to compensate the former owners for the Africans' value, but when Beeston and the Jamaican masters sent their agent, instead of the money they believed they were owed, they received a reiteration that the "great and merciful" king of Spain promised "that all persons that fled to him or his territories" would be "wholly emancipated from any pretenders."[48] Beeston thus quoted to his superiors the Spanish officials' language claiming their own greater justice and mercy. In doing so he echoed his own observation three decades earlier in Cartagena, that elite Cartageneros opposed the English disposition to see all people of color as movable commodities rather than as members of local communities. At the end of the century, Beeston remained comfortable contrasting Spanish officials' claims to offer protection to "all persons" with English demands for return of their property.

But Beeston also accused Cuban colonists of using the policy to bolster their own labor force. He predicted that "by this rule they may rob us of all our slaves, for Cuba is to be seen from the north side of this island in fair weather, and therefore there needs not much navigation for them to run thither." Beeston worried that the Spanish not only cheated the English but played them for fools in the process. He also believed that the Spanish duped some enslaved Jamaicans by enticing them to flee only to re-enslave them upon their arrival in Cuba. However, when he complained that the Spanish policy produced "great disturbance" and "loss" among "His Majesty's subjects," he referred only to slave owners.[49] If Governor Beeston believed enslaved Jamaicans to be subjects of William III, he did not concern himself with the loss they would experience in seeking freedom only to be re-enslaved.

Even as Beeston doubted Spanish motives, he repeated Spanish officials' argument to him that the matter was one of "justice." Despite sanctuary seekers' and Spanish officials' reference to the English as heretics and "pretenders," the moral issues at stake went beyond the orthodoxy of Catholicism over Protestantism. Both English and Spanish officials knew that the English made little effort to convert enslaved Africans or Natives to Christianity, a moral failing that contrasted with Spanish practice, and Spanish officials used the occasion of refugees' border crossing to make a case (perhaps to themselves as much as to an international audience) for their own commitment to ensuring justice to "all people."[50] While we might not now regard Spanish and French imposition of European colonial religion on African and Indigenous people as evidence of ethical superiority, by colonizers' shared standards, it would have been. The opportunity to extend sanctuary provided Spanish officials a useful moral counterweight to the exploitative plantation society that increasingly defined many of their own colonies, including in southern Cuba.[51]

Moreover, in a region that depended on militias for defense, these sanctuary seekers were strategically valuable because their experiences of seizure and enslavement motivated them to defend Spanish colonies against foreign invaders.[52] Throughout Spanish America, Spanish, Black, Native, and mixed-race men served in militias, separated into companies by race. Like their (qualified) jurisdictional separation into "republics," such segregation reflects the limits to incorporation into one body politic; but as Pérez de Guzmán revealed in Panama, they often garnered significant respect from colonial authorities and in some colonies boasted rights comparable to those of White militias, including the right to select their own officers.[53]

Imperial conflict similarly gave some free and enslaved Black people the chance to move from English to French territory in search of freedom or, French officials claimed, greater religious and political inclusion as slaves. French Caribbean officials, like the Spanish, argued that enslaved and free people of African descent were colonial subjects entitled to protection from crown officials, and that their political personhood and right to crown protection were inextricably tied to their Catholicism.[54] Like Spanish officials, they did so during moments of conflict with the English over the return of African-descended prisoners of war and runaways. The examples that follow, from the eastern Caribbean, suggest that the people who fled Jamaican captivity for sanctuary in Cuba or Nueva Granada participated in a larger debate about whether people of color—including those who were enslaved—were members of colonial bodies politic and by extension subjects of European sovereigns, and whether being Christian could ensure such belonging.

In the Leeward Islands, land changed hands and people crossed borders during multiple imperial and local wars and postwar chaos—as enslaved plunder, as prisoners of war, and of their own free will. In 1697, the Treaty of Ryswick, which ended the War of the Grand Alliance, required authorities to return prisoners of war and property confiscated during the war.[55] However, local English officials argued that when they acquired land as part of the settlement, they acquired as well the men and women who lived there enslaved to the French. Many of the captives so detained disagreed and fled to French jurisdiction. Two years after the conclusion of the peace, the president and council of English Nevis demanded that the Marquis d'Amblimont, governor general of the French Antilles, return twenty-one "negroes" who supposedly belonged to two English elites from Antigua. The twenty-one people had been enslaved to French masters prior to the war and were captured by the English during the war. But they had fled across the sixty miles of sea from English Antigua to French Guadeloupe, choosing French enslavement over English. The Nevis Council "daily" feared that others enslaved in the Leeward Islands would follow them. The escapees and the French officials had the law on their side whether officials defined enslaved people as property or prisoners, since the treaty required that both be returned. But the Nevis Council complained that allowing the French to harbor those who had fled would "prove of very pernicious consequence to many of His Majesty's subjects."[56] Like Jamaica governor Beeston, the Nevis Council appealed to London officials' rightful concern for "His Majesty's Subjects" by using the term exclusively for colonists, in this case slaveholders, implying that enslaved people were neither subjects nor entitled to the crown's concern.

D'Amblimont saw the relation between crown officials and people of color more expansively. He first demanded that the English return several *free* Black people they had taken and enslaved during the war, enclosing a list of their names. As did Spanish officials, d'Amblimont argued that the English propensity to turn free Black prisoners of war into hereditary slaves reflected English moral incompetence and that the English failed to show the prisoners the "justice, charity and humanity" they were due.[57] An English memorial responded that the English would release prisoners of war who had been free under French rule, but only after the French returned the people who were already enslaved when the English seized them, and who had since gotten themselves back to French jurisdiction.[58] D'Amblimont, however, refused to send back to the English *any* people who had made their way from English to French territory, insisting that "slaves who have risked their lives to return to their former masters in accordance with the liberty secured to them by the Treaty" "should be allowed" to remain with or return to their French masters, referring perhaps to Article 6 of the Treaty of Ryswick stipulating that all property taken during the war be returned.

While he invoked treaty law, religion formed the crux of d'Amblimont's argument: "The negroes who have returned to their French masters have been baptised and received into the Roman Catholic Church: if they were restored [to the English], they would be deprived of those opportunities of practising their religion, to secure which was, perhaps, the main object of the risks they ran."[59] His argument, that people ought to be able to practice their religion freely, may seem surprising so soon after the revocation of the Edict of Nantes and the ensuing persecution of Protestants. Perhaps, however, it makes sense as a justification for the enslaved Catholics' boundary crossing: practicing their religion entailed living in a place where it was practiced, just as for the Spanish sanctuary seekers wishing "to live in a land of Roman Catholic Christians."

D'Amblimont's demands and the English rejection of them reveal that even as law-of-nations language was gaining traction, colonial contexts undermined it. Those who appealed to a law of nations presumed it to rest on mutually understood political categories such as "subject." But French, Spanish, and English officials in the Caribbean disagreed about who fit into the category. When d'Amblimont demanded the return of free Black men and women, he wrote (ignoring transatlantic human trafficking) that the English governor must be "aware that it is part of the Law of Nations that free negroes in any country must not be sold but enjoy the same prerogatives as men born free." While the 1685 French Code Noir (specifically meant to regulate slavery and race in France's American colonies) granted former slaves the same rights as freeborn French subjects, I have not found any treaty law or treatise on the law of nations that did so.

Moreover, those people who fled across borders to escape various forms of captivity increasingly insisted that such categories did *not* translate. The people of color who found themselves captured by the English and subsequently defined as enslaved property without political or religious identities or rights fled with the conviction that blackness or indigeneity and membership in the body politic (even if as a slave) could coexist in the Spanish and French Caribbean worlds. When Spanish and French officials accepted such fugitives' professions of membership within the French or Spanish worlds, they confirmed definitions of race, enslavement, and belonging that they knew to differ from those of the English. When they employed the universalist languages of Christianity and the law of nations to do so, they sometimes seemed to conflate the two to suggest that Christianity's ethical requirements constituted the law of nations. Even if an emerging law of nations diverged from Christianity, Spanish and French officials could invoke both, with their presumptive universal applicability, to point to English colonial exclusion of people of color as a moral failing.

D'Amblimont's language, that French slaves taken by the English be "allowed" to return, assumed that enslaved captives preferred their former French masters to their current English ones. The former French slaves who evaded their new English masters to return to French enslavement seem to support d'Amblimont's claim.[60] D'Amblimont saw no irony in his insistence that enslaved Africans' treaty right to choose their enslavers constituted a "liberty," testimony to his confidence in the benefits conveyed by Catholicism. If d'Amblimont was correct that people fled English for French enslavement in the Leeward Islands, then the individuals he described made a remarkable choice. Unlike cases where enslaved people fled from Carolina to Florida and from Jamaica to Cuba, people in the Leeward Islands ran from English enslavement to French enslavement on islands whose sugar-based economies were relatively similar.

Colonel Christopher Codrington, one of the two Antigua elites who claimed to own the twenty-one people who had fled English for French enslavement, dismissed the importance that the escapees and d'Amblimont placed on enslaved persons' religion. He attributed their flight to "a natural desire of changing their masters upon the least severe usage" and to "the encouragement of these many holy-days the French allow their slaves."[61] Codrington saw freedom from labor on Catholic holy days in strictly materialist terms. But to French lawmakers, masters, and enslaved men and women, slaves' ability to rest (or perhaps even worship) on holy days may have been inseparable from and constitutive of a Catholic and therefore French allegiance in this Caribbean plantation world.

When the Board of Trade requested additional information from Codrington, he countered d'Amblimont's contention that treaty law required the return of slaves captured during war. Indeed, "no such treaty" existed because none was needed: rather, the law of nations covered such cases and, according to Codrington, stipulated that "the negroes became the property of the conquerors," exactly as with "cattle, etc." He argued in essence that enslaved people were entailed to the estates on which they lived and worked so that when territory changed hands, so did the enslaved people living on it. He held that such an "understanding" superseded the Treaty of Ryswick articles providing for the return of both property and prisoners of war.[62] Regardless, returning them would have been impracticable, because as plunder, captives had been "fairly divided" between the navy and army and then sold to purchasers in Barbados, Jamaica, North America, the Leeward Islands, and "probably to the Spaniards"—in other words, scattered beyond recovery. Codrington called d'Amblimont's appeal to religious principles "idle" "pretence."[63]

Codrington further pointed out that civil law (the basis for French law) confirmed the right to hold Christians as slaves and that French practice followed accordingly, with baptized people of African descent "as much slaves as those in the English colonies."[64] He was correct that civil law permitted the enslavement of Christians, as did the Code Noir. But he was incorrect that enslaved Christians of color were "as much slaves" in French as in English colonies. The Code Noir required slaves' baptism and, consequently, theoretically recognized their inclusion among the king's subjects. On that basis, the law protected the integrity of slaves' families and their right to purchase their freedom.

In the Caribbean, French slave owners and officials violated those rights with impunity, including selling people away to Protestants. But in moments of interimperial conflict, enslaved men and women might seize an opportunity created by the Caribbean's close and changing borders to assert those rights. French law, like Spanish, precluded the legal definition of slaves as chattel that Codrington was pushing for in the international legal arena. So while Christians in French colonies could indeed be owned by other people in hereditary perpetuity, their Christianity ensured that the law would recognize their humanity and that they would possess rights not accorded to chattel livestock. Even though we know that French (like Spanish) slave owners and officials violated those laws, we should listen to the individuals who fled, telling us that they chose enslavement to Catholic Caribbean masters over enslavement to Protestant ones.

As for the free people whom the English had captured, and whose return d'Amblimont demanded, Codrington, like other English officials, rejected their membership in the French body politic. Therefore, even if the English had captured "all the free negroes in the French colonies," "I say then no injury is done to the French nor have they a right to demand them." He did, however, "allow a very barbarous injury is done to the negroes themselves." They should be "restored to their freedom, and suffered to dispose of themselves," choosing whether to "stay amongst us or return to the French." People of African descent could be free, but to Codrington they could only be nonstate actors, not constituents of colonial societies or of imperial bodies politic.

Codrington recognized the threat to English slave law. When French officials claimed that they demanded the return of Catholic slaves as a matter of conscience, they challenged the "the point of property" in human beings that he believed the institution of slavery depended on. In this, he revealed English dualistic thinking regarding race and slavery: if someone was property, they could not also be a prisoner of war. If the French could demand the return of enslaved Catholics even when a treaty stipulated the return of property, it would render the treaties meaningless with regard to the Caribbean's most important form of property, "because no treaty can oblige men to act contrary to their consciences." Codrington imagined that as soon as the enslaved people in the English Caribbean colonies got wind of such a policy, they would depart en masse for nearby French jurisdictions.

Codrington's fear only made sense if French enslavement was preferable to English. If "five hundred or a thousand or ten thousand negroes should get off Barbados to Martinique" and presented themselves to "the Monks," the clergy "would undoubtedly admit them to baptism." And because it would help them escape their English enslavement, "the negroes would of course be good Roman Catholicks." Codrington even imagined that the French might have legal qualms about benefiting from the labor of "men and Christians desiring to live as good Roman Catholicks" and therefore offer liberty, and that "the negroes in pure gratitude might be persuaded to resign [voluntarily!] their freedom and become slaves to the French."[65]

Like William Beeston, Christopher Codrington recognized the role Catholicism played in enslaved people's preference for Spanish or French over English colonial society. Unlike Beeston in Jamaica, Codrington may have accepted the comparison as critique, and responded with efforts to provide religious instruction for captives in Barbados.[66] But most English Caribbean planters and assemblies took the Spanish and French cases as a warning. Christianizing the enslaved might not render them free, but it made it harder to deny their humanity, and it required protections and inclusion that English slave owners preferred to avoid. Instead, empowered by their representative legislative assemblies, they chose to maximize the border separating free from slave, "white" from "negro," and Christian from heathen, which excused more inhumane treatment and discouraged evangelizing.

As a result, enslaved men and women continued to flee Jamaica for Cuba into the eighteenth century, even as sugar production grew on the southern coast of Cuba. Jamaican governor Beeston had been correct at the turn of the century when he perceived that Spanish colonists possessed considerable economic incentives to re-enslave escapees. But the refugees themselves, some of their Spanish neighbors, and many Spanish officials insisted that the runaways' claims to freedom as Catholic subjects of Spain were legitimate.

In 1723 in Santiago de Cuba, Miguel Caravali and Gaspar Moco petitioned for themselves and on behalf of several others who had fled with them from Jamaica to gain their freedom under the sanctuary policy. Cuban records identify both men by their nation of origin (as perceived by the Spanish) as well as by race. Miguel was "casta Caravali," identifying him as from Calabar, and Gaspar was "casta Moco," also from what is now southern Nigeria. Both were also identified as "negros." Unlike the earlier sanctuary seekers who escaped Jamaica to seek freedom in Spanish jurisdiction, Miguel and Gaspar seem to have been born in Africa rather than in other parts of Spanish or Portuguese America, so they did not petition on the basis of prior inclusion in a local Spanish American community. Nor did they claim capture by pirates. The sanctuary policy, which initially responded to pirated Spanish American vassals' desire to return, now attracted and incorporated into the Spanish colonial body politic others wishing to escape English (or Dutch) enslavement.

When Miguel and Gaspar and their fellow refugees made it to Cuba, initially its developing slave-based economy seemed to win out. On their arrival, the group of refugees found themselves re-enslaved to the widow Francesca Modesta de Silva, apparently with the knowledge of Governor Lopez de Cangas. Other residents of Santiago, however, objected to the escaped Jamaicans' re-enslavement. Several colonists testified on their behalf and may have aided Miguel and Gaspar in presenting their petitions to Judge Gregorio Lopez de Navia y Quiroga, who decided that justice demanded the refugees be freed for their "good faith."[67] The judge described Miguel and Gaspar as "seeking Christianity," without mentioning their desire to become free. Unlike the earlier cases, in which Catholics expressed their wishes to return to a place where they could practice the religion of their upbringing, Miguel and Gaspar instead framed their journey as one in search of Christianity. The sanctuary policy had evolved to include potential converts as well as Catholic refugees, making freedom the just reward for the efforts they had made to pursue Catholicism.

The same investigation that freed Miguel and Gaspar also reprimanded Governor Lopez de Cangas for failing to address residents' complaints that *cimarrones* (Maroons) from the town of El Cobre, only twelve miles away, were committing unspecified depredations on the people of Santiago. El Cobre was unusual because its population of royal slaves (slaves of the crown working in copper mines) and free Blacks had negotiated royal status as a Black town with a unique identity based on sightings of the Virgin Mary.[68] At least one local official complained that it was very difficult to explain to royal slaves the difference between slaves and vassals, suggesting conflict between his own vision of slaves as outside the body politic and the royal slaves' insistence on their inclusion within it.[69]

The complaints against Governor Lopez de Cangas documented colonists' concern about frequent interactions between free Blacks of Santiago de Cuba and the people of El Cobre, and their concern that El Cobre provided refuge for enslaved people escaping from Santiago.[70] Perhaps leaders of El Cobre did so for a combination of ethical and material reasons, similar to those of Spanish leaders granting sanctuary to refugees from Jamaica. The proximity of El Cobre to Santiago de Cuba (as well as the presence of the Maroon town of Trelawny in northwestern Jamaica) suggests that Miguel, Gaspar, and their fellow escapees chose Santiago de Cuba over other possibilities. Their options theoretically included Maroon communities in both Jamaica and Cuba, but they instead sought Spanish Cuban society and a life as Spanish vassals over what might seem to be greater autonomy in free Black towns, a choice that seems all the more notable in light of their surnames marking likely African nativity.

Because the Caribbean's geography provided its denizens so many opportunities to cross political borders, the region became a crucible for working out the changing meanings of subjecthood within Atlantic empires. Like the Jamaican escapees who testified in the 1667 and 1680 cases, the French Antilles governor d'Amblimont and the Cuban judge Lopez de Navia emphasized enslaved people's desire to practice their Catholicism as reason for colonial administrators to act on their behalf. In both cases, Catholic officials reinforced sanctuary seekers' efforts to define the boundaries of subjecthood in religious terms. For officials, such definitions became a means of policing geopolitical boundaries. Governor d'Amblimont and Judge Lopez de Navia both insisted that the religious nature of imperial boundaries in the Caribbean held significant meaning for individuals of African and Indigenous descent. Both colonial officials could only advance such theoretical claims because people of color had already enacted them—first via their interimperial flights and then by their requests that imperial officials make good on French and Spanish promises that Catholicism formed a sufficient basis for imperial allegiance, crown protection, and membership in the body politic. The lingering corporate nature of the Spanish Atlantic and to a lesser degree the French, where membership in the church body and the ties of local community carried rights and protections, made it possible for people of color to develop loyalties for which the English Caribbean offered little parallel. English officials' silence regarding the rights or humanity of Black or Indigenous war captives (free or enslaved) is made louder by Spanish and French officials' repeated invocations of Christianity, justice, and legal protections. The universalist ideals of Roman Catholicism thus offered potent ideological mobilization that French and Spanish officials deployed when they wished to attract subjects to destabilize nearby enemies or to highlight their own justice in contrast to English heretics' inhumanity. The commitment to such ideals was expedient, however. It diminished when such geopolitical concerns receded.

English officials used very different language than did Spanish and French officials to discuss people of African descent who had crossed colonial borders. The English in the Caribbean argued that people of African and Indigenous descent were properly understood to be outside not only the English body politic but also the Spanish and French. English officials emphasized the owners whose property rights were at stake. The Spanish and French, if only rarely referring explicitly to enslaved or free Blacks or Natives as subjects, did stress that they were people to whom the crown owed protection—just as it did to its subjects. They discussed the rights and humanity and allegiance of the enslaved in terms of their relationship to the crown—the essence of subject identity—and in terms of their networks of family and service that tied them to other crown subjects. These cases show a Caribbean that put people in motion and made political belonging a question of process, and they allow us to see what we, too, often can only surmise—how individuals at many levels of society understood the region's jurisdictions, geopolitics, and economies.

CHAPTER 4

"Amongst the White and Civilized People of the World"

Jews in the Caribbean moved in the opposite direction from enslaved and free people of color, into the English and Dutch Atlantic from the Spanish and Portuguese empires, often via the Netherlands. Their situation in the Caribbean was precarious, in part as a result of the generation-long Dutch rule of Pernambuco in Brazil that began in 1630. Sephardic Jews, whose ancestors were from Spain and Portugal, had moved to the Dutch colony of New Holland, drawn by unprecedented toleration and pushed by crowded conditions in Amsterdam. In New Holland, they joined families that had lived for generations as New Christians under Portuguese rule and who now found themselves free to practice Judaism openly, to operate retail stores, and to own sugar plantations. By the mid-1640s, around 1,500 Jews lived in Dutch Brazil.[1] But when Portugal regained control in 1654 (one year before England's conquest of Jamaica), Jewish residents were given three months to leave. Many migrated to Dutch and English colonies (sometimes following an initial flight to the Netherlands), where they found varying degrees of discrimination but could openly practice their religion and live in community.[2]

Migration into Jamaica and land grants in the first decade after the English conquest reveal that Jews and crypto-Jews living throughout the Atlantic world saw opportunity in the newly English island. Some of those had fled the Portuguese reconquest of Dutch Brazil the year before the Western Design came to Jamaica, and Jamaica's location further attracted Jewish merchants who had commercial and familial connections in the Spanish and Portuguese Caribbean. The poet Daniel Lopez Laguna, born in Portugal to New Christians and imprisoned by the Inquisition in Spain, escaped in the 1660s and headed for Jamaica, where he celebrated that there, he could "s[i]ng The Psalms of my joy."[3]

Jews occupied an uncertain place within and alongside European bodies politic. They and others understood them to belong to the "Hebrew nation" rather than any European nation. *Nation*, derived from the Latin *nasci*, "to be born" (also the derivation of *native* and *natural*), had both ethnic and political meaning in the seventeenth century. It was most commonly used as we might use "a people"—to refer to those with shared culture, language, descent, and history.[4] Most nations coincided with a geographic space that often also comprised a polity such as a kingdom or republic. The English nation, therefore, was composed of people who were ethnically English and descended from people born within the borders of the kingdom of England. Composite monarchies such as Great Britain and Spain created a larger category of political belonging, in which individuals of multiple nations (and multiple kingdoms) shared one monarch. The sovereign's subjects thus came from several nations.[5] While a monarch ruled each kingdom separately, and each retained its own laws and administrative structures, those distinctions between a sovereign's subjects were often invisible when they ventured into the international arena, and treaties referred uniformly to the ways in which the agreement bound all of each sovereign's subjects. When the kingdoms within composite monarchies maintained considerable domestic autonomy, the composite nature of the body politic gained visibility primarily as subjects traveled outside their nation's (or kingdom's) borders, a phenomenon that increased with Atlantic colonization and trade. Treaties and diplomatic correspondence thus referred to "Great Britain" and to "British" subjects well before the 1707 Act of Union that made the designation appropriate within Britain. Even so, contemporaries often ignored the misalignment of nation and body politic unless conflict forced them to acknowledge it.

The relationship between "nations" and kingdoms within a composite monarchy defies easy description. Some kingdoms (Scotland, Aragon) retained that designation as they incorporated. Others, such as Wales or Viscaya/Biscay, were folded into the dominant kingdoms of England and Castile. Nonetheless, in the late seventeenth century, all retained a sense of persistent national identity, often reinforced by separate languages, even as Atlantic colonization increased the importance of composite-monarchy subjecthood. In the Americas, Spain further created the vice-kingdoms of New Spain and Peru, whose Spanish residents were theoretically but not actually limited to Castilians. They, along with people from various Indigenous and African nations, retained national identities such as Castilian, Miskito, or Caravali/Calabar.

The Hebrew nation was unlike any other. It lacked a state or sovereignty, and its members lived dispersed throughout much of the world. Their presence therefore challenged European visions of nations that aligned with sovereign kingdoms. The creation of British and Spanish composite monarchies had included efforts to force religious conversion (of Muslims in the Kingdom of Granada, for example, or Catholics in Ireland). In Spain and Portugal, some Jews converted and became conversos/new Christians, or outwardly conformed and were crypto-Jews, but many European Jews did not or could not incorporate into Christian European empires, in part because Jews themselves and their Christian neighbors believed that Jewish corporate, national, and religious identities were inextricably woven together. Their ethnicity made full conversion impossible. European sovereigns regarded Jewish residents as perpetual foreigners, regardless of how many generations of their ancestors had lived in, owned property in, paid taxes to, fought to defend, or sworn loyalty to the polity. As a result, medieval and early modern Jews suffered violence and serial expulsions in Europe, which drove frequent border crossing that further exacerbated their outsider status.[6]

Foreigners could become subjects of a sovereign and thereby members of the body politic by acquiring naturalization or denization that included an oath of loyalty.[7] This process did not, however, alter Jews' nationality. Jewish residents' political subjecthood within European polities therefore contained a serious tension: subjects of a sovereign were defined by both birth and loyalty. Although nationality and subjecthood were distinct categories, birth usually created both. Heredity determined one's nation, and parents (as subjects themselves) and place of birth (within the geographic bounds of the sovereign's dominions) determined one's subject identity. Even though birth did not confer subjecthood in the same way that it did nation, Europeans imagined them as linked. The linguistic reference to birth in both "nation" and "natural born" (subject) illustrate the connection. But the reality was messier. Officials and others often conflated the two categories unless an event forced them to consider the distinctions.

In composite monarchies, the status of naturalized or denizenized subjects was further complicated by the strain between the sovereign's relationship to subjects as individuals and as members of constitutive kingdoms. In England, for example, theoretically only an Act of Parliament could grant full naturalization. This limitation made sense for a process that was meant to confer the benefits of being "natural" (or native-born), since each nation within the composite monarchy maintained its own parliament, and nations were also understood to be "natural," created by the collective members' births within the geographically defined dominion. Full naturalization suggested retroactively changing the circumstances (place and parents) of one's birth. Although the process of naturalization made people subjects and not nationals, the word *naturalization* itself suggested slippage between theoretically distinct concepts of political belonging (subjecthood) and ethnic membership (nation).

In Britain, the sovereign and his or her representatives (such as colonial governors) could, through letters patent, theoretically grant only denization. While a grant of denization from the crown also made recipients into the sovereign's subjects, denizen status was not supposed to pass to children, nor could the children of denizens inherit real property, although in practice both happened. Moreover, there was no legal clarity in the seventeenth century about whether denizen status granted by lesser officials moved with an individual who traveled beyond the administrator's jurisdiction. In the English Atlantic, there was little consistency in maintaining distinctions between naturalization and denization, and disagreement over the extent and portability of colonial naturalizations caused considerable conflict both within empires and between them.

Jews' serial expulsions and resulting searches for refuge were among the events that required disentangling nationality from political subjecthood. So were the frequent conquests and changing jurisdictions in the Caribbean. Because Spanish and Portuguese (and after 1685, French) officials disqualified Jews from political subjecthood on religious grounds, Caribbean conquests upended Jewish colonists' lives, and their attempts to find new homes or to stay put and negotiate a place within a new colonial order forced officials repeatedly to articulate Jews' place within (or outside of) colonial bodies politic. Sometimes they explained their rationale for inclusion or exclusion.

Imperial officials sought to retain or acquire experienced colonists, even if they disagreed about whether such individuals should enjoy religious toleration. Despite prejudice against Jews from officials and colonists alike, English and Dutch administrators competed for Jewish settlers by expanding freedoms, hoping that if Jewish people established roots within a colony, they would strengthen it against foreign invasion and against the continual threat that enslaved people would rise against their oppression.[8] In Jamaica, officials noted Jews' interest in protecting the island against Spanish or French attack and therefore their likelihood of loyalty to the English.[9] The desire for loyal colonists thus explains English conquerors' 1655 hope "to make good subjects of" the Portuguese Jews they found in Spanish Jamaica, while planning to expel the Spanish.[10] Some possessed expertise growing sugar. Others brought Spanish or Portuguese language skills and commercial contacts in Spanish port towns, making them especially valuable to colonies competing for Spanish American trade.

Even if the toleration that Jews had experienced in New Holland rested on strategic rather than ethical concerns, it provided them with a precedent from which to negotiate in other colonies. In the years following their expulsion from Portuguese Brazil, though they met with resistance and prejudice, they successfully claimed expanded rights in several Dutch, English, and (before 1685) French jurisdictions. In 1655, Rabbi Menasseh ben Israel (Manoel Dias Soero) traveled from Amsterdam to London, where—expressing confidence that English people would heed "that Command of the Lord our God" to "*love . . . strangers*"—he successfully petitioned Oliver Cromwell for Jews' readmission to England.[11]

Jewish immigrants to the English Caribbean thus sought partial inclusion within colonial bodies politic. They professed loyalty to the crown and wanted subject status that would enable their full participation in imperial commerce. They included whiteness among the traits that made them compatible with English Christian society, whether metropolitan or colonial. But they aimed to find places that would let them live as Jews, which necessarily entailed a significant degree of separation from the majority Christian population. They repeatedly requested the right to govern themselves by Jewish law. When Menasseh described to Cromwell the benefits Jewish settlers provided to other places that had welcomed them, he stressed that an autonomy to decide civil (and in some instances criminal) cases among themselves was key to attracting and retaining Jewish immigrants. Because, according to Menasseh, Sephardic Jews maintained kin and commercial contacts throughout the Atlantic, "those neighbour Nations, where the Iewes shall finde liberty to live according to their owne Iudaicall Lawes" would "most easily draw that benefit" of Spanish riches "to themselves by meanes of the industry of our Nation."[12]

What would it mean for Jews to govern themselves by their own law? Much of the Jewish law in question governed religious and dietary practice. Given the context of Iberian persecution, requesting permission to live by Jewish law may have been driven by a desire to receive assurance that they would be able to practice Judaism openly. But Jewish law also governed economic or criminal behavior and would necessarily overlap with the jurisdiction of local courts, in Jamaica or elsewhere. In Menasseh's Amsterdam (the temporary home also of many of Jamaica's future Jewish residents), the Sephardic community had agreed in 1639 that "community leaders and judges should follow, except where it will conflict with Torah, mercantile law or the law merchant." Such a decision reflects the fact that (as Menasseh noted in his petition) many of those community leaders and judges were merchants, integrated into European and Atlantic legal and cultural practice.[13]

Permitting Jews to settle such affairs among themselves echoed contemporary theories about how unequal composite sovereignties could function. A corporate body—such as a Jewish community in Jamaica—might owe allegiance to a sovereign but still govern itself and its members. The seventeenth-century English world used such frameworks to grant limited sovereignty to corporate bodies as diverse as the East India Company, Juan de Bola's town, and the Powhatan Chiefdom.[14] It created a form of inclusion seemingly in tension with grants of naturalization that brought people into the body politic as individuals. Nevertheless, for Jews in the Atlantic world, the two forms of incorporation could apply simultaneously. We tend to look back on elements of uneven composite sovereignty, such as tribute or communal taxation, as a failure to fully incorporate people as subjects, but such a view may be imposing a post- Enlightenment (or post-Lockean) view of belonging and in any case overlooks the desire of contemporaries for the elements of corporate autonomy included in such relationships.

The decision allowing Jews to return to English jurisdiction encouraged Portuguese Jews who had fled Brazil for the Netherlands, but who wished to return to the Caribbean, to consider moving to just-conquered Jamaica. Shortly after the Restoration, Jacob Jeosua Bueno Enriques, "of the Hebrew nation," petitioned Charles II for license to work a rumored copper mine in the island with his kinsmen Josef and Moise Bueno Enriques. The project failed, but their proposals reveal their sense of what living in the English colony might allow. They requested permission to build synagogues and govern themselves by Jewish ("our") law.[15]

In the course of making commercial, historical, religious, ethical, and political arguments for Jewish admission to England, Menasseh included Jews together with English people as living "amongst the white and civilized people of the world" and "not amongst the Blacke-moores and wild-men." This—one of the earliest English-language invocations of whiteness to categorize people as superior—derived from his own or his Amsterdam associates' experiences in Dutch Brazil. He asserted a familiarity with "the Negros of Guinea and Brazil" to explain a supposedly universal human inclination to despise the afflicted and thus to explain why Jews were falsely accused of scandalous cruelties such as the killing of Christian children.[16]

But he drew a sharp distinction between "white and civilized people" and "Negros" by providing starkly different examples of the human propensity to kick those who were down. He claimed that Black people on both sides of the Atlantic attacked shipwreck victims because they saw wrecks as evidence of a divine curse. His example of the same tendency in "civilized" people was of ancient Romans accusing Christians of "sl[aying] their children to celebrate their Ceremonies." Both examples sought to draw Jews and European Christians together. Both populations engaged in Atlantic shipping (and would therefore supply many of the shipwreck victims supposedly vulnerable to attack from local Black people). And, more explicitly, both were falsely accused of sacrificing others' children: "even the very same ancient scandall that was cast of old upon the innocent Christians, is now laid upon the Iewes."[17]

Caribbean governors shared Menasseh ben Israel's opinion that Jewish settlers would benefit their colonies. They highlighted Jews' valuable commercial connections, and they shared the rabbi's identification of Jews as White. The competition for settlers can be seen in Governor Thomas Modyford's 1664 suggestion that only Jamaica be permitted to offer naturalization to foreigners.[18] Evidently his proposal failed, because the following year, Jewish colonists succeeded in acquiring naturalization and significant privileges in English Surinam (the colony of Willoughbyland on the northern coast of South America). A number of these were Jews who had fled Brazil for Amsterdam and then, in 1659, received license from the Dutch West India Company to go to Dutch Cayenne, where they were permitted to worship and use their own law. When the French conquered Cayenne in 1664, they guaranteed freedom of worship for Jews, but most (about one hundred) apparently left for English Surinam, where their previous experience may have aided them in negotiating a blanket naturalization with significant privileges. English officials were perhaps conscious of competition with Jamaica for additional Jewish settlers from surrounding colonies when they agreed that Jews would enjoy "freedom to plant and trade, free practice of religion," exemption from public service except militia, "a tribunal of their own" for minor causes, and ten acres in the capital for a synagogue, school, and cemetery.[19] Unlike individual patents of naturalization that stressed individual loyalty to the monarch, this group naturalization reinforced the corporate community of Sephardic Jews. The strategy succeeded in drawing immigrants: 10 percent of English Surinam's population was Jewish in 1665, including both planters and merchants.[20]

But just two years later, during the Second Anglo-Dutch War, the Dutch seized Surinam, and the question of what the turnover meant for the colony's residents rested on incompatible interpretations of the language of belonging. Local English and Dutch officials in the colony negotiated an agreement, and in the conventions of the time, the official version was in Latin. An English negotiator later admitted that "the Treaty was tedious, we not understanding Dutch well, neither they English, so that all things were twice translated," from Dutch to Latin to English and back again. The double translation, and negotiators' limited understanding of one another's languages, allowed them to come away with conflicting ideas about what they had agreed on with regard to Jewish residents. Article 5 specified that "subditos" or subjects of Charles II could leave the colony, and that they could take their movable property, including enslaved people, with them. The English translation made at the negotiations translated the "subdito" of Article 5 into "any Inhabitants." Earlier articles specified that "the English" who stayed would not be required to fight against "Subjects of the King of England" who might attack Dutch Surinam (nor could they aid the attackers), and that "all persons whatsoever, & of what Nac[i]on soever, whether they be English, Jewes, &c.," would have "confirmed unto them, ther Estates, Lands, Goods . . . to enjoy, inherit, and possess."[21] Whereas the English translation had expanded the category of "subject" into "inhabitant," the Dutch translation narrowed it to "the English." The 1667 Treaty of Breda ending the war ratified those local Articles of Capitulation. Initially the distinction mattered little because many, including apparently all of Surinam's Jewish residents, at first chose to stay, responding to generous terms of surrender that offered the same rights to foreign as to Dutch colonists and permitted them to avoid the significant costs of uprooting.[22]

By the end of the decade, some English (though apparently not yet any Jews) wished to leave, but Dutch officials in the colony balked, afraid to lose the planters and enslaved men and women who made the colony valuable. In response to English complaints, the Dutch States General resolved in the summer of 1670 that, as specified in the capitulations, the people in question could leave, but again the language differed. Dutch diplomats stated that "all those English who will" could "depart at pleasure with their persons and transportable goods," including sugar-making equipment and any people they owned at the time of the surrender. The English commission sent to

Surinam to facilitate the move again employed the more expansive language that "his Majesty's subjects in that Colony" were free to leave Surinam "with their slaves and goods."[23]

Although that decision came in response to non-Jewish residents' desire to leave, conditions in the colony were deteriorating, and Surinam's former English deputy governor William Byam (now governor of Antigua) believed "even the Jews" were, by 1670, "highly dissatisfied with the country" and likely would depart. He predicted that Dutch Surinam would fail when Jewish and English colonists departed, leaving Surinam "but a sad colony." Then, with the continued arrival of "great supplies of negroes" but "no whites," Surinam would face the additional danger that "the blacks . . . will make the colony theirs," which would "be the end of it." Byam, in predicting the flight of Surinam's Jewish and remaining English residents, articulated whiteness as a category of belonging in English Caribbean society. He clearly considered Sephardic Jews valuable to English and Dutch colonies because their whiteness and property ownership, including their ownership of human property, placed them alongside English planters in upholding the plantation- and slave-based colonial order. For Jews, those markers of colonial belonging operated alongside their negotiated corporate autonomies and their individual naturalizations as subjects of Charles II. While "the Jews" were distinct from both "the English" and "the Dutch," together all were "whites."[24]

As Surinam lost its appeal, Jamaica's prospects had improved. Perhaps the 1670 Treaty of Madrid had made Jamaica more appealing to Sephardim wishing to maintain family and trade contacts in Spanish America. A few months after the treaty's arrival, as Jamaican officials aimed to open trade with Spanish America, they recognized that the island's Jewish residents and their commercial networks could help them do so. Modyford requested further authority to naturalize "any persons of what nations soever," acknowledging that it would be "for that island only." In order to continue luring settlers, he recommended that Charles II maintain "Liberty of conscience and a free exercise of Religion to all persons" in Jamaica.

Moreover, Modyford folded Jamaica's need for "persons . . . to settle" into arguments against the Royal African Company's monopoly on slave trading. Opening the slave trade to "the whole nation & forrayners also" would advance the king's interest because "Mankinde is ye principall, Gold ye accessory, encrease ye first considerably & ye other must follow."[25] By mankind, Morgan referred to slave traders, not the people they trafficked. Opening slave trading to all would lure merchants away from the colonies of England's competitors, and then their families and associates would follow. Surinam had made obvious to the English that Sephardim sought places to settle and that many possessed enslaved laborers, sugar and indigo processing equipment, and connections in Spanish American ports that would rapidly swell colonial revenues. They could benefit both Jamaica's merchant and planting economies.[26]

The following year, Modyford's replacement Thomas Lynch stressed the importance of Jews' merchant and kin networks when he wrote that he "cannot find any but Jews that will adventure their goods or persons to get trade." Obliquely noting the advantages they enjoyed through their connections in Spanish American ports, while at the same time enlisting anti-Jewish stereotypes, he suspected that Sephardic merchants "may connive at some little underhand trade" with their partners in Spanish America, beyond that which they reported to Jamaican officials or paid taxes on. Lynch, however, intended to ignore his suspicions because he believed "it . . . better than a public and open trade," which Spanish American officials could not condone and which therefore would, if the English pressed it, "infallibly destroy what we have with Spain."[27]

William Beeston similarly depended on Jewish linguistic and cultural fluency in Spanish America during his 1671 diplomatic voyage to Cartagena. One of the first two envoys he sent ashore was the Jewish merchant David Gomez, whose wealth, like his language skills, made him a useful agent.[28] By this point, significant numbers of Jews had been naturalized in Jamaica, though the earliest Jewish naturalization patents do not survive. Extant records begin in 1672, but the previous year the Jamaica Council ordered that "an exact account be taken of those Jews" who could produce their naturalization letters, vowing to take up the question of "what to do with those that have none."[29] Those naturalizations reflect Jewish immigrants' efforts to acquire the official belonging that could protect their estates. It also indicates their need to do so, as foreigners, members of "the Hebrew nation." In 1672 Governor Lynch repeated his support for extending full welcome and "begged orders about the Jews and Hollanders that came to plant." He considered it in "the interest of the island to encourage" them, as they brought "great stocks" and "aversions to the French and Spaniards."[30]

After the third Anglo-Dutch war (1672–1674), the Treaty of Westminster again confirmed the 1667 local Articles of Surrender for Surinam. By this time, many more people wished to leave Dutch Surinam, including Jewish residents. Indeed, Surinam Jews considered sending representatives to Jamaica to negotiate terms of settlement.[31] When London officials sent commissioners to facilitate departure and provide transportation, among those who sought to leave were ten Jewish families, who between them wanted to take 332 enslaved people to Jamaica.

Hoping to convince revenue-producing potential colonists to move (with their enslaved laborers and equipment) to English jurisdiction, English officials offered prospective immigrants generous terms, especially if they chose to go to Jamaica. In addition to transportation of "famillies Servants and Merchandizes" as well as any equipment for processing sugar and indigo, those choosing Jamaica would receive double the land usually allotted by headright to newcomers "as well for yo[u]r Slaves as your Selves," and the promise of provisions at moderate rates until they could produce their own.[32]

When English commissioners arrived in Surinam in 1675 to help English subjects migrate, however, the Dutch governor refused to let any Jews depart. The English commissioners, the Dutch governor in Surinam, and the potential Jewish migrants disagreed about the Surinam Jews' political identity. At this point, the competing translations of the original local Articles of Surrender and subsequent confirmations suddenly mattered. The Dutch governor sought to keep Jews in Surinam and insisted that the various agreements permitting emigration excluded them. He worried that the flight of colonists would weaken the colony militarily and that the departure of Jewish colonists (and the enslaved African people they planned to take with them) would ruin the colony's plantation economy.[33] Officials also disagreed about whether planters moving could take Indigenous slaves along with those of African descent. Both controversies derived from security concerns: Dutch officials worried that the disappearance of Indians who labored as servants or slaves among the colonists would provoke attack from their relatives.

But while economic and military concerns may have reflected the Dutch governor's underlying fears, his argument focused more narrowly on how Jewish people fit into colonial and Atlantic bodies politic. At this point, officials realized how crucially the English and Dutch translations differed. When the Dutch governor read the Dutch versions of the local articles and the States General's resolution confirming those articles, specifying that "the English" could leave, he focused on distinctions between nations. He argued that "Jews could not be English" and therefore he could require that they stay. The English commissioners, who had "the originall in Latin" with them, noted that it specified "subjects" (*subditos*). They expressed disbelief that the word "Subjects" might not be a "Generall word of comprehension," and insisted that they "were not to be Governed by Dutch translation." To prove how ludicrous the Dutch governor's arguments were, they pointed out that his interpretation would exclude Scots and Irish, both "nations" distinct from the English.[34] Underscoring the distinction between nation and body politic, between "the English" and Charles II's "subjects," the commissioners outlined the conditions for transport, addressing the "Gentlemen" who were "his Ma[jes]t[ie]s Subjects in Surinam as well the Hebrew Nation as English." Here, the commissioners treated Byam's 1665 blanket naturalization of Jews as granting full subject status.

Despite differing assumptions in London and the English Atlantic about the mobility of colonial naturalizations (which strictly ought to have been temporary and local denizations), an international competition for White colonists encouraged a capacious interpretation of colonial naturalization. English officials in London and the colonies commonly denied the broader applicability of colonial naturalizations, but demand for European colonists with property and connections prompted a concession in Jamaica that was not yet fully articulated in London.[35] The Dutch governor was not so sure. When the English commissioners pointed out that the question was not one of "English" nationhood but of political subjecthood, the governor pressed the argument further, "deny[ing] that the Jewes were his Majesties subjects *or* free denizens." Moreover, he seemed aware of an English distinction between the theoretically limited colonial letters patent and the more complete naturalization by Act of Parliament.[36] While he succeeded in preventing the Jewish petitioners from leaving with the commissioners, he allowed one exception for a man who had been naturalized in London by Parliament.[37]

A Jamaican Act for Naturalization, likely from 1670 given its resemblance to Modyford's writings from that year, intending to spur "the speedy settling & peopling" of the island, encouraged "persons of different Nacons" to come to Jamaica "with their ffamilyes and stockes . . . to settle plant or Reside." The island's government would draw immigrants "by Incorporating . . . them with all the Rights & priviledges of any of his Ma[jesty']s naturall borne subjects." The language of the act explicitly brought foreign immigrants of multiple nations into the body of subjects who made up the political society of the island. The act therefore permitted the governor and his successors to declare any alien or foreigner "already settled or . . . such as shall heerafter come" who took the oath of allegiance or "otherwise" gave "sufficient security" of allegiance to the governor "to be to all Intents and purposes fully & Compleately naturalized."

The Jamaica Assembly thus enacted more thorough naturalization legislation than English law allowed. Naturalized individuals and their heirs would possess the same "Immunities & Rights . . . as fully & amply as any of his Ma[jes]ties naturall borne subjects, . . . as . . . if they themselves had beene borne within any of his Ma[jes]ties Realmes or Dominions." The act would protect the naturalized subject from any "Laws Acts Ordinance usage or custome to the contrary," surely referring to London's practice of regarding colonial naturalizations as denizations no matter their language, and limiting colonial naturalizations to the colonies that granted them. In order to reduce the difficulty of obtaining naturalizations, the act lowered the fees to the still considerable ten pounds sterling for the governor plus ten shillings for the clerk.[38]

This act meant that foreign newcomers to Jamaica could acquire full naturalization locally rather than having to travel to England. This status would be especially important for merchants, because England's Navigation Acts prohibited foreigners from oceanic trade. Regardless of whether London approved it, Jamaican naturalizations used the act's capacious language. Patent books in the Jamaica Archives, which record land patents, naturalizations of all foreigners, and birth records for Jews (whose births, unlike those of conforming Protestants, would not appear in parish records), indicate that Sephardic immigrants to the island began patenting small parcels of land (urban lots in Port Royal or Spanish Town) as early as 1664, and large plantations (up to 1,620 acres, in various parishes) beginning in 1669. Recorded naturalizations began in 1672 and used the language of full naturalization. Nonetheless, many Jews in Jamaica who could afford to do so sought further security by applying in London for affirmation, which came in the form of denizenship. In 1670 and 1671 London officials issued several warrants, each making a specific "inhabitant of Jamaica," almost all with Sephardic names, "a free denizen of England," stipulating that the benefits of denizenship would commence as soon as he had "taken the oaths of allegiance and supremacy before the Governor of the island."[39] Through the end of the century at least, Jamaica governors, with no apparent objection from London, used the language of naturalization in patents that, theoretically, should only have conferred denization on foreigners.

Between 1672 and 1715, when this study ends, Jamaica patent records contain about 150 Sephardic naturalizations, roughly half of all Jamaican naturalizations during that period. However, despite the language of those naturalizations declaring that the recipients would receive all the rights and privileges of natural-born subjects, they apparently did not (or at least they feared they would not), because naturalized Jewish parents, whose children born in the island would have been natural-born subjects according to the act, nonetheless paid to have those children naturalized separately. Naturalized foreign parents who were Christian did not take the like precaution.[40]

When Sir Thomas Lynch departed for Jamaica to replace Modyford as governor, his instructions went even further to stimulate non-Anglican immigration. Not only was he "to give all possible encouragement to persons of different opinions in religion," but also to "dispense with the oaths of supremacy and allegiance" except to members and officers of his council, "finding some other way of securing allegiance." The Jamaica Act for Naturalization had aimed at a similar end, permitting either the oath of allegiance or other evidence of loyalty, and the subsequent naturalizations state that Jews swore their oath on the Five Books of Moses rather than on the English Protestant Bible, more evidence of flexibility to attract immigrants. But Lynch's instructions to "dispense with" the oath entirely reveal an even stronger commitment to bypass customary forms of assuring loyalty in favor of increasing "the number of . . . subjects." He was to ensure that "no man . . . be molested, in the exercise of his religion" as long as he remained "content with a quiet and peaceable enjoying of it."[41]

Sephardic Jews who moved to Jamaica to take advantage of these easements faced not only discrimination in the island but also, if they had ever lived as Iberian Christians, outright danger sailing to and from it. Spanish officials challenged conversos' identities as English or Dutch Jews, much as English officials demanded the return of people of color who had fled Jamaica for Spanish jurisdiction. In both cases, the officials who had lost people claimed that those individuals had had no right to flee, that their new incorporation into sanctuary spaces was illegitimate, and that their correct legal status was under the control of prior jurisdictions, either as slaves (in the English case) or as Catholics subject to the Inquisition (in the Spanish). As when Spanish Jamaican officials tried to detain former conversos fleeing Brazil in 1654, Spanish officials stressed Caribbean Sephardic Jews' prior lives as Catholics to claim jurisdiction over them. Colonial officials (not church leaders) asserted that the church's religious authority over Catholics in the region superseded English or Dutch jurisdictional claims over particular geographic spaces, over English or Dutch ships, or over people who sought subjecthood in those Protestant empires.[42] Catholicism, as a fundamental basis for Spanish political identity, could not be renounced. This Spanish tenet created specific risks for Jewish merchants, whose travels exposed them to the danger of capture by guardacostas and delivery to the Inquisition.

In 1683, the Jewish merchant Benjamin Baruch Carvallo moved from Dutch Curaçao to English Jamaica, where he was naturalized.[43] That summer, as he returned to Curaçao to retrieve his family, the Spanish guardacostas captain Agustín Alvares, holding a commission from the governor of Havana, seized the English bark on which Carvallo sailed, robbed him of his goods, tortured him, and retained him as prisoner. Alvares then sailed into Curaçao with his prize and told Governor Jan van Erpecum that he had "a Jew called Benjamin Carvallo" and that he intended to keep him because "Carvallo used to call himself a Christian."[44]

Alvares demanded 22,000 pieces of eight for Carvallo's release. When Carvallo's friends in Curaçao petitioned van Erpecum for help, the governor convinced Alvares to lower the ransom (to 3,500 pieces of eight) and return the English bark to its owner, but did not demand Carvallo's goods, much less arrest Alvares for unlawful seizure. While the Dutch official claimed to be "ashamed" of Alvares's "cruelty and piracy" and acknowledged the ransom payment "to be unjust," he did not force him to return the money, despite having Alvares and his crew, sixteen of whom were Dutch, "in his power." Carvallo and van Erpecum both wrote to Jamaica governor Lynch, who demanded that van Erpecum restore Carvallo's ransom, suggesting that the Dutch governor could, in turn, ask it of the governor of Havana if he wished. Van Erpecum acknowledged Alvares's behavior as "evil" but defended his own inaction by claiming that when Alvares "refuse[d] to submit to our jurisdiction in this case," the guardacostas commission from the governor of Havana tied his hands. Even in promising to send a vessel to Havana to complain, van Erpecum denied full responsibility, instead informing Lynch that he would have it stop in Jamaica on the way to procure Lynch's assistance.[45]

Lynch wrote to the Lords of Trade and Plantations about Carvallo, whom he described not by name but as "a Jew, naturalised here."[46] All three authorities—the Dutch governor, the Spanish privateer, and the English governor—claimed jurisdiction over Carvallo: van Erpecum because the man and his goods were present in his port, Alvares and Lynch because each claimed the right to assign Carvallo membership in their own colonial body politic. Doing so placed the merchant within the boundaries of their respective sovereign's political communities, boundaries that had to follow mobile members as they traversed maritime spaces beyond any sovereign's jurisdictions. Lynch emphasized Carvallo's naturalization in Jamaica, and while the designation did not necessarily make Carvallo a subject of the English monarch, Lynch behaved as though English officials owed Carvallo the protections due a subject. Not until the 1740 Plantation Act would Parliament acknowledge colonial naturalizations as effective throughout the empire, but Surinam provided a precedent that endorsed such an interpretation seventy years earlier, and the Caribbean context provided occasions to test it.[47] Jamaican officials and the people they naturalized acted as if their membership in the body politic was imperial and not merely Jamaican.

The guardacostas captain Alvares claimed that under Spanish law he could impose Spanish vassalage on Carvallo. Once an individual declared himself a Catholic loyal to the Spanish crown, Spanish officials held themselves duty bound to police that identity. The crown and its representatives could force individuals to remain within the cultural borders it had constructed to define its subjects and thereby its empire, even as those subjects traveled beyond its jurisdictional borders. If Spanish Catholics, especially rich ones, could transform themselves into English Jews, those borders threatened to dissolve. Spain would lose significant material wealth and see its colonial evangelizing mission compromised. Both threats raised anxieties about the religious and political loyalties of New Christians in the Iberian Atlantic.

In his letter to the Lords of Trade and Plantations, Lynch referred to the Spanish guardacostas captain Alvares as "a pirate." The allegation was appropriate if Alvares possessed no genuine authority (via commission or otherwise) over Carvallo. The answer to that question depended on who could define Carvallo's political and religious identity as he traveled through the uncertain jurisdiction of Caribbean waters. If Spanish imperial officials had their way, he was a Spanish converso who had repudiated his lawful identity and his obligation to loyalty. In that case, Alvares acted as an arm of Spanish crown authority. But if English officials prevailed, then in approving Carvallo's application for naturalization, they accepted his own definition of himself and took on a responsibility to protect him. Moreover, Lynch insisted, once Carvallo and Jamaica officials agreed to (and recorded) Carvallo's new English subjecthood, other empires' officials were obligated to respect it. Lynch believed that Curaçao governor van Erpecum should therefore have done more.[48]

Van Erpecum may have begrudged Curaçao's loss of Carvallo to Jamaica, but the English captain of the seized bark maintained that Curaçao's slave trade to Spanish America explained van Erpecum's leniency toward Alvares. The captain complained that "the Assientista's factors govern[ed]" Curaçao. In

1683 in Spain (as Chapter 5 details), two different merchant companies, one Dutch and the other Genoese but supplied largely by English slave traders, vied for the asiento license. In the Caribbean, tensions ran so high among merchants whose livelihoods were at stake that the Dutch "rogues" in Curaçao, according to the English captain, "threatened to murder every Englishman they met."[49] They knew that regardless of the decision reached in Madrid about which company would receive the coveted license, already-established local trade patterns might continue illegally if parties could continue to cultivate good regional relationships. Therefore, van Erpecum had every incentive to appease Alvares, clearly already enmeshed in Dutch networks (even if Lynch exaggerated the number of Dutchmen in the Spaniard's crew). Given Anglo-Dutch competition to profit from the presence of Jewish merchants in the region, van Erpecum may even have connived with Alvares to prevent Carvallo's migration out of his own jurisdiction to Jamaica. The English captain, concerned for his own vessel and livelihood, focused less on Alvares and Carvallo and more on the context of Curaçao, which he saw as so focused on trading slaves to Spanish America during a period of intense international competition that the merchants conducting that trade controlled the island.

Lynch said he was not surprised that the Dutch behaved in such self-interested fashion, blaming the Dutch character as epitomized by their "proverb" that "'Jesus Christ is good, but trade is better.'"[50] He accused the Dutch of abandoning the moral scruples they ought to hold as self-identified Christians in order to avoid making any waves that could upset their commerce.[51] Thus Governor Lynch, a slave trader himself, used an assumed universal Christian code of morals to disparage Dutch devotion to commerce. At the same time, he worked to protect Carvallo's ability to live and trade in the Caribbean as a Jew rather than as an adherent to any of the Christian sects upheld by the region's European powers. He could thus claim English moral superiority in welcoming and protecting Jews, not only compared to the Spanish, who so obviously denied toleration, but also compared to the Dutch. Jews had found refuge from Iberian expulsion and forced conversion among the Dutch in both Europe and the Caribbean, but here Lynch implied that Dutch toleration boiled down to commercial and not ethical concerns.

Dutch protections for Jews were, according to Lynch and the English captain, at the mercy of commercial interests (in this case appeasing the Spanish in order to secure slave trading contacts). Although English Jamaican officials themselves explicitly welcomed Jewish immigrants and "their estates" to "strengthen" the island, Lynch framed that welcome here as one that reflected and confirmed English Christian values. The English and Spanish both used their expansion of the body politic to admit others as a sign of moral superiority and humanity, the Spanish including people of color on the ground that they were Christian, and the English including Jews on the ground that they were White.

The language of belonging—of subjecthood—that English officials deployed in their contest for Jewish colonists carried especial weight in the international arena. It was, however, distinct from the issue of civil or political rights within a colonial or metropolitan society. Those rights were important to drawing immigrants. (In 1670, Jamaica governor Thomas Modyford had described the admission of foreigners and the provision of liberty of conscience as "very needful . . . baits . . . to increase the number of his Majesty's subjects here.")[52] But officials' subsequent defense of Jewish subjects (like Spanish protections for Indigenous and Black vassals) was compatible with significant discrimination against them. The English commissioners in Surinam could speak in 1675 of the "full liberty" of all Charles II's "subjects of w[ha]t degree, or condicon w[ha]tsover inhabiting in Surinam."[53] The king was protecting his subjects' liberties vis-à-vis his rivals. Nonetheless, although in England and its dominions subjecthood implied liberty, it did not suggest equality. Subjects could be ranked by "degree." They lived under varying "condicon[s]." Such gradations of membership determined all sorts of privileges and rights, many of them decided locally.

Just as the Spanish crown vowed to protect even enslaved vassals from heretics, all subjects of the British sovereign, regardless of their local struggles against economic, political, and civil disabilities, were to enjoy crown protection against rivals who threatened their liberty. Belonging as it operated internally was distinct from subjecthood in the interimperial arena. Their separation helps explain why contemporaries usually referred to freedom from imposed disabilities as "privileges" rather than "rights" for subjects who could expect protection outside their sovereign's dominions. However, the occasional appearance of "rights" language in these discussions also suggests the possibility that external protections and internal rights for subjects might merge.

Jewish immigrants in Jamaica remained distinct from their Christian neighbors, largely by choice. Although they bought land throughout the island, they cultivated a Jewish community through synagogue membership and schooling, marriage ties, and commercial networks.[54] English records in

Jamaica use the ethnopolitical term "nation" to refer to Jews, even as they included naturalizations that declared them "natural-born," revealing complications in the process of incorporating Jewish residents. Jews' ability to live openly as a partly self-governing community was part of what drew them to English (and Dutch) colonies.[55]

In many ways, Jewish people in Jamaica had become part of the social fabric of a distinctly Caribbean colonial society. Although the urban centers of Port Royal and later Kingston contained visible Jewish neighborhoods, Jewish individuals and families also lived dispersed throughout the island and were especially likely to own shops in small villages or at crossroads.[56] They bought, sold, and owned slaves and thus participated in and benefited from the Caribbean creation of whiteness. However, the ability to live as a Jewish community also made them visibly distinct from Christians and therefore vulnerable to continued othering, especially in moments of conflict.

There were limits to English colonists' willingness to accept the inclusion of Jewish people into the local body politic.[57] Some English merchants objected to the welcome extended to their Jewish counterparts and, in 1671, submitted a "petition of the English merchants against the trading of the Jews." The island's council responded by confirming that Jewish merchants who had letters of denization or naturalization possessed the right to trade, as they did all the other "rights of natural-born subjects" that their naturalization papers promised.[58]

Rival European officials proclaimed expansive declarations of belonging as they competed with one another for people in the war-torn and disease-ridden but profitable Caribbean. Multiple jurisdictional contests provided ample opportunities for both officials and the individuals whose lives were at stake to assert new schemas of inclusion. But because there was slippage, then as now, in the language and concepts of belonging, such inclusion in the interimperial realm also encouraged people to petition for rights and full belonging within the societies that claimed them as (lesser) members. In contrast to the early modern distinction between subjecthood (or vassalage), which promised protection outside the sovereign's dominions, and stratified forms of local belonging that afforded varying levels of privilege, modern citizenship entails civil rights within the polity and protection outside of it.

That linking of the two emerged during the Age of Revolution as the rights of individuals within a polity became a constitutive part of sovereigns' legitimacy in the eyes of the world.[59] Thereafter, citizenship came to define both rights within the body politic and protection without. As a result, we may not readily comprehend the ways in which early modern people could separate the two. But being able to imagine that separation is important if we are to understand that imposing significant disabilities on valued subjects was less contradictory for seventeenth-century inhabitants of the Atlantic world than it would be for us.

Nevertheless, the idea that sovereigns drew their legitimacy in part from their fair and humane treatment of those they ruled had a long history alongside more absolutist impulses. We can see such arguments in the ways Spanish officials defended sanctuary seekers from their English would-be owners, and in the ways English and Dutch officials protected Jewish people from Spanish guardacostas and the Inquisition. Just as Spanish American officials used clemency toward freedom seekers as a means of constructing a merciful identity for themselves and their king, so English colonial leaders touted their offers of "sanctuary" to Jews.[60] In both cases, officials tied (if implicitly) their own power to act to their praiseworthy recognition of refugees' political personhood, and then used their own self-proclaimed humanity as illustration of their nation's or empire's superiority.

At the same time, individuals petitioned for privileges on the basis of their value to their sovereign in the international sphere. While they did not always acquire the privileges they sought, in seeking them they voiced—publicly and for the record—the idea that locally recognized privileges should accompany membership in the body politic (which in turn came partly from community belonging). As in the case of slaves who escaped to freedom in Spanish America, Jews' migrations, and petitions like Carvallo's, were propelled by geopolitical conflicts and then changed the stakes of those conflicts by creating debates over the terms of belonging.

Sephardic Jews, searching for a place to practice their religion openly and prosper economically, found that to the English in the Caribbean, they had become a valuable means of filling the demand for "white" (Governor Byam) "subjects" (Governor Modyford) in Caribbean plantation colonies. In creating plantation economies, planters and officials knew that they created dangerous societies. They fully expected men and women held in bondage to resist, and they therefore sought to bolster the population of people who had a stake in creating and preserving a colonial order. In the English Caribbean, where assemblies and slaveholders had opted to exclude Black and Indigenous people from Christianity and limit their access to freedom or subjecthood, elites employed multiple strategies to increase the number of White men. In 1681, Jamaica lawmakers, following Barbados's example, enacted (but could not enforce) a deficiency clause requiring slaveholders to keep "one White Man-Servant, Overseer, or hired Man" for every five enslaved people.[61] And they subsumed foreign nations within White subjecthood, incorporating people of the Hebrew nation along with those of the Scottish, French, and Palatinate.

All naturalized foreigners in Jamaica might face skepticism about their loyalty. In the case of Jews, such doubts were compounded by the endogamy that perpetuated an ongoing sense of their national difference, as well as their desire to maintain Portuguese and Hebrew languages, separate schools, a distinct weekly calendar, a kosher diet, and their own law. These efforts to preserve a distinct culture and community in Jamaica and other European colonies also averted dilution of their religious otherness. In contrast, Protestant foreigners' religion fostered intermarriage with English colonists and assimilation that gradually allowed their descendants to be absorbed into the English "nation" as well as the Jamaican body politic.

The earthquake that plunged half of Port Royal into the sea in 1692 destroyed the Jewish section of the town, taking with it people's records of their naturalizations. Losing their proof of belonging created special risks for Jewish merchants, who needed the status to trade legally, and several immediately petitioned to have their status confirmed.[62] Despite their defense of the island when the French attacked two years later, Jewish Jamaicans faced increasing discrimination in the 1690s.[63] In 1695, just a year after the French attack, in a bill to raise moneys for continued defenses (against both foreigners and Maroons), the Assembly assessed an additional tax on "the Nation and People of the Jews, residing within this island" "over and above" the increased taxes they shared with other island taxpayers. Twelve named men from the Jewish community were to deliver £750 within a month. In the following three years, the Assembly imposed additional assessments of £1,000, £350 (the reduction a response to learning that London disapproved of the previous year's increase), and £437. In 1699, the Assembly reportedly intended to demand £5,250, but it was dissolved before passing the tax, "otherways this would have concluded the utter ruin and destruction of our poor nation."[64] The governor at the time, William Beeston, claimed that he and his council were powerless to oppose the Assembly, "for if they do not raise money as they will themselves, they will not do it at all," and the island needed revenue.[65]

In 1699, the Baron de Belmonte, a converso representing the interests of Spain in Amsterdam, intervened on behalf of the overtaxed Jews, writing to William III that because they could not access their letters of denization and naturalization from the king and his predecessors (destroyed in the earthquake), "they have been obliged to pay three times the particular taxes . . . beside the general taxes made." Belmonte revealed his precise understanding of the distinction between grants of belonging by letters patent and by Act of Parliament (an understanding more complete than that of many English colonial officials) when he requested that William give "sovereign orders" that Jamaica "maintain for the Jewish Portuguese Nation the privileges they have always enjoyed in the Island of Jamaica under the letters patent . . . which your Majesty and the preceding Kings have had the grace to accord."[66] Communal (and even extra) taxation could be consistent with a tributary relationship that in some ways resembled the kind of semi-sovereignty Jews often sought in Jamaica and other colonies. But Jamaican Jews saw these extra taxes as "break[ing] . . . the law and their Patent of Naturalization."[67] In their view, their naturalizations made each of them individual subjects of the English crown.

In the early eighteenth century, the Jamaica Assembly imposed additional disabilities on Jamaican Jews. In 1707 it prevented Jews from voting for members of the Assembly. In 1711 it prohibited any non-Christians from voting and stipulated that "no Jew, Mulatto, Indian or Negro shall be capable to officiate or employed to write in or for any offices upon any pretense whatsoever."[68] Petitions supporting such disenfranchisement argued that Jews had renounced their right to government by opposing Jesus, and justified Jamaica's exclusions by pointing out the context that Jews did not have "a share in governing any country upon earth," highlighting their precarious relation to sovereignty, as political theory increasingly pinned rights to individuals rather than to members of corporate bodies.[69] English efforts to incorporate Jews met with local resistance from colonists (as did Spanish sanctuary). But those who supported their inclusion and limited member ship prevailed, and visitors remarked on the island's Jewish presence.[70]

In the case of Jews, as with people of African and Indigenous descent seeking sanctuary, Spanish officials insisted on ecclesiastical jurisdiction over spaces (Cuba, the Caribbean Sea) and the people who occupied them. Because Spanish imperial officials enforced that ecclesiastical jurisdiction, it created imperial jurisdiction. The sanctuary seekers in Chapter 3 sought "the land of Roman Catholic Christians," not Spanish territory or law or the beneficence of the Spanish monarch. Imperial officials, however, turned to their English counterparts and claimed those individuals as faithful dependents. In both cases, the Spanish church's sense of its own *geographical* domain proved important to the people who lived within its proclaimed borders. Although it was not precisely synonymous with Spanish imperial jurisdiction, as we will see in the next chapter, imperial officials used the ecclesiastical geography to press imperial claims to protect or control individual people.

CHAPTER 5

"Our Holy Catholic Faith and the Asiento"

During the 1680s, as they worked to build an international slave trade, English and Spanish merchants and officials in the western Caribbean tried to create a shared legal community that they could use to resolve disputes and prosecute maritime criminals. The multiple overlapping jurisdictions and the differences in imperial and local legal cultures made it difficult to pursue disputants or goods across borders. Despite the existence of merchant law (lex mercatoria) meant to settle trade disputes between Europeans throughout the world, the local judges and courts that heard cases in the Caribbean often lacked extensive legal training, and they followed the law that they knew, which likely meant some admixture of Spanish civil law or English common law with treaties, treatises, royal decrees, and local laws.

In order to operate in multiple jurisdictions with unevenly trained judges, Caribbean merchants and officials dealt with conflicts ad hoc, handling disputes in ways that were both personal and contingent. They depended on individuals who could straddle English and Spanish colonial worlds and who had a vested interest in doing so. Judges, governors, and other officials in Caribbean port towns negotiated with merchants, ship captains, seamen, planters, colonial consumers, and clergymen as they determined how law would govern the international relations that could hinder or facilitate trade.

These Caribbean denizens rarely used a language of international law (*law of nations* in English, *ius gentium* in Latin, *derecho de gentes* in Spanish) during the seventeenth century. Rather, they struggled within a mental framework of mutually bounded jurisdictions to increase cooperation so they could deal with realities too messy for one jurisdiction to contain. The effort proved impossible: bounded jurisdictions could not comprehend Caribbean realities. Thus, while they did not acknowledge it, those who sought to facilitate international trade began to loosen the beliefs that commercial behavior, political allegiance, and religious identity ought, ideally, to share the same borders; and that all activities should fall within the jurisdiction of only one authority, determined by virtue of the individuals who took part in them, the space in which they interacted, or the nature (religious, economic, political) of the activity.

People who crossed borders to trade challenged the boundaries that officials drew to isolate English and Spanish places from one another. Their movements also challenged the borders separating military from civilian jurisdictions, and religious from secular. Imperial officials and religious authorities disagreed about the nature and shape of imperial and religious jurisdiction over places and over mobile merchants and clergy. Those officials' arguments over who could trade where revealed unresolved jurisdictional tensions that up to that point had remained invisible.

This chapter explores three incidents that show how imperial claims (religious as well as political) over Caribbean spaces and people depended on local decisions made on the ground and at sea. The first arose when a Cuban guardacostas took a New England ship as prize. The second hinged on an English governor's liberation of French pirates who had preyed on Spaniards. While recorded only briefly, the pirates' release colored the third incident, involving a Spanish merchant's Catholic chapel in Jamaica. Underlying all three controversies was a rivalry initiated in Spain between Dutch and Genoese slave traders over the asiento. That competition for the Spanish slave-trading contract provides the key context for understanding all three stories, illustrating, on the one hand, the crucial importance of interimperial human trafficking to geopolitics in the Caribbean and, on the other, how actions on the ground proceeded despite European decisions, and then necessarily influenced those decisions.

Because the asiento provided cover for slave traders to smuggle textiles and other manufactured goods into Spanish America, the European demand for sugar and other plantation crops and the increasing trade in the human beings who produced those goods also opened more markets for European manufactures. Economic historians have estimated that by the middle of the seventeenth century, foreigners carried over half of Spain's American trade, and by the end of the century, extralegal trade was the norm in Spanish American ports.[1]

The increasing volume of Caribbean shipping—laden with human cargoes, bullion, plantation products, European textiles, and North American foodstuffs—provided everyone involved with powerful incentives to curtail conflict. But trade produced conflict even without human interference, especially in an age with little insurance. Crops failed, cargoes spoiled, and natural disasters destroyed ships and storehouses. Moreover, while some Spanish American officials tacitly condoned interimperial trade or engaged in it themselves, others enforced Spanish laws prohibiting such commerce. Caribbean trade therefore depended on the presence of a few individuals who could mediate conflicts and repair ruptures.[2] This chapter follows one such individual, the slave trader Santiago del Castillo/James Castile, as he negotiated legal, commercial, and religious accommodations in the western Caribbean and in Europe, on his own behalf and for the benefit of his many business associates.

During the second half of the seventeenth century, asiento subcontractors ("factors") in the Caribbean acquired slaves from Dutch, Genoese, English, French, Portuguese, and Danish traders who used Caribbean ports on Dutch, English, Danish, or French islands as transshipment points. When the Dutch acquired Curaçao in 1634 and the English conquered Jamaica in 1655, both strategically situated close to the four legal Spanish American ports of Cartagena, Vera Cruz, Portobelo, and Havana, they gained advantage over other Europeans competing for this Spanish trade.[3]

In their efforts to establish shared (or at least translatable) legal practices in the region, Caribbean residents and sojourners debated the nature of religious and subject identity and the proper constitution of a colonial body politic. They usually took for granted a world of separate imperial jurisdictions whose overlapping claims were incompatible. But sometimes they gestured toward a shared legal community requiring flexibility. Some merchants and mariners who operated in this Caribbean world of dozens of legal codes learned to negotiate between and across jurisdictional borders and emphasized shared rules of treaty law and more general common values—as Christians or as members of "trading nations"—in ways that foreshadowed the articulation of a "law of nations" in the eighteenth century.

In 1683 the Genoese merchant Nicolas Porcio, who had shared the asiento contract with his father-in-law, Juan Barroso del Pozo, since 1676, inherited it outright. That contract was supposed to last until 1689, but when Porcio fell into debt in 1684, Balthazar Coymans, a Dutch merchant living in Cádiz and representing the Amsterdam merchant company Jean Coymans and Company (in turn backed by the Dutch West India Company), saw in Porcio's debt an opportunity to acquire the Spanish slave trade contract. The

Dutch West India Company had already been selling enslaved Africans to the Genoese company's factors, who came to Curaçao to purchase them and then resold them in Cartagena, Portobelo, Vera Cruz, and Havana. Coymans hoped instead to sell slaves directly from Curaçao to Spanish American customers, so he wrote to the Spanish crown accusing Porcio of mismanagement. Offering immediate cash, Coymans had the support of the Council of the Indies and letters from Cartagena governor Juan Pando corroborating his complaints against Porcio.[4] Because the asiento paid the salaries of some members of the Council of the Indies, Coymans's Dutch West India Company backing and promise of solvency proved attractive.[5] In March 1685, the crown sent royal orders instructing its Spanish American officials to facilitate the transfer of asiento property from Porcio and his representatives to Coymans's employees. Porcio immediately protested, and Porcio and Coymans became embroiled in a dispute that spanned the Atlantic and lasted until the end of the decade.[6]

Coymans received the contract notwithstanding the crown's reservations about giving a Protestant access to Spanish American ports. Despite such fears, the agreement specified that Coymans supply two men-of-war to serve as guardacostas against pirates in the Caribbean, under Spanish governors' authority but with Dutch and Flemish crews. (As we have seen from guardacostas captain Agustín Alvares's Dutch crewmembers two years earlier, this was not as much of an innovation as it might appear to be.) While the common seamen could not disembark, they nonetheless filled the role of maritime Spanish police in the region supposedly closed by Spain to foreign navigation. Anticipating objections based on Coymans's "defect" as a foreign heretic, the council granted him a temporary pardon so that he and his immediate representatives could disembark to trade. Such a procedure resembled English grants of denizenship—local grants of residency to foreigners to live in English jurisdiction.

Officials recognized the advantages of doing business with foreign merchants who had cash or commodities on hand. But, unwilling to change exclusionary laws or unable yet to imagine such change, they granted impermanent openings that might last for the duration of a contract, as in this case, or for the length of one individual's life, as in denizenship. By making such grants temporary and uninheritable, Spanish officials insisted on the immutability of *natural* subjecthood and on imperial economies bounded by both religion and such natal political identities. They could allow trade to cross borders while (for a time) maintaining the fiction that it did not.[7]

Multiple Spanish authorities and administrative bodies debated awarding Porcio's unexpired contract to Coymans. The king, his confessor, the Council of the Indies, the House of Trade, the Inquisition, and the papal nuncio all weighed in.[8] Porcio himself, in Panama at the time of the decision, enlisted the help of his brother-in-law Pedro Francisco de Barroso, dean of the Cádiz Cathedral, who traveled to Madrid on Porcio's behalf to object to Coymans on religious grounds.[9] The Council for the Inquisition wrote to the papal nuncio (the pope's ambassador) at Madrid that because so many American vassals were "weak converts from barbarous infidelity" they were especially "liable to contamination through association with the foreign heretics."[10] Church officials believed that Indigenous and African vassals, as converts or descendants of converts, would be especially susceptible to the dangers of Protestant contagion if Coymans's ships with their Dutch merchants and mariners entered Spanish American port towns to trade. The nuncio reminded the king (and the king's confessor) that Spain's entire colonial expansion project rested ethically and legally on its success in converting non-Christians to Catholicism. Even though the asiento agreement specified that common seamen could not go ashore, once a vessel docked that restriction was difficult to enforce, especially with complicit or bribable officials. Moreover, someone had to unload cargoes, which ensured contact between mariners and residents of port towns. Transferring human cargo required close cooperation between dockworkers and ships' crews. For all these reasons, the papal nuncio was certain the pope would object to the Coymans asiento.[11]

Carlos II was swayed, and he appointed a special committee to examine the issue. But it was dominated by members of the Council of the Indies drawing their salaries from the asiento moneys, and instead of sharing the church officials' concerns, they complained that the nuncio had interfered in commercial and political issues outside his proper range of concern. The special committee asserted that Coymans's contract was legally sound and that the king was obligated to fulfill it.[12] But objections continued, and a year later the Council for the Inquisition decided that Coymans's contract granted him too many privileges, that it did not safeguard the Catholic faith, and that it opened the door for English merchants to request similar privileges. In October 1686, Carlos II created a special permanent board, the *junta particular del asiento de negros*, which this time did not include Coymans's supporters from the Council of the Indies. In March 1687, it recommended that Coymans's contract be annulled, and in July determined that it should go back to Porcio.

In September, the crown agreed and sent proclamations to the Americas reversing its previous instructions.[13]

At this point, the Dutch West India Company protested. The Council of the Indies, which had supported Coymans's Dutch company, nonetheless rejected its larger backer's attempts to interfere. Because the West India Company operated under a license from the Dutch republic, the Council of the Indies feared that its involvement in the Coymans-Porcio conflict risked inflating a commercial contract and trade dispute into a question of state between Spain and the Netherlands. The council insisted instead that the asiento was a contract between the king and the independent merchant Balthazar Coymans, who as a resident of Cádiz was subject to the jurisdiction of the Spanish king and council.[14] Thus, even the Council of the Indies, some of whose members stood to gain from Dutch West India Company support, grew nervous when the asiento threatened to create foreign entanglements. They argued that the temporary pardon they had given Coymans to trade had been fundamentally different because it had enveloped him within Spanish jurisdiction. While he brought welcome Dutch financial backing from the West India Company, the council believed that Coymans's license in no way provided the company any role in Spanish commercial policy.

During this contest for the asiento in the mid-1680s, both Porcio's Genoese firm and Coymans's Dutch company had factors living in Port Royal, Jamaica: Santiago del Castillo (for Porcio) and Antonio Lazertoza (for Coymans).[15] Both factors, Spanish men working for the Genoese and Dutch firms, subcontracted with the English Royal African Company to supply slaves at Port Royal for transshipment to Spanish American ports. Thus, even though English slave traders regarded their Dutch counterparts as rivals, the English Royal African Company (and independent slave traders violating the Royal African Company's monopoly) stood to profit from the business of both Lazertoza and Castillo.

While debate raged in Spain over the fate of the asiento, in Jamaica the representatives of both the Dutch and Genoese firms continued to purchase newly arrived captives for Spanish American customers. Porcio's factor Santiago del Castillo played a major role in creating and protecting the conditions that allowed merchants to trade between Jamaica and Spanish American port towns. Castillo, who arrived in Jamaica in November 1684, acted as both a linguistic and cultural translator. He worked to overcome the restrictions enforced by scrupulous officials and to repair damage to commerce caused by pirates (or commissioned privateers) so that trade could continue.[16] His wide-ranging efforts show us how the asiento demanded such fixers, who possessed both the knowledge and the influence to operate between Spanish and English imperial spaces in the Caribbean.[17] The slave traders who competed for asiento contracts and subcontracts during the 1680s operated in an arena where competing imperial claims to exclusive bounded trade were supposedly breached only by licensed exceptions. In theory, those exceptions, most obviously the asiento, did not challenge the commercial boundaries between rival jurisdictions, but in reality, such trade thoroughly entangled the English and Spanish Caribbean—financially, culturally, diplomatically, and legally.

Therefore, the people who made that trade work increasingly belonged to a regional commercial world that needed shared procedures. In the seventeenth century, they strove to identify such procedures without a formal international community of law that might have accompanied more explicitly open interimperial trade. People like Castillo could bridge multiple worlds and were willing to take the risks entailed to gain the profits promised by human trafficking. That lucrative trade would have foundered without them. The officials who promoted the regional slave trade recognized the necessity of men like Castillo and did what they could to ease their entry into Caribbean and European societies. In 1685 Jamaica's lieutenant governor Hender Molesworth, who had been a factor of the Royal African Company and who supported the asiento, naturalized Castillo, assuring Castillo's right to trade and own property in Jamaica.[18] Although he traveled widely, Castillo made Jamaica his home, acquiring multiple urban lots and rural landholdings totaling well over a thousand acres. He married (Mary), had at least one son (Joseph), and died on the island between 1710 and 1715.[19]

Castillo became embroiled in the conflict between his employer, Nicolas Porcio, and Porcio's Dutch challenger, Balthazar Coymans. At the same time, he worked to make Jamaica more accessible to Spanish merchants and mariners who came there to buy enslaved African women and men. In 1686, as things trended his way in Spain, Coymans received authority to proceed against persons "hiding" asiento property, a reference to Porcio and Castillo. Despite Porcio's debts to the Spanish crown, and despite his loss of the license to Coymans, he and Castillo continued to operate in the Caribbean as though they still held asiento privileges. To do so, they kept in motion goods and money that the crown thought should go to pay Porcio's overdue crown licensing fees and other debts. Coymans "procured orders" to arrest Porcio, then in Panama, and Castillo, in Jamaica.[20] Castillo, who claimed to be a personal creditor to the asiento, likewise pursued Porcio for debts owed to English Jamaicans, who in turn blamed Castillo. Castillo wrote to Panama officials for help in extracting the payments from Porcio, so that Castillo could clear his own name. Although Jamaican officials impounded Castillo's property when they received notice of the Spanish arrest order, they did not arrest Castillo when they had opportunity to do so.

Castillo prevented Coymans's representative from seizing the Genoese company's asiento property in Jamaica, and he sent at least some of it to Spain via London, to aid Porcio's brother-in-law (the dean of the cathedral) in building Porcio's defense against Coymans. Over the course of several months in early 1686, Coymans protested to the Council of the Indies, the council reported to Carlos II, and the Spanish king instructed his ambassador in London to protest to James II, who told Jamaica lieutenant governor Hender Molesworth to admit Coymans's shipping.[21] In this instance, the Council of the Indies did not hesitate to make an issue of commerce into a question of state. Moreover, they believed that their own oversight of the asiento extended to the activities of subcontractors operating in an English colonial jurisdiction that neither fell under Spanish authority nor shared nationality with either company (Dutch or Genoese) in question. At that point, Porcio fled Panama for Madrid, where he took asylum in a monastery.[22]

Castillo's efforts to protect Porcio's (and therefore his own) interests in the region extended beyond the direct guarding of company assets to a more general allaying of Anglo-Spanish conflict in the region. In working to mitigate interimperial disputes, he at the same time tried to show how indispensable he was to the slave trading that officials and elites from both empires desired. One such conflict arose in 1685, when Matheo Guarín, the commander of the Havana guardacostas fleet, seized a ketch sailing from New England for Jamaica. Needing repairs to his own ship, Guarín sought shelter in Port Royal, bringing with him the New England vessel, which he claimed as legal prize. But English officials accused him of seizing the ketch illegally and condemned Guarín and his *mulato* crewman Juan Christian to hang. Guarín's imprisonment and threatened execution triggered an interimperial incident involving the two asiento rivals resident in Jamaica, and produced a flurry of communications between English and Spanish officials, merchants, and mariners about the meaning of treaty law and the rules of interimperial negotiation.[23] Santiago del Castillo took Guarín food while he was in prison and petitioned Governor Molesworth to grant Guarín clemency, actions that later provided Castillo with leeway to plead on behalf of English interests in Cuba and in New Spain.

Repercussions from Guarín's arrest began when the Spanish ship captain Juan de Jenes, who worked for Coymans's asiento factor Antonio Lazertoza, took the news of Guarín's imprisonment and sentence to Vera Cruz. Jenes and twelve of his crew members had been in Jamaica to witness Guarín's treatment. The asiento required that English, Spanish, and Dutch ships spend time in one another's ports, although neither the English nor the Spanish dismantled protective restrictions prohibiting foreign shipping. In Jamaica foreign mariners and merchants such as Jenes's crewmen lived ashore while awaiting cargoes. The asiento's condoned interimperial trade thus created markedly different grounds for interaction than did clandestine smuggling, which avoided port towns or long stays.

Jenes and his men testified to the court in Vera Cruz that English Jamaicans treated Spaniards poorly, and that Jamaica governor Molesworth condoned Guarín's mistreatment in prison. Further damning the English governor, the Spanish mariners reported that Molesworth had permitted the pirate John Coxon to escape prison, despite Coxon's known predations on the Spanish and England's treaty obligations to punish pirates. In Vera Cruz, Spanish officials responded to Jenes's anti-English accusations by imprisoning Adrian Scroope and Derrick Cornelisen, "vecinos" of Jamaica (though from their names, "natural" Dutchmen), as ransom for Guarín's release.

Meanwhile, Guarín's crewmen in Jamaica petitioned Governor Molesworth on their captain's behalf. Molesworth, moved by the crewmen's pleas and perhaps also by Castillo's influence, wrote to Charles II, requesting and receiving a pardon for Guarín and setting him and the crewman Juan Christian free. Nonetheless, even after Guarín returned to Cuba, Scroope and Cornelisen remained imprisoned in Vera Cruz. In January 1687 Castillo traveled there to seek their release and to repair Jamaica's reputation as a place to do business. Castillo underscored his own role in smoothing the way for Spaniards in the colony, noting that he helped Guarín as "I have helped all the Spanish in Jamaica—as is notorious throughout the Indies." He had six witnesses with him in Vera Cruz who could confirm Jamaican officials' fair treatment of Spanish slave traders, refuting the accusations that Juan de Jenes and another of Coymans's asiento ship captains (Luys de Arriaza) had leveled against the English governor. As Castillo and Arriaza debated one another in the Vera Cruz court, Castillo accused both the Spanish ship captains of spreading false reports. They had impugned not only Governor Molesworth but also "the Island and the English nation" in order to "discredit the island" so that Carlos II would keep the asiento in Dutch hands "for lack of good correspondence with the English."[24]

The two Spanish rivals—the Genoese merchant Porcio's asiento factor Castillo, and the Dutch merchant Coymans's ship captain Arriaza—argued before the Vera Cruz court about exactly what had happened in Jamaica. They disputed the relative significance of treaty law and English law in determining what procedures bound English Jamaican officials, and therefore whether Spanish officials were justified in retaliating for Guarín's imprisonment. Rather than assuming that such questions possessed preexisting imperial answers that would come from Madrid or London, judges and governors in Caribbean port towns listened as the merchant and ship captain debated how (and what) law should govern the international relations that could hinder or facilitate trade. Coymans's ship captain Arriaza made clear that he perceived this conflict through the lens of the asiento rivalry, referring to Castillo by his position as "Porcio's factor" in this imprisonment case that, on its surface, had little to do with slave trading.

Captain Arriaza asserted that although Governor Molesworth had in fact suspended Guarín's punishment and appraised his king of the sentence, as the Treaty of Madrid required, he had to be pressured to do so. Arriaza asserted that Molesworth would have hanged Guarín had Guarín's crew not pleaded for him. Although Arriaza acknowledged that "Porcio's factor" Castillo had sustained Guarín while he languished in prison, he used that occasion, too, to criticize Jamaicans, claiming that Castillo had to bribe "the heretics" for permission to push food under the prison door, which the guards would not even open enough to let in any light.

Castillo defended Molesworth and tutored the Vera Cruz court on English law, explaining that if in Jamaica a jury of twelve upstanding men convicted someone, the governor could not intervene. Such information was inapplicable in this case, which was heard by Jamaica's vice admiralty court, as was common in piracy cases.[25] Nevertheless, because Guarín's men had pleaded so effectively for their captain, Molesworth had successfully petitioned Charles II to pardon Guarín. Moreover, Molesworth had released Juan Christian as well, even though the king's pardon had not mentioned him. Castillo thus took the same facts Arriaza had used to emphasize the island's danger to Spaniards and instead made a case for his own influence and the governor's flexibility and clemency.

Arriaza then repeated Jenes's accusation that the pirate Coxon, with a crew that included "vecinos" of Jamaica, robbed Spaniards throughout the West

Indies, that the governor did not prosecute them, and that they were now cutting wood for Jamaica at the Bay of Campeche. Castillo acknowledged the truth of these facts, without noting that the word *vecino* that Arriaza used to describe the pirates and logwood cutters had no English cognate. Although the men in question made Jamaica their home base, likely few of them possessed the property or local standing that *vecino* implied. Nonetheless, Jamaican officials should have stopped their crimes. But they needed Spanish help.

Castillo defended Molesworth partly on the ground that the Spanish witnesses in Jamaica had tied his hands by failing to give their depositions in court according to the requirements of English law. A successful asiento, depending on officials' ability to clear the Caribbean of maritime criminals, would require that Spanish mariners follow English legal procedure when under English jurisdiction. Finally, Castillo denied Jenes's claim that his sailors and cabin boys had suffered in Jamaica. Rather, he insisted that they had enjoyed good treatment, and that English officials had in fact overlooked several incidents for which they deserved punishment.

Castillo failed to secure the release of Scroope and Cornelisen from their Vera Cruz jail, but his daily visits to Guarín during his Jamaican imprisonment had developed into a friendship, which indirectly aided English officials as they decided their next move.[26] When Guarín returned to Cuba, he spread word of Castillo's aid to him. That relationship helped English officials and Castillo to find out why Vera Cruz officials held Scroope and Cornelisen even after Molesworth had released Guarín. They were then able to craft an appropriate response.

The information came along with additional evidence of Castillo's influence: when a Cuban guardacostas brought an English sloop as prize into Trinidad, Cuba, the town's deputy (*teniente*) wrote to Castillo in Jamaica. The guardacostas' captain (who likely worked under Guarín) had renounced the right to the English sloop "because of the attention Don Santiago del Castillo had given to Guarín," remarking that the Spanish so depended on Castillo's protection in dealing with the English that they could "call him father." The teniente thanked Castillo profusely for the shelter and protection he provided for Spaniards in general and for his help to Guarín in particular, and forwarded to Castillo a set of decrees that the viceroy of New Spain had issued about Scroope and Cornelisen.[27] Castillo shared them with Jamaica governor Molesworth, who wrote to the viceroy of New Spain pleading for the release of Scroope and Cornelisen, "vecinos of this island." Because Molesworth had succeeded in gaining pardon for Guarín, he insisted, Spanish officials should release the two men they had taken in retaliation. Moreover, both Porcio's factor (Castillo) and Coymans's factor (Lazertoza) had testified that Jenes's and Arriaza's statements included "false slanders" "to which all other Spaniards that at present are found in this Island" would attest if necessary. Jenes's sailors had even sworn that the denunciations against Jamaica that they had earlier signed in Vera Cruz were false; Jenes had pressured them and had read them only part of what they signed.[28]

In February 1686, the secretary of Jamaica and a Royal African Company asiento factor went to Antonio Lazertoza's Port Royal house to ask Coymans's factor for help. Together they read a decree from the viceroy of New Spain that contained Jenes's crew members' original anti-English depositions. Lazertoza then spoke with those crewmembers in person and, "after having seen, recognized, and understood," he agreed to provide a sworn declaration "of my good will and without pressure." He testified that not only was Jenes's deposition libelous and his crewmembers' original testimony false, but that the men so feared Jenes that they had fled his employment and remained in Jamaica. One claimed to fear for his life sailing under Jenes.

After attacking Jenes's credibility, Lazertoza praised Governor Molesworth, who had only been doing what the law required of him when he put Matheo Guarín on trial. Molesworth, with his "accustomed beneficence to strangers," had given Guarín all the liberty possible to defend his cause, ensuring that Guarín had a lawyer and returning to him his papers and his commission which had been confiscated upon his arrest. A tribunal of the Admiralty heard the case and, according to Lazertoza, the testimony they heard left the judges no choice but to condemn Guarín to death. Lazertoza said that he, Jenes, and Castillo had all petitioned Molesworth to grant a stay of execution until Guarín could write to the Spanish ambassador in London to request a pardon. Exhibiting the patronage (*señoria*) appropriate to his office, Molesworth granted a stay of one year. Finally, Lazertoza added, he had never heard that the governor had had any part in the pirate Coxon's escape, but that he had always aided the Spanish nation in this island and tried to destroy pirates.[29] If Castillo was correct that Jenes and Arriaza made up their negative testimony in order to draw the asiento away from Porcio to Coymans (or away from Jamaica to Curaçao), Lazertoza, as Coymans's factor and therefore an employee of the same company as Jenes and Arriaza, was an especially useful witness for the interests of Porcio, Castillo, and the Jamaicans.

I have not found whether Scroope and Cornelisen were released. The apparent irony that "Dutch" Jamaicans were imprisoned as ransom for the behavior of the Genoese firm illustrates the fungibility and complexity of Caribbean identities. Regardless of the men's fates, the case shows how Castillo crossed political, legal, cultural, and linguistic borders to serve his own interests and those of others wishing to traffic men and women between Jamaica and Spanish America. Because that regional slave trade was so valuable to so many, Castillo's abilities as legal, linguistic, and cultural translator gave him considerable influence among both Spanish and English officials and mariners in the western Caribbean.

Castillo leveraged that influence to gain cultural as well as economic, political, and legal privileges for himself and fellow Spaniards in Jamaica. He established a public chapel in his estate near Port Royal and then built a Catholic church that could hold three hundred people, "although" according to his own report, "there was no liberty of conscience" for Catholics. He employed seven Catholic clergymen at his own cost. They lived on Castillo's estate, where they "always" celebrated divine offices.[30] The bishop Diego Evelino Hurtado de Compostela of Cuba claimed to believe that England's king James II had sent all seven of the priests.[31] The principal clergyman John Baptist/Juan Bautista Dempsy had traveled to Cuba shortly after his arrival in Jamaica, perhaps at Castillo's urging. He applied to the dean of the diocese (the Cuban See) for permission to serve in Jamaica, as validation for his ministry. The diocese responded by granting Dempsy the title of vicar-general, an office of considerable jurisdictional authority. If true, Dempsy apparently had believed James II's approval of him insufficient to validate his own ministry and that further validation from the overseeing diocese—which he understood to be Cuba—was needed. Dempsy was able to live in Jamaica as Bishop Hurtado's vicar-general without incident, due, in Castillo's opinion, to Castillo's own "influence and wealth."[32]

Those who attended services in Castillo's church could have included Spanish, English, Irish, French, or Black seamen or residents, or enslaved Africans awaiting transshipment. Spanish ships that arrived to purchase slaves sometimes appeared in advance of the Royal African Company ships or interlopers and might wait weeks or months for the ships to arrive. Merchants and seamen, such as Juan de Jenes's crew, spent time ashore, but their desire to attend mass could not alone explain the size of Castillo's church, whose clergy may have been baptizing captives held there for transshipment (a practice that English officials would have little cause to oppose). If Castillo's church held anywhere near the three hundred people he claimed, it was one of the largest buildings in the Anglican colony. Castillo's estate sat above the town on a hillside overlooking the port, visible from below. English authorities surely knew about it and the services held there, given the frequent presence of merchants, ship captains, and colonial officials at Castillo's house. But initially neither the chapel nor the clergymen's presence caused concern in the English island.

Although two Jamaica governors, along with other local officials, supported Castillo's efforts to claim a local belonging in Port Royal, he never achieved the community membership that would make those claims secure from political or economic rivals, as became clear in 1687 with the arrival of Christopher Monck, Second Duke of Albemarle, as James II's new governor of the island. In April 1688, Castillo and Albemarle clashed over their differing interpretations of James's general pardon for pirates. This incident was brief but important, because it illustrates Castillo's willingness to antagonize the new English governor in order to protect Anglo-Spanish slave trading. He perhaps felt confident that the asiento had by then become important enough to influential Jamaicans and London officials that he risked little in alienating Albemarle.

The king's pardon, like others that had preceded it, offered clemency to any pirates who turned themselves in and gave security not to return to piracy. On that news, according to Castillo, thirty-seven French pirates came to Port Royal from the South Sea, where they had been preying on Spanish shipping. Castillo accused the governor of accepting a bribe when he "took all the silver that they brought and left them in liberty." They took it as a tacit approval, and "much encourage[d] they went again to pirate." Albemarle's leniency toward French pirates attacking Spanish shipping put Anglo-Spanish trade at risk. While the silver the French pirates brought into Jamaica enriched those who received it, English support for French pirates threatened both licit and illicit trade between Port Royal and Spanish ports.

Albemarle countered that because the pirates were French, English Jamaican officials possessed no jurisdiction over them, which was incorrect: if indeed the men were pirates, Jamaica's Act for Restraining and Punishing Privateers and Pirates required Albemarle to bring them to trial. Furthermore, Albemarle continued, the island did not have enough jail space for so many pirates, but if Castillo liked, he could give the governor a new jail. Castillo, in writing to Spanish authorities, explicitly accused Albemarle of letting the pirates go so that he could collect security from them repeatedly.[33]

In describing his responses to Albemarle's actions, Castillo revealed the strategies he used to influence those in power in both empires. When he objected directly to the governor, he emphasized that in failing to prevent the French pirates' departure the governor had disregarded James II's wishes. But when writing to Madrid, Castillo claimed that he had objected to the governor's pardons because releasing the French pirates would produce "considerable damages to the vassals of our King and Lord."[34] He thus appealed separately to two distinct imperial worldviews. He stressed the English king's interests (and the Jamaican governor's responsibility to pursue them) with Albemarle, but to his Spanish correspondent he depicted himself (despite his Jamaican naturalization) as a loyal Spanish subject, protecting Spanish interests.

The tensions between Castillo and Albemarle escalated when a new Catholic priest, Thomas Churchill, followed Albemarle from London to Jamaica, arriving in May 1688. The conflict that ensued between Churchill and Governor Albemarle, on the one hand, and Castillo and John Baptist Dempsy, on the other, drew in the bishop of Cuba and England's Lords of Trade and Plantations. Both priests claimed the right to minister to Anglican Jamaica's Catholic residents, and their clash raised questions of religious jurisdiction, just when James II's Catholicism challenged England's religious identity, and threatened to blur an important boundary separating English spaces in the Atlantic from Spanish (and French) ones.

As with trade and privateering conflicts, the rivals argued over what administrative hierarchy governed Caribbean spaces and people. Did the treaty law that contributed to an emerging law of nations (specifically the 1670 Treaty of Madrid) supersede Spanish, English, and church law at the human and spatial borders of the two empires? Was it possible for jurisdictional spaces to overlap? Specifically, could a Spanish church jurisdiction (the Cuban bishopric) include an English imperial space (Jamaica)? Or could one administrative body (the Cuban bishopric) govern individual people (Catholics) in spaces governed by other administrative bodies (the Church of England)? Could one person belong to both an English colony and a Spanish colonial church? The presence of these rival Catholic clergymen in Jamaica exposed the overlap of multiple jurisdictional boundaries—not just between Spanish Cuba and English Jamaica, but also between colonial and religious administrations within each empire.[35]

James II, on his ascension in 1685, tried to provide toleration for Catholics within the English empire: in 1687 he pressured judges to excuse Catholics from the Test Act (which required that anyone who was to hold military or civil office deny transubstantiation and take the Oath of Supremacy affirming the crown's control over the Church of England). The king also published the Declaration of Indulgence, providing liberty of conscience for Catholics, among others. But Governor Albemarle's patronage of the Catholic priest Thomas Churchill may in fact have eroded toleration for Catholics in the island. Jamaican elites voiced considerable opposition to Albemarle during the short time between his arrival in 1687 and his death in the early fall of 1688. They asserted that he did not understand the Caribbean and that he was tyrannical. His service to James II may have provoked the accusations of tyranny, commonly associated with Louis XIV's absolute monarchy and with popery. English use of the word *popery* conveyed Catholicism *and* tyranny, and suggested that Catholicism produced tyrannical governments whereas Protestantism worked against them.[36]

According to Thomas Churchill, despite Castillo's church and its clergy, Jamaican Catholics had asked him to petition on their behalf in England for a priest, and he generously offered to go himself. James II provided him a salary of £200 per year, and Governor Albemarle added a supplement.[37] According to Albemarle, Churchill enjoyed official recognition as "chief Pastor of his Ma[jes]ties Catholick subjects of this Island." By limiting Churchill's ministry to the "Catholick subjects" of James II rather than all Catholics in the colony, Albemarle asserted government hierarchy over church hierarchy, as would have been the case in the Church of England.[38] This formulation was at odds with Catholic universalism, though Spanish American administrators also placed imperial over church officials. According to Albemarle, the king ordered the governor to "encourage & Countenance . . . Churchill, with the rest of his persuasion." Again violating the tenets of universalism, the governor was to encourage Catholics who were "recommend[ed] by" Churchill "and no other."[39]

Churchill readily accepted the role of "chief Pastor" of Jamaica's Catholics, trying to establish his authority over the clergymen already there. But that brought him to Castillo, the patron of the seven Catholic clergymen already on the island. When Churchill first arrived in Jamaica in May 1688, he stayed for eighteen days in the Spanish merchant's house, at Castillo's invitation. While there, Churchill tried his best to establish authority over John Baptist Dempsy and the other six priests employed by Castillo. He called a meeting of the island's Catholic "laity as well as clergy" to establish "such rules & orders amongst them, as should be most consonant, and agreeable to the Canons & doctrine of his Church."[40]

Churchill's intrusion offended Dempsy and Castillo. Castillo decided that Churchill was "more heretic than Catholic" and expelled him from his house, thus setting off a controversy intertwining religious jurisdiction with the jurisdiction of the asiento.[41] Governor Albemarle, whom Castillo painted as "a grand heretic and a great enemy of the Spaniards and Catholics," began proceedings to charge Castillo's seven priests, "suspending" them and banning them from Castillo's chapel, although there was no other Catholic church in the island. Castillo sent two of the clergymen to Cuba to inform the chapter that Governor Albemarle and Father Churchill were trying to remove Jamaica from the Cuban bishop's ecclesiastic jurisdiction, thereby challenging an authority that rested on apostolic succession.[42]

Governor Albemarle, in relating these events, called Castillo "a subject to the King of Spain." Albemarle knew that Castillo had been naturalized in Jamaica three years earlier but instead tied Castillo's political identity to the Spanish crown.[43] Albemarle thus linked Castillo's appeals to Bishop Hurtado with allegiance to the Spanish empire, in contrast to Castillo's behavior and the bishop's claims, which asserted a separation between political and religious authority. Castillo apparently did *not* write to the governor of Cuba or to the viceroy of New Spain, who governed the Caribbean. Nor did he involve political authorities in Cartagena, where his strongest trade connections lay. Catholic religious hierarchies represented a geographically distinct but overlapping administrative network that linked Jamaica to Cuba without necessarily involving New Spain or New Granada. Castillo's communications could therefore reflect his religious identity as a Catholic without deriving clearly from a political allegiance to either crown.

Castillo did know that the debate in Spain over whether Coymans could hold the asiento contract turned in part on the Dutch merchant's Protestantism; he wrote to the bishop that Porcio "as a Catholic" had obtained restitution of the asiento.[44] Castillo's efforts to curry favor with the Catholic Church hierarchy in Cuba could have constituted a commercial strategy. If he could prove that Porcio's asiento served Catholic Church interests, even as it bridged borders between the Spanish and English Caribbean, Castillo might sway Spanish officials to return the contract to his Genoese employer, who was a foreigner but a Catholic one.

In response to Castillo's news from Jamaica, Hurtado sent a decree to Castillo, addressed to the English government of Jamaica. Castillo immediately made the proclamation public in his church, and (according to Castillo) Father Churchill gave it to Governor Albemarle.[45] The Cuban decree asserted that any Catholic ministry in Jamaica required the approval of the bishop of Cuba because prior to 1655, when Jamaica had been a Spanish colony and therefore fallen under formal Spanish jurisdiction, it had been part of the Cuban diocese. Although Spain's Carlos II had, in the 1670 Treaty of Madrid, "ceded temporal right" over Jamaica to England, the treaty "did not touch, nor could" it, "the spiritual right." Diplomats negotiating on behalf of their sovereigns Charles II and Carlos II had no spiritual authority over the island, even had they thought to include such a clause. "Only the See of the Bishopric of Cuba" could have renounced spiritual jurisdiction over Jamaica.[46]

Indeed, the 1670 treaty did not mention religion. It stated that "the . . . King of Great Britain . . . shall have, hold, and possess forever, with full right of sovereignty, ownership, and possession, all the lands, regions, islands, colonies, and dominions, situated in the West Indies or in any part of America, that the said King of Great Britain and his subjects at present hold and possess."[47] The question of religious authority rested on the definition of "full right of sovereignty, ownership, and possession." The Spanish crown possessed greater control over the Roman Catholic Church in its American colonies than it did in Spain. Crown officials, rather than church officials, controlled clergy appointments, so it seems surprising that religious officials in Cuba would act with such jurisdictional confidence.[48]

Earlier Jamaican authorities may not have known that Dempsy had forged a connection with the Cuban bishopric and that Cuban clergymen were keeping tabs on Jamaica, but Hurtado's proclamation made Dempsy's Cuban correspondence impossible to ignore. Even if Cuban ecclesiastical authorities had not regarded the English colony as part of their jurisdiction before Dempsy's arrival, his willingness to regard himself as part of the Cuban See, along with Castillo's patronage, allowed them to claim religious jurisdiction. The bishop's decree suggests that Cuban church officials believed, or at least thought they could plausibly pretend to believe, that they and King James II were working together as Catholics not only to minister to Catholics in the English Caribbean but to increase their numbers. Hurtado claimed that James II had sent John Baptist Dempsy and the other clergymen as "missionaries" to Jamaica, suggesting that they were not just to tend to Catholics on the island but to win converts. According to the bishop, they were succeeding. The work of the seven clergymen at Castillo's estate, and the "zeal" of Castillo in opening his home to them and building the chapel, had advanced "the propagation of the Christian religion" in Jamaica. While ridiculing Thomas Churchill for his Greek ordination, Bishop Hurtado praised "his majesty the most Christian King of Great Britain" for sending "Don Juan Baptista Dempsy" and the other clergymen to Jamaica. Just as some English

Protestants feared, then, foreign Catholics saw James II's reign as an opportunity to make inroads into areas where Protestant churches were weakly established.[49]

This Cuban bishop's claim to govern the Jamaican Catholic Church defied English law that gave the monarch religious supremacy. However, James II's decision to let the Oath of Supremacy expire called into question his authority over English ecclesiastical matters. The Oath of Supremacy affirmed the English sovereign's ultimate authority over the Church of England and denying "foreign princes" (originally the pope) any jurisdiction over the church. While James II may indeed have intended to relinquish such control to the pope, he likely did not predict that existing Catholic administrative structure would place his Caribbean colonies under Spanish Cuban authority. Separation from Roman Catholic hierarchies was a founding principle of the Church of England's identity and one invoked every time public and military officials took or administered the Oath of Supremacy. The Roman Catholicism James II espoused carried with it hierarchical ties to Rome that complicated the king's authority over religious appointment of Catholics such as Churchill and Dempsy.[50]

Governor Albemarle called Hurtado's claims "contemptible" and "very much derogatory to his Ma[jes]ties Prerogative & dignity."[51] Indeed, the Cuban document was a "forreign Ecclesiastick power" that signaled the "introduction of forreign authority into this Island."[52] Father Churchill denounced Santiago del Castillo for bringing "the manifesto" to Jamaica. He, like Albemarle, emphasized the challenge to James II's prerogative. Governor Albemarle went on to call Castillo's actions "so barefac'd a contempt to authority" and "of so evill a consequence to the governmt" that he called on the council to investigate. The council summoned Castillo, who acknowledged that he had sent to Cuba for the document and that he had made it public. The council ordered the provost marshal to arrest Castillo and hold him until instructions came from James II.[53]

While the governor and Council of Jamaica took issue with Hurtado's declaration, neither Jamaica's officially Protestant affiliation nor the anti-popery that would shortly drive James II into exile appear in the documents surrounding the case.[54] Even taking into account the religious toleration that had characterized Jamaica's quest for colonists and trade, such apparent latitude for Catholic "missionaries" engaged in "propagation" suggests a surprising degree of acceptance, given anti-Catholic fears circulating elsewhere in the English Atlantic in response to James II's reign. When the governor and council did object, it was only at the behest of a rival Catholic. Although Albemarle could not have ignored the challenges contained in the bishop's decree, he had not raised questions about the priests at Castillo's house before Churchill's arrival, even when quarreling with the Spanish merchant over his release of French pirates, a moment that he could have used to challenge the seven Catholic missionaries' presence at the foreign merchant's estate. The Anglican clergy in Jamaica appear to have remained silent about Dempsy (seven of the dozen or so parishes on the island were supplied with Anglican ministers in the 1680s).[55] Rather, the primary objection came from their fellow Catholic Churchill and from Governor Albemarle.

Castillo, by using his "wealth and influence" as a slave trader to harbor the Catholic missionaries, illustrated the dangers open trade posed to those who saw imperial identities as bound up with specific religious adherence. Traders' interimperial activities did more than just challenge the notion that imperial or even religious borders ought to dictate the movement of goods. If the asiento was to proceed, merchants had to be able to construct lives around their border-crossing traffic. Castillo's life in Jamaica, combined with his own religious convictions, then gave Spanish religious authorities a toehold that they could develop into a firmer footing during James II's brief tenure on the English throne.

Questions of jurisdiction had very practical implications for traders, merchants, and other residents who needed to know what rules would govern them and what freedoms and privileges they could expect. But jurisdictional questions also possessed important symbolic value because mobile inhabitants of the Caribbean might exhibit political and religious allegiances that challenged any imagined clean alignment between control over space and control over people. Jamaican officials, in their zeal to promote slave trading and attract wealthy European settlers, did not hesitate to naturalize Castillo, a partner in the interimperial colonial project of transforming the Caribbean into an assemblage of slave societies. But he leveraged his influence primarily in his own interest, which included Spanish or English imperial concerns only insofar as they furthered Anglo-Spanish slave trading.

Castillo's economic importance to Jamaica's trade in human captives, and the relations he had cultivated to promote that commerce, meant that he retained considerable support from elite Jamaicans and officials even after Bishop Hurtado's decree became public. When the council ordered the provost marshal to arrest Castillo, the provost marshal and several other high-ranking officials instead helped Castillo escape the island.[56] Many residents of the port town were complicit in the slave trader's escape. When the provost marshal later faced trial for ignoring many opportunities to arrest Castillo, several witnesses testified that they had seen the well-known merchant appear in public in Port Royal at various times between 6 a.m. and 10 p.m. on the day following the order for his arrest and immediately before his flight.

As Castillo prepared to flee the island, former governor Hender Molesworth informed him that in three days he (Molesworth) was leaving for London with a fleet of several ships. If Castillo could reach a safe location, they would pick him up on their way, and in London Molesworth would put Castillo "at the feet" of James II, from whom Molesworth was sure Castillo would obtain justice. Moreover, Molesworth told Castillo that he had in hand a memorial signed by "all" of the eighty most important gentlemen of Jamaica, addressed to the king and affirming their universal support for Castillo. So Castillo and Molesworth agreed that Castillo would flee to Havana, and the English fleet would wait in sight of the port for Castillo to join them.[57] Molesworth and Castillo carried enough weight with the fleet's captains to put such a plan into motion, even though it defied the current governor Albemarle's authority.

Castillo wrote that the Jamaican arrest orders were for himself, Vicar-General Dempsy, and the two priests who had gone to Cuba to procure the memorial, as "traitors to the King for having introduced the ecclesiastical jurisdiction of Cuba."[58] If he reported correctly, the arrest order's language suggests that English officials recognized Castillo's Jamaican naturalization as entailing some degree of loyalty to the English sovereign. Without such allegiance, he could not have become a "traitor."[59]

The case thus brought to light the still unresolved meaning of naturalization. English colonial governors who naturalized foreigners, like Spanish colonial officials granting foreigners *vecindad* (local citizenship) or *naturaleza* (nativity), did not possess the authority—at least in theory—to grant subjecthood, which in England came only from Parliament.[60] However, Jamaica governors used the imperial (or at least national) language of naturalization and subjecthood rather than local denization. Left unsaid was whether a Spaniard like Castillo, naturalized in Jamaica, had thereby renounced his Spanish subjecthood, becoming a subject of the English crown. But although the Jamaica patents specified that the recipient would enjoy all the rights and privileges of a "natural born subject" and in the name of the king, officials outside Jamaica did not always accept naturalization as a trait that adhered to the recipient (as we have seen with Jews) if he traveled beyond the jurisdiction of the official who had signed the deed (or even if the granting official had been replaced by another).

When Castillo fled Jamaica, he was only able to bring two clergymen: "the friar from Our Father San Juan de Dios" and a Jesuit. The other priests, including Dempsy, were hiding in fear, and so Castillo left them at his house with his family. He also left "in" his house 182 enslaved individuals whom he had begun to purchase from English transatlantic slave traders to fulfill an order from Porcio. All the captives had been impounded until instructions arrived from James II.[61] Castillo and the two priests slipped out of Port Royal under cover of night in a small sloop with seven mariners, arriving in Havana May 27.

The governor there, Don Diego de Viana, initially received them with great fanfare and promised all assistance, assuring them that when the English ships arrived, they would be allowed to board and continue to London. Castillo was to take the two clergymen with him to testify to James II that he had increased the "Holy Catholic Faith" in Jamaica "by a considerable number." (Castillo believed the king already knew this, because he had written of it to the Spanish Council of the Indies president Velez and expected that Velez had relayed the information to the English monarch.)[62] However, the next day Governor Viana surprised Castillo with Carlos II's two-year-old order to arrest Castillo (and Porcio) and send them to Madrid for Porcio's defaulted asiento payment. Castillo pleaded that he himself remained creditor to the asiento and could prove it with "authentic and original documents."

Fearing that Jamaican authorities would condemn Dempsy to death and that the other clergy and lay Catholics in Jamaica faced "evident danger," Castillo begged Governor Viana to give him license to leave the port to meet the English ships. Time was of the essence. Moreover, he could better serve "His Majesty" (Carlos II) and the asiento by going to London than to Spain, especially because if Carlos II had returned the asiento to Porcio (as rumor had it), Castillo had to convince James II to ensure enough Africans in Jamaica to meet the contract. The governor's secretary told Castillo that "the Governor would expect a good gift" from Castillo or send him to Spain. Castillo offered five hundred pesos, which he claimed was all that he had available, but Viana demanded six thousand pesos and kept him imprisoned.[63]

The following day the governor visited Castillo and suggested he write a memorial outlining all of the services he had done for Carlos II and for the king's vassals, to explain why the Cuban officials ought to help him. Castillo did so and presented the memorial to the governor's advisor, who argued (according to Castillo) that the governor ought to let Castillo go to London, because the voyage would serve God and king. The bishop and several lawyers added their support, but the governor said it would be impossible to do anything without another thousand pesos. The exasperated bishop said that were he willing to be party to such corruption, he would supply the bribe himself.[64]

Castillo then petitioned the governor to at least let the two priests go to London to plead on behalf of "the poor priests who remained in the jail and in my house." They could also prepare the English to help him meet the asiento contract's requirements if the news was correct that the Spanish crown had returned the contract to Porcio. This the governor permitted, but Castillo reported that he found it "shameful" to see how "the Governors work in the Indies with neither fear of God" nor any consideration of whether their actions served his Majesty. Rather, they operated from "pure interest," thereby neglecting many opportunities to support "our Holy Catholic Faith and the Asiento."[65]

Castillo explicitly painted the rise of international slave trading as a means to foster the growth of Catholicism by providing inroads into English colonies. He implicated Spanish and English officials alike, claiming that the most disgraceful part of the ordeal was that when Albemarle's officials had come to arrest him, they had broken the doors of the church and the tabernacle where the sacrament was kept.[66] Havana governor Viana should, according to Castillo, have recognized that Porcio's asiento benefited church and crown and granted Castillo license to go to London despite Spanish royal orders to the contrary. When official word of the asiento's return to Porcio reached Cuba, Castillo was released, and he made it to London by 1689.[67] There, the Royal African Company and Jamaican merchants complained that Albemarle and his officials discouraged Genoese and Dutch asiento trading alike, disobeying the governor's explicit instructions to encourage it and neglecting royal interest in the company. But slave traders' objections to Albemarle were rendered moot when news reached London that shortly after Castillo escaped, the governor had died. At the same time, James II, faced with the invasion of William of Orange and the defection of many political elites and most of his army, fled to France.

Upon the ascension of William and Mary, the Royal African Company and Jamaican merchants immediately pushed to realign Jamaica policy with their own interests. The company petitioned the Board of Trade to repeal two acts passed in Jamaica under Albemarle, one raising the value of pieces of eight and the other outlawing trade with Spanish America.[68] A group of thirty-seven "planters and merchants of Jamaica" added their voices to the request.[69] In response to a widely reported perception that Albemarle had, during his brief time on the island, "ruined and destroyed" Jamaica's trade with neighboring Spanish ports, William III reappointed Castillo's ally Hender Molesworth as governor. Molesworth understood the region's geopolitical dynamics and already possessed a network of connections. London officials believed that Molesworth not only "knows the interests of the French and Spaniards in the West Indies" but also enjoyed the approval of "all the merchants and planters concerned in Jamaica," which would help him reestablish trust in the government after Albemarle's "arbitrary rule."[70]

Recommitment to the Spanish American slave trade and the need to draft instructions for the new governor prompted a discussion among multiple English officers about trade regulations. In June 1689, Molesworth requested clarification about several questions, including "how far Assiento ships may sell trifling goods without infringing the Acts of Navigation."[71] As soon as the Lords of Trade and Plantations read his queries, they forwarded them to the king for his instructions.[72] But as crown officials considered his questions, Molesworth died in London, leaving the island's governorship again empty. About eighty "Merchants Planters & Traders" in London "conserne[d] in Jamaica" quickly signed a request for the appointment of "a Governour well acquainted with the Place & People," either Colonel Peter Beckford, Colonel William Beeston, or Samuel Bernard, slave traders all.

In a new political climate that made it safe to attack James II and his appointees, the petitioners suggested that Albemarle had promoted the "wicked contrivance of evill counsellours, judges, & ministers" to "subvert the Lawes & liberties" of the island and introduce "the Popish Religion," putting people without estates or reputation into office. These supporters of Molesworth also supported Castillo. They did not object to his Catholicism, nor did they mention John Baptist Dempsy or the other priests under Castillo's protection. Rather, they opposed the "Popish Priest" Thomas Churchill and the role he had played in the island by advising and consulting with the governor and other officials.[73] Albemarle had "appoint[ed] the King's house" in Port Royal for Churchill "to say Mass in." They objected to Albemarle for advancing popery, both with his official support for Churchill and with what they saw as his arbitrary rule. A Catholic king raised the specter of tyranny to English Protestants, who believed that Catholic rulers took orders from the pope and necessarily opposed representative governments. Such "popery," evinced by Churchill's influence over Albemarle, should be fought at all costs. But Catholics such as Castillo, who shared the petitioners' commercial goal to maintain the island as a slave-trading hub, presented little trouble if they kept their religion out of government office. Thus he and his priests, though Catholic, were not popish.[74] Nor did religious issues arise even when officials were particularly exasperated with their Spanish American counterparts, suggesting that the anti-Spanish anti-popery of the sixteenth and early seventeenth centuries had given way to the anti-French anti-popery of the eighteenth century.[75]

Meanwhile, planters in Jamaica who opposed the Royal African Company's monopoly took advantage of the upheaval to protest the asiento, wishing not to compete with Spanish American buyers for the captive Africans brought in by transatlantic slavers. From Jamaica, Assembly member Ralph Knight offered a more positive account of Albemarle's tenure in his "state of this Island." Not yet aware of William and Mary's ascension to the throne, Knight addressed his letter to James II on behalf of the Jamaica Council and Assembly. The memorial complained that Jamaicans had only been able to purchase a small portion of the thousands of Africans the Royal African Company had imported during the previous six years because of bad "usage" the island's planters had suffered at the hands of Governor Molesworth and other company factors. The factors, including Molesworth, "grasping all into their own hand," had favored reexporting captive Africans over selling them in Jamaica.[76]

Even before the asiento "was settled" in Jamaica, royal frigates convoyed "shiploads of the choicest negroes to the Spaniards." After Jamaica became an official asiento entrepôt, "the negroes were picked to suit the Spaniards, the factors and their particular friends still reaping all the benefit." In the island, published lists named the local merchants who profited by buying up captives for the asiento, alongside the amounts they received in "paybacks," "as though it were a public concern." Indeed, asiento factors received so much in interest (thousands of pounds) that it sometimes exceeded the principal. In contrast, "the most eminent [English] merchants" received small sums. "Thus foreigners get the best of the negroes, and we only the refuse at £22 a head." When planters boarded ships to buy Africans, "their ready money has been refused because it was not pieces-of-eight." An act requiring that two planters and two merchants always be present for the "equal lotting of the negroes" was meant to ensure Jamaica slaveholders fair opportunity to purchase the most desirable captives, but the factors always "appointed their own creatures."[77]

The Royal African Company preferred to sell to asiento factors offering coin rather than to local planters who frequently needed credit, but Knight accused the Royal African Company of exaggerating planters' failure to pay their debts to justify their preference for asiento buyers. According to Knight, after Albemarle's "happy" arrival, the new governor had sought to aid the planters, twice demanding from Royal African Company factors an itemized list of all debts that planters owed to verify the Royal African Company's claims. Molesworth and another factor each promised such a list but never delivered. Knight concluded from this failure to produce itemized accounts "that it is not the planters but the factors' favourites who are the debtors." Moreover, Knight claimed that planters lost the money they did pay for enslaved Africans because, being unable to purchase individuals of their own choosing, they bought "refuse negroes of Jews and beggarly sub-brokers" who had acquired sick captives at low prices and resold them, "so that" barely a third "bought by the planter from the Company are now alive."[78]

Although Knight acknowledged that the greatest beneficiaries of the practices he described were "favorites" or employees of the Dutch company, he opposed Castillo as well. He complained that Porcio's asiento had paid bribes in 1684 and 1685 to Governor Molesworth, to the captains of the frigates used for convoys, and to Royal African Company factors to purchase their favoritism. Thomas Lynch, governor before Molesworth, had voided Charles II's assurance that Africans be delivered to Jamaica at no more than £17/head, and thereby had "ruined" several planters, forcing them to leave the island. Knight begged for renewal of Charles's "order that we may be provided with good negroes at reasonable rates," asking the king to consider how much he would have received by customs duties if planters had been able to purchase viable slaves, given that one third of the net proceeds of Jamaican produce went into the Royal Exchequer.[79] Thus the dispute between merchants and planters in Jamaica was also a debate over the place of international commerce. Was the Royal African Company obligated first to English buyers, or could it sell across international borders to the highest payer with the best form of ready cash?[80] That battle included a debate over the place of foreign merchants (including Catholics and Jews) in the island.

In 1689, at the start of the War of the Grand Alliance (and as London officials debated who should replace Albemarle as the new Jamaica governor), Castillo submitted a remarkable petition to the English Lords of Trade and Plantations. Although Castillo was in London at the time and could have delivered the petition himself, the Royal African Company submitted it for him, with their own endorsement attached. In the petition, Castillo requested numerous safeguards to protect his continued use of Port Royal as a base for transshipping enslaved people to the Spanish Caribbean. He stressed that the concessions he requested would help "settl[e] that Trade in his Ma[jes]ty's Dominions" and let him fulfill the contract he had made with the Royal African Company. Castillo framed his project as one designed to benefit England. He emphasized Jamaica's location within William's "Dominions," reminding the king that the Dutch and increasingly the French stood poised to corner Spanish American markets should William refuse to give asiento traders the encouragement they sought.[81]

Much of what Santiago del Castillo asked for in his petition merely confirmed long-standing practice. But given the repercussions of the Coymans-Porcio contest in Spain and the difficulties Castillo had experienced under Governor Albemarle, it probably seemed wise to verify the new English administration's continued support for the asiento. The start of a new war, with Spain and England as military allies, provided an opening to secure official approval.[82] Perhaps the changing political context encouraged merchants' optimism that Caribbean practice might become imperial policy.

Castillo began by asking explicitly for approval of the asiento trade, requesting permission to buy captive Africans from the Royal African Company or "other his Ma[jes]ty's Subjects" in order to export them, and also permission to import into Jamaica money, bullion, jewels, or other commodities of the Spanish West Indies without paying more duties than existing law already required. Although this request would merely formalize existing practice, it challenged the Royal African Company's legal monopoly on importing slaves into English colonies. He also requested liberty to purchase provisions, ship furnishings, and other supplies for the asiento's vessels or employees, and permission to unload and reload cargoes if ships needed to careen for repairs, normally violations of the Navigation Acts' prohibitions against foreign shipping in English ports. Castillo also requested protections for the asiento so its merchandise would not be liable to seizure if its officers or seamen privately smuggled goods.

Castillo's final request was for "free exercise of his Religion in his owne House," as long as he did not include William III's subjects "contrary to Law." Sensitive to English anti-Catholic fears in the wake of James II's reign, Castillo departed from his earlier boasts to Madrid of spreading Catholicism in English Jamaica. Instead, he seemed to accept that religious bodies should remain separate from (yet align with) national identity. In referring explicitly to English law as "law," Castillo advertised his understanding that in all cases without specific dispensation, he would be subject to the jurisdiction of Jamaica's and England's laws and officials.

Perhaps that assurance was meant to persuade London officials to consider Castillo's most remarkable request. While allowing that the laws of England should apply to any legal disputes involving the asiento's debts contracted in English dominions, he asked that when any other differences arose involving "Spaniards or other Forreigners" employed by the asiento, the English governor of the colony where the offense occurred should judge the case, acting as a "Judge Conservator according to the way of Spaine." Thus, asiento employees would not have to appear before an English jury or local judge but would rather seek justice from the governor.[83] In fact, he was requesting that the English official in an English colony use Spanish legal process to try cases involving Spanish subjects. Using such a process in Jamaica would amplify Castillo's voice. While he might or might not have exercised influence over a local jury or an admiralty judge, he certainly could secure audience with anyone likely to be appointed governor in Albemarle's wake.

In endorsing the petition, the Royal African Company emphasized that Castillo intended "to make his cheife settlement" at Jamaica and had agreed to purchase "a Considerable Quantity of slaves" from the company. Company officials argued that Castillo's residence in Jamaica would be "of great advantage" not just to the company but also to Jamaicans who would likely be paid in specie for provisioning the ships' crewmembers and the captive men, women, and children who awaited transshipment. On these grounds, the company proposed that the new king issue "instructions . . . to the several Governors of the English Plantations" to abide by the specifications Castillo had outlined.[84]

Castillo's petition set off a debate about the relationship between the asiento and the Navigation Acts, generating opinions from five administrative bodies: the Lords of Trade and Plantations, the Attorney and Solicitor General, the King in Council, the Commissioners of Customs, and the Lords of the Treasury.[85] Some of the opinions were predictable: the Attorney and Solicitor General rejected Castillo's proposal that a special (Spanish) process govern asiento employees. Instead, they stated, the "laws and customs of the place must be observed." Legal procedure attached to place (in this case English colonies), rather than following mobile people (the Spanish merchants and mariners who traveled to those colonies). However, they anticipated "due regard" for Carlos II's orders and for his subjects' contracts. They affirmed the right to "private exercise of religion," allowing Castillo to maintain his chapel.[86]

Surprisingly, given how long English merchants had been working to gain a greater share of the asiento, the Attorney and Solicitor General objected to the use of Port Royal or any other English port as conduit for an Anglo-Spanish asiento. They stated bluntly that "Negroes are merchandise" and therefore could "no more be exported under the Act than other goods." This interpretation may have reflected their sympathy for the Jamaica planters who resented having to compete against the reexport trade. In contrast, the Customs Commissioners were ready to change English regulatory law in order to encourage profitable human trafficking. They suggested that "the prohibition of alien ships, crews and factors to trade in British countries be dispensed with" so that "a Spanish factor" could do business "in Jamaica as requested." To the Customs Commissioners, Jamaica's central place in the Caribbean's international slave trade warranted repeal of the Navigation Acts.[87]

In early November 1689, the Lords of Trade and Plantations laid the petition and all the reports before William III, who forwarded it all yet again, this time to the Judges of the Kings Bench. They repeated the Attorney and Solicitor General's opinion that "Negroes are merchandise" and that therefore giving liberty to "any Alien, not made Denizen, to Trade in Jamaica" or other English colonies violated the Navigation Acts. They ignored the Customs Commissioners' support for doing away with the Navigation Act. Neither aliens nor their ships could legally trade in English colonies, nor could aliens "export thence Negroes" or even "provisions for shipping."[88] This opinion demanded that foreigners acquire denizenship in the place they wished to trade, as Castillo had done in Jamaica.[89] But he could only have used his own or English ships, with majority English crews, which would have rendered his trade illegal in Spanish American ports.

At this point, the Spanish ambassador Pedro de Ronquillo pointed out that while London officials debated, valuable trade opportunities were lost. Castillo was ready to start for Jamaica; Ronquillo hoped that until the issue was settled, the king might in the meantime "at least . . . permit the practice which has already existed more than twenty years to continue" and instruct Jamaica and other governors "not to trouble" Castillo or "his dependents in the execution of" the buying and selling of human beings that was "their duty."[90]

William III granted the ambassador's request, instructing the new Jamaica governor to "receive protect and Countenance" all ships and merchants "employ'd for buying of Negroes" for the asiento, and to encourage the commerce in African people "in all due and fitting manner." The king noted that Nicolas Porcio held the asiento from "our Good Brother the Catholick King," and that Porcio's "chief agent Sr James Del Castillo" had contracted with the English Royal African Company (made up of "our subjects") and with other English merchants to supply "all or majority of Negroes for that purpose."[91] He accepted the argument Castillo and the Royal African Company had offered over those of the Jamaica planters: trading captive Africans to Spanish American buyers benefited England and its American colonies. Despite the legal consensus that the asiento and the Navigation Acts were legally incompatible, William's instructions left no room for doubt: slave trading was too valuable to jeopardize.

The king also signaled Castillo's value to England by knighting the Spanish merchant: the man who had appeared in English and Spanish documents up to this point as Don Santiago del Castillo became "S[i]r James" in this letter. In subsequent English correspondence he further Anglicized his name to Sir James Castile.[92] That transition addressed an important realization that had become clear in all the legal debates surrounding Castillo's petition. If both Spanish and English empires were to maintain protective commercial legislation, keeping foreign merchants and shipping out of their ports, interimperial trade like the asiento could not proceed unless there were people who could claim inclusion in two or more empires. While the Customs Commissioners' recommendations made clear that doing away with regulatory protections had become thinkable (following decades of Caribbean practice), most imperial officials were not ready to endorse open trade. More commonly, they issued special licenses, using the crown prerogative to grant limited exclusions, as Carlos II had done to grant the asiento to the heretic Coymans, and as William now did for Castillo. William's decision to knight Castillo provided a means of circumventing the Navigation Acts in order to support the growth of the international slave trade and the Royal African Company. At this moment, when England and Spain were entering a war against France, and French Caribbean traders threatened English merchants' Spanish American markets, Castillo's proven abilities as a Caribbean negotiator promised extra value.[93]

CHAPTER 6

"The Trading World"

In 1695, twenty-one men incorporated themselves into the Company of Scotland Trading to Africa and the Indies, a joint-stock company intended to provide markets for Scottish merchants and manufacturers. Although Scots could reside and own property in English colonies, England's Navigation Acts prohibited them from trading with English colonies, and the East India Company and Royal African Company monopolies excluded them from commerce in much of the rest of the world.

As the company's name suggests, the Scottish Parliament's act approving the company did not specify an intent to establish a colony in Panama, as they eventually would do, or even in the western hemisphere. Rather, the act chartering the company, which William III's chancellor of Scotland approved without the king's knowledge, permitted the Company of Scotland to trade anywhere in the world "not being at War with His Majesty" and to plant colonies, towns, or forts anywhere in Asia, Africa, or America "not possest by any European Soveraign, Potentate, Prince, or State," so long as the place was uninhabited or "the Natives and Inhabitants thereof" gave the Company of Scotland consent to settle.[1]

The act specified that Scottish law ("the Laws of this Kingdom") would govern the company, but it acknowledged that treaty law determined the international context within which the company could trade or colonize. Because William III, like his predecessors, acted in the international arena as king of Great Britain (rather than separating his kingdoms as he did when acting domestically), the 1670 Treaty of Madrid, establishing peace between Charles II and Carlos II in the Americas, applied to Scots as it did to Englishmen. Article 2 of that treaty declared "that there be a Universal Peace ... in America, as in the other parts of the World, between the most Serene Kings of Great Britain and Spain, their Heirs and Successors ... and between

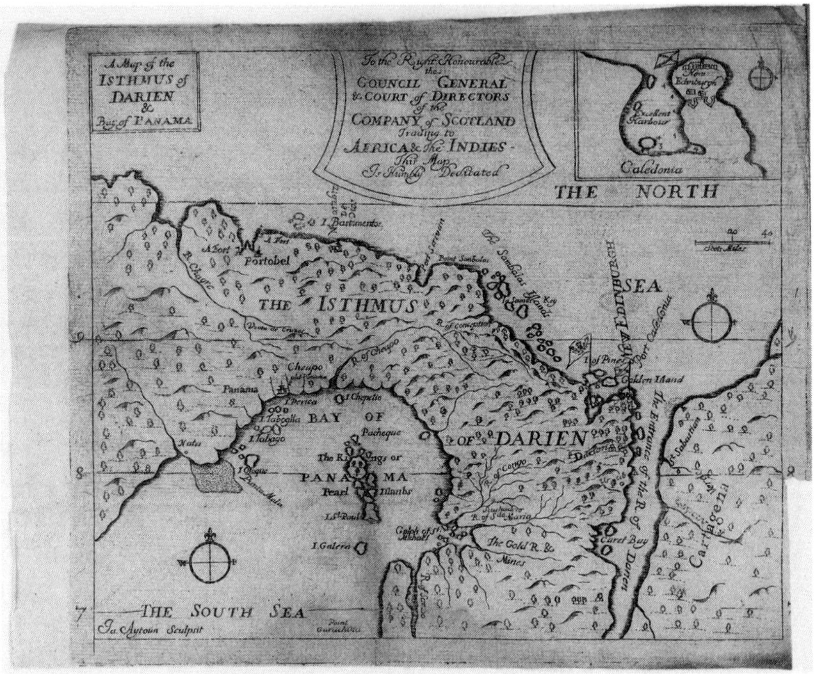

Map 6. *A Map of the Isthmus of Darien & Bay of Panama*. By Ja. Aytoun, 1699. Courtesy of the John Carter Brown Library.

the People and Inhabitants under their respective Obedience." The phrase encompassing all the people under the two crowns' obedience was more expansive than "subjects," which does not appear in this article but does occur in another section of the treaty stating that "the Subjects of the King of Great Britain shall not Sail unto and Trade in the Havens and Places which the Catholick King holdeth in the said Indies," much less try to colonize them.[2]

Nonetheless, in October 1697 the Company of Scotland's directors chose to invest most of the company's capital to establish a colony named New Caledonia at Darién, on the Caribbean coast of the Isthmus of Panama. Darién lay between the Spanish ports of Cartagena and Portobelo, where Peru's treasure crossed the isthmus from Panama City on the Pacific for loading onto Spanish ships at Portobelo on the Caribbean coast. It was situated in territory Spain had long claimed and other Europeans had long recognized as Spanish. In choosing Darién, the Company of Scotland's directors broke their own Act of Incorporation and violated the Treaty of Madrid.

The Company of Scotland planned to establish New Caledonia as a free port, open to all merchants and shipping regardless of political allegiance or religious affiliation. According to their far-fetched promotions (based on the vision of the merchant and banker William Paterson), doing so would usher in an extraordinary expansion of commerce that could benefit the entire "trading world."[3] The Isthmus of Panama was the ideal place for such a port because there, merchants could tap into the riches of American mines by meeting Spanish colonists' unmet demand for textiles and enslaved laborers.

The Isthmus of Panama, as the "most convenient" location "for an Emporium or seat of trade," would promote "considerable Improve[ment] . . . in trade and navigation," especially in the transatlantic slave trade. When "the merchants of all nations" brought "their negroes to this setlment," they could "expect a certaine m[a]rk[e]t," from "the planters of the place or from the one or the other sea." They could avoid the frequent delays that killed "vast numbers" of enslaved people and that "has allwayse been an almost insuportable discouragm[en]t to that trade." Even if a delay did occur between the arrival of captives and their purchase, the merchants who brought them could "in the mean while imploy them to advantage in the country, where there need never want worke, untill" the captive people could "be disposed of to satisfaction." The sure market and available employment would "at once ease the merchants of these great expenses and uncertaintys they now are lyable unto."[4]

The Company of Scotland's plan to engage in human trafficking underscores that when the Scottish planners anticipated worldwide benefit from opening the isthmus to free trade, they envisioned a limited community of trading nations. Far from including all trading peoples, their world included only those polities whose merchants engaged in long-distance maritime shipping, increasingly with naval protection. Indeed, the opportunities were greatest for those who made other people into merchandise. But in predicting the project would bestow universal benefit, the Scottish company's founders evoked a global commercial society that foreshadowed more formal articulations of international commercial and legal community in the next century, one that went well beyond excluding multitudes of people from membership in this community of "all nations." Their project rested on the commodification of the excluded.

Nonetheless, Paterson and the company stressed that their colony's triumph would stem from its offers of radical economic and political freedoms. Those freedoms would draw immigrants from nearby Caribbean colonies, who would ensure the settlement's success. The English "would Incline thither to the freedom of the government and trade," and French planters, "in as great slavery, as those of the English or other nations," and "as sensible of their conditions as any," would readily depart their own colonies for "a better place as this will be." France would be left with "but few subjects" in its own Caribbean colonies. New Caledonia would not be "a prostitute to tyrany and oppresion like the rest of the Indies," but "a free port and a free government for the people of all nations," at least all nations trading in human captives.[5]

Answering the potential objection that "all Europe" would oppose their plans for "a free government and port in the Indies; and would joyntly endeavour to root it out," company directors acknowledged that while it would indeed be "terrible to have all Europe that never yet agreed in any thing else to joyne against us," such an outcome was unlikely because the inclusivity of their project would win such wide support. If the "designe were a meer scotts collony exclusive of all others like those of others nations," then the fear might be justified. But people were tired of the "tyraneys and exclusive setlemts [of] the Spanyards English and others in America." A free port could survive because it was "desired by all."[6] In planning to establish New Caledonia as a free port, open to all interested merchants, company directors endorsed Paterson's advice that they "make no distinction of Parties . . . but that of whatever Nation or Religion a man might be (if one of us) he ought to be looked upon to be of the same Interest and Inclination."[7] Membership in the company (making a merchant "one of us") would supersede national or religious identity.[8]

The Scots' relations with the Indigenous people of Darién were more complicated than their proposed commodification of Africans. To legitimize their colonization project, company defenders portrayed the Tule as a self-governing people who qualified as "the Natives and Inhabitants thereof," whose consent would enable the Company of Scotland to settle legally in the area. But they did not imagine them as equals or as people who might shape a shared society, even though in reality the Tule possessed considerable power over the Scottish outpost. As had some of the 1680–1682 Coxon/Sharpe privateers, the Scots defended their right to settle in Darién by insisting that Indigenous Tule "Supreame Leaders," rather than the Spanish crown, were sovereign in the region and had invited the Scots to settle.[9]

Because the Isthmus of Panama was a nexus for merchandise from Europe, Asia, Africa, and America, it had long drawn various actors to the international western Caribbean. New arrivals and individuals born in the region tested the limits of European empire and the definitions of subject identity. New Caledonia was no exception. In establishing the colony, the company rejected British regulatory policies that reserved the commercial benefits of empire for only one of the kingdoms—England—that composed Great Britain. William III and his English Caribbean officials, unsurprisingly, sought to remove New Caledonia. But the structure of his composite monarchy hampered their efforts, because the English governors of his English colonies had uncertain jurisdiction over the Scottish company. The realization that their hands were tied pushed England to co-opt Scots into Britain more fully: Scots could share in commercial empire but would lose much of their independence.[10]

As Ignacio Gallup-Diaz has shown, the Indigenous Tule living in Darién had already developed a strategic response to living in a place that drew so much attention. They—as individuals and villages but not as a unified polity—used the comings and goings of various Europeans to confirm the space as their own, controlling the terms of engagement with all intruders, including the Spanish.[11] After the 1680 Tule-buccaneer alliance against Spanish Panama discussed in Chapter 2, Spanish and Tule leaders reaffirmed their earlier policies for dealing with one another. Spanish officials tried to enforce the long-standing ban on Spanish colonists in Darién, a policy meant to restrict the colonial presence in the region to friars, who would use religious instruction and gift giving to secure conversion to Catholicism and submission to Spanish sovereignty.

For their part, some Tule people continued to accept gifts and sometimes evangelizing, agreeing in exchange to participate in baptism and oath-taking ceremonies, which the Spanish regarded as signs of permanent loyalty. Sometimes Tule people agreed to *reducción*: resettlement into new towns that, while Indigenous, were colonial. The Indigenous rulers of those towns held precarious authority contingent on both the cooperation of those they led and the approval of Spanish officials. Once such "reductions" had occurred, Spanish officials regarded the Tule as Christians obligated to orthodoxy and as vassals owing perpetual loyalty to the crown. They were to help repel any invaders, as the Tule had done during Juan Pérez de Guzmán's unsuccessful defense of the isthmus against Henry Morgan in 1670–1671. Like Indigenous polities elsewhere in the Atlantic world, the Tule did not believe one-time ceremonies signified perpetual allegiance. Rather, they saw their relationship with Spanish colonizers as requiring continual maintenance with repeated gift giving. Not only would diplomacy be ongoing, but alliance would not, in Tule eyes, necessarily preclude similar relationships with other peoples.

Indeed, many Tule saw the presence of Spain's European rivals, who brought their own gifts and trade items, as opportunity rather than threat.[12]

English, French, and Dutch traders (some of them merchants from nearby colonies and some of them pirates seeking markets for their pillage) brought goods into Darién just as the Spanish did. Tule who took oaths of loyalty to the Spanish crown and then also entered into agreements with other Europeans expressed surprise (perhaps disingenuous) when Spanish officials objected. Spanish officials grew frustrated and considered abandoning their offers of goods to the Tule; but ultimately, needing Tule defense forces, they redoubled their efforts to secure Indigenous loyalty in the Darién region and the isthmus as a whole. In part, they did so by ramping up efforts to Christianize them.[13] Although they had misgivings about this course of action, the Spanish thus reaffirmed a vision of colonization that rested on Indigenous inclusion within the body politic on the basis of shared Christianity, though only some of the Indigenous peoples of the region accepted that vision. Those who did included the residents of Chepo. Spanish officials increasingly depended for the region's defense on Chepo and Palenque. Chepo was a "reduced" Tule town, and Palenque was, as its name indicates, a nearby town of free people of African descent.[14]

Colonists and soldiers from the Company of Scotland Trading to Africa and the Indies arrived at Darién to establish New Caledonia in 1698, just after the Treaty of Ryswick, as English, French, Dutch, and Portuguese merchants and officials jockeyed for Spanish American favor throughout the Caribbean. As a result of that international competition to bring enslaved people and textiles into the region, the Scots faced opposition not just from Spain but from an international conglomeration of officials and merchants. Those Europeans, each hoping to win the prize of the asiento for themselves, rejected the Company of Scotland's plan to establish a free port between the Atlantic and Pacific that would welcome merchants of all religious affiliations, national identities, and imperial loyalties. New Caledonia's location at a crucial global shipping passage ensured the international opposition that led to the colony's downfall: the Spanish would quash the colony in 1700, with English complicity and French offers of aid.[15]

Although Tule opposition, a Spanish policy of limiting colonial settlement, and Darién's disease-promoting climate had prevented a significant Spanish presence in Darién, Spanish officials in the Caribbean and in Europe called the Scottish colony an invasion; Carlos II possessed sovereignty over the region and the Tule were among his vassals. English opponents of New

Caledonia, fearing the settlement would disrupt Anglo-Spanish trade, made similar legal arguments: the Scottish colony had violated the Spanish King's sovereignty and therefore British king William III should disallow it. They knew that the Spanish would blame William and likely inflict reprisal on his English subjects in the Caribbean. No matter how internally divided or contentious was a composite monarchy, when one of its nations transgressed treaty agreements it could bring interimperial repercussions down on the rest. Moreover, the French positioned themselves to obtain the asiento, then under the Portuguese Cacheu Company but contracted out to English and Dutch traders. So London officials had to respond to the Company of Scotland within the context of Spanish objections, in part because Spanish anger over New Caledonia threatened English merchants' access to Spanish American silver through the slave and cloth trades. Appeasing the Spanish was even more crucial on the eve of the Spanish king Carlos II's much anticipated death, amid fears that the increasingly powerful French would designate the new Spanish monarch and thereby gain the asiento.

As was the case for other joint-stock corporations, the Company of Scotland's charter granted it powers associated with sovereign polities.[16] It could defend its settlements and trading posts, "make Reprisals," "seek and take Reparation of Damnage done by Sea or by Land," and "make and conclude Treaties of Peace and Commerce with the Soveraigns, Princes, Estates, Rulers, Governours, or Proprietors" anywhere outside Europe.[17] It could purchase or negotiate any "Rights, Liberties, Priviledges, Exemptions, and other Grants" that would benefit its trade, from any foreign princes at peace with William III. The "General Treaties of Peace and Commerce" between William and other sovereigns would provide the company both "Security" and "Authority" to negotiate with them.

By granting such broad authority to conduct international diplomacy in Asia, Africa, and the Americas, Scotland's Parliament and William III's Scottish chancellor delegated to the company sovereignty over Scottish affairs and over William's Scottish subjects in much of the world. The company would possess "Free and Absolute Right and Property" over both its colonies and their products. It would owe only one hogshead tobacco per year as a token duty to the crown, as "Acknowledgment of their Alledgiance," but could determine and exact its own duties and customs on its colonists and on merchants, to be used for public projects. The company would also possess "Right of Government and Admiralty" rather than being subject to other Admiralty courts.[18] William's ultimate authority surfaced when it could benefit the company, however: if anyone seized the company's ships, goods, or people, "His Majesty promises to Interpose His Authority" in order to help the company gain "Restitution, Reparation and Satisfaction" for any damages.[19] In reality, William, angry that such promises were made in his name, would not intervene as the charter stipulated.[20]

While holding a monopoly on global trade by Scots, the company directors also made shares and licenses readily available to foreigners, as they pursued their plan that New Caledonia would operate as a free port and attract merchants from all over the "trading world."[21] The company's sovereignty over Scots who traveled beyond Europe helps explain how it could seek monopoly status, on the one hand, and favor free or more open trade, on the other. While one scholar has called the Company of Scotland a "state within a state," it was perhaps more accurately a "state outside a state."[22] The crown held clear sovereignty over Scots within Britain, and the company possessed jurisdiction and practical sovereignty over Scots (and its other shareholders) abroad. The company enforced Scottish law, could tax its colony's inhabitants, and through its monopoly over Scots' trade, possessed authority to police William's Scottish subjects' economic activity outside Europe. This arrangement did not necessarily contradict the Act of Incorporation's recognition that the company was bound by William's treaties. But, as was the case with other corporate sovereignties, the arrangement invited conflict by establishing multiple British interpreters of treaty law in arenas beyond the practical reach of William's immediate authority.

The act passed on to the corporation the ability to confer political belonging and opened a route for foreigners to acquire British subject identity that would then hold within the kingdoms as well as outside it. The act exhibited the same linguistic vagueness that characterized naturalization and denization in Jamaica and elsewhere in the British Atlantic. All who invested in the company, whether Scots or not, would become "free Denizons of this Kingdom."[23] It then more expansively specified that those who "shall settle to Inhabit, or be born" in the company's colonies or factories, and even foreign shareholders, would become "Natives of this Kingdom [Scotland] and have the Priviledges thereof."[24] Residence, birth, and even investment conferred membership in the body politic.[25] The company could thus grant membership in the Scottish kingdom to non-Scots who then possessed the rights and responsibilities of William III's subjects as they went out into the world to interact with foreigners.[26] The Company of Scotland, like Jamaican officials, used naturalization language that granted more thoroughgoing conveyance of political and economic rights than English naturalization law technically allowed.

In its initial public offering, the company made 49 percent of shares available to non-Scots and actively pursued investment outside Scotland, making its first efforts to raise capital in London in November 1695. The East India Company, Royal African Company, and Levant Company monopolies and London's sugar merchants protested vigorously, insisting that the privileges granted the Company of Scotland would ruin English trade. English shareholders in the Scottish company would be able to trade legally from Scotland, including to Asia, and the East India Company regarded these English investors as interlopers.[27]

In November 1695, the East India Company announced that if any of its own shareholders had also subscribed for shares in the Company of Scotland, the East India Company considered them to have broken their oaths and acted against the East India Company's interest. Framing the issue as one of loyalty was in keeping with both companies' semi-sovereignty: purchasing membership in these companies could confer political belonging and entry into foreign markets by way of company officers' overseas negotiations and treaties. In exchange, members owed a loyalty that was likewise modeled on that which subjects owed to polities. England's Parliament agreed that William should disallow the Company of Scotland and argued that by threatening English merchants' trade, the Scottish company would hurt England as a whole.[28]

The attacks from the East India Company elicited equally vociferous defenses. Company of Scotland shareholder Roderick MacKenzie published a pamphlet just three days later arguing that Scotland lagged far enough behind England in world trade to justify the privileges. Furthermore, the "New Scotch-English, or English-Scotch Indian Company" would benefit English consumers by bringing down prices on imports from Asia. But the crux of MacKenzie's defense was his argument that Scots and Englishmen were too similar to occupy such unequal places within an expanding commercial world. The opportunities presented by companies and colonies should be British, not English. The Company of Scotland should "bury in oblivion the distinguishing Names of Scotch and English," ushering in a unification that "Nature seems to have intended" by placing the English and Scots within the same "Liquid Walls." They were "the Subjects of one King" who shared language and religion and whose "Lawes point at the same End, to distribute Justice, and defend Liberty and Property."[29] MacKenzie thus suggested union, although as justification for a Scottish company distinct from existing English trading companies.

Despite East India Company objections, the London directors of the Company of Scotland took an oath of allegiance to the company and established committees to investigate sending ships to the East Indies. In response, in 1696 the East India Company insisted to the House of Commons that when the Company of Scotland administered an oath of loyalty to itself within the borders of England, it overstepped its jurisdiction and challenged English sovereignty. The Scottish company's London directors had therefore committed high crimes and misdemeanors by "administering and taking an oath de fideli in England" and by raising money in England.[30]

English investigations into the Company of Scotland, at the urging of the East India Company, illustrate three points. First, they confirm what the Scots expected, that English politicians and English merchants with monopoly privileges wished to preserve a composite monarchy that excluded Scots from profitable trade with the rest of the world. However expansively William III might figure as a British monarch in foreign treaties, his colonial empire (as the Navigation Acts had specified) was to remain English. Moreover, the East India Company's complaints asserted that England's Parliament and the merchants who lobbied it should dictate the terms under which Scotland could create its own colonies or trading companies. When their common sovereign and his Scottish Parliament negotiated with one another about issues beyond Scotland's borders, they should do so under English oversight.

Second, English elites opposed the weakening of Anglo-Scottish economic borders that the Company of Scotland envisioned when it tried to attract shareholders in London. The East India Company's accusation that such weakening constituted high crimes and misdemeanors posited maintaining financial boundaries between the two kingdoms as a crucial part of political loyalty and identity.[31] Finally, the breadth and vigor of the opposition—not only from the East India Company but also from the Royal African Company—suggests that London monopoly merchants were both uncertain where the Scottish company would focus its settlement efforts, and unwilling to see them settle anywhere.

Although English corporations such as the East India Company and the Royal African Company possessed sovereign powers similar to those granted in the Company of Scotland charter, William III balked when he realized exactly what his Scottish chancellor Tweeddale had approved in his name. One Scottish official warned Tweeddale that the act "does vex and perplex the King more th[a]n can be Immagined" because it granted "powers priviledges and soveraignties" that challenged William's authority as "King of Scotland." The king dismissed Tweeddale from his post but did not revoke the act, and the company turned from London to Scotland to raise capital. Scots responded with enormous enthusiasm, reflecting both a nationalist response to English obstruction and their hopes of reaping fantastic returns. Between February and August 1696, the company raised pledges totaling £400,000, an amount that represented at least four times Scotland's annual government revenue.[32] Scottish investors opened their pockets not yet knowing that the company's directors were narrowing their focus to Darién. Their optimism rested on a more general sense that expanding trade opportunities throughout the world promised great financial returns.

In July 1696, during the midst of the subscription drive in Scotland, company directors began considering Darién as a focus of operations, though they tried to keep their deliberations secret. That month, William Paterson proposed to his fellow company directors "several designs and schemes of trade and Discovery" including "places of trade and settlement." The directors agreed to keep Paterson's plans under consideration, and ordered him to write them down and seal them, to be opened only by special order.[33]

Paterson had begun promoting a colony at Darién in the 1680s, trying unsuccessfully to raise capital in Amsterdam, Hamburg, and Berlin.[34] In 1688 he and three other merchants sought funding from the elector of Brandenburg.[35] Paterson's long-standing desire to establish a colony or trading post at Darién stemmed from his argument that open global commerce offered the miraculous promise of alleviating poverty throughout "the trading world." Paterson was the source of the Company of Scotland's decision to allow any merchants or colonists to trade or settle in New Caledonia. He believed it "manifest that trade is capable of increasing trade, and money of begetting money to the end of the world."[36] The Isthmus of Panama presented the greatest opportunity for "trade to increase trade" because it linked the Atlantic and Pacific. Opening that link to all interested traders, rather than restricting it to the merchants of one company, nation, or empire, would best connect all the worlds' markets so that "the trading world shall need no more to want work for their hands, but will rather want hands for their work." What he left unsaid was that as unemployment disappeared among commercial nations, the "hands" who would do all the labor would belong to men and women stolen, enslaved, and forced to work for the benefit of trading nations and their subjects.

Paterson and other promoters were correct in predicting that eighteenth-century commercial expansion would improve Europeans' material standard of living. They failed to predict the suffering, among Europeans as well as among Africans and Indigenous Americans, that would accompany the production and distribution of new consumer goods, a failure perhaps consistent with their uncertainty about *how* trade created wealth. A "Poem upon the Undertaking of the Royal Company of Scotland" reveals the haziness of their notion that open trade would create widespread prosperity out of thin air:

> Freedom draws such, and where there's many found,
> It is most certain, Riches will abound.
> One hundred such, ten thousand do imploy,
> Who find their *Wealth* increase, but know not *Why*

The author, who knew that the Company of Scotland's plan focused on Darién, reiterated that unfettered commerce would provide ample employment and plenty for all.[37]

A 1696 promotional pamphlet likewise revealed both confidence in and wonder at the promises of global commerce: "there is such a Mystery in Trade, that Trade createth Trade, and one Trade createth another, and encreaseth another."[38] That was why Paterson saw the isthmus, along with Havana, where ships assembled before crossing the Atlantic for Europe, as the "doors of the seas and the keys of the universe."[39] The metaphors of door and key that he used were not original. But Paterson expanded on the imagery when he called Panama and Havana the keys not only to the oceans, the Indies, or the world, but even to the universe, emphasizing the cosmic power he saw in global trade. It could lift onto a new plane that part of humanity that could claim membership in the trading world.

Paterson believed the Scottish colony would make the world more just and humane as well as more wealthy. He argued that controlling the isthmus would allow the Scots to "give laws to both oceans, and to become the arbitrators of the commercial world."[40] The most straightforward interpretation of the impulse to "give laws" is that it signaled a desire to exert power, and indeed the goals seem consistent with contemporaneous imaginings that an absolute monarch might conquer the world. But in the context of Paterson's essay, "to give" is also consistent with the bestowal of a gift. The economic hegemony afforded by a Darién-based colony would allow the company to rule the world peacefully, "without . . . contracting the guilt and blood of Alexander and Caesar."[41] Britons very much believed in the superiority of their own laws "to distribute Justice, and defend Liberty and Property," as Roderick MacKenzie's 1695 pamphlet had emphasized.[42]

Paterson's fantasy of wealth without "guilt and blood" ignored the violence of the transatlantic slave trade that underpinned his plans.[43] Company discussions of potential settlement locations repeatedly mention the desire to find a place that would allow them to sell enslaved Africans to various European colonists, including Spaniards.[44] When he proposed global commerce as a cure for poverty, Paterson thus excluded African laborers from the beneficiaries. Rather, they figured in his equation as nearly invisible producers of trade goods ("the labouring man in America"), and as merchandise themselves.[45] His views epitomized a British ability to envision colonization as universally beneficial because they presumed a "universe" that did not include people who were commodities rather than commodifiers.

The 1697 "Poem Upon the Undertaking of the Royal Company of Scotland" unapologetically linked the creation of wealth via free trade with the enslavement and forced labor of African captives:

This Company designs a Colony.
To which all Mankind may resort
And find quick Justice in an open Port.
To that the weary Labourer may go,
And gain an easie Wealth in doing so.
Small Use of tiresome Labour wil be there,
That Clyme richly rewards a little Care,
There every Man may choose a pleasant Seat,
Which *poor Men* will make Rich, & *Rich Men* Great.
Black Slaves like bussie Bees will plant them Canes
Have Juice more sweet then honey in their *Veins*
Which boil'd to Sugar, brings in constant gains
. . .
Ships thence encrease to fetch these Goods away,
For which the Stock will ready Money pay.
By Manufactures here the Poor will live,
So they that go and they that stay will thrive.[46]

Enslaved Africans were not among the "every Man" who could "choose" a place from which to "live" and "thrive." Rather, they were "bussie Bees," outside of the body politic and indeed outside of "all Mankind."

Wooed with such promises of easy living, public opinion in Scotland endorsed the loosening of trade restrictions. One ballad wishing "Courage to the Scotch-Indian Company . . . To fetch Home INDIAN Treasures" bore the title "Trade's Release."[47] Cries to "release" trade from imperial strictures no doubt reflected some Scots' nationalist desire to enter expanding global commerce, or their personal resentment against their individual exclusion. But they used the language of free trade, articulating a principled commitment to a political economy that they could claim to support as a universal good.[48]

According to Walter Herries, a surgeon who traveled to the colony and afterward became a critic of the project and an informant for Spain, Paterson drew inspiration from the pirates Henry Morgan, William Dampier, and Lionel Wafer when he made his case that interimperial boundaries should not constrain trade. Herries thus discredited Paterson's and the company's design for open trade by associating it with pirates who had likewise rejected the claims of empire. According to Herries, pirates had also provided Paterson with evidence that Darién was the best place to begin opening such trade.[49] Whether or not such accusations were true, the Company of Scotland's challenge to Spanish sovereignty and its opposition to imperially bounded trade tarred it with the same brush as piracy in the eyes of England's political and mercantile establishment and others such as Herries, who rejected Paterson's utopian globalization vision.

When, in late 1697, company directors agreed to pursue Paterson's plans for Darién, they anticipated legal challenges and dealt with them in two ways. First, they tried to keep the location of their intended settlement secret (from King William, the Scottish Parliament, their own stockholders, and even from the voyage's seamen and colonists) as long as possible. Clearly they realized that they planned to violate their own charter, Spanish sovereignty, and Anglo-Spanish treaty law. Their second strategy, employed after the voyage's location became public, was to advance natural law arguments by securing the welcome of the Tule, who, they argued, had never submitted to the Spanish and were therefore just the sort of "Natives or Inhabitants" who could, under their charter, grant the company permission to settle in a place "not possest by any European Sovereign."[50] By denying Spanish sovereignty over Darién, they implicitly rejected treaty law (one basis of the developing law of nations) in favor of natural law (a very different theoretical basis for a law of nations). In doing so, they, like the pirates before them, took advantage of Indigenous resistance to Spanish sovereignty and strategically made a principle of it.[51]

As early as the previous spring, some English officials had known that the Company of Scotland was considering Darién, and they acted on their knowledge before the company directors had even arrived at their final decision the following September.[52] In July, the Board of Trade examined former pirates William Dampier and Lionel Wafer regarding the company's designs.[53] The same month, a Spanish resident in Hamburg wrote to the Spanish crown about Scottish plans for Darién.[54] In September, the Board of Trade recommended that England send an expedition from London or Jamaica to possess Darién for England and preempt the Scottish company. Accordingly, on December 5, 1697, London officials dispatched Captain Richard Long from London to Darién.[55] Long's departure suggests that in 1697, London officials were determined to prevent an independent Scottish toehold in global trade, even at risk of angering the Spanish.

In July 1698, five ships containing twelve hundred people and numerous trade goods left Edinburgh for Darién.[56] Although numerous English and Spanish government officials knew of the colony's location, many shareholders and even many of those who sailed on the venture did not. At least one ensign later claimed that when the ships left Edinburgh on July 14, 1698, he thought he was going to Africa.[57] Company directors apparently did not realize that English officials knew their plans. On August 29, 1698, "the Committie of Secreets" in Scotland sent a letter to the council in New Caledonia reporting that after the fleet had sailed, the company's Council General in Scotland had "in a very dutyful manner acquainted the King with . . . the place of your setlement."[58] Knowing that as subjects of William III they had violated both British treaty law and a Spanish claim to sovereignty that was widely acknowledged among Europeans, company leaders decided it safer to ask forgiveness (or plead ignorance) after the fact than to ask permission (or even inform their sovereign) beforehand.

After divulging New Caledonia's location to William III, the Committee of Secrets believed that they had "reason to hope; and doe believe that his Ma[jes]tie will give us and you his gracious Countenance and Royall protection." These hopes seem audacious, given the company's violation of its own Act of Incorporation specifying that it settle only in places not possessed by any European sovereign, and its underhanded failure to disclose its plans earlier. Nonetheless, the committee also anticipated that the "Government of England" would help maintain New Caledonia "against ye attempts of any forraign Enemies," reporting news from Cádiz that Spain was preparing to send a force of one thousand men, to be joined by as many recruits as they could get in the Indies "to make head ag[ain]st you." After a decade of military alliance and immediately after the Treaty of Ryswick reconfirmed British-Spanish peace, company officials turned the Spanish into "forraign enemies" in 1698. What's more, in predicting English aid they presumed that Britishness should prevail over national (Scottish or English) allegiance.[59]

For its first voyage the company had purchased textiles and shoes, among the items most frequently smuggled from England via Jamaica to Spanish America, in line with the directors' intent to engage in "smuggling and sloop trade" with Spain's colonial and Indigenous subjects. To a colony of 1,200 men and women, the Company sent 2,347 pairs of men's shoes, 603 pairs of women's shoes and 553 pairs of pumps, along with 6,802 combs and 52,848 buttons.[60] While not specified in the inventory, one observer noted an abundance of "Spanish Bobs" among the periwigs in the cargo.[61] They also took iron goods to exchange for captives in Guinea, though they never made a voyage to Africa.[62]

When the Scots arrived in Panama, they courted the local Tule before trying to trade with Spaniards because legally they needed the local "consent" that their charter required of them. Andreas—perhaps the same man who had engaged Coxon and his men sixteen years earlier—"promised to defend the Scots to the last drop of blood." In February 1699 the colony's local directors signed a more formal treaty of "Friendship, Union, and Perpetual Confederation" with the "Excellent Diego . . . Chief and Supreame Leader of the Indians Inhabitants of the lands and possessions in and about . . . Dariéno." The treaty allowed for other Tule leaders to join.[63] New Caledonia thus reflected the limits of both William III's and Carlos II's sovereignties. Because William III's English empire excluded his Scottish subjects, they sought their own empire, expressing their limited allegiance to their sovereign by breaking his treaty laws. Likewise, Tule alliances with Scots reflected Tule people's belief that they remained free to act independently of Spain. In both cases, imperial sovereigns' policies failed to compel obedience from those they claimed as subjects.[64]

The Scottish colony provoked near panic among Jamaican slave traders and smugglers; one Jamaican at the start of 1699 reported that the Scottish settlement was "the only news and discourse in these parts."[65] The English in the region disabused the Scots of their expectation of English aid. Instead, Jamaica governor William Beeston swiftly reached out to the Spanish in hopes of keeping the Scottish settlement from damaging Jamaica's asiento trade. In late December, just weeks after the Scots' landfall, he wrote to the governors of Cuba and Cartagena, stressing that the Scots were not English and that their colony should not affect Anglo-Spanish relations. He insisted "that although the Scottish nation recognized the King of England as its lord, it is nevertheless a nation distinct from the English and the English are in no wise accomplices in this design, or a party to the scheme of the Scots, or in correspondence with them; nor shall the Scots receive any aid from me." He pointed out that he had heard nothing from London officials about the project, suggesting its illicit nature.[66]

Suspecting that Spanish officials nonetheless viewed the Scottish settlement as an *English* challenge to their sovereignty, Beeston begged the governor of Cartagena "not [to] attribute culpability to my nationals," pressing the Spanish official to accept the domestically meaningful distinctions between Scottish and English on the interimperial stage as well. With considerable hyperbole, he pointed to "the amity and good relations which have always prevailed between the crowns of Spain and England" and expressed hope that the friendship "may continue in the future, which relations I assure your lordsh[i]p shall with due care be maintained on my side." Beeston asked his counterpart to share the information with "his Catholic majesty's other governors."[67]

Unpersuaded, Spanish officials filed Beeston's letter with a reference to "His Britannic Majesty" that implicitly lumped together Scots and English as British. Despite Beeston's protestations, they saw the Scots as rogue British subjects whom English officials in the region ought to have kept within the law. Their view, and not Beeston's, was in keeping with treaty law. Richard Long, the English captain sent to preempt the Scottish settlement, told the Scots that the Spanish were planning to attack them. Long, who at that point was spying on the Scots for England, said he had established an English claim to the Gulf of Urubá for the "English crown," but there is no other evidence that he did so or that Spanish officials or English Jamaicans (both of whom would have objected) suspected him of doing so.[68] Moreover, in 1698 William III's printers reissued the 1670 Treaty of Madrid, removing any excuse for his subjects to claim ignorance of its terms.[69] Whether responding to the Spanish ambassador's complaints, the Board of Trade's concerns, or the Royal African Company's objections, London officials (despite their earlier instructions to Long) now prioritized preserving peace with Spain in the western Caribbean.

Just as Jamaicans feared, Spanish officials captured Scottish and English vessels alike as reprisal for the colony. When the Company of Scotland's *Dolphin* hit rocks en route to Curaçao to trade with the Dutch, it sought relief in Cartagena. But Spanish officials seized the ship and its goods and imprisoned its crew.[70] Cartagena officials also detained three colonial vessels (one from Jamaica and two from New York) as well as two English ships that carried human captives for the asiento, in retaliation for the Scottish colony. The master of a New York vessel that had escaped seizure reported that "the Spaniards told them they took them because there was war with the English."[71] Even if Cartagena officials understood that the Scottish settlement did not represent an English act of war, they believed that William's closest agent in the region—the governor of Jamaica—must possess the authority to control his sovereign's subjects, whatever their nationality. The fact that the Scottish company also signified a challenge to English claims of sovereignty over Scottish economic activity mattered little to Spanish American officials. They believed they understood composite monarchies, and they held local "British" officials responsible for the invasion.[72]

The Company of Scotland's decision to invade Darién thus interrupted the legal human trafficking of English and Spanish asiento merchants and the extralegal trade that the seized New York and Jamaican vessels carried on with Spanish American merchants and consumers. While Cartagena officials frequently overlooked or took part in contraband trade, they also understood that both contraband and the asiento mattered to Jamaica's economy, to New York's, to the Royal African Company's, and to England's.[73] Because they also certainly understood Scotland's weakness relative to England, they knew that capturing English merchant shipping gave Spanish officials a powerful bargaining tool to oppose New Caledonia. The Royal African Company had been correct that the Scottish company would hinder its trade though not, as they had anticipated, via competition in West Africa, but rather by undermining the reexport of newly arrived African captives from Jamaica to Spanish American ports.[74]

Cartagena officials hoped to hold the captured ships for ransom to demand that the English in the Caribbean exert appropriate control over William's Scottish subjects and quash their Darién invasion. In Governor Beeston's view, Spanish American officials could legitimately expect such policing from English officials in the Caribbean. Moreover, they could afford to make such demands in a competitive situation where French and Dutch merchants offered Spanish Americans alternatives to English trade. The Scottish invasion gave Spanish and English Caribbean merchants, as well as Spanish officials in Europe, cause to doubt London's support for Anglo-Spanish Caribbean peace and trade.

In February 1699 Beeston predicted that Spanish naval ships would continue to capture all the English ships they could "on account of the Scotch settling in Darien." Frustrated, he blamed the Scots for the Spanish attacks but complained, too, that English merchant ships were an unfair target.[75] When Admiral John Benbow sailed his English naval squadron into Portobelo to retrieve English prizes, Dionisio de Artunduaga, commander of the Spanish fleet there, suspected him instead of planning conquest in league with the Scots. Beeston lectured Artunduaga on the relationship between sovereigns and their subjects who ventured beyond the sovereign's borders: "Princes," he explained, "keep ships and Forces to preserve their Honor and their Subjects Welfare." Benbow was performing William's duty to his subjects in demanding the return of seized English ships. The Spanish had taken the English prizes on the pretext that they carried Spanish money. But that situation was unavoidable because it was the legal payment that English merchants "receive from you for Negroes and Provisions," a trade undertaken "by order from his Catholick Majesty, or by his Licence at Least."[76] What neither man knew was that Benbow carried private instructions from William III directing him to ensure New Caledonia's defeat.[77]

Governor Beeston, though he had stressed Anglo-Scottish separation to Spanish American governors, contemplated an explicit assertion of English jurisdiction over the Company of Scotland. In April he informed the Board of Trade that he had "published a proclamation forbidding any Trade or Correspondency in any kind with the Scotch at Darien." Beeston noted that the Scots had begun to run out of provisions and other supplies, and he thought that many of them would leave voluntarily if he could receive permission to send a ship to bring them to Jamaica. That, he suggested, would prevent them from "go[ing] amongst the French or Dutch where they will be lost to His Majesty or his service."

The threat of losing Scottish colonists loomed large at a time when the impending Spanish succession crisis threatened to plunge the region back into war. Beeston did not anticipate that the Scots would exhibit any particular allegiance to the English over the French or Dutch. Indeed, their venture constituted an explicit protest against an English empire that had made them unequal subjects, in an international Caribbean that offered alternatives. Because colonial officials worried about the dangers inherent in the plantation political economies they were creating and competed to attract White settlers, individual Scots could entertain multiple options when the Spanish drove them out of Panama. But Beeston also recognized the Scots as William's subjects, whose defection to another sovereign's dominions would weaken the body politic of his monarchy. The Jamaican governor believed that in a world on the eve of war and in a colony desiring White inhabitants, it would "be much better" if they came to Jamaica "to strengthen this country."[78] The potential loss of Spanish trade led Beeston to conclude the need for a more uniform British sovereignty, in which all of William's subjects would be equally subject to the same hierarchy of authority wherever in the world they traveled, settling questions of belonging brought on by individuals' commercial goals.

At the same time, English American officials elsewhere wondered whether Scots in English colonies, as subjects of the British monarch but living under explicitly English legal jurisdiction, possessed equal *political* rights, though they were, under the Navigation Acts, denied equal economic rights. In the midst of the Darién crisis, in 1698, the governors of both Virginia and Barbados wrote to the Board of Trade asking whether Scots could serve as Assembly members in English colonies. The Board of Trade met these queries with uncertainty, appealing to the Attorney and Solicitor General, who concluded that Scots "being in law natural-born subjects of England" were indeed qualified to hold office under the new Act for Preventing Frauds and Regulating Abuses in the Plantation Trade.[79] A decade before the 1707 Act of Union, then, events in America spurred reconsideration of the nature of Britain's composite monarchy.

However, far from governing all Britons in the western Caribbean, Beeston could not even keep Jamaicans out of Darién. While Governor Beeston saw the Scots at New Caledonia as "a nation distinct," harming English interests in the region, some English merchant ship captains saw opportunity in trading with the Scots. In early 1699 the Jamaica merchants John Sadler and Jacob Mears, on advice from Joseph Cohen D'Asevedo, drew up detailed plans to trade enslaved Africans to Spanish America through New Caledonia, unsuccessfully approaching James Castile/Santiago del Castillo for help. The Assembly discovered their plans and shut them down. However, despite their "endeavouring to subvert and turn the current of the trade of this island" and their "contempt of his majesty's authority and government," they were merely fined and released.[80]

In London, Spain's new ambassador the Marqués de Canales, perhaps having gotten wind of Joseph Cohen D'Asevedo's involvement, expressed particular concern about the role Jews played in the project. Their presence, he stressed to his king, gave New Caledonia "the aspect of Conquest." This was not only because they brought necessary capital to the project, but Jews were "altogether unchecked by Law, Divine or human."[81] In contrast to William Paterson, who categorized people as outside law on the basis of their failure to engage in long-distance trade, Canales excluded those who were not Christian.

English merchants and captains in the region pursued a variety of commercial interests that did not align neatly to suggest a single English foreign policy for the Caribbean. While some lost their cargoes and found themselves imprisoned in Cartagena in reprisal for New Caledonia, others succeeded in trading with the Scottish invaders there. When the Scots learned that Cartagena officials had detained their councilor Captain Robert Pinkerton as a pirate, there happened to be "2 Jamaica Sloups (then in the Harbour)," despite Beeston's orders to stay away. The Scottish colony commissioned the Jamaican sloop captains to sail for Cartagena to demand the return of Pinkerton and his men. If their negotiations failed, the company authorized the two captains to attack Spanish shipping or settlement in retaliation. Endorsing English pirates' practice of seizing Spanish American people of color as plunder, the Articles of Agreement between the Council of New Caledonia and the English captain specified their expectation that resulting pillage might include "slaves."[82]

Several other English North American governors shared Beeston's concern that the Scottish invasion would damage English trade. New York governor Richard Coote, Earl of Bellomont, reported in 1699 that the Spanish had taken twenty-four ships of logwood cutters "belonging to this and the other colonies" in the Bay of Campeche. Rumor had it that "the Spaniards are provoked . . . by the Scotch late settlement on Golden Island near Darien."[83] English logwood cutters once again found themselves tools for Spanish officials hoping to compel English cooperation to oust the Scots from Darién.

As Beeston and Bellomont discussed the Caribbean's shifting political economy, they commiserated about the difficulties of trading with Spanish America. The two English governors noted the specific end-of-the-century geopolitical context that encouraged Spanish Caribbean officials to favor French trade. An interimperial Caribbean awash in rival traders gave Spanish merchants and officials the freedom to vent their outrage at Scottish invaders or English-born pirates by turning to French suppliers and by enacting revenge on English traders. In June 1699 Beeston promised Bellomont that he would forward a letter from the New York governor to Saint-Domingue governor Jean-Baptiste du Casse. Beeston cautioned, however, that few ships sailed from Jamaica to Saint-Domingue, because since the Peace of Ryswick, the French had forbidden trade with all but the Spaniards "whom they are much in love with, supposing them and their country to be their own as soon as the King of Spain dies." Beeston fumed that even after the previous decade of Anglo-Spanish alliance against the French, the Spanish seemed just "as fond of" the French and admitted them into their ports to trade, and Beeston complained that the Spanish showed a complete lack of gratitude to "the English, who have been so long fighting for them and spending their blood and treasure to defend them." Instead of responding with the favored trade status he believed the Spanish owed the English, the Spanish "refuse[d] all civility and common respect, and call 'em ill names."[84]

Beeston attributed the new Spanish "love" of the French entirely to "the Scotch . . . settled at Darien." The governor may or may not have known that du Casse and other French officials in the region were trying to exploit Spanish anger at New Caledonia and had approached the governors of Cartagena and Portobelo with offers to help rout the Scots.[85] But he definitely understood the wider context: French merchants and officials courted Spanish Americans, and Beeston blamed the Darién colony for what he characterized as Spanish officials' incorrect interpretation of Anglo-Scottish relations. The Spanish refused to believe the Company of Scotland had proceeded without William III's "consent or connivance," even though Beeston had written to "all the Governors" and had sent them duplicates of his proclamation forbidding Jamaicans from going near the Scots, trading with them, or sending them provisions. Beeston also linked the Franco-Spanish affinity to their shared Catholicism, suggesting that French Caribbean merchants and officials had "gotten such an interest in them by reason of their Churchmen and religion." Once they had the Spanish officials' ear, the French convinced them that the English and Scots were "all one people" and that English avowals of Scots' independent action were "a blind."[86]

Beeston's opinions about the Scottish colony contained a contradiction. On the one hand, he objected to the idea that the English and Scots were "all one people," but on the other hand, he pushed for permission to "fetch" them. If he, as an English governor of an English colony, exercised their mutual sovereign's authority over Scottish colonists living under a Scottish charter, his actions would have suggested the convergence of English and Scottish people into "one people."[87] Such a convergence would mirror the treaty language that Spanish officials employed in referencing *Gran Bretaña* rather than *Inglaterra* in their disputes with Jamaica governors. Scholars have argued that Darién paved the way for the 1707 Act of Union, which made Scots full participants in an empire that thereafter was British. They point to the enormous loss of Scottish capital in the venture, which lowered Scots' patriotic resistance to integration when London offered remuneration, and to Scots' realization that their options on the world stage were limited.[88] But the Company of Scotland's short-lived venture also clarified the risks for England of continuing to refuse Scots admittance into empire. Scottish efforts to create their own empire threatened to thwart English commercial diplomacy in the interimperial Caribbean and perhaps also globally, in part because Spaniards, themselves members of a composite monarchy, rejected English Caribbean efforts to deny affiliation with or responsibility for their fellow Britons.

Even though pirates were multinational bands who resorted to French, Dutch, and Danish jurisdictions as well as to English, Jamaica governor Beeston and New York governor Bellomont saw them as problematic in many of the same ways that the Company of Scotland was problematic. Both groups were composed of insubordinate subjects who impeded English merchants' trade. The governors discussed the two populations in the same letters as they tried to coordinate their anti-piracy efforts. Turn-of-the-century colonial and metropolitan English officials worried about how to rid the Caribbean (and the globe) of pirates and how to subordinate Scots to England's commercial empire.[89] Both efforts were part of English attempts to outcompete their French rivals for Spanish American trade. While Beeston and Bellomont envisioned increased interimperial trade and decreased religious barriers to commerce, their vision did not permit unbridled international competition or a free port like that the Company of Scotland planned for Darién. Rather, they hoped to gain access to Spanish markets and bullion at the expense of the French and Dutch (though perhaps in cooperation with the Portuguese), through controlled, legalized commerce modeled on an expanded license system like the asiento.[90]

New Jersey governor Jeremiah Basse went even further in linking Caribbean Scots and pirates. Not only did the two groups pose similar threats to English economic interests and imperial goals, they were in fact tied to one another: he had gotten the East Jersey Assembly to pass the Jamaica Act for Restraining and Punishing Privateers and Pirates, as the Board of Trade had ordered, even though the act met fierce opposition from "the Scotch gentlemen" in East Jersey. He found himself "discouraged in my zeal for the common good and H[is] M[ajesty's] service" because even his supporters faulted him for his "discountenancing the Scotch and pirates." Basse believed that the East Jersey Scots drew their confidence to resist the Jamaica Act from news of New Caledonia and from rumors (true) that the new governor of East and West New Jersey would be a Scot. Some of the Scottish merchants in the Jerseys and Pennsylvania had "publicly asserted" that William III "dare not interrupt them in their settlement of Golden Island [New Caledonia], lest it should make a breach between the two nations" of England and Scotland. If they were correct that their king worried that Darién would provoke Anglo-Scottish conflict, the Pennsylvania and Jersey merchants discounted his unease at a possible breach with Spain. Given William's overriding concern to stem French expansion, the specter of Franco-Spanish alliance overshadowed a potential Anglo-Scottish rupture.[91]

According to Governor Basse, the Scots in East Jersey openly corresponded with the Darién settlement, contrary to royal orders, and even encouraged North American colonists to trade and settle there. Basse cautioned that "if some speedy course be not taken for the stopping of their growth," "the English trade must fall . . . and that of the Scotch nation" advance. The only remedy was "a total exclusion of [Scots] from any share in the Government of these Plantations."[92] Basse thus rejected the Attorney and Solicitor General's year-old ruling that Scots could serve as officials in English colonies. He argued that Scots' "prosperity," the result of control over trade in the Jerseys and Pennsylvania, "cannot but extremely prejudice the general interest of our own nation."

Basse even foresaw North American Scots' "subjection to their so much applauded Caledonia," rather than to England. In this period of potentially massive geopolitical upheaval surrounding Spanish succession and before the Act of Union, Basse imagined a Scottish settlement on the Isthmus of Panama that could grow to such importance that Scots throughout the Atlantic would become subjects of New Caledonia rather than of Great Britain or even of Scotland. He voiced the fears of others, that Darién's location "may in time collect to it the riches of the Eastern and Western Indi[e]s, the one safely transported through the famous South Seas over the Isthmust [*sic*] of Darien and the other from the two adjoining Empires of Peru and Mexico."[93] Like Beeston, he believed that leaving Panama under the control of the Spanish better served English interests than allowing Scots to gain it.

Under pressure from Ambassador Canales and from English merchants, crown officials in London, like colonial administrators in the Americas, objected to the Company of Scotland's Darién colony as an affront to both

English and Spanish sovereignty. In the spring of 1699 London officials had ordered its American governors to publicly forbid all trade or correspondence with the Scots at Darién, as Beeston had already done. Canales told William III that Spain regarded the Scottish incursion "a rupture of the alliance between the two Crowns."[94] Concern spread that English merchants were on the verge of losing what Spanish American trade they still had. Josiah Heathcote wrote from Portobelo in October 1699, reporting changes in Spanish attitudes and behavior. He warned that despite Jamaica merchants' efforts to maintain their trade with the Spanish, it "decays every day" because "the French Court neglects no occasion to establish the trade in America with the Spaniards."[95]

Supporters of the Company of Scotland wrote numerous pamphlets defending the colony, reiterating arguments that Tule independence provided them legal standing. A "Memorial in defence of the legality of the proceedings of the Scots Company at Darien," probably written in 1699, used Barthlomew Sharpe's 1682 trial for piracy as legal precedent to justify the company's incursion into Darién.[96] The author recalled that Sharpe had successfully defended himself against accusations of "Pyracy and robbery committed upon the Spaniards" with his "Commission from independent native Indians then at war with Spain," but acknowledged that many at the time regarded Sharpe's "defense . . . as a jest." Indeed, Sharpe had intended his courtroom listeners to see a legal claim based on an Indigenous sovereign's commission as so ludicrous that it could only be a joke, and "it was not for that reason he was acquitted."[97]

Nonetheless, the 1699 "Memorial's" author believed that Sharpe's defense served as legal precedent because Sharpe *had* in fact "jointed with the Dariens [and] commit[ed] great acts of hostility & carried away much booty," and he *had* in court offered the "deffense that he acted by a commission from an independent people," and the trial *had* resulted in his being "acquitted by a competent judiciary in England." Even if Sharpe had not meant his defense seriously, a precedent was a precedent: "it must be thought that a decision in the way of Justice was no jest but according to the Law of the Nation."[98] According to that precedent, the Company of Scotland's negotiations with the Tule rendered their colony legal in the interimperial arena. Although Sharpe's trial had taken place in an English court, the Spanish ambassador had brought the case to trial, and the natural law principle that Sharpe had offered transcended English law.

Members of the Board of Trade rejected such defenses and reached conclusions about New Caledonia similar to Jamaica governor Beeston's, but not because they dismissed natural law claims as a "jest." They noted that the Company of Scotland's charter forbade claims to any land possessed by a European prince or state, and they disputed the company's insistence that it had settled in a place under Tule and not Spanish possession. According to the Board of Trade, "the whole weight of the controversy turns upon this." If the Spanish possessed Darién, the Company of Scotland had defied not only their own Parliamentary Act of Incorporation but also Articles 7 and 8 of the 1670 Treaty of Madrid, thereby challenging their own sovereign's authority over them and Spain's sovereignty over its American dominions. While the Scots at Darién may not have fallen under English Jamaica governor Beeston's jurisdiction, they were indeed under British sovereigns' treaties.[99]

The Board of Trade regarded as immaterial whether the Tule had invited the Scots. "Darien Indians" were "a wild sort of people, sub-divided into small clans," in no position to challenge "the supreme sovereign of the whole country, which the Spaniard hath from the first discovery claimed to be."[100] The Board of Trade noted the lack of a Tule prince or emperor who, under European legal theory, could have permitted Scottish settlement or transferred dominion over Darién to the Company of Scotland. The Board of Trade's characterization of the Tule as politically fragmented was more accurate than Sharpe's or the Company of Scotland's, and reflected the London officials' willingness to accept Spanish assessment of Panama's geopolitics. Thus they concluded that the Spanish monarch was sovereign in the region. Rejecting the sovereignty of a "sub-divided" people dovetailed with their own efforts to impose control over Scots and privateers, as they expanded their imperial presence in the region and sought equal footing with Spain in America.

Although the Board of Trade acknowledged that the Spanish themselves "are the best able to prove the validity of their title," it declared itself able "by the printed books of good authority" to document Spanish claims to Darién as long-standing and valid and to identify in detail Spain's jurisdictional borders, dividing the region at the Darién River between the audiencias of Panama and Cartagena. It was not "ignorance of those parts" that had kept other European princes from attempting plantations in the strategically crucial isthmus, but rather the knowledge that "such a thing could not be compassed without an open rupture with Spain." Panama's situation "betwixt the two Empires of Peru and Mexico" and its role as conduit for Peru's treasure ensured "that the Spaniards will unavoidably be ever jealous" of any who entered the "neighbourhood" and threatened to interrupt Spanish monopoly over communication and commerce between the Pacific and the Atlantic—precisely what made the region "key." The Board of Trade thus addressed Scots' natural law claims seriously but found them to rest on suspect pretense. What mattered instead was that the Scots' settlement violated the Treaty of Madrid, which governed British-Spanish relations in the region.

The board expected the Spanish to take "just . . . offence" at the Company of Scotland's attempts to justify their colony. Since no "European Prince or State" had challenged Spanish claims to Panama for nearly two hundred years, why should the Spanish "now of a sudden, after an open invasion, . . . be required to prove their title and possession"? The board tried to envision Spanish officials' perspectives on New Caledonia in order to reach a decision that would reflect and reinforce European consensus on the legitimate bases for sovereignty. Acting in accordance with widely accepted norms was all the more necessary if they hoped to reach a peaceful conclusion despite the lack of a shared legal structure: as they noted, "What tribunal can be erected?"[101] In the absence of interimperial courts, sovereigns who wished to maintain peace with one another had to police their subjects' behavior beyond state borders. Doing so proved especially difficult in a Caribbean region that offered so many opportunities for defection. Moreover, the region's commercial promise as a center of interimperial trade in textiles and enslaved people heightened English incentives to maintain stability by recognizing Spanish claims, especially at a moment when French merchants seemed poised to overtake them.

The board noted Spanish officials' recent objection even to foreign logwood cutters in Campeche as evidence that the Scottish company's claims to legality were especially brazen. In Campeche, a place the board presumed far less important to Spain than Darién, Spanish forces had recently seized and destroyed a settlement of about three hundred English logwood cutters who had been "disavowed by the Government of England," killing many of them on the spot and enchaining the rest to build forts in Mexico. According to the Board of Trade, Spanish officials resorted to such brutality to prevent the English from "habituat[ing]" themselves to the region. Because Darién was "the most sensible and vital part" of Spain's American possessions, the English should expect an even more violent response if the Scottish colony persisted. New Caledonia would "inevitably . . . involve his Majesty in such misunderstandings with Spain as may prove fatal to the peace and good accord betwixt the two Crowns."[102]

Like Beeston, then, the English Board of Trade accepted Spanish claims to the Isthmus of Panama and argued that England must reject the Scottish company's colony in order to promote Anglo-Spanish commerce. Just as England had "disavowed" but did not remove the three hundred English logwood cutters, permitting (and seemingly condoning) brutal Spanish policing, London officials similarly ordered the king's subjects not to help the Scots as they ran short of provisions and began to starve. England did nothing actively to remove them, leaving that task instead to the Spanish, who secured the Company of Scotland's surrender of Darién in 1700.[103]

Thus, in pursuit of the profits of human trafficking and its associated trades, the English, by "disavowal," ceded to their Spanish imperial rivals and trade partners the right to patrol British subjects' illegal behavior. Offering up British subjects to likely violent foreign justice was a price worth paying for continued access to lucrative markets for enslaved people and for textiles. The temptations of the slave trade encouraged legal cooperation and submission to foreign jurisdiction, not just for merchants such as Santiago del Castillo seeking courts to adjudicate commercial disputes, but also for metropolitan officials deciding the fate of rogue subjects. Moreover, the events surrounding Darién convinced many English officials that they must gain jurisdiction over Scots if they were to protect their access to Spanish American silver and expand global trade in the period of shifting power they anticipated would follow Carlos II's death.

Both empires responded to events in Darién with efforts to more fully incorporate people whose endeavors to trade freely and engage in their own diplomacy made them (in the eyes of imperial officials) rebellious subjects or vassals. The Spanish, despite repeated failures to obtain functional rather than theoretical loyalty from Darién's Indigenous inhabitants, nonetheless persisted in their strategy of incorporating the Tule through reduction to an explicitly Catholic political order. In the 1720s, as Tule in the northern Darién began killing priests and desecrating churches, Spanish officials blamed it on their repeated interactions with Protestants. When the Scots and the Tule in Darién challenged the definitions of subjecthood that English and Spanish officials had imposed on them, imperial responses affirmed the differences between the English and Spanish Caribbean worlds.

Spanish officials responded inconsistently to Tule displays of diplomatic independence, fluctuating between what Gallup-Diaz characterizes as a policy of "gradual missionization and diplomatic co-optation" and violence combined with withholding of gifts. But even the violence was expressed as punishment of rebellious vassals—individuals who rejected their inclusion into the Spanish body politic and the loyalty they supposedly owed to it. On the eve of the Scots' arrival, the president of Panama (the conde de Canillas), angry over the murder of three Franciscans, had instructed Luis Carrisoli, the colonial liaison to the Tule, to "give up your blind foolish thought that you have Indian friends" and recognize that the Tule were only attached to the Spanish for the gifts they received. But when he realized the simultaneous threats of New Caledonia and French pirates, he reverted to past Spanish practice and instructed Carrisoli to increase gift giving to any Indians who would "reduce" themselves to existing Indigenous Christian towns. He then backtracked, complaining to the Council of the Indies that while the Spanish spent a lot of money on gifts for Tule people who had "accepted, by their own admission," vassalage to the king, "the truth is that the Indians are only the vassals of the last person to give them gifts."[104]

In 1700, once the Scots were safely dislodged, Canillas granted to Carrisoli lands that would form the center of a new *reducción*, an appointment that also conferred membership in a prestigious military order. The Council of the Indies was concerned about granting a position of such authority to Carrisoli because he was Mestizo. However, deciding that he "was not an Indian through the male line," they approved the appointment. This did not end the conflict between Spanish officials and the Tule but did confirm Spain's dependence on Indigenous vassals, seen in Panama's reliance on Chepo and Palenque during the following decades.[105]

While the Spanish sought to bind Indigenous vassals to Spain with a shared religion, the English strove to bring the Scots to heel (and add valued White subjects in the Caribbean) by offering them greater inclusion in a British colonial and commercial empire. Because the western Caribbean was so central to European economic thinking and geopolitics at the turn of the century, when Scots chose Darién to assert their right to global commerce and establish a free port, they so threatened English plans for commercial expansion that the English response ultimately facilitated unification in 1707. By merging the two kingdoms and fully including Scots in what was now British rather than English empire, they hoped to gain the allegiance of those they sought to control as subjects.[106]

Scots could be folded into English empire, making it British, because the Scottish nation was part of "the trading world," as its Darién propaganda proclaimed. New Caledonia failed. But its promoters' attempt to create a free port at Darién, where merchants from all nations in the trading world would together build a global commercial network with human trafficking at its core, helped assure Scottish merchants their place in Britain's commercial empire. The growing importance of slave trading to Atlantic commerce reified the distinction between a legal community of trading nations, for whom a law of nations required give and take, and the rest of the world, subject even to being traded. British planners intended to "give law" to the rest of the world—trading nations and traded nations alike—and Scottish merchants in the eighteenth century helped create the commercial dominance that would in fact give Britain an outsized influence on global law.

CHAPTER 7

"In the Hands of Creoalians"

For over two decades at the turn of the eighteenth century, war roiled the Atlantic world. In the Caribbean, English, French, and Dutch rivals all sought cooperative commerce with Spanish Americans as the ultimate goal of the War of the Grand Alliance (1688–1697) and the War of the Spanish Succession (1701–1714). At the same time, Europeans in the region shared a commitment to a future dependent on the labor of captive Africans and their descendants. As soldiers, sailors, merchants, and colonial officials fought over markets and maritime power, they bolstered a political economy built on mining, plantation production, and their surrounding trades.

This chapter explores how those military contests—with slave trading as the local spoils—raised questions about commerce and the conduct of war, and about security, loyalty, and belonging. The Caribbean military goals of preserving and increasing interimperial slave trading led English and Dutch officials to dispense with customary restrictions against trading with enemies, and wartime trade disruptions pushed English officials to press for more open foreign trade. In the War of the Spanish Succession, Spanish American elites took sides according to their economic interests; their Spanish, French, English, or Dutch trading partners helped determine their support for Habsburgs or Bourbons. English merchants and colonial administrators observed Spanish Americans' willingness to trade with enemies and built a fantasy Spanish American identity in which Spanish American elites were "naturally" Habsburg, independent of Bourbon Spain, and commercially linked to England. Far into the war, English officials in the Caribbean pursued an economic and geopolitical strategy based on this delusion.[1]

English and Dutch efforts to maintain and expand trade networks in the Spanish Caribbean during both wars made privateering even more problematic than it had been in prior decades. Slave trading had already driven a wedge between interimperial merchants and peacetime privateers (and their respective supporters). But governors still depended on privateers for defense, and during the two wars, privateers repeatedly used their relative independence to pursue their own gain over the goals of their commissioning officers. Colonial officials soon recognized that even wartime privateering threatened the commerce they hoped to secure by the war. By the middle of the War of the Spanish Succession, the problem grew so vexing that Jamaica's governor sought to end English wartime reliance on private men-of-war in the region. When his superiors rejected his suggestion, privateers continued to violate prohibitions against attacking Anglo-Spanish trade, spurning the war's aim of preserving merchant shipping. In their efforts to hold on to familiar models of themselves as imperial agents who could identify enemies and advance their sovereign's interests, privateers instead found themselves labeled pirates and thus outcasts from the body politic, even during wartime.

During both wars, as merchants and officials from multiple empires brought ever more captive laborers into the region, colonial administrators tried to shore up the ranks of loyal subjects who could defend colonial societies against both foreign invaders and captives resisting their enslavement. The English in Jamaica renewed concerted efforts to bolster the population of free White people. They campaigned to attract and naturalize immigrants who fit (or could be made to fit) into the category of White, including European foreigners. They also worked to prevent the loss of White people from the region by opposing the impressment or "defection" of mariners (including privateers) or colonists to other jurisdictions. Jamaican officials expressed growing fear of both the enslaved majority and of Maroons during war years.

Spanish American elites throughout the Caribbean also sought to increase their exploitation of the labor of enslaved Africans during this decade. But the Spanish Atlantic's more expansive concept of the body politic meant that defense needs during the War of the Grand Alliance and the War of the Spanish Succession gave people of color opportunities to assert their rights of belonging. As we have seen, Panama officials repeatedly confirmed their reliance on Indigenous and African-descended soldiers when facing invasions from Scots and multinational pirates as well as two declared wars. During these two decades of war, Cuban officials likewise strove to ensure the allegiance of free Black and Indigenous populations and militias.

The Anglo-Spanish military alliance of the 1690s motivated merchants and officials to figure out how the English and Spanish could share some aspects of Caribbean jurisdiction. These efforts led some (such as Santiago del Castillo) to call for a loosening of English regulatory law, and English officials largely complied. But the very trade that they hoped would improve local relations could stymie would-be alliances. Because joint military efforts provided new cover for the already-flourishing illicit trade, Spanish officials in both the Caribbean and the metropole, despite depending on English military aid against French forces, worried about their allies' encroachments. Spanish American officials, often with good reason, suspected English naval ships of smuggling and refused overtures for military coordination. Spain's Council of the Indies likewise saw the war's potential to provide cover for increased smuggling between allies. In 1694 it expressed concern that English military squadrons would carry clothing to sell to Spanish colonists, and instructed governors to use extra care in protecting their ports from illegal trade.[2]

In 1694, English forces prepared to invade the western parts of Hispaniola to try to expel the French from Petit-Goâve and its surrounds. Spanish imperial officials saw French settlement on the island as an invasion of Spanish dominions (even though many local Spanish colonists were willing to trade with French slave traders ensconced there).[3] The English favored Spanish claims to dominion over the entire island over the claims of their French competitors for the asiento. The English saw protecting Spanish dominions from French conquest as a way to preserve their own trade with Spanish America and prevent French inroads in the region that could put all English shipping at risk. Jamaica governor Beeston worried that the French might take Cartagena in addition to Saint Domingue. If they did, they would have Caribbean possessions on two sides of Jamaica, and "all the Spanish navigation and ours from the Island will be intercepted."[4]

Although English and Spanish governors' efforts at coalescing around their shared military alliance faltered, they did correspond regularly with one another and share strategic knowledge, regularly dispatching "expresses" to one another.[5] In at least one instance, officials in Spain used English shipping to communicate with their own colonial administrators, sending packets to Jamaica for Beeston to forward to Spanish governors and other officers in Cartagena and Portobelo.[6]

Wartime cooperation did not produce mutual respect, however. Indeed, over the course of the two wars, Dutch, English, and French competition for access to Spanish America led English officials and merchants to portray Spanish Americans as pawns who could be manipulated. In 1696, echoing his earlier disdain for clergy as weakening Cartagena, Beeston warned that the

French could easily take that Spanish port (as indeed they did the following year) if they were able to surprise "a people not used to war, who never saw a bomb, and who are mostly made up of churchmen and a few wornout old soldiers."[7] The anti-Catholic stereotypes that the English used to target the Spanish changed as they redirected their fear of tyrannical Catholic power (popery) toward the French. These English portrayals of clergy-centric Spanish colonies as weak, in part because they overvalued religion, tempered contradictory Black Legend image of Spaniards as cruel and inhumane.

As illegal trade increased or became more flagrant during the war, some English colonists resented Jamaica's persistent focus on Spanish American trade, and portrayed Spaniards as unreliable allies. In 1695, for example, the Jamaican George Kast protested to William III that Spanish vessels traded openly in Jamaica and had done so for several years, contrary to the Acts of Navigation and the Treaty of Madrid. If he was aware that William III had just condoned Santiago del Castillo's asiento trading, Kast's petition carried an implicit rebuke of the king's decision. Repeating the earlier objections of the Jamaica Council and Assembly, he complained that the asiento represented an "abuse" of the planters because the factors of the Royal African Company reserved the best Africans for their Spanish customers, leaving "only the refuse, who either died on their hands or were little able to do the work required of them." According to Kast, that trade policy resulted in an underpopulated and underdeveloped Jamaica, keeping potential planters from choosing to settle in Jamaica and denying those who did enough laborers to work their land.[8]

Echoing Jamaica governor Lynch's criticism of the Dutch West India Company's control in Curaçao a dozen years earlier, Kast argued that the Royal African Company had been able to get away with its preferential treatment of Spanish customers because it exercised too much control over "the Court." The planters, "inexperienced men far from home," had little chance of overcoming the company's lobbying. "Now, to the end that the planters may be supplied with negroes," he argued that they should have first choice of Africans brought to Jamaica. But if "the [Navigation] Acts and the Treaty are to be winked at" so that Spanish American merchants could continue coming into Jamaica to buy the Royal African Company's captives, then the company should be required to import enough Africans to meet the demands of both Spanish American and Jamaican slaveholders.[9]

If we can believe Kast, the planters also displayed a rare concern for seamen. They complained that Spaniards, "construing the Treaty strictly, seize and condemn vessels on very slight pretences, and barbarously ill-treat the sailors, so that some die in prison and others are sent to the mines and heard of no more." Kast lumped together two very different groups as "the Spaniards": those who broke the Treaty of Madrid to sail into Port Royal for condoned commerce of enslaved Africans, and those who enforced the treaty too "strictly" and took English prizes. The first sought peace with their English counterparts; the second supported zealous guardacostas who treated English shipping as plunder. Kast, in representing them as united in aiming to harm English interests, refused to acknowledge that Spanish actors in the Caribbean pursued goals as diverse and independent of one another as did he and his English antagonists.[10]

Although slave trading persisted through the war, hostilities did disrupt commerce between English and Spanish merchants and between the English Caribbean and mainland North America. The lack of shipping from the mainland created a shortage of provisions in Jamaica serious enough that Governor Beeston tried to buy food from Santo Domingo and begged relief from the Navigation Acts so that he could purchase provisions from the Dutch at Curaçao. Beeston also worried that the English, by failing to protect Anglo-Spanish trade in the region, had lost the asiento. Nicolas Porcio had died and his contract had expired. As his company remained in arrears (to both the Spanish crown and to Jamaicans), Beeston feared that Spain would reassign the license to a merchant with fewer interests in Jamaica. In June 1696, he requested information from London: "We hear nothing about the Assiento, whether it be again disposed of or to whom, nor have I had . . . a word as to the money due from Porcio to the merchants here." He believed that if Spanish officials harbored good will toward the English, Jamaicans would have received the moneys owed them. The president of Panama could have impounded Porcio's goods for his Jamaican creditors if he had so chosen.[11]

When Governor Beeston lamented that English failure to protect Anglo-Spanish shipping produced Spanish ill will, he pointed out how jurisdictional and administrative conflicts among officials within empires could unravel alliances between those empires. He complained repeatedly that England's naval ships hurt Jamaica more than they helped it. In presenting to his council updated muster rolls indicating a decline of 1,050 men (from 2,440 to 1,390) during ten months in 1695–1696, Beeston blamed "the harassing and ill-using of the men of war, who have frightened away not only our own people but also those of the Northern Colonies from bringing us provisions." He and his council warned that "all our privateers and seamen (who were a great guard and strength to the Island)" "run away as fast as they can" to avoid impressment.[12] The council thought that 1,500 additional men were needed to defend the island against "a foreign enemy [during war] or [to] secure it from a domestic one if the slaves should make any attempt," noting that there were 40,000 people held in bondage on the island. The councilors, like Beeston, could "see no remedy" unless William III entrusted the governor with power to stop naval officers from impressing, "as former Governors have had."

The councilors thus agreed with George Kast that a loss of free men had endangered the island while it was at war and as its enslaved population grew. They disagreed about the cause of the loss; where Beeston and his council saw impressment driving away men and shipping, Kast saw the difficulty purchasing slaves and Spanish guardacostas seizures as the deterrents.[13] The lack of soldiers drove even land-based civilians away: martial law requiring ordinary people to work on defenses instead of working "to earn their bread" spurred them to "retire to the Northern Colonies for greater quiet and ease." Proprietary colonies in particular "entice our people away daily, telling them of living there easy and quiet," and grew rich by entertaining the Red Sea pirates, "by which means they fill, while the King's own Colonies dwindle to nothing." London should send provisions along with soldiers and sailors; merchants could not help provision naval ships because "the Assiento and all other trade being gone, the merchants have little money and I have none." The governor needed more supplies and greater authority over the navy.[14]

Beeston had the ear of powerful lobbyists in London, who pleaded his case in person. The London merchant (and future mayor) Gilbert Heathcote served as Jamaica's paid agent from 1693 to 1704. In 1696, when asked to advise the Lords of Trade on a course of action for Jamaica, Heathcote deferred to Beeston as possessing the "greatest knowledge of affairs in these parts of anyone." Heathcote further argued that ignoring Beeston's longstanding familiarity with the international Caribbean to grant independent authority to naval officers who were newcomers to the region made for bad strategy, especially given the island's dangerous demography. The ships' officers illegally impressed freemen, servants, and debtors from an already underpopulated island that needed to retain "freemen and servants" for its own security against the French and against the laborers whose continued bondage depended on armed White men to police them. "Thus," he wrote, "each man-of-war sent to strengthen the Island renders it weaker." Beeston was powerless to do anything about the situation. Rear Admiral Benbow had set such an example of disrespect for the governor that "even the Captain of a fire-ship" felt free to respond to requests from the governor with "such a hectoring, saucy letter" that a lesser man than Beeston would have "throw[n] up his command."[15]

The impressment continued even after the war ended in 1697. Despite William III's "express commands" to the contrary, confirmed by the Admiralty, Benbow ordered his men in 1699 to press Jamaica inhabitants. Doing so not only frightened away needed seamen but it also upended "all authority," undermining other aspects of Governor Beeston's command. According to Heathcote, fear of impressment—during this period of peace—sent "ordinary people" packing to the Scots at Darién "or any place else where they think they can be easy, so that it seems to me this island can never be well settled."[16] An island "unsettled" by "ordinary people" invited foreign attacks and slave uprisings and threatened England's competitive advantage over France in supplying slaves and manufactured goods to Spanish American ports.

When the war ended in 1697, the Board of Trade sent copies of the Treaty of Ryswick to all English colonial governors, who were to familiarize themselves with it.[17] The treaty affirmed Anglo-Spanish peace as it also ended both empires' hostilities with France. Even so, rumors circulated among both English and Spanish officials in the Caribbean of new Anglo-Spanish enmity and of renewed enforcement of trade laws. Many in (and interested in) the Caribbean expected a short-lived peace. The Anglo-French struggle for Spanish American trade created much of the context in which Carlos II's death would precipitate the Spanish succession crisis. Caribbean officials anticipated the Spanish king's death and understood that it would reshuffle the asiento, and so competition for Spanish American favor in the region perpetuated Anglo-French enmity over more peaceful rivalry, despite Ryswick. This competition between English and French merchants was a clear source of tension in the Caribbean late in the War of the Grand Alliance. It would become an explicit source of conflict at the start of the eighteenth century.

As formal hostilities ended, Governor Beeston feared that Jamaica merchants would lose out to their French rivals if imperial officials failed to promote the island's commercial potential. He stressed how important it was at that crucial juncture to maintain lenient trade policies, and he reminded his superiors of Jamaica's central position relative to Spanish America. When royal instructions ordered adherence to the acts prohibiting trade with foreigners, Beeston defended the practice instead. While he had followed orders and done all he could to prevent smuggling, "the want of necessary supplies and the scarcity and dearness of all things" during the war had led Jamaicans to buy from "the foreign importers of necessaries." Such traders were, in any case, impossible to stop given "the size of the island and the number of harbours and rivers for landing." He believed "nothing is so ruinous to the settlement of these Colonies as these [Navigation] Acts," because Jamaica did not receive sufficient supplies from England nor enough shipping to export Jamaica's produce. Without the commercial outlet provided by foreign shipping, "the people" lost the fruits of their labor and investment, and the king lost his customs. He estimated that without the Navigation Acts, Jamaica "would be settled and peopled" with no charge to the king, and customs would triple. English manufacturers would gain profits, and "many thousands of pounds of gold and silver" would flow into England. But if the laws were enforced, "these islands will dwindle to nothing."

England could ill afford to lose Jamaica, as its location made it "capable of anything for war or trade." Indeed, its location relative to the Spanish port cities meant that (echoing William Paterson's language) Jamaica could "easily be made to give laws to the Spanish West Indies."[18] Beeston knew that Spanish colonists would continue to depend on international trade. If the English did not act, they would lose their chance to profit from it. Instead, France would gain economic and diplomatic power in the region. While Beeston exaggerated Spanish American weakness, he perceived a truth: long-term Spanish reliance on foreigners to provide enslaved laborers, European manufactured goods, and military protection had rendered Spanish officials less able to dictate the terms of engagement than they had been a decade earlier. He also predicted another reality, that dominance in interimperial trade would increase legal influence as well. While England would not directly "give law" to Spanish Americans, England and France eroded Spanish protective regulations during the first two decades of the eighteenth century. Great Britain wielded its commercial dominance to shape the law of nations, which would become increasingly meaningful over the next century.

The English and Spanish distrusted one another and vied for the upper hand in their dealings with one another. Spanish officials continued to seize contraband traders and put them to hard labor as they had for decades, regarding the entire Caribbean as their own jurisdiction. In 1699, Gilbert Heathcote's brother complained from Jamaica that Spanish officials and the asiento factor in Cartagena robbed English ships trading Africans at the Spanish American port, and predicted that two English ships then sailing from Cartagena to Vera Cruz would "meet with the same civilities" there.

"The Spaniards are, in all things where they have the advantage and power, very rude to us." Far from envisioning the kind of joint efforts that Castillo had tried to foster, Heathcote felt it a "pity" the English were not free "to make them sensible of their indignities." While he wanted to profit from selling more Africans to Spanish Americans, he resented the need for local cooperation and shared jurisdiction. Rather, he conceived a commercial relationship in which the English dictated the terms and enforced them by violence if necessary.

In his calls to violence, he did not suggest a return to an Elizabethan or Cromwellian conquest mindset or to the forced trade engaged in by some privateers. Rather, he presumed an English superiority that conferred the rights to determine proper behavior and discipline transgressors. He noted that Rear Admiral Benbow was accompanying several merchants to Cartagena in an attempt to regain some English vessels taken "without any reason" and to free hostage English traders and imprisoned seamen who suffered abuse. Heathcote wanted permission to retaliate rather than "tamely be obliged to suffer their insults."

He also complained that Spanish Americans engaged in unfair trade practices: Cartagena merchants had paid an English shipmaster about £250 for a cargo of eleven Africans, then turned around and sold them for over £400, behavior Heathcote blamed on the "impudence" and "roguery" of Cartagena officials, who paid their king's duties only on the £250 recorded payment to the English slave trader. Heathcote grudgingly admired their ability to cheat their king ("it's pretty") but wanted it "laid before their Ambassador," railing against Spanish merchants who succeeded in buying low and selling high—behaving as though they operated in an unregulated market.[19] It was perhaps an ironic position for an independent slave trader who had opposed his own crown's historical support for the Royal African Company monopoly.[20] Less attached to specific economic principle than to increased profits, Heathcote wanted London and Madrid to enforce rules for international trade in the western Caribbean that would benefit English slave traders. If Spanish American buyers were willing to pay £36 for one enslaved person, Heathcote wanted regulation in place to ensure the English sellers would receive more than £22.

At the turn of the eighteenth century, the Caribbean was in a state of upheaval that derived from many sources. The asiento's future was uncertain. The Peace of Ryswick released seamen into the region to seek employment, which some of them found in piracy, logwood cutting, and illegal enslavement of

Indigenous peoples.[21] The Royal African Company's 1698 loss of its monopoly further rearranged merchants' commercial connections. Merchants throughout the Atlantic eyed the slave trade to Spanish America. Some targeted the Isthmus of Panama, the main transit route linking the Caribbean (the entry point of enslaved Africans) to Andean sources of silver. The Company of Scotland invaded Panama. And everyone knew that the king of Spain was about to die without heir.

Shortly before Carlos II's death in 1700, he and his advisors named as his successor the Duke of Anjou, grandson of the French king Louis XIV. After almost two centuries of Habsburg monarchs, a Bourbon would rule Spain, as Felipe V of Spain. The following year, in a move consistent with the new Franco-Spanish alliance, the new king of Spain awarded the asiento to Jean-Baptiste du Casse, a French naval officer and the governor of Saint Domingue, on behalf of the French Guinea Company. Unlike previous asiento licenses, this one would not be subdivided; the French Guinea Company held a monopoly on trading captive Africans to Spanish America.[22] To check the expansion of French economic and political power, England, the Dutch Republic, and the Holy Roman Empire allied against France in 1701, only ten days after the asiento went to the French Guinea Company.[23] They aimed to put the Habsburg archduke Charles (son of Holy Roman Emperor Leopold I) on the Spanish throne as Carlos III. Spain would then have a sovereign beholden to the English and Dutch and favorable toward their merchants. During the War of the Spanish Succession that followed, Dutch and English merchants continued to smuggle slaves and textiles into Spanish America in exchange for coin and bullion, despite increased risks. Although Spanish American customers may have benefited from fierce competition between European traders, they chose sides in the war depending on who their own trade partners were, rather than explicitly favoring free trade.

Caribbean elites during the first decade of the eighteenth century believed that the region's future rested on the outcome of the War of the Spanish Succession, because that outcome would dictate the contours of commerce in the region and affect access to captive laborers. The Spanish, French, English, and Dutch all understood that the asiento was at stake, and many merchants in the region believed the awarding of that license—to either an English or a French company (which would subsequently either subcontract or monopolize the trade)—would be the most important outcome of the war.[24]

London officials, like their Bourbon counterparts in France and Spain, initially assumed that allegiance forbade trade with enemies. When she

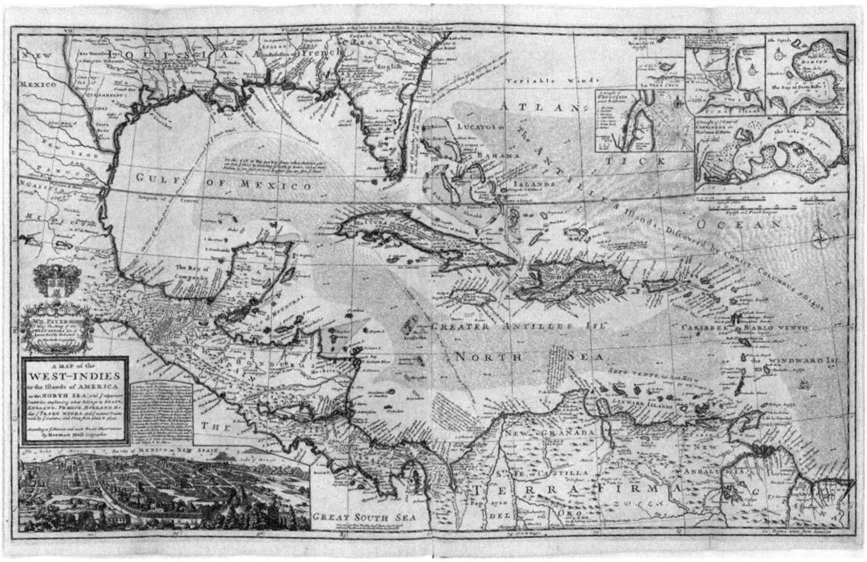

Map 7. *A Map of the West-Indies.* By Herman Moll, [1709]. Moll's map bears striking resemblance to Pierre Mortier's 1708 *Teatre de la Guerre en Amerique.* Both the French and British maps emphasized the economic opportunities provided by accessing Spanish ports and shipping, with insets of the Havana, Portobelo, Vera Cruz, Cartagena, and St. Augustine ports in the upper right, and of Mexico City in the lower left. Dotted lines trace the route of the Spanish fleets, and detailed text notes describe the fleet's behavior. Moll dedicated the map to Darién promoter William Paterson, acknowledging Paterson's role in promoting British designs on the region. I am indebted to Jacob Batts for bringing my attention to Mortier's map. Courtesy of the John Carter Brown Library.

announced her official declaration of war to English American colonists in 1702, Britain's new monarch, Queen Anne, prohibited trade with French or Spanish subjects and authorized governors and naval commanders to issue privateering commissions against French and Spanish shipping and ports. Her subjects' "duty" was to "annoy the subjects of France and Spain."[75] So in May 1702, Vice Admiral Benbow returned to Jamaica, with royal instructions prohibiting commerce with the French or the Spanish and authorizing privateering against both.

The political economy of the Caribbean, however, suggested an alternative formulation of wartime loyalties, initiated by the Dutch. They eschewed customary bans against trade with enemies and instead fostered commerce with Spanish Americans to undercut Spain's alliance with France. English officials and merchants from the Caribbean and from North America, who saw the Dutch as both military allies and commercial rivals, opposed letting them expand their slave trading at English expense. When Benbow arrived in Jamaica, he and the Jamaica lieutenant governor (and Royal African Company factor) Peter Beckford agreed that Benbow should send letters to the governors of Cartagena and Cuba and the viceroy of Mexico, informing them of Anne's alliance with the Habsburg emperor, "hoping 'twill bring them over to the House of Austria, and relinquish that of Bourbon." Benbow noted that if the Spanish officials refused his offer, he would "immediately" follow the royal orders. Benbow and Beckford, who had received royal instructions for war, overrode them to offer local peace first.[26]

Benbow and Beckford hoped that mere news of the English alliance with the Habsburgs would lead Spanish American officials to renounce the Bourbon succession. European notions of sovereignty—as embodied in the person of the monarch—encouraged the belief that a new king or queen required the sovereign's subjects to reaffirm their loyalty. Public celebrations of ascension were meant to create affective bonds toward new rulers, and incumbent officials took new oaths of loyalty on the ascension of a new monarch (even one in the hereditary line of succession), to acknowledge the required shift. If the new monarch represented a new ruling family, the requirements for an intellectual and emotional change in loyalty increased. Benbow posited that Spanish Americans would prefer the continuity of a Habsburg monarchy because he imagined that it would let them hold on to their loyalties and their political identities.[27]

But Benbow also understood that Spanish American officials and merchants would weigh their economic interests and their personal safety in making any public declaration of loyalty. He believed that "the Spaniards in these parts will be soon brought over to the House of Austria and relinquish that of Bourbon" *if* his forces at Jamaica could defeat an expected French fleet and *if* a member of the Austrian family could "be set up . . . in old Spaine." Spanish Americans would face serious repercussions from Bourbon victors for publicly supporting the Habsburgs, so "they will be very cautious to declare without a certainty" of Habsburg ascendancy.[28] Vulnerable Spanish American officials and elites might act less on any deep-seated Habsburg or Bourbon loyalty and more on their best guess at who would win the war.

Jamaica lieutenant governor Beckford also defended his and Benbow's decision to disobey their orders, pointing out to London the advantages of following the Dutch example. Not only would the English gain immediately by preserving their access to Spanish American silver during the war, but they would also help the war effort by keeping that money out of French coffers. Additionally, they would set the stage for what they hoped would be a settled Anglo-Spanish trade as part of the postwar peace. They had work to do, because the French had made significant inroads; they had "prevailed wonderfully with the Spaniard both in amity and trade" for the previous twelve months, and in Spanish port towns had installed "their" officers, who were receiving instructions from the French court rather than from Madrid. He was unsure whether the Spanish cooperated with the French from "Love or Feare." Linking Spanish Americans' commercial behavior ("trade") with their felt relationship ("amity"), Beckford worried about Spanish Americans' feelings toward their French affiliates. If their cooperation with their Bourbon superiors derived from "love," then the English could anticipate much more difficulty in changing their behavior. But if the Spanish obeyed their Bourbon rulers only out of "feare," their loyalties might yet lie with the Habsburgs. Beckford did, however, conjecture that Spanish colonists were "uneasye" with the Bourbon-imposed officers. He consistently identified those officers as "French" as he tried to imagine that Spanish Americans would resent their new superiors as foreign.[29]

Governor Beckford, as a slave trader, worried about Spanish American loyalties because he feared English loss of the slave and cloth trades. But even as he used the language of loyalty, he doubted that merchants would voluntarily limit economic gain for political allegiance. To prevent a French monopoly on the slave trade, the English needed not only to attack French merchant shipping, but also to keep English and French slave traders apart. The French transatlantic slave trade could not meet Spanish American demand unless French traders were "assisted by both English and Dutch." Beckford recognized English merchants' readiness to sell to any buyer, but nonetheless countered that realism by upholding the ideal that a natural and persistent loyalty should prevent trade with the enemy. Perhaps believing that Spaniards possessed stronger scruples or less freedom, Beckford expected them to trade illegally with the English only if the French failed them. If the French, without English or Dutch sources for enslaved Africans, proved "incapable to furnish the quantity contracted for," then their asiento contract would "break" during "the first year," at which point the Spaniards would "be glad" to purchase enslaved Africans directly from English merchants.[30]

Letters arrived in London from elsewhere in the Caribbean and from North America echoing Jamaicans' concerns that the Dutch, in refusing to treat their local Spanish trade partners as enemies, were poised to overtake the English in Spanish American trade.[31] Rather than letting the Dutch lay hold of Spanish American markets, the English should follow their example, keeping their established networks and trying to block out the French. Vice admiralty judge Robert Quary wrote from Philadelphia that the Dutch at Curaçao had recalled all their privateers "and have now a free and open trade with the Spaniards" that exceeded peacetime levels. Anne's subjects chafed at having "their hands tyed up whilst the Dutch engross all the trade."[32] William Penn feared that "because [of] not tradeing with the Spanish dominions as formerly," his colony's trade would dwindle for lack of coin.[33] The Barbados governor added that Curaçao officials required all vessels to "give security not to molest the Spaniards," and instructed them "to traffick with them as formerly." He noted that Curaçao received these orders from the Dutch West India Company, underscoring the policy as one that served mercantile interests.[34]

The Jamaican agent Gilbert Heathcote believed that even if Anne hesitated to publicly condone trade with a declared enemy, the English should "conniv[e] at a Trade betwixt our people at Jamaica and the Spaniards." The commerce was too valuable to neglect: in exchange for "onely wearing apparell and negroes" the English received "nothing but gold and silver." Moreover, the commerce would cultivate good relations and promote the queen's "glorious designe of re[n]ding ye Spanish Monarchy out of ye hands of ye House of Bourbon, without which we are undone." If France got hold of Spain's American silver, it would threaten England and the world with its tyranny. To prevent that outcome, London officials could have the Jamaica governor "wink or looke through his fingers" when merchants brought in silver and "ask noe questions" about the trade.[35] Colonial merchants had traded with enemies during prior wars, when they thought they could get away with it. What was different here were the imperial officials' contortions as they tried to conceive of Spanish Americans not as enemies but as neighbors with whom loyal subjects could openly trade. Heathcote seemed unconcerned that a proposed solution that required Anne's subjects to disobey her orders might weaken their allegiance. If official policy, based on traditional wartime practice, clashed with an imperial interest increasingly understood to align with globalizing trade, Heathcote clearly favored the latter.[36]

After receiving the opinions of Caribbean administrators and merchants, London officials reconsidered both that policy and their assumption that Spanish Americans were by default Felipe's subjects. In 1703, as the Secretary of State prepared to prohibit trade with both the Spanish and French, the Board of Trade interjected, forwarding an anonymous essay laying out all the reasons to allow trade with Spanish America, though they acknowledged that "in time of war" it would be better to carry on such trade "in a private manner."[37]

The Board of Trade also summarized all the advice it had received for the queen: her colonial subjects, "in strict observation" of her declaration of war, had foregone the "correspondence and commerce which they formerly had with the Spanish Nation in America." The Dutch, taking a less traditional view of "their interest," called in their privateers to "ingratiate" themselves with Spanish Americans in the Caribbean and as a result, "enjoy[ed] a free and open trade." Seeing the Dutch prosper tempted Anne's subjects to violate the Navigation Acts and sell their goods to the Dutch and the Danes, who then carried them on not only to the Spanish in the region but also to the French or to Europe. To stop smuggling that ultimately benefited France, the queen should allow her subjects "equal advantage of Trade" with the Spanish and shut down the illegal trade with Curaçao and St. Thomas. She should also prohibit privateering against the Spanish: "long experience" had taught that it "irritat[ed]" the Spanish to the point that they denied trade to English merchants, with no "real advantage" to English interests. Rather, privateering "turn[ed] that trade into the hands of our Neighbours."[38] It had therefore become "more than ever necessary" to recognize "a distinction between the French and Spaniards in America." While both might be declared enemies, "in point of trade" Spanish Americans occupied a different place entirely. They and their trade were the prize to be gained by the war, so treating them as enemies made no sense.[39]

Meanwhile, the new Jamaica governor Thomas Handasyd, frustrated at the situation that put Dutch rivals (and allies) at such advantage, commissioned privateering against Dutch and Danish shipping.[40] He framed those seizures as efforts to police allies' conduct during the war, observing his orders to prevent "all trade with H[er] M[ajesty's] enemy."[41] When Dutch complaints about the seizures reached Europe, they reinforced the arguments that the English would better emulate the Dutch than try to stop them. After the Dutch States General echoed the advice of her colonial officials, Anne ordered that the English resume all "trade and commerce with the Spaniards in those parts . . . in all commodities" except war stores. Governors were to permit Anne's subjects and Dutch traders alike free and open trade with Spanish America in any goods that had been legal prior to the war.[42]

Thereafter, English colonial officials and naval commanders were to attack French and Spanish transatlantic shipping. But they were to draw Spanish subjects in America to Habsburg loyalty, with trade, promises of protection, and arguments that Habsburgs were more legitimately "Spanish" than were Bourbons. Some English officials even hoped that if the Bourbons prevailed in Spain, Spanish America would separate from Spain to choose the Habsburg sovereign and English and Dutch trade. But better to sway Spaniards everywhere: in September 1703, London instructed Handasyd to assure all the Spanish governors that Anne would not allow them "to suffer" while she was "succouring their countrymen in Spain and rescueing them from a French tyranny, and restoring their country to their lawful soveraigne of the House of Austria." Handasyd should promise Spaniards in the Caribbean that Anne's subjects would "live in a friendly manner" and "keep a good correspondence and commerce" with them, as long as they were willing to pursue "friendship" with the English.[43]

Handasyd developed a plan to send secret letters to the governors of Santo Domingo, Cartagena, Portobelo, and Havana under cover of prisoner exchanges.[44] After several false starts, he succeeded in sending letters and emissaries at least to Cuba, where Jamaica's offers of support gave some elite Habaneros courage to resist Bourbon leaders.[45] Only the arrival of a French fleet quelled a 1704 outbreak of pro-Habsburg resistance that included members of the cabildo and of the military.[46] Former French privateers such as Jean-Baptiste du Casse and Lorenzo de Graff (Lorencillo), who had terrorized the Spanish Caribbean during the 1690s, now arrived with convoys sent to "protect" the Spanish. Cubans were less than reassured but apparently curious, because when Lorencillo arrived, his infamy brought "all of the city" out to see him. The fleet's admiral suspected that Habaneros' continued enmity for their former nemesis endangered him, and he forbade Lorencillo from disembarking.[47]

Despite English confidence that Spanish Americans would see Bourbons as French tyrants, they also understood that Spanish Americans would more likely risk trading with English enemies if those enemies could meet their market demands and provide them with protection. Handasyd ordered Jamaicans to give "no injury or spoile" to "any plantations belonging to Spaniards." Jamaican sloop captains found Spaniards "very well inclined to trade with the English and Dutch" if they could be protected from French retaliation, but the English lacked "enough of the commodities the Spaniards wanted." If they had had enough captives and textiles, "they might have had an extraordinary trade." To further reassure Spanish Americans, Handasyd requested "proclamations in Spanish" from Carlos ("the King of Spain") approving Anglo-Spanish trade. Such a document might provide Spanish American merchants, ship captains, and local officials with legal cover if Bourbon officials caught them. London officials envisioned Handasyd and Jamaican traders accessing wide-reaching Spanish American networks and sent him fifty copies for distribution.[48]

While some Spanish Americans clearly welcomed English commerce, English observers were wrong to interpret willing trade as evidence of a general pro-Habsburg stance. As Aaron Alejandro Olivas's work makes clear, Spanish American merchants' and administrators' loyalties followed their networks of patronage, trust, and commerce, whether Spanish, French, English, or Dutch.[49] On the one hand, English rear admiral William Whetstone might find some Cartageneros "very weary of ye French yoak and tyranny" and "mighty desireous of a trade and correspondence with Jamaica," treating English sloops "with great kindness and permitt[ing] them to trade, even under the walls of their fortifications."[50] But on the other hand, Spanish officials took numerous English smugglers as prisoners of war. Those prisoners complained of mistreatment at the hands of Spanish captors, challenging arguments that the Spanish waited eagerly for the English to save them from the French. One former prisoner wrote that the Spaniards sent English captives to dig mines, row galleys, and build forts and churches. Some of them had died of exertion or bad treatment, and some had been "killed in cold blood."[51]

Despite evidence that many Spanish Americans supported the Bourbon succession and French trade, the English intensified their efforts to recruit Spanish Americans, and began to emphasize the Habsburgs as the "natural" occupants of the Spanish throne. Although the word conveyed birthplace in English and even more so in Spanish, the Habsburg House of Austria was centered outside Spain, as was the French House of Bourbon, and the would-be King Carlos III was born in Vienna. To encourage Spanish Americans to cooperate in their "rescue," Handasyd was to tell them that "their natural Sovereign" Carlos III was sending to them "succours of naturall Spaniards" to serve as military and civil officers who would replace Bourbon administrators, thereby returning Spanish Americans to "the good government of those parts in [Carlos's] own Royal name." English officials characterized the Bourbon monarchy as unnatural, in part because it lacked "ancient" roots to give it legitimacy, rendering Bourbon officials incapable of providing "good government" for Spain's American colonists. While such language seems carefully composed for Spanish consumption (English officials were not in the habit of identifying Spanish Habsburg bureaucracy as "good government,") neither do these writings suggest irony. Anne, her advisors, and Jamaica officials seem to have believed that Spanish Americans would accept such a framing of events.[52]

In January 1706, London officials took recent English military successes in Spain as an opportunity for "inviting and encouraging the Spaniards in the West Indies to shake off the French servitude, and follow the example of their friends in Old Spain." Handasyd should seek "any disposition in the Spaniards in America to declare for King Charles III," and if he found any hint of Habsburg leanings, he should promise English ships, land forces, arms, ammunition, and whatever else they deemed necessary for "rescuing them from the yoake of France, and restoring their trade to the ancient Channel between Old and New Spain."[53] London officials made clear here, if perhaps unintentionally, that the rescue was intended for commerce as much as for people.

The English increased their persuasion efforts; they painted Bourbon rule as French and foreign, and connected French tyranny to restricted commerce. Handasyd was to relay to Spanish Americans a full description of French "practices and designs . . . for monopolising their trade," making sure they understood that Jean-Baptiste du Casse, who had so recently fought against Spanish interests in the region, had now persuaded Louis XIV to divide the asiento into three shares: one for Louis XIV, one for Felipe V, and one for du Casse himself, to distribute among his own French and Spanish associates.[54] Other Spanish merchants (let alone the English or Dutch) would be shut out.

Moreover, according to the English, the Bourbons sought to displace Spanish officials, merchants, and even clergy with French replacements. They were even reorganizing the galleon and flota voyages for their own benefit, which the English trusted if "well known and understood in the Indies" would "provoke" Spanish Americans "to a revolt, to which they are otherwise sufficiently inclined." Surely they would prefer "their former correspondencies and dealings with their own factors and countrymen of Old Spain." The English insisted that they themselves presented no such threat, merely wishing to trade alongside Spanish merchants and otherwise leave Spain to govern itself and its Indies. Thus London officials framed the issue as one of identity—linking Spaniards on both sides of the Atlantic as "countrymen."[55] This linkage ignored the long-standing importance of international smuggling in Spanish America and instead created a fictional past in which Spanish Americans traded mainly with Spaniards. The English erased the foreign smugglers ubiquitous in Spanish American ports during the previous half century, a rewriting perhaps intended to obscure their own designs on future Spanish American trade. In the same year (1706), the English signed a wishful asiento contract with would-be King Carlos, the Archduke Charles. The treaty reserved even more benefits for the English than the then-current French contract did, and did more to conflate the private contract and diplomatic treaty aspects of the agreement. It made Queen Anne, rather than a company, the supplier of slaves, and provided no shareholding for the Spanish king. The English intended to exclude all rivals, including their Dutch allies, and to monopolize the trade ("to stand alone in the whole trade of America"), just as they publicly criticized the French for doing.[56]

But English propaganda had some effect. Some Cubans, wishing to protect established commercial networks that bound them to the English, took courage from the promises of English help to resist the French presence in Havana. The new Bourbon monopoly outlawed the connections that they had built with Jamaican slave traders, but a pro-Habsburg ideology provided them with justification for pursuing their commercial interests.[57] When news arrived in 1706 that the northern Spanish kingdom of Catalonia had revolted against Felipe V, pro-Habsburg Cubans killed some French mariners in Havana. Bourbon officials there responded with military patrols and a curfew, threatening anyone found out after midnight with exile to Florida, and anyone who insulted the French with torture. The day after authorities posted the new policy, someone anonymously appended an addendum, threatening the governor with death if French ships remained in the bay, and vowing to rise up, seek help from Jamaica, reject continued French presence, and acclaim the Habsburg Empire.[58] The threat to solicit Jamaican assistance indicates that Handasyd's messages proffering aid had gotten through. According to Levi Marrero, such "English secessionist propaganda" continued in Cuba until the war ended.[59]

In contrast to the anti-French Cubans, most Spanish Americans weighed English reports of victorious Habsburgs in Spain against competing news from other sources and exercised caution. Jamaica governor Handasyd lamented that French messengers often beat him in the information race. Pro-Bourbon reports of conditions in Europe had "mightily discouraged King Charles' party here and encouraged those of the Duke of Anjou's." Handasyd tried "to undeceive" Spanish Americans by publicizing Bourbon losses in Savoy and Milan and by assuring Spanish Americans that a "powerfull force" of Habsburg allies would return Spaniards "to a true obedience to their lawfull King."[60] The Jamaica governor promulgated an imaginary standard of loyalty as immutable: only one king could be "lawfull" and only obedience to him could be "true," ignoring his own (and everyone else's) knowledge that individual Spanish Americans chose sides strategically, as English, French, and Dutch merchants offered trade neither lawful nor "true" to Spanish American political theory but in accordance with decades-long practice.

Handasyd could not, however, ignore the rebuff he received from Cartagena governor José de Zúñiga y la Cerda, who informed him that English reports were "wholly made void by letters . . . from the Catholick Majesty, Philip V" announcing his control over Madrid and "all the other towns." Spanish Americans stood ready to "spill the last drop of our blood" in the Bourbon king's defense.[61] Despite the Cuban governor's clear rejection, Handasyd believed the merchants of Cartagena and other Spanish American port towns "as willing as ever to continue a private trade with us," if the English could increase supplies, especially of woolens, to meet demand.[62]

However, Spanish Caribbean markets threatened to decline because French merchants increasingly sailed directly to Pacific ports, carrying both enslaved Africans and European textiles. English Jamaicans' connections in Cartagena and Panama, with arduous overland routes to Peru, might no longer link them to Pacific buyers if ships bearing captives and cloth regularly made Pacific voyages.[63] Still, Jamaicans, outfitted for short-distance trade and dependent on already-established networks, retained their focus on nearby commerce and on cultivating trade, alliance, and even "friendship" as integrated goals. When a Spanish ship sailing from Caracas wrecked on Jamaica's coast in the summer of 1710, Handasyd quickly sent the survivors ("native Spaniards") to Cartagena and Portobelo "in hopes" that his aid to them would help "mend upon us" Spanish trade. Two or three sloops had just arrived in Jamaica from the Spanish American coast, having made "pretty good voyages," and eight or nine more were headed out.[64] Those vessels returned with £80,000 but on the way home fought off French privateers for three days, losing Captain Charles Gandey. Handasyd recognized the personal relationships that still underpinned commerce, and he feared that "this Island will suffer a great loss by [Gandey's] death, since the Spaniards had an entire friendship for him, and he esteem'd amongst them a fair Trader."[65]

During the War of the Grand Alliance and the War of the Spanish Succession, privateers on both sides targeted slave-trading ships and raided sugar plantations, seizing thousands of enslaved people as wartime plunder and selling them where they could.[66] In doing so, they embraced a Caribbean political economy that identified people of color as commodities and underscored the importance of slave trading to the two wars, which officials and merchants acknowledged more explicitly during the latter conflict. At its start, London merchants complained that French privateers from Martinique had "taken so many ships from Guinea with negroes" and ships bringing provisions that they had "ruin'd many Merchants and disabled the Planters from carrying on their works for want of strength and food." Such seizures had, moreover, "much enriched" the French "by enabling them to supply the Spaniards with a very great number of negroes."[67] The ultimate prize of the war—access to Spanish silver via a trade in captive Africans—became prize during the war as well. Even if French privateers did not expressly pursue the interests of French merchants, French merchants and French colonies nonetheless saw immediate gain and improved their position as reliable suppliers of men, women, and children to labor in Spanish American mines, plantations, and households.[68]

Although privateers acquired far more captives when they seized slave ships than when they raided plantations, Jamaica governor Handasyd saw the capture of enslaved Jamaicans as a primary indicator of the war's effects on the island. He reported in 1703 that, "as to the enemy's attempts against us, I thank God we have hitherto escaped very well," which he measured as "having not lost since the warr above 27 or 28 slaves," even though French privateers in small craft had "much infested" Jamaica's coasts.[69]

Captive people, unlike goods, could resist or flee their own capture, and while they conceivably could have participated in their own abduction, there is no evidence to suggest that they did so. Unlike the men and women who fled Jamaican enslavement for sanctuary in Cuba or Cartagena, those captured as wartime plunder almost certainly remained slaves. Their fate on sugar plantations in French Saint Domingue would have been no better than in Jamaica. Enslaved Jamaicans did not run to their French captors; Handasyd wrote that the raids depended on privateers' ability "to surprize the negroes," describing how "the enemy . . . land in the night by sloops and barquelongos, running [the boats] into small cricks and covering them with b[ough]s, lying themselves in the woods till they have an opportunity of surprizeing the Plantations." The raids were impossible to prevent, "since they can run over from Cuba in one night." During the previous two months there had been three such attempts. However, Handasyd "thank[ed] God" that French privateers had "not got 50 slaves" since his arrival, "for which we have gott three times the number from them." In 1708, a French privateer snuck past the patrols on the north side of the island and took a sloop with its cargo of dyewood "and 10 or 12 negroes that were at work" on the sloop or on shore. Handasyd attributed the loss "altogether to the carelessness of the people there," perhaps in leaving enslaved men at work alone, and likely unarmed, in an area known to be the target of French attacks.[70] In mentioning no other form of war spoils, the governor signaled that people were the primary plunder in the region.[71]

As early as 1704, Governor Handasyd worried that Jamaica's own privateers, if not stopped from attacking Spanish American targets, would "ruine our correspondence" with them. After the revisions to English wartime policy enacted earlier in the year, privateers could still take either Spanish or French ships at sea, though only French ships in port. But some, "under pretence of faith in tradeing with the Spaniards, intice[d] them from the land and ma[d]e prey of them."[72] These privateers' feigned trade should not cause us to conflate smuggling with privateering. Caribbean merchants trading across imperial borders (almost always smugglers from someone's perspective) saw privateers as both direct and indirect threat. If English privateers continued to operate with their historical autonomy and follow the traditional practice of targeting all enemy shipping, they would "wholly ruine our trade." And because Dutch governors had proved better able to impede Dutch privateers' predation on Spanish shipping, "they will draw the whole trade to themselves."[73]

Handasyd requested some means to further control privateers, but London officials refused; they had already drawn instructions designed to encourage Anglo-Spanish trade "without disabling ourselves from annoying the Spanish ships and galleons in the open sea." Nothing more could be done. Governors should instead require privateers to post bond guaranteeing that they would not "break faith with such of the Spaniards as they shall trade with" nor "make a prey of them." Handasyd should again send out letters to renew Spanish confidence that the English desired a "mutual trade."[74]

However, the commercial goals of war and English efforts to balance differing strategies toward the French and the Spanish guaranteed trouble. Privateers refused to forego attacks on Spanish American towns, estates, or coastal trade because the terms of their commissions, granting them a proportion of their plunder, provided such strong incentive to seize any vulnerable ship or port. English privateers even seized Spanish and English Caribbean vessels trading with one another, the very commerce the war was intended to secure. In July 1707, news reached London that two Jamaican privateers "lye concealed on the Spanish coast and there intercept the Spanish canoes as they come from trading with our ships," taking the money they brought or the goods they had just purchased. By disobeying their orders so flagrantly, the privateers had turned pirate well before the war ended. Worse, "several of the principal traders of Jamaica" were owners or investors in these illicit ventures. "Such evill practices" damaged "the honour" of the queen's government, violated the "publick faith," hurt "the interest of King Charles III," and "ruin[ed] . . . our present trade with the subjects of the Spanish nation." Because "trade" and "interest" depended on "honour" and "faith," privateers' traditional activity of plundering wartime enemies became "evil," threatening the war goal of cross-border trade. (Given the uncertainty of the Spanish succession at that point, English officials broke with their normally precise formulation that individuals were subjects of a particular named sovereign—or in the case of the Dutch, a republic—and instead identified subjects of a Spanish "nation.")[75]

Hoping to avoid altogether the trouble privateers presented, the governor again insisted on the need to control them, this time requesting "an order not to grant any more Commissions for privateers" at all.[76] By 1707 the Jamaica governor, trying to maintain conditions conducive to border-crossing trade, concluded that private men-of-war possessed too much autonomy, which mattered because their interests failed to align with those of their empire, even during wartime. But the Board of Trade placed the burden on Handasyd to control the privateers using existing regulations, confident that if he took care "that the privateers be kept within just bounds, as is provided by the last mentioned Act . . . trade will flourish again."[77]

Other observers echoed Handasyd's argument that privateers no longer made useful agents of state in the region, even during wartime. English packet-boat operator Edmund Dummer testified to "very great complaints against privateering on the coast, which will infallibly destroy all our correspondence with the Spanish West Indies."[78] Dummer argued that to keep privateers from targeting Spanish Americans, more rules were needed: English privateers should receive instructions to attack only ships "mann'd and sailed with French men," and to keep the prisoners alive as "evidence [of] the lawfullness of the capture." If they took any "Spanish coasting vessell mann'd with Spanyards on the said shore," they should repay the victims double the value of the seizure, in identical goods. Copies of these instructions should be sent to the Spanish to "revive the trade."[79]

Some of Dummer's suggestions prevailed in Parliament's 1708 Act for Encouraging Trade to America but were undercut by the Cruisers and Convoys Act of the same year, which encouraged privateering. In January 1709, Dummer reported "great complaints" coming from the Caribbean against the second act, which Dummer called the "Act for Privateers." It "tend[ed] to ye ruine of all trade with the Spanish West Indies," lured seamen from both the men of war and merchant vessels, "and when Peace shall come, leave to the world a brood of pyrates to infest it." In short, it thwarted "the most publick and honest interest of the Nation," trade "with the Spanyard." Jamaica was already suffering from the act: a Kingston correspondent wrote to Dummer that trade "seems at a stand" and that the only thing "on foot" was privateering.

Even the British navy could not constrain the privateers to their commissions. On the promise of naval convoys, Jamaican slave traders had "bought negroes for the trade." But after they delivered the captive people ashore, a Jamaican privateer took several Spanish canoes loaded with money right under the nose of the convoy, just as they had reached the English slave traders at anchor. The same privateer then captured another vessel "with a good summ of money on board" and claimed it was a Spanish oceangoing vessel, liable to seizure. Dummer feared that, even worse, the victim had been English, but because the privateer had failed to bring any of the captured crew to Jamaica to testify, as the act required, there was no telling. Lax oversight meant that privateers could follow English ships out of port, seize their valuables, kill the crew, and burn the ship, with officials "never the wiser." Although Dummer called these men privateers, the actions he described were piracy. He acknowledged as much in reporting the widespread belief that "this cursed" practice "will breed so many pirates" when peace came that they would present more danger than the French did during the war.[80]

Already some of these privateering vessels operated in the democratic manner pirates became famous for in the decade following the peace. Some Jamaicans thought it was those egalitarian shipboard politics that caused them to behave more like pirates than privateers. They attacked English shipping because "their captains have no command, every man is allowed a vote, and so most votes carry the vessell where they please." If governors instead issued commissions that required privateering captains to hold sole command, those captains could better keep the seamen "in subjection" (as were mariners on merchant and naval shipping). Then captains, who had put up security for their own behavior, could more easily obey the instructions that prohibited them from attacking Spanish ports or coasting vessels or any

English targets.[81] The Board of Trade endorsed the suggestions coming from Jamaica and instructed Handasyd to insert a clause into all commissions for private men-of-war "giving the Captain the sole power of the ship, and restraining the seamen from having anything to do in the command thereof." This would, on paper, allow a captain to thwart "irregularities [even] when the majority is against him."[82]

For his part, Governor Handasyd continued to insist on the impossibility of reforming privateers, and by 1709 he began to interchange the words *pirate* and *privateer* to refer to men who held commissions but who acted more as free agents than state agents. He reported over three hundred men on the San Blas Islands, whose numbers threatened to increase without active suppression (and were estimated at five hundred or nine hundred individuals by others). Though the men refused to accept Britain's new privateering model as less lucrative and more obviously serving the interests of merchants, neither did they wish to sign on with the Bourbons. The governors of Havana, Portobelo, Santiago de Cuba, and Cartagena as well as the French governors of Port Louis, Petit-Goâve, and Léogâne had "all offered to give them a generall pardon if they'll come in and serve them against H[er] M[ajesty] and her Allies, but they have utterly refused." Handasyd, despite labeling the men as pirates, tried to understand their choices in terms of national identity and loyalty, noting that their refusal of service to the Bourbons came "notwithstanding the chief of them is a French man." They had sent Handasyd several messages that if the queen would grant them pardon and protection, they would come to Jamaica and serve Anne and her allies "faithfully."[83]

Handasyd offered the men pardons, but most of them had "either perished for want of support, or disperced." About one hundred had come in, "sorry miserable creatures" who arrived naked and starving. With trade in the region "dead," perhaps through their own activities, maritime predation offered diminishing returns. Nonetheless, it still appealed to hundreds of men who preferred its risks to naval service, and British law required Jamaica governors to continue to commission them.[84]

Keeping those privateers bound to the terms of their commissions required judges committed to interimperial legal processes. In 1712 Archibald Hamilton, who replaced Handasyd as Jamaica governor, informed the Board of Trade of "several disorders and crueltys" that privateers had committed against Spaniards along the coasts of both Cartagena and Cuba. Prosecuting them proved difficult because the principal evidence came "from ye Spaniards themselves," and some English judges were unwilling to accept their testimonies. Although Hamilton "believe[d] ym too true," the judges chose to accept the word of the privateers, who denied any guilt. They resisted the move toward global commerce that required an interpolity law designed to serve the merchants of all trading nations.[85]

Further complicating the cases, the royal men of war who had arrested the privateers had not followed proper procedure when they brought them into Port Royal. The owners of the privateering vessels sued the captain of the man-of-war for having seized their goods and detained their men without due process. Both the privateering vessels' owners and the captain's commanding officer (the admiral of the fleet) appealed to Hamilton, who had no sympathy for either. The naval captain had "gone farther than he could well justifye" because, however guilty the privateers might be, they still had to be tried according to law "and this they insisted on." The privateers, whose international lawbreaking caused governors, merchants, and diplomats such trouble, guarded their own legal rights closely. Because the naval officers had a history of pressing men from the shore as well as from merchant ships, "the whole Island," like the judges, sided with the privateers.

Though the privateers might have escaped both legal penalties and public censure, Hamilton thought he saw merchants' fears of losing Spanish American trade realized. In 1712, Jamaicans witnessed the "entire decay of trade." Merchants "live[d] in hopes" that the trade would "revive again upon ye establishment of a peace" that would permit wholehearted suppression of private men-of-war. When Governor Hamilton received the queen's proclamation for a four-month cessation of arms, he planned to "call in those [commissions] that are out as soon as possible"[86] Instead, the island's mariners, legally pirates if acting without commissions during this truce, continued to prey on Spanish America. Their crimes "being national," Hamilton sought London's involvement. One had been "robbing ye Spaniards" near Cartagena as they traded with Dutch merchants. The other had seized Spaniards trading with English vessels off the Cuban coast and tortured them to extort their goods and money. Hamilton had received complaints from the respective Spanish governors and from Spanish, Dutch, and English traders. He prosecuted the first case, of theft near Cartagena, and planned to order restitution out of the privateer's goods, which were in custody. The second case, of torture, was "not so well prooved" and less clearly violated any statute. Hamilton vowed to do all he could by law but bemoaned his "inability effectually to redress these disorders."[87]

By November, the governor had acquired good evidence that the privateers suspected of torturing Cuban Spaniards had indeed committed "those cruelteys." The case heightened the tension between the governor and the navy admiral. Although Governor Hamilton had arrived recently, he adopted the view of Jamaican residents and Caribbean seamen who saw themselves as integral to the body politic—subjects protected by British law. They saw their incorporation into empire as fundamentally constitutive, insisting that "whatever [they] had done . . . they were to be tryed by the law for it" and not "press'd or detained as prisoners on board the men of warr." In contrast, Rear Admiral Hovenden Walker, in illegally impressing as his predecessors had done, exhibited a utilitarian view of colonial male subjects as manpower during war. He delayed releasing the privateers, "alarming the inhabitants, and particularly the seafaring men." When they were finally set ashore and Hamilton could have them interviewed, he concluded that they were in fact "guilty of . . . tying a Spaniard and a mulatto and severely whipping them to make them confess where they had hid their mony" and their goods, which they had just purchased from an English vessel. Because the privateers' captain had been killed in this encounter and because his crew members alleged they had acted "by his command," Jamaica lawyers advised Hamilton that they not be convicted of having broken the law. All the governor could do was collect the bond money that the privateers' investors had pledged "for performance of the instructions" the governor had given the now-dead captain.[88]

As these cases demonstrate, Caribbean privateers hewed to a seventeenth-century geopolitical model in which Spaniards and other foreigners remained natural enemies of the English and in which declared enemies, whether military or civilian, presented legitimate targets for attack and plunder. English merchants in the Caribbean and London, and the officials who supported them, sought a radically different model that would, in the interest of inter-imperial slave trading, curb privateers' historical autonomy and limit their role as legitimate geopolitical actors. Anemic English legislation paid lip service to the new model but provided room for privateers to spurn Anglo-Spanish truce, encouraging them to turn pirate well before the Treaty of Utrecht ushered in peace that outlawed their activities altogether.[89]

During both wars, people of African and Indigenous descent took advantage of upheavals to create spaces of inclusion for themselves in Spanish and English colonial societies. They employed a variety of strategies to do so. In 1690, at the start of the War of the Grand Alliance in Jamaica, five "Spanish Negroes," men "borne out of our allegiance," saw their chance to claim belonging in an island desperate for loyal subjects. In a rare clear example of Black subjecthood in the colony, they requested and received naturalization in Jamaica.[90] During the War of the Grand Alliance, Governor Beeston worried that a successful French invasion would "leave us exposed to the insults not only of the French but also of our blacks, who are twenty to one white and know their strength so well that they might be encouraged to reduce Jamaica to another Guinea."[91] In 1693, the slave trader Santiago del Castillo received permission to construct a fortress on his estate overlooking Port Royal, to protect his "House and plantacion and Negroes" from "their Maj[es]ties Enemy's." The grant noted that the fort would serve the colony more generally, *and* that it would help protect Castillo's own estate, where he had "sett[led his] factory of the Assiento for the Introduction of Negroe Slaves into the Spanish Indies."[92] Newly arrived African people being held for transshipment would provide an especially tempting target for French men-of-war and might also seek to resist or escape their captors.

In 1702, at the start of the War of the Spanish Succession, Jamaica's windward (eastern) Maroon communities recruited and captured enslaved people from neighboring plantations and "mightily increased . . . their numbers," which emboldened them "to come down armed and attack . . . settlements."[93] Colonial officials responded quickly, raising forces "to pursue and destroy" them. Rather than recognizing their independence, officials labeled them "rebellious and runaway slaves."[94] Colonial militias engaged the Maroons at least once during the war, "killing and taking many of those negroes and burning and destroying their towns and houses" and provisions, but the community persisted.[95]

Enslaved Jamaicans may well have been motivated by Maroon activity, as well as by the context of war, to resist their own bondage. In 1704, more than thirty enslaved people equipped themselves with "firearms plunder'd and took out of houses," attacked several sites, burned a house, and wounded one colonist before colonial forces captured and killed twelve of them and the rest fled. Even as Jamaica suffered repeated French attacks, Governor Handasyd "own[ed]" to fearing "some bloody design" from enslaved resisters "more . . . than any other enemy." He readily acknowledged their incentive to fight their oppression: "Their numbers being so very great and the whites so few, makes me wonder that they have not before this destroyed us all, there being in some Plantations 200 or 300 negroes to one or two white men."[96] Seven months later Handasyd reported the "Insurrection . . . quite quelled," some of the "Ring Leaders" executed, and the rest "sent off the island."[97]

Even when the disruptions of war abated, White Jamaicans feared that the slave society they pursued increasingly endangered them. In October 1712, in worrying that so "scatter'd a body of men" could not "defen[d] . . . so large . . . an Island," Governor Handasyd stressed that even without any "forreign enemy[,] ye planters could not conceal their apprehentions from their negroes." Slaveholders believed they perceived among the enslaved an increase in bold, violent resistance ("insolence," in the governor's view), such as the killing and dismembering of "two white persons" "in open day." The governor asked London officials to keep soldiers in Jamaica "at least for some time after a peace or untill wee can reap ye benefit of it by an addition of white people amongst us." "Otherwise," the colony was liable to "some very unlucky disaster by an insurrection."[98] Although his prediction depended on his knowledge that slaves had just cause to resist, his explicit attribution of insurrections to bad luck attempted to remove blame from slaveholders and agency from the enslaved.

Jamaican officials made various efforts during the War of the Spanish Succession to keep White men on the island and to bring more men and women of European descent to the colony as permanent settlers. In objecting to navy officers' frequent impressment of local mariners and land-dwelling residents, governors stressed the island's need to defend itself. "Of greatest concern" to the Council and Assembly, naval officers pressed "not only . . . ye seafaring men of ye Island but even ye civill officers in ye discharge of their duty."[99] Jamaica lost men to impressment both directly and indirectly, because some fled to Dutch and Danish islands to flee the threat of impressment.[100]

These opinions spread to London, where in 1703 "Merchants and Planters concerned in the Island of Jamaica" urged Anne to send regiments to save Jamaica from rumored French attack. The island needed such reinforcements because yet another vice admiral (John Graydon) had requisitioned its warships and pressed all the "most useful people."[101] In 1704 two merchants called on the Board of Trade to send military recruits to Jamaica immediately because the naval officers had caused for "many yeares . . . such havock in the Island by pressing," that too few (White) men remained "to defend themselves agains thei[r] own negroes." The problem was not just the men they impressed "but the vast numbers they have frighted away" from Jamaica, which included "many hundred English seamen fled to the Dutch Settlement at Curassoa." For fear of impressment, "neither English seamen nor seamen of any other Nation will come near" Jamaica. This, the merchants argued, was the worst reduction of the island since the 1692 earthquake and disease outbreaks that followed it.[102]

Vice Admiral Graydon countered that he had had no choice. English subjects in the Caribbean so lacked "zeal" for the queen's service that they overcharged the naval forces for provisions and lured soldiers and seamen to quit their service. He blamed their failings on their immersion in an interimperial Caribbean political economy rather than an English Atlantic one. Graydon believed that Jamaican colonists, under cover of privateering, "carr[ied] on a sinister trade with H[er] M[ajesty's] enemyes" and even warned those enemies of English military "preparations and designes against them." As Graydon saw it, the problems stemmed from the fact that "the Government of these Islands" rested "absolutely in the hands of Creoalians," whose ties to residents of Spanish, French, and Dutch colonies weakened their sense of obligation to their sovereign and her empire.[103] Frequent commerce (fostered by proximity) connected creole residents of rival and enemy empires to one another and permitted an independence that weakened their loyalty. Even if Graydon's aspersions contained a grain of truth, Jamaica colonists nonetheless retained their sense of themselves as members of the English body politic, though they perhaps focused more on the privileges than the responsibilities of such membership. As naval officers continued to press mariners and landmen during the war, Jamaica's Council and Assembly complained that the officers exceeded their authority, threatening the "prosperity of trade" and violating the "rights and libertyes of ye subject."[104]

In addition to trying to hold on to the people they had, Jamaica governors had long supported naturalizing European foreigners as a means of increasing the island's loyal population. Early in the War of the Spanish Succession, Governor Handasyd and many merchants in Jamaica grew concerned about the loss of White men even while they engaged in a competition to increase the enslaved population of their own island and of the region, and so supported efforts to attract and naturalize foreigners. Over one hundred Christian foreigners and Jews were naturalized in Jamaica during the war.[105]

But some of these Caribbean efforts to ease White immigrants' integration into colonial society ran afoul of London officials, who were cautious about controlling the boundaries of the body politic. In a 1703 case involving individuals whose Englishness may seem to us unproblematic, the Jamaica Assembly naturalized several children who had been born to English parents at sea, en route from England to Jamaica. To avoid having to repeat the task, the Assembly passed a broader naturalization act encompassing "all other persons whatsoever already born, or who shall at any time hereafter be born on the High Seas of English parents in an English bottom navigated according to the law of England and sailing from any of the Queen's dominions to Jamaica."

Making English ships sailing under English law between English places into mobile legal extensions of England was consistent with jurisdictional theory reflected in much of maritime law.[106] But London officials refused to approve the act, noting that no similar "general naturalization" had ever passed in England. The closest recent relevant act (passed during the War of the Grand Alliance) was one naturalizing children born abroad to officers, soldiers, and others directly serving the government, but it had lasted only for the duration of the war. The Jamaican act in question naturalized all children, "whether their parents had been in the service" of the government or not, and was perpetual.[107] It perhaps ran aground on the question of *how* nativity created belonging.

The "natural" belonging that resulted when someone entered the world on English land could not extend to movable or maritime jurisdictional spaces because ships could not support permanent residence or denizenship. They therefore could not provide the basis for a "natural" subjecthood, even though they could function as English jurisdictional space for property transfers or criminal prosecutions.[108] Jamaica's high immigration and mortality rates meant that a far greater percentage of Jamaica's children of English parentage would fall under such an act than would children in England. That context, and Jamaican lawmakers' awareness that the racial demographics they were creating endangered the island's colonial society, made them more willing than London administrators to expand jurisdictional theory to increase the numbers of Englishmen on the island.

Handasyd was even willing to accept French deserters into Jamaica. In 1705 a group of seventy or eighty French people "revolted from the French and Spanish Governments in the West Indies" and requested Anne's protection. Because they "behave[d] themselves as they ought to do" and were willing to take "the oaths," Handasyd sent them promise of refuge.[109] But before he could send a sloop to collect them, French and Spanish forces "had fallen upon them" and forced them to surrender.[110] During wartime and in plantation societies, colonial officials sought to keep potential subjects, even those who wished to flee.

When some members of the Jamaica Assembly resisted extending so indiscriminate a welcome, Governor Handasyd responded with an explicit appeal to racial politics. In 1705, the Assembly passed an act excluding foreigners from either civil offices or militia service, thereby disqualifying "severall Scotch, Dutch and French Gentlemen" who had served the island "in both capacities" during the previous twenty years. Governor Handasyd found the act ill conceived because the men in question were all wealthy, a quality that helped make them "as good subjects to H[er] M[ajesty]" as any other men on the island. In colonial society "where white people are so much wanted," Handasyd believed the English should do all they could to attract European foreigners (especially "substantiall" ones) to the island and fully incorporate them.[111] On the Board of Trade's recommendation, Anne complied with the governor's recommendation and disallowed the act.[112]

Concerns about how to integrate non-British foreigners complicated the demand for White immigrants. In August 1709, as officials considered a proposal to settle up to one thousand Palatines in Jamaica, one promoter argued that the crown should provide transport and "make room" for them. They would help defend the island, would buy English commodities, and would pay customs on their own products. But English or Scottish settlers should be "mixt with them on the same foot and encouragement" to ensure that they not remain separate but combine with Britons into a creole White colonial population.[113] British officials planned to ensure the Palatines settlement among and interaction with Anne's "natural" subjects on the island, with the assumption that if prohibited from maintaining a distinct community, their lives would come to match their confessions of loyalty to their new sovereign, remaking their identities.

The queen approved the project, and the Board of Trade instructed the Jamaica Council and Assembly to provide cleared ground and housing for the arrivals. "For their further encouragement," the governor was to grant them letters of naturalization without the usual fees, that they "may enjoy all such priviledges and advantages as are enjoyed by the present inhabitants of Jamaica." The Board of Trade anticipated support for the project among "the present inhabitants" because the population boost would augment the island's trade and boost its security. This plan, too, explicitly identified the island's "security" in racial terms. The board expected planters to willingly "give" the Palatines "land [and] help them to settle it, as 'tis their interest so to do, they being sensible how much they want numbers of white people in that place." If the initial plan to settle on Lynch (Navy) Island off the north coast proved unsuccessful, the Palatines should be distributed among thinly populated parishes to address the frequently ignored deficiency law that masters of slaves keep a proportion of White men relative to slaves on their plantations.[114]

Unlike in Jamaica, in nearby Santiago de Cuba, communities of color aimed to use colonial defensive needs during the war to underscore their value to crown and colony, with mixed success. The Company of Indians from the town of San Luis de los Caneyes fought to defend the southern coast against English invasion, but the governor put them under a Spanish captain in 1708, claiming he could not identify a Native man with the necessary military discipline to lead the unit. This was a militia that had been "recognized since time immemorial" for its aid in keeping the coast of Santiago free from "pirates, smugglers, and evildoers," but in their case, Bourbon reorganizations provided colonial officials with a chance to impose greater oversight.[115]

The royal slaves who constituted the town of El Cobre not only retained their corporate status but successfully defended their role as military protectors of crown interests. Moreover, they used the courts to get a governor who challenged them removed from office, jailed, and recalled to Spain.[116] Felipe V's ascension to the Spanish throne in 1700 held especial import for Cobreros because they belonged to the king as his personal property, as well as owing him the same loyalty as did all other vassals. If they discussed among themselves any questions about the new king's legitimacy, they concluded such conversations before presenting themselves to the colonial authorities who recorded their words for us. Publicly, Cobreros shifted their loyalty to the new Bourbon regime without hesitation. Indeed, they performed their allegiance to the king as a means of resisting the directives of the governor who served as the king's representative.[117]

Jose Canales Caballero, who took office as governor in 1708, immediately sought to punish Cobreros for illegal but customary economic activities, particularly mining and selling the king's copper on their own account. To put a stop to the practice, Governor Canales sent an officer with cavalry to El Cobre to disarm the Black militia company there. In the process, the soldiers raided Cobreros' houses (presumably looking for copper and mining equipment) and set fire to some of them. Cobreros initially fled to the surrounding countryside but returned to protest, relying on the same networks of patronage and clergy support that had aided them earlier and that allowed slaves elsewhere in Spanish America to access the courts.

In 1709, with the support of a former governor and lieutenant, and carrying a letter from the parish priest, the Cobrero Diego de Rosas traveled to Madrid.[118] Rosas presented a memorial in which he testified to the royal slaves' dedication "to the armed defense of the Port of [Santiago de] Cuba and its coasts" and their constant readiness to defend the region against "the enemy" by their "punctuality and valor and their knowledge of the backcountry."[119] Thus he attested to the slaves' willingness to risk their lives to protect the colony. Rosas made a plea for arms so that Cobreros could protect themselves from English privateers who could capture and sell them in English colonies if they were left unable to defend themselves. Cobreros, like people of African and Indigenous descent throughout the Caribbean, knew all too well that English privateers indiscriminately took people of color as plunder and sold them in English colonies as slaves. The request also perhaps speaks to a regional wartime power imbalance that had led Jamaica governor Handasyd to boast that the English had captured three times more slaves than their enemies had.

As María Elena Díaz emphasizes, Rosas not only claimed the slaves' "legal right . . . to protect their master's [the king's] property in their own persons," but also "an entitlement to defend with arms their social prerogatives, including their right to live as a pueblo [and] their identity (including their Catholic identity against infidels)."[120] Because of the wartime context, which was playing out as a civil war in Cuba, Cobreros could call attention to their loyalty as especially valuable to the king at that moment. It provided the king with grounds for reaffirming his royal slaves' customary rights and for considering even more expansive privileges.

Rosas argued that the governor intended to disarm the slaves in order to leave the port of Guaycabón "defenseless so that the enemies can attack it," at which point the governor would sell the royal slaves to "the English enemies of this Crown" as part of his "friendship . . . with the Governor of the Island of Jamaica," to whom he gave gifts and with whom he traded. This accusation of treason spurred an investigation whose judge interviewed multiple people in the jurisdiction, including enslaved *regidores* (members of El Cobre's town council) and many of Governor Canales's other political enemies. The investigation found plenty of evidence that Canales had participated in contraband trade, but most of it pointed to commerce with the French or with other Spanish American ports, which while illegal did not carry the stain of treasonous wartime behavior. His gifts to the Jamaican governor had gone in a boat full of English prisoners destined for exchange—a practice that some criticized but that fell within normal diplomatic protocol. Canales was thus cleared of the most serious charges, though he died soon afterward in Spain.[121]

Canales's defense argued that the royal slaves of El Cobre were pawns of the former governor and his political allies. Even if Canales's rivals sought their own ends in joining forces with the Cobreros, the slaves' grievances and their framing of those grievances—as a violation of rights stemming from their corporate identity—reflected long-term strategies of the town to claim local ties and thereby membership in the larger body politic. In this, they echoed the claims of those individuals born in Spanish America who fled Jamaican captivity to seek sanctuary in Cuba and Cartagena.[122] Their strategy worked inasmuch as the crown reaffirmed the Cobreros' protection from sale, although their suggestion that their wartime service to the crown ought to earn them their freedom failed. However, their ability to frame the claim within language describing the Spanish American body politic reflected openings in Spanish Caribbean legal and political culture that did not exist on English islands. These openings permitted not just free people of African and Indigenous descent but even enslaved men and women to be heard as loyal vassals of the crown. They delegitimized the governor by accusing him of scheming to sell them away from their local belonging and into an interimperial marketplace for human beings, represented by the English and Dutch enemies. At the same time in English America, no court system permitted slaves to make such claims, and Jamaican officials in need of loyal subjects looked to foreigners, ranging from members of the same composite monarchy to enemy nationals, whom they could deem White.

Conclusion

"The Law of Nations"

In the summer of 1697 (at the end of the War of the Grand Alliance), off the coast of Cuba, the English navy vice admiral John Nevill wrote to the general of the Spanish galleons that officials in Spain had sent him to the Caribbean to escort the Spanish ships to Cádiz. He also wrote to Cuba governor Diego Córdoba Laso de la Vega begging permission to bring his own vessels into Havana before the transatlantic voyage, as he was "in great want of water and refreshment." Governor Córdoba refused; it was illegal for foreign ships to enter Havana, but Nevill could instead go to the Matanzas River, well east of Havana. Angry, Nevill claimed himself "mightily surprised" by the rebuff, since he had come "so many hundred leagues" to the region to serve the Spanish king. Because the Matanzas River did not provide a fleet as large as his with room to maneuver, the governor's offer amounted to a denial of water and a violation of "the law of nations."[1]

In trying to justify his indignation, Nevill waffled between asserting the supposed universality of the law of nations and drawing boundaries between peoples. He accused Córdoba of "use[ing] us more like Turks and Moors than Christians and Englishmen." Shared membership in European Christendom, along with the recent military alliance, should have led Córdoba to apply shared legal norms that encompassed the English navy, rather than Spanish imperial law that excluded it. Shared membership in a community of nations required better treatment; he noted that even "if we were Turks or Jews we could not, by the law of nations, be refused admission into any port for . . . water." But Nevill then pivoted back to boundary making, using Córdoba's refusal to denigrate Spaniards as unworthy of inclusion in a legal community that included not just "Turks or Jews" but also Indigenous Americans.

The vice admiral would instead "seek water among the Indians, from whom I doubt not that we shall find more friendship than from you."

At the same time, though, Nevill tried to break down barriers separating the English and Spanish in making his case for admission to port. He emphasized English service to the Spanish during the war. The messenger delivering his letter was to reiterate that Spanish officials had ordered Nevill and his English fleet "secretly to these seas for the security of the galleons," and to stress that the vice admiral had just come from Cartagena, where he had lost all his longboats chasing the French commander Baron de Pointis after his sack of Cartagena. It was because of that loss (in service to the Spanish) that he could not get water at the Bay of Matanzas. Admonishing the governor to appreciate his English allies, Nevill boasted that the English had landed a thousand men at the French settlement of Petit-Goâve on Hispaniola and burned it, destroying nine French privateer ships and carrying away five hundred privateersmen as prisoners to Europe. As had Nevill's letter, the messenger was to invoke "the law of nations" explicitly. Membership in the legal community of nations required admission into "port to water, in case of distress," as long as the ships were gone within forty-eight hours. He understood the Spanish king's refusal to allow ships of other nations to enter his ports "on account of trade," but protested that his men-of-war carried no merchandise, implying that therefore the governor could allow them in while still obeying Spanish law. According to Nevill, Spanish law and the law of nations agreed with one another in condoning the English fleet's entrance into Havana.

Neither Nevill's letters nor his messenger swayed Córdoba. The exchange ended with the Cuba governor protesting Nevill's depiction of him but standing by his decision, saying he had no choice. He ignored the English admiral's comments about Turks, Moors, Jews, and Indians, but he did respond to Nevill's invocation of the law of nations, by offering a pilot to help the English fleet navigate Matanzas Bay.[2] In doing so, he acknowledged the obligations of international norms that prohibited him from closing the island to (European) foreigners in need. The governor's written offer of a pilot could serve as protection against later accusations of violating treaty law or the law of nations.[3]

Like Nevill, people who lived in and traveled through the archipelagic Caribbean in the late seventeenth and early eighteenth centuries encountered others whose specific law (imperial, colonial, local, religious) differed from their own. Their interpretations of the supposedly shared legal and ethical codes provided by natural law, the law of nations, treaties, or religion likewise often diverged. In the Caribbean, there was little agreement about who had jurisdiction where, or over the criteria for political belonging that would define peoples' interactions with various forms of law. Individuals and groups nonetheless appealed to shared legal and ethical standards that they believed ought to govern their interactions in peace and at war, sometimes calling those shared standards the law of nations.

When merchants and ship captains appealed to the law of nations, they proposed common membership in a community that transcended empire. The idea of such a community derived from several sources. One was natural law, a concept that Europeans inherited from the ancient world. It rested on a belief in humans' inborn (natural, natal) capacity for reason, and was therefore understood to be shared by all people. In the early modern period, Europeans tried to use natural law to understand and govern their interactions with one another and also with people outside Europe and outside Christendom.[4] However, the definition of "everyone" was subject to revision; when Europeans folded elements of Christianity into their concepts of universal law, the results could justify the exclusion of non-Christian peoples, sometimes even after their conversion to Christianity.[5] Knitting merchant law into the law of nations condoned further exclusion of people who lived within nations that were recognized but not part of "the trading world." Britons claimed an ever-expanding place in that world, which suggested the incorporation of Scots and Sephardic Jews but not Tule or Kongolese into the body politic.

The law of nations also rested on bases that Europeans understood as less universal. In the most limiting sense, they might use the term to refer to specific treaty articles. In these cases they assumed a legal community whose membership included only the subjects of the specific sovereigns party to the treaty. Sometimes, Europeans in the seventeenth-century Caribbean used the term to refer to the behaviors demanded of Christians toward other Christians. They also might refer to standards outlined by merchant law, contributing to a sense of commonality among nations engaged in long-distance trade. That community was larger than Christiandom because it included the Hebrew nation (and might include Asian or North African "nations"), but it was not universal.[6]

The law of nations would come to have a more precise meaning in the mid-eighteenth century, especially with the writings of Emer de Vattel, but in the seventeenth-century Caribbean, people used the term to mean a variety of things, and the question of whether and to whom it applied was unclear.[7] Spanish and English translations of the phrase carried different connotations.

The original Latin *ius gentium* was translated as *derecho de gentes* in Spanish and *le droit des gens* in French. While there is overlap, *ius* in Latin, *derecho* in Spanish, and *droit* in French stress "rights," whereas the English translation into *law* (*ley* in Spanish) emphasizes rules and regulations. *Gentes* in both Latin and Spanish (and *gens* in French) meant hereditary groups whose members were related and who shared a history that usually tied them to a place. In English the closest translation might have been *peoples*. While the word *nation* in English continued to connote a hereditary people, it moved toward a definition more akin to nation-state, suggesting a people bound by a structure of governance in addition to a common birthplace, language, culture, and ancestry. In the English translation, *the law of nations* suggested the relation between polities. Its protections for the individual derived from their relationship (as a subject) with a sovereign head of state. *Derecho de gentes* connoted something closer to "the rights of peoples" than "the law of nations." If the Spanish had translated it as the English did, it would have been *la ley de las naciones*. While such distinctions may have mattered little to diplomats in Europe drafting treaties in Latin, the differences in emphasis aligned with differences in interpretation and application in the Caribbean. The language in which law was expressed necessarily affected the way people on the ground and at sea received it.

In the early modern Caribbean, when individuals invoked interimperial standards of justice (sometimes calling them the law of nations), the ways they did so were telling. As Chapter 3 illustrates, Spanish and French officials claimed that the law applied to free and even enslaved Africans and Indigenous people living within their polities and could protect them in the international arena. This interpretation was consistent with their more expansive translations of *ius gentium* into the rights of peoples. Seventeenth-century English people also presumed shared ethical practices (and sometimes used the term *law of nations* when they did so) to insist on humane treatment. But when they did so to protect someone vulnerable to persecution in another empire, as in the case of the merchant Benjamin Baruch Carvallo, it was for a fellow member of the "trading world." The English emphasized merchant and treaty law aspects of the law of nations along with shared Christianity (from which they had excluded enslaved people), while the Spanish and French emphasized natural law and shared Christianity (into which they had forced everyone).

Competing ideas about who belonged within colonial Caribbean societies set up conflict in the international arena. As people increasingly expected interpolity procedures to govern cross-border conflict, they had to determine which members of each society warranted protection.[8] When lawmakers within a polity excluded categories of people from the political personhood that gave them full membership within their own society, they could try to prevent them from exercising the rights supposedly accorded by *ius gentium* to "peoples" in the international arena. We can see the process at work in officials' efforts to coordinate (or dictate) prosecution of pirates, when English slaveholders sought to retrieve former captives who had fled, and when Spanish guardacostas captains endeavored to force the return of new Jews.

Questions of race and religion remained contentious. When the creation of race accompanied and enabled the enslavement of Africans and Indigenous Americans, in the eyes of enslavers it gradually came to replace national designations (such as Caravali or Miskito) for the people who were enslaved. For English colonizers, the process of enslavement that separated captive people from their nations justified denying them the protections that law afforded. The English rendering of *ius* into "law" rather than "right" and *gente* into "nation" and not "people" facilitated stripping peoples (*gente*) of their natural-law rights (*ius*). In Spanish and French law, as in English, the process of enslavement and transportation severed people from their ancestral nations and labeled them with racial identities. But Catholic colonizers incorporated people of color into the colonial body politic as constituents. In moments of cross-border negotiation, Spanish and French officials might regard enslaved people of color as *gente* with *derechos*—people owed justice, and not mere slaveholders' property.

All Caribbean colonizers maintained hierarchies of rights within the boundaries of their political communities. The Spanish included all Catholics, ranked according to race and wealth. The English included all Whites, ranked according to religion and wealth. Establishing these hierarchies of rights in the Caribbean perhaps proved easier for the Spanish than for their English contemporaries because in Spanish American societies, political belonging included vassalage in addition to subjecthood. The word *vassalage*, which had originally described a medieval peasant's relationship to a lord, evolved very differently in English and Spanish as that relationship disappeared in early modern societies. In Spanish, it came to describe the relationship between individuals and the monarch. The original meaning did not disappear; within the Spanish world, people emphasized their obedience and loyalty as vassals. *Subjects* (*subditos*) was a term mostly reserved for diplomacy, so it applied to individuals primarily when they traveled outside their sovereign's dominions, where they owed obedience to his treaties and could expect protection from foreign abuse.

In English the word *vassal* became a term conveying subjugation and a lack of rights. In the English Atlantic, where *subject* was the only functioning category to describe the relationship an individual had to the sovereign or the polity, it applied both within the body politic and outside it. But whereas the Spanish emphasized their loyalty and obedience as vassals, the English stressed their rights as subjects. The higher stakes of English political ideals, with no middle ground (combined with the more exacting demands of many forms of Protestantism), perhaps made inclusion of colonized peoples into the body politic less likely in the English world than in the Spanish. While intermediate degrees of belonging existed (for religious minorities, for non-freeholders), a growing English emphasis on the rights of individual subjects (and a concomitant move to tie those rights to property ownership) suggested an increasingly exclusive political belonging. Indeed, Barbadian lawmakers made the overt claim that people of African descent were unqualified for the jury trials that many English people saw as a prime marker of their subject rights.[9] It is a similar irony that in the English Caribbean, toleration (for Jews, foreigners, and Catholics) and even, in the case of Castillo and his networks, something approaching cosmopolitan welcome, served the interests of slave trading.

At the end of the War of the Spanish Succession, Great Britain acquired a thirty-year asiento license for the South Sea Company. Feverish investment in the South Sea Company, generally remembered as a cautionary tale for investors, also revealed an ongoing British commitment to profit by selling men and women into slavery. This willingness came during the era that the economist Albert Hirschman has identified as the period when Europeans came to accept individuals' pursuit of their economic interest as commendable rather than censurable.[10] This profound shift followed and was perhaps enabled by the emergence of "a vocabulary of private rights," which Martti Koskenniemi has attributed to sixteenth- and seventeenth-century Spanish Scholastics. When the flood of American silver and gold expanded the scale of global trade and dramatically swelled merchants' profits, those legal scholars argued that the commerce was morally permissible. Despite the Christian view that "profit making for private gain . . . constituted the mortal sin of avarice," the commerce benefited the commonwealth, and the innovative economies of scale seemed necessary to address complexities of global exchange.

The Scholastics outlined a private right of property, "together with the derivative rights of travel and trade, enforced by just war." Koskenniemi argues that we should think of the Scholastics "not so much as reluctant advocates of a formal Spanish lordship over distant peoples but as articulators and ideologists of a global structure of horizontal relationships between holders of the subjective rights of *dominium*." In other words, they were concerned with relations *among* European colonizers, and saw "private-law relationships of contract and property" as the means to govern those relations.[11] Much of this new *ius gentium* thus drew a distinction between trading peoples who made use of such private law and peoples who did not.

Though in a different vein, Antony Anghie also makes a powerful case that we should look to Europe's colonial expansion for the origins of international law, and that we should recognize international law's role in the repeated re-creation of the global inequalities of colonialism. He identifies Europeans' self-declared civilizing mission as the primary means by which Europeans imposed their historically and geographically specific laws on the rest of the world, as supposedly universal.[12] Other scholars likewise have noted that the criteria for civilization—the standard for inclusion within the law of nations—changed continually and were, until the late nineteenth century, often unstated.[13] Much of this analysis, however, leaps from Francisco de Vitoria in the sixteenth century to Emer de Vattel in the mid-eighteenth century, or even to nineteenth-century positivism.

If we look to the Caribbean in the late seventeenth and early eighteenth centuries, we can see that participation in commerce came to be regarded as a marker of civilization, as the Company of Scotland's promotional writings attest. Such elevation of profit seeking, by individuals and nation-states, overrode Christian teachings that saw an individual's focus on material self-interest as dangerous to one's soul and community. Because that shift coincided with the escalation of Atlantic and Caribbean slave trading, it was inextricably entangled with Europeans' commitment to the commodification of people as producers of wealth and as trade goods themselves.

Britain's monopoly on the slave trade to Spanish America contributed to its overall commercial expansion, increasing its influence over the Caribbean, the Atlantic, and indeed the world's oceans over the course of the eighteenth century. By the late eighteenth and into the nineteenth century, British maritime power allowed British imperial agents to engage in what Lauren Benton describes as a "purposeful confusion of English law and the law of nations."[14] As a result, the significance of English attachment to whiteness and commerce extended beyond the British empire. The "ordering of international relations by recourse to private property, contract, and exchange" was not only a means for Europeans to exert power over other peoples directly, but became a basis (alongside profession of Christianity) for membership in the international legal community.[15] While Europeans surely traded with Africans and Indigenous Americans, they did not include them among the trading peoples who could have recourse to all parts of *ius gentium*. As William Paterson had imagined in 1701, the international slave trade had so enriched the British king that he could presume to be "the effective guardian of the sea and protector of the commercial world."[16]

Much of the literature on the law of nations, in examining Europeans collectively as colonizers participating in a shared process, misses the distinctions in the ways the Spanish and English imagined their own claims to universalism. Those distinctions, so visible in English Jamaica's late seventeenth- and early eighteenth-century relationship with the Spanish American ports that surrounded it, show how European legal universalism began to move from being based in Christianity to being based on a combination of whiteness, participation in global commerce, and a Christian identity.

Multiple scholars have shown us how seventeenth-century colonizing Europeans' initial use of Christianity to mark difference (both within their colonial societies and between themselves and the people they sought to exploit) contributed to the evolution of categories of race.[17] They have also noted that in the international arena, the basis for inclusion within the shared community of international law "shifted from the religious to the civilizational," and by the late nineteenth century, "'civilization' became tightly tied to whiteness."[18] But the way that Christianity figured in interpolity law also changed. Initially, demands to include other Christians in shared law invoked a shared community whose members should treat one another humanely. As Julia Gaffield notes, by the nineteenth century Christianity became a key component of "civility" as a means of excluding non-Europeans from full admission to the international arena.[19]

These moves were not merely processes whereby Christianity provided the groundwork for concepts of whiteness or civilized nations to develop. What we see in the Caribbean is that the English, whose definitions would come to dominate, began to exclude Spanish Americans as less White and less civilized *because of* their adherence to Christian universalism. They would likely have denied it: Jamaica governor Lynch criticized the Dutch for their supposed maxim "Jesus Christ is good but trade is better," even as the English came to a similar affirmation of mercantile success, not just as a valuable means to political, diplomatic, or religious ascendance but as virtuous. They subverted the messages that the religion's sacred text repeated so frequently: that people should "love" others—strangers and enemies as well as "one another"—and that pursuit of material wealth was not only incompatible with that love but was in fact the "root of all evil." In this way, the universalism of the law of nations effectively rejected the universalism of Christianity. Nineteenth- and twentieth-century international lawyers who "continued to insist . . . on the distinctively Christian character of international law" neglected that past.[20]

The notion that interpolity law encompassed only "nations" that demonstrated commercial aptitude persisted into the nineteenth and twentieth centuries, when full inclusion in the international legal community depended on polities' display of a sufficient "standard of civilization." Ntina Tzouvala argues that that the standard (originally rooted in adherence to principles of Christianity and natural law) became synonymous with conformity to capitalist modernity, which polities could theoretically achieve, even as it retained racist assumptions that some (non-White, non-Western) political communities could not achieve such standards. The very integration of these disadvantaged communities into the global capitalist economy, supposedly a precondition for full inclusion in international law, in reality perpetuated economic inequalities that made it difficult to achieve the political stabilities also needed to demonstrate the necessary "standard of civilization."[21]

We can see the roots of the "seemingly contradictory" two standards—whiteness on the one hand and embrace of capitalism on the other—in the seventeenth-century Caribbean and specifically in slave trading. Not only did that commerce reduce enslaved people of color to objects rather than subjects, but it foreshadowed the complicated place of Spanish America in the international community. As Spanish American nation-states gained their independence, European jurists and diplomats recognized them as treaty-worthy members of the international community, but not as equal ones. They were subject to extractive exploitation at the hands of Europe and the United States, who disregarded their sovereignty and used racism to justify their contempt. By the end of the seventeenth century, the English, who had so recently exhibited deference born of necessity toward Spanish America, could refer to it as "the great Carcass, upon which all the rest doe prey."[22] In English eyes, Spain's commercial failure—to supply its colonists with the goods they desired—relegated it to a peripheral source of imperial wealth for others. At the same time, as we have seen in Chapter 2, the English disparaged Spanish America's residents as "mongrels" too degraded by their racial impurities to meet the standards of behavior—such as giving quarter to captured enemies—that the law of nations required.

Elena Schneider provides us with a forceful example of how profoundly eighteenth-century Britain's growing maritime power shaped race relations beyond its borders. Its 1762–1763 occupation of Havana had lasting consequences for the island's enslaved and free Black populations. In response to their surprising and devastating defeat, Spanish officials and elites set into motion a series of changes that stripped Afro-Cubans of many traditional privileges. Those privileges, affirmed in Spain's earlier Caribbean conflicts with the English, now fell victim to a Spanish determination to develop their own transatlantic slave trade, in order to sever themselves from their dependence on British merchants. But to do so they adopted the slave-trading logic of those same enemies and increasingly denied African-descended Cubans a place in the body politic that earlier had been ensured by their Catholicism and their contributions as loyal subjects to their sovereign.[23] Despite these shifts, however, we should recognize that Cuban society, like that of other Spanish American colonies and new nations, remained, in theory and in reality, more committed to an inclusive (though unequal) body politic than those of British American colonies or the new United States.[24]

It makes sense that the United States became the first nation-state outside Europe to gain inclusion into the law-of-nations community.[25] In limiting new citizenship to "free white person[s]," U.S. lawmakers modeled their nation's membership rules on the British Atlantic's exclusionary body politic.[26] In the British Atlantic over the course of the eighteenth century, and in the United States at the end of the eighteenth century, the exclusion of people of African and Indigenous descent from the body politic rested on work undertaken at the end of the seventeenth century. That earlier effort permitted racial exclusion to persist and seem natural, even as increasing numbers of enslaved and free Africans and Natives converted to Christianity, and as abolitionists challenged the legitimacy of the transatlantic slave trade on legal and ethical grounds.

Spanish American nations, as they struggled during the Age of Revolution to create republics, contended with histories of slavery and racism that they shared with the United States. But they also had a tradition of unequal, but still significant inclusion of people of color. True to their colonial past in other ways as well, many new Spanish American nations retained Catholicism as a precondition for citizenship, or demanded outward religious conformity. European nations (especially Great Britain) and the United States responded with great ambiguity toward Spanish American independence and sovereignty in the nineteenth century. As "Europe evaluated and categorized states legally and politically as 'civilized,' or 'semi-civilized' or 'uncivilized,'" Europeans (and North Americans) called Spanish American civilization into question, often on racist grounds, as justification for commercial or military conquest. We can see a forewarning of that dismissal in seventeenth-century English officials' denigration of Spain's American vassals as "mongrels." The international community's rejection of Haiti, despite its explicitly Christian constitution, presaged that community's ambiguous reception of Spanish American independent nations.[27] In the new bodies politic of the Age of Revolution we can see the long shadows of seventeenth-century Caribbean political economies. And in the international order that grew over the following century, we can see how those political economies, resting as they did on the transatlantic slave trade, set the stage for an exclusionary law of nations.

NOTES

The following abbreviations appear in the notes.

AGI	Archivo General de Indias, Seville
BL	British Library
CO	Colonial Office series, The National Archives of the UK
CSP	Colonial State Papers, ProQuest. Most of the material that I have cited from this database is also available in the *Calendar of State Papers, Colonial, America and West Indies* (London: HMSO, 1860–1969).
EEBO	Early English Books Online
JA	Jamaica Archives
NRS	National Records of Scotland
NLS	National Library of Scotland
PARES	Portal de Archivos Españoles

Introduction

1. Sir Thos. Modyford to Sec. Sir Henry Bennet (Lord Arlington), May 10, 1664, Barbados, TNA CO 1/18, no. 65, p. 7.

2. Richard Blome, *A Description of the Island of Jamaica* (London, 1672), 54–55.

3. Deputy Governor Sir Henry Morgan to the Lords of Trade and Plantations, Port Royal, January 27, 1681, CSP. Two years later a published collection of the island's laws described Jamaica as "commodiously seated in the midst of the Spaniards." *The Laws of Jamaica* (London: H. Hills, 1683).

4. Additionally, European efforts to create empire in the region drove most record keeping. Colonial officials created and preserved most of the documents that survive. Their concerns, not ours, structure the archives and influence what we can know. Ann Laura Stoler, *Along the Archival Grain: Epistemic Anxieties and Colonial Common Sense* (Princeton, NJ: Princeton University Press, 2009); Marisa J. Fuentes, *Dispossessed Lives: Enslaved Women, Violence, and the Archive* (Philadelphia: University of Pennsylvania Press, 2016).

5. I take as a starting point, following the work of many scholars, that English Caribbean colonies influenced English North America and the English Atlantic as a whole, especially with regard to slavery and race. See Susan Dwyer Amussen, *Caribbean Exchanges: Slavery and the Transformation of English Society, 1650–1700* (Chapel Hill: University of North Carolina Press, 2007); Richard S. Dunn, "The English Sugar Islands and the Founding of South Carolina," *South Carolina Historical Magazine* 72 (1971), 81–93; April Lee Hatfield, *Atlantic Virginia: Intercolonial Relations in the Seventeenth Century* (Philadelphia: University of Pennsylvania Press, 2004); Peter H. Wood, *Black Majority: Negroes in Colonial South Carolina from 1670 Through the Stono Rebellion* (New York: Alfred A. Knopf, 1975); Simon P. Newman, *A New World of Labor: The*

Development of Plantation Slavery in the British Atlantic (Philadelphia: University of Pennsylvania Press, 2013). For the specific importance of Jamaica, see Leslie Theibert, "Making an English Caribbean, 1650–1688" (Ph.D. diss., Yale University, 2013); Abigail L. Swingen, *Competing Visions of Empire: Labor, Slavery, and the Origins of the British Atlantic Empire* (New Haven, Conn.: Yale University Press, 2015); Trevor Burnard and John Garrigus, *The Plantation Machine: Atlantic Capitalism in French Saint-Domingue and British Jamaica* (Philadelphia: University of Pennsylvania Press, 2016).

6. Julius Scott first recognized the possibility for such communication networks in *The Common Wind: Afro-American Currents in the Age of the Haitian Revolution* (New York: Verso, 2018).

7. Two distinct legal principles underpinned European thought regarding allegiance and subjecthood. *Jus sanguinis*, the right of blood, saw the status and its obligations and privileges as hereditary, passing from one or both parents to their (legal) offspring. *Jus soli*, the right of soil, saw place of birth (within the sovereign's dominions) as conferring subjecthood. Brook E. Newman, *A Dark Inheritance: Blood, Race, and Sex in Colonial Jamaica* (New Haven, Conn.: Yale University Press, 2018); Holly Brewer, "Slavery, Sovereignty, and 'Inheritable Blood': Reconsidering John Locke and the Origins of American Slavery," *American Historical Review* 122 (2017), 1038–1078. Without the Latin terminology, people in the Caribbean appealed to both principles as well as to the idea that one could choose one's allegiance and formalize a tie with a sovereign by performing a ceremony that usually involved taking an oath. All of these principles also met opposition.

8. Much scholarship has emphasized the Caribbean as an arena of war, with "no peace beyond the line." See Chapter 1 for a fuller discussion of the concept and literature. *Boundaries of Belonging* shows that those who adhered to the concept represented a minority of people living and involved in the region.

9. A similar study could well have been done on the Spanish and French or the Spanish and Dutch. The Spanish, because they controlled the people and territory that provided the bullion and were therefore the target of other Europeans, are a necessary part of the story. Subjects and officials of other empires entered (willingly or unwillingly) into entanglements, first with Spanish America and secondarily with one another. For the persistence of this pattern, see Eliga H. Gould, "Entangled Histories, Entangled Worlds: The English-Speaking Atlantic as a Spanish Periphery," *American Historical Review* 112 (2007), 764–786.

10. Frank Tannenbaum, *Slave and Citizen* (New York: Knopf, 1946), vii.

11. María Elena Díaz, "Beyond Tannenbaum," *Law and History Review* 22 (2004), 371–376. However, it is important to note that we can see the persistence of meaningful differences in political theory in U.S. constitutions that sought to exclude people of African and Indigenous descent, and in Spanish American efforts (however problematic) to include them. Robert J. Cottrol, *The Long, Lingering Shadow: Slavery, Race, and Law in the American Hemisphere* (Athens: University of Georgia Press, 2013).

12. Evan Haefeli offers a correction to overblown portraits of English tolerance in *Accidental Pluralism: America and the Religious Politics of Expansion, 1497–1662* (Chicago: University of Chicago Press, 2021), and Stuart B. Schwartz argues for greater religious toleration in Spanish and Portuguese America. My findings (more in line with a traditional interpretation) reflect the oppositional posture of Caribbean officials, who operated in border areas threatened by violence at the hands of Protestant rivals. Schwartz, *All Can Be Saved: Religious Tolerance and Salvation in the Iberian Atlantic World* (New Haven, Conn.: Yale University Press, 2008).

13. Lauren Benton notes Europeans' "widely shared legal repertoire," emphasizing especially their shared familiarity with Roman law. *A Search for Sovereignty: Law and Geography in European Empires, 1400–1900* (New York: Cambridge University Press, 2010), 23.

14. Alejandro de la Fuente stresses that individuals who "made claims and pressed for benefits . . . gave concrete social meaning to the abstract rights regulated in the positive laws," while criticizing Tannenbaum for granting social agency to the laws themselves. "Slave Law and Claims-Making in Cuba: The Tannenbaum Debate Revisited," *Law and History Review* 22 (2004), 339–369. See also de la Fuente and Ariela J. Gross, *Becoming Free, Becoming Black: Race, Freedom, and Law in Cuba, Virginia, and Louisiana* (New York: Cambridge University Press, 2020); de la Fuente, "From Slaves to Citizens? Tannenbaum and the Debates on Slavery, Emancipation, and Race Relations in Latin America," *International Labor and Working-Class History* 77 (2010), 154–173; and Jane Landers, *Black Society in Spanish Florida* (Urbana: University of Illinois Press, 1999). Brian P. Owensby and Richard J. Ross note the "inclusion of indigenous people in the social and legal order" in Spanish America, which, though "always contested and often violated," stood in contrast to their legal separation in English America. "Making Law Intelligible in Comparative Context," in Owensby and Ross, eds., *Justice in a New World: Negotiating Legal Intelligibility in British, Iberian, and Indigenous America* (New York: New York University Press, 2018), 8.

15. They had inherited the language and concept of the body politic from medieval political theorists, who drew on both Plato and Paul for the metaphor. Joëlle Rollo-Koster, "Body Politic," in Mark Bevir, ed., *Encyclopedia of Political Theory* (Thousand Oaks, Calif.: Sage, 2010), 1:133–137.

16. For a seventeenth-century English colonial use of the metaphor to explain human inequality, see John Winthrop's 1630 "A Modell of Christian Charity," widely available, including at https://www.masshist.org/publications/winthrop/index.php/view/PWF02d270 and in *Winthrop Papers*, Vol. 2 (Boston: Massachusetts Historical Society, 1931), 282–295.

17. For distrust, see María Elena Martínez, *Genealogical Fictions: Limpieza de Sangre, Religion, and Gender in Colonial Mexico* (Stanford, Calif.: Stanford University Press, 2008).

18. María Elena Díaz, *The Virgin, the King, and the Royal Slaves of El Cobre: Negotiating Freedom in Colonial Cuba, 1670–1780* (Stanford, Calif.: Stanford University Press, 2000).

19. This process is better known in the Florida-Carolina border region, where refugees and officials drew on the earlier Caribbean precedents that I describe in Chapter 3. Landers, *Black Society in Spanish Florida.*

20. Although my analysis differs from a Weberian argument that Protestantism facilitated capitalism, it is compatible. I argue that the multiplication of Christianities within Protestant England and the consequent severing of the body politic from any one religious body permitted English lawmakers to make enslaved people's legal definition as property more important than their legal personhood. In the Spanish world, where similar tension existed, the continuing ability to see church and state unified in one mystical body encouraged lawmakers to emphasize the legal personhood of enslaved people, especially in relation to their English and Dutch rivals. Max Weber, *The Protestant Ethic and the Spirit of Capitalism* (1905; New York: W. W. Norton, 2009).

21. This separation was legally articulated earlier, in a colonial context, in Maryland's 1649 Toleration Act.

22. Travis Glasson, *Mastering Christianity: Missionary Anglicanism and Slavery in the Atlantic World* (New York: Oxford University Press, 2012); Katherine Gerbner, *Christian*

Slavery: Conversion and Race in the Protestant Atlantic World (Philadelphia: University of Pennsylvania Press, 2018). Barbadians feared enslaved New England Indians precisely because they had been exposed to Christianity. Linford D. Fisher, "'Dangerous Designes': The 1676 Barbados Act to Prohibit New England Indian Slave Importation," *William and Mary Quarterly*, 3rd ser., 71 (2014), 99–124.

23. Rebecca Goetz shows that in Virginia, English slave owners initially used Christianity to exclude Africans as non-Christians, which required that they resist converting slaves. Enslaved people's lack of Christianity then allowed colonists to justify to themselves their exclusion of African-descended people from the body politic. In other words, by equating Christianity with whiteness, Virginia colonists created a means to exclude on the basis of race. Even though they wrote laws specifying that conversion did not preclude enslavement, they preferred the greater gulf that they could maintain by not evangelizing, and they expressed concern that shared Christianity would require better treatment. English lawmakers only then accepted Christianizing efforts in the eighteenth century, after the process of denying legal personhood was complete. Rebecca Anne Goetz, *The Baptism of Early Virginia: How Christianity Created Race* (Baltimore: Johns Hopkins University Press, 2012). See also Gerbner, *Christian Slavery*.

24. Throughout the manuscript I capitalize all racial categories in English, including White, Black, Mulatto, and Mestizo. I argue in the book that the creation and assignment of legal and political meaning to such categories was an important means by which imperial officials included or excluded people from the body politic. Racial identities also shaped individuals' sense of their place within local communities, colonies, and empires. English officials may have wished to see whiteness as an absence of race, a default category that could operate as shorthand for the full personhood they wished to deny other people. I capitalize the word "White" to remind myself and readers that it was a time- and space-specific legal creation with considerable import, as were the other racial categories that people claimed and were assigned in the early modern Caribbean.

25. Such distinctions rested on long-standing differences between English and Spanish political practice. Spain's long history of medieval *convivencia*, along with its uneasy incorporation of forced converts, many of North African descent, during the *reconquista*, left Spaniards familiar (if not comfortable) with the possibility of a visibly diverse but religiously homogeneous body politic. In contrast, England's greater distance from the Mediterranean and Africa limited English Christians' exposure to Muslims, Jews, and phenotypic diversity. The Caribbean's particular political and economic geographies made those differences both more obvious and more relevant.

26. The religiously weighted language of Anglo-Spanish rivalry is clear in both sides' propaganda surrounding Cromwell's Western Design. Carla Gardina Pestana, *The English Conquest of Jamaica: Oliver Cromwell's Bid for Empire* (Cambridge, Mass.: Harvard University Press, 2017).

27. Steve Pincus has argued that economic regulations aiming to close imperial borders were not nearly as ubiquitous during the seventeenth or eighteenth centuries as the term mercantilism suggests. See "Rethinking Mercantilism" forum, *William and Mary Quarterly*, 3rd ser., 69 (2012), 3–70, especially Pincus, "Rethinking Mercantilism: Political Economy, the British Empire, and the Atlantic World in the Seventeenth and Eighteenth Centuries," 3–34.

28. Ignacio Gallup-Diaz, *The Door of the Seas and the Key to the Universe: Indian Politics and Imperial Rivalry in the Darién, 1640–1750* (New York: Columbia University Press/

gutenberg-e, 2004), underscores the importance of the Isthmus of Panama. The central place of Panama in Caribbean, Atlantic, and global history is the focus of "An ARTery of EMPIRE: Conquest, Commerce, Crisis, Culture and the Panamanian Junction (1513–1671)," headed by Bethany Aram. Scholarship supported by this project includes Alejandro García-Montón, "The Rise of Portobelo and the Transformation of the Spanish American Slave Trade, 1640s–1730s: Transimperial Connections and Intra-American Shipping," *Hispanic American Historical Review* 99 (2019), 399–429; García-Montón, *Genoese Entrepreneurship and the Asiento Slave Trade, 1650–1700* (New York: Routledge, 2022); and Bethany Aram, "¿Entre dos mares? Reflexiones a partir de la Historia Atlántica y hacía tres conceptos de la Historia Global," *Nuevo Mundo, Mundos Nuevos* (2019), n.p.

29. Smuggling of rival Europeans' manufactured goods to Spanish America occurred both through southern Spain and through those Europeans' Caribbean colonies. Nuala Zahedieh, "The Merchants of Port Royal, Jamaica and Spanish Contraband Trade, 1655–1692," *William and Mary Quarterly*, 3rd ser., 43 (1986), 570–593; Curtis P. Nettels, "England and the Spanish-American Trade, 1680–1715," *Journal of Modern History* 3 (1931), 1–32; Stanley J. Stein and Barbara H. Stein, *Silver, Trade, and War: Spain and America in the Making of Early Modern Europe* (Baltimore: Johns Hopkins University Press, 2000); Wim Klooster, *Illicit Riches: Dutch Trade in the Caribbean, 1648–1795* (Leiden: KITLV Press, 1998); José Ignacio Martínez Ruiz, "¿Cádiz, Jamaica o Londres? La colonia británica de Cádiz y las transformaciones del comercio inglés con la América española (1655–1750)," *Studia Historica: Historia Moderna* 33 (2011), 177–202; Aaron Alejandro Olivas, "Loyalty and Disloyalty to the Bourbon Dynasty in Spanish America and the Philippines During the War of the Spanish Succession (1700–1715)" (Ph.D. diss., UCLA, 2013); Jesse Cromwell, *The Smugglers' World: Illicit Trade and Atlantic Communities in Eighteenth-Century Venezuela* (Chapel Hill: University of North Carolina Press, 2018).

30. Georges Scelle, "The Slave-Trade in the Spanish Colonies of America: The Assiento," trans. Edna K. Hoyt, *American Journal of International Law* 4 (1910), 612–661. The requirement that all Spanish shipping to the Americas depart from Seville (and later Cádiz) would have added fatal time to the transatlantic voyage. The word *asiento* simply meant contract, and the crown granted asientos for things other than slave trading, but the *asiento de negros* became so important in the international Atlantic that the word came to be understood as a synonym for the specific *asiento de negros*.

31. Pestana, *English Conquest*, 98.

32. J[ohn] Daniell [to William Daniell], "A letter from Jamaica," June 3, 1655, in Thomas Birch, ed., *A Collection of the State Papers of John Thurloe, Esq.*, 7 vols. (London, 1742), 3:504–508, 507.

33. Apparently no one showed up to learn the details of the "favourable concessions." Andrew Carter, who had been acting governor of Providence Island when the Spanish reconquered, "relish[ed] his opportunity for revenge" in the negotiations over Jamaica and used the terms the Spanish had offered the English as his model. Pestana, *English Conquest*, 125–126, 208.

34. Barbara Klamon Kopytoff, "The Early Political Development of Jamaican Maroon Societies," *William and Mary Quarterly*, 3rd ser., 35 (1978), 287–307.

35. Cornelius Burough to Robert Blackborne, April 10, 1660, CO 1/33, no. 69; Pestana, *English Conquest*, 194–205.

36. James Robertson, *Gone Is the Ancient Glory: Spanish Town, Jamaica, 1554–2000* (Kingston: Ian Randle, 2005), 42.

37. Despite de Bola's death later in 1663, the palenque (with his name) persisted at least on paper, appearing on John Ogilby's 1671 map and Charles Bochart and Humphrey Knollis's 1682 "A New & Exact Map of the Island of Jamaica." David Buisseret and S. A. G. Taylor, "Juan De Bolas and His Pelinco," *Caribbean Quarterly* 54 (2008), 95–102. But, according to Robertson, after his death "individual members of his group established themselves in Spanish Town, receiving grants of urban properties." *Gone Is the Ancient Glory*, 50.

38. Pestana argues that the English discounted African contributions because they "flew in the face of their own self-image as 'protectors of the Atlantic world,' not to mention the emerging discourse of African inferiority." Pestana, *English Conquest*, 205, 211, cites Michael Guasco, *Slaves and Englishmen: Human Bondage in the Early Modern Atlantic World* (Philadelphia: University of Pennsylvania Press, 2014) , 195–199.

39. Abstract of letter from Ysassi to the king, August 10, 1660, in Frank Cundall and Joseph L. Pietersz, *Jamaica Under the Spaniards, Abstracted from the Archives of Seville* (Kingston: Institute of Jamaica, 1919), 101–102. Ysassi made clear that these were free men. Pestana, *English Conquest*, 203, 225. For the 1656 decree, Pestana cites Edward Doyley, "Journal," 17 Add. MSS 12423, British Library.

40. Pestana, *English Conquest*, 200, 227, cites Proclamation 18 August 1661, Doyley's Journal, 108. She notes that in 1670, Modyford said only Indians were prisoners of war.

41. Spanish Jamaica's status as patrimony of the Columbus family rather than a royal colony, as well as its sparse settlement, excluded the colony from prohibitions against Portuguese immigration, and the absence of an Inquisition office on the island may have made life safer for *conversos* who continued to practice Judaism. Robertson, *Gone Is the Ancient Glory*, 30–31.

42. Robertson, *Gone Is the Ancient Glory*, 46, cites Vincent T. Harlow, ed., "The Voyages of Captain William Jackson (1642–1645)," in *Camden Miscellany XIII* (London: Offices of the Society, 1924), 19. For identification of "Portugals" as Jews or New Christians, see Daviken Studnicki-Gizbert, "*La Nación* among the Nations: Portuguese and Other Maritime Trading Diasporas in the Atlantic, Sixteenth to Eighteenth Centuries," in Richard L. Kagan and Philip D. Morgan, eds., *Atlantic Diasporas: Jews, Conversos, and Crypto-Jews in the Age of Mercantilism, 1500–1800* (Baltimore: Johns Hopkins University Press, 2009), 75–98.

43. Mordechai Arbell, *The Portuguese Jews of Jamaica* (Kingston: Canoe Press/University of the West Indies, 2000), 11.

44. Richard Venables to Secretary Thurloe, June 13, 1655, in *Interesting Tracts, Relating to the Island of Jamaica . . . to the Year 1702* (St. Jago de la Vega: Lewis, Lunan, and Jones, 1800), 47–48.

45. Arbell, *Portuguese Jews of Jamaica*, 11–12.

46. Simon de Caseres to Cromwell, September 1655, in Thomas Birch, ed., *A Collection of the State Papers of John Thurloe, Esq: . . .* 7 vols. (London: Executor of Fletcher Gyles, 1742), 4:61–63, emphasis added.

47. Cromwell's millenarianism prompted his welcome for Jews, whose dispersal throughout the world he believed a necessary precondition for the second coming of Christ.

48. Gregory E. O'Malley, *Final Passages: The Intercolonial Slave Trade of British America, 1619–1807* (Chapel Hill: University of North Carolina Press, 2014).

49. Swingen, *Competing Visions of Empire*.

50. Gerald Horne, *The Apocalypse of Settler Colonialism: The Roots of Slavery, White Supremacy, and Capitalism in Seventeenth-Century North America and the Caribbean* (New York: Monthly Review Press, 2018).

51. For the colonial Caribbean development of a plantation political economy see Díaz, *The Virgin, the King, and the Royal Slaves*. For the Caribbean's varied economy, see Jesse Cromwell, "More Than Slaves and Sugar: Recent Historiography of the Trans-Imperial Caribbean and Its Sinew Populations," *History Compass* 12 (2014), 770–783.

52. For discussion of the Atlantic as a commons, see Michael J. Jarvis, *In the Eye of All Trade: Bermuda, Bermudians, and the Maritime Atlantic World, 1680–1783* (Chapel Hill: University of North Carolina Press, 2010), 185–256.

53. Cromwell, "More Than Slaves and Sugar."

54. The sovereigns of composite monarchies such as Spain and Great Britain acted in the international arena as such, rather than as sovereigns of constituent kingdoms, even when, as in both of these cases, colonization was officially restricted to the subjects of one kingdom only (Castile or England). See Chapter 6 for further discussion.

55. For the importance of *vecino* status, see Tamar Herzog, *Defining Nations: Immigrants and Citizens in Early Modern Spain and Spanish America* (New Haven, Conn.: Yale University Press, 2003), 17–63.

Chapter 1

1. The most obvious examples of such celebration were Richard Hakluyt's *The Principall Navigations, Voyages and Discoveries of the English Nation* (London, 1589) and Samuel Purchas's *Hakluytus Posthumus or Purchas his Pilgrimes* (London, 1625), collections of travel narratives. Mark Hanna provides a summary of such attitudes in *Pirate Nests and the Rise of the British Empire, 1570–1740* (Chapel Hill: University of North Carolina Press, 2015), 21–101.

2. Much scholarship has emphasized the Caribbean as an arena of war. Eric Williams, *From Columbus to Castro: The History of the Caribbean, 1492–1969* (1970; New York: Vintage Books, 1984), especially chapter 7, "The Cockpit of Europe." Carl Bridenbaugh and Roberta Bridenbaugh, *No Peace Beyond the Line: The English in the Caribbean, 1624–1690* (New York: Oxford University Press, 1972); Richard Pares, *War and Trade in the West Indies, 1739–1763* (1936; reprint, London: Frank Cass, 1963). For a history of the phrase, see Elizabeth Mancke, "Empire and State," in David Armitage and Michael J. Braddick, eds., *The British Atlantic World, 1500–1800* (New York: Palgrave Macmillan, 2002), 175–195.

3. Karen Ordahl Kupperman, *Providence Island, 1630–1641: The Other Puritan Colony* (New York: Cambridge University Press, 1993), 26.

4. Pestana, *English Conquest*, 19–41, 98–102, Cromwell quote 99; cites Garrett Mattingly, "No Peace Beyond What Line?" *Transactions of the Royal Historical Society* 13 (1963), 145-162.

5. Pestana, English Conquest, 25, 111; Kristen Block, *Ordinary Lives in the Early Caribbean: Religion, Colonial Competition, and the Politics of Profit* (Athens: University of Georgia Press, 2012), 122.

6. The term *privateer* first appeared in English in 1660 or 1661, referring to Jamaica. Hanna, *Pirate Nests*, 106.

7. The most thorough treatment of the Stuart royal family's promotion of and investment in slave trading remains George Frederick Zook, *The Company of Royal Adventurers Trading into Africa* (Lancaster, Pa.: Press of the New Era Printing Company, 1919).

8. O'Malley, *Final Passages*; Zahedieh, "Merchants of Port Royal"; Andrés Reséndez, *The Other Slavery: The Uncovered Story of Indian Enslavement in America* (New York: Houghton Mifflin, 2016); Karl Offen, "Mapping Amerindian Captivity in Colonial Mosquitia," *Journal of Latin American Geography* 14 (2015), 35–65.

9. The first of these men, buccaneers from Hispaniola and Tortuga, were initially courted by Jamaican officials to hunt the island's feral cattle. Pestana, "Early English Jamaica Without Pirates," *William and Mary Quarterly*, 3rd ser., 71 (2014), 321–360.

10. Nuala Zahedieh, "Trade, Plunder, and Economic Development in Early English Jamaica," *Economic History Review* 39 (1986), 205–222; Zahedieh, "'A Frugal, Prudential and Hopeful Trade': Privateering in Jamaica, 1655–89," *Journal of Imperial and Commonwealth History* 18 (1990), 145–168; Zahedieh, "The Capture of the Blue Dove, 1664: Policy, Profit and Protection in Early English Jamaica," in Roderick A. McDonald, ed., *West Indies Accounts: Essays on the History of the British Caribbean and the Atlantic Economy in Honour of Richard Sheridan* (Kingston: University Press of the West Indies, 1996), 29–47.

11. Merchants had long traded with one another across national and religious boundaries in Europe. Heather Dalton, "Negotiating Fortune: English Merchants in Early Sixteenth-Century Seville," in Caroline A. Williams, ed., *Bridging the Early Modern Atlantic World: People, Products, and Practices on the Move* (New York: Routledge, 2009), 57–74. The Spanish crown enforced the exclusion of Protestants (and new Christians) from their American possessions in part to protect Indigenous and African converts, whom Spanish officials regarded as susceptible to corruption from heresy. Karoline P. Cook, *Forbidden Passages: Muslims and Moriscos in Colonial Spanish America* (Philadelphia: University of Pennsylvania Press, 2016), 2–3, 73–74.

12. Scholars have noted that privateers brought human plunder into English colonies and sold those captives. Because some of those men and women had been enslaved when captured, either on slave-trading ships or in other colonies, it is less recognized that many individuals so sold had been free in Spanish or Portuguese America. Hanna, *Pirate Nests*; Wood, *Black Majority*, 44; St. Julien Ravenel Childs, *Malaria and Colonization in the Carolina Low Country, 1526–1696* (Baltimore: Johns Hopkins University Press, 1940), 207, for information that pirates captured almost two hundred Black people in their 1683 raid on Vera Cruz and sold them in Carolina. Some later escaped to Florida.

13. When Modyford sent his own slave-trading ship to Cartagena, his captain sold captive Africans for pieces of eight. From there the ship sailed to Boston rather than returning to Barbados, perhaps in illustration of one of the disadvantages of carrying on a slave trade to Spanish America from Barbados. Having sailed west from the island, ships wishing to return had to battle contrary currents and winds. Thomas Modyford to his brother, September 13, 1662, enclosure in entry for February 26, 1663, CO 1/17 nos. 7, 8, 9; J. K. Laughton, revised by Nuala Zahedieh, "Modyford, Sir James, baronet," *Oxford Dictionary of National Biography*, 2004, 2008, https://doi-org.srv-proxy2.library.tamu.edu/10.1093/ref:odnb/18870.

14. Thomas Modyford to his brother, May 26, 1662, CO 1/17, no. 8, one of four letters appended to the February 26, 1663, entry, CO 1/17, nos. 7, 8, 9. The letters are dated between March 30 and September 13, 1662. Modyford addressed the letters "Deare Brother," either to his brother-in-law Thomas Kendall or his brother James Modyford.

15. Thomas Modyford to his brother, April 30, 1662, May 26, 1662, September 13, 1662, enclosures in entry for February 26, 1663, CO 1/17, nos. 7, 8, 9.

16. Thomas Modyford to his brother, September 13, 1662, enclosure in entry for February 26, 1663, CO 1/17 nos. 7, 8, 9.

17. Proposals in the handwriting of Col Thomas Modyford, CO 1/18, no. 2, likely 1663. See also several 1662 extracts from Modyford's letters, discussed below, enclosures appended to the February 26, 1663, entry, CO 1/17, nos. 7, 8, 9.

18. Proposals in the handwriting of Col Thomas Modyford, CO 1/18, no. 2 [before January 11, 1664].

19. Propositions which it is humbly conceived will be for his Majesty's service, CO 1/18, no. 3 [1664]. These are in the same handwriting as the propositions concerning Jamaica that are endorsed "Mr. Kendal's," CO 1/18, no. 4 [1664?]. For Kendall's relationship to Modyford, see Richard S. Dunn, *Sugar and Slaves: The Rise of the Planter Class in the English West Indies, 1624–1713* (Chapel Hill: University of North Carolina Press, 1972), 81. See also the King to Col. Sir Thos. Modyford, CO 1/18, no. 7 [1664] [January 11].

20. Instructions for Coll. Muddiford, February 18, 1664, CO 1/18, no. 26. Susan Amussen notes similar values in Barbados by the 1640s and 1650s. *Caribbean Exchanges*, 31.

21. Instructions for Coll. Muddiford, February 18, 1664, CO 1/18, no. 26.

22. For Charles II's co-opting of his father's former opponents, see Ronald Hutton, *Charles the Second, King of England, Scotland, and Ireland* (New York: Oxford University Press, 1989), 134–139.

23. Instructions for Coll. Muddiford, February 18, 1664, CO 1/18, no. 26.

24. Propositions concerning Jamaica, endorsed "Mr. Kendal's," CO 1/18, no. 4 [1664?].

25. Instructions for Coll. Muddiford, February 18, 1664, CO 1/18, no. 26.

26. Sir Thos. Modyford to Sec. Sir Henry Bennet (Lord Arlington), May 10, 1664, CO 1/18, no. 65. Enclosures ii and iii are his commission (April 30) and instructions (May 2) to Col. Theodore Cary and Capt. John Perrott to treat with the president-general of San Domingo, instructing them to "obtain some testimonial from the Governor" of Cartagena to recommend the English in Jamaica as slave traders, August 20, 1662, CO 139/1, fol. 19.

27. There was Dutch precedent for what Charles proposed, but Modyford's instructions do not mention it. Klooster, *Illicit Riches*; Linda M. Rupert, *Creolization and Contraband: Curaçao in the Early Modern Atlantic World* (Athens: University of Georgia Press, 2012).

28. Instructions for Coll Theodore Cary and Capt John Perrott touchinge theire Negotiation with the Spanyards at Sta Domingo, May 2, 1664, CO 1/18, no. 65iii. (This is an enclosure included with a May 10, 1664, letter from Modyford to Sir Henry Bennet Lord Arlington.)

29. The only commissions allowed were those "authorized by Power derived from Our Dearest Brother the Duke of Yorke Our High Admirall." This was a renewal of instructions from the previous year. CO 1/18, no. 26, February 18, 1664.

30. Minutes of the Council of Jamaica, August 20, 1662, CSP. In both earlier and later periods, smugglers sometimes forced trade with threats of violence. However, during the late seventeenth century, when most English smugglers in the region who traded with Spanish Americans depended on building networks of trust, they opposed privateering. For the later period, see Casey S. Schmitt, "Virtue in Corruption: Privateers, Smugglers, and the Shape of Empire in the Eighteenth-Century Caribbean," *Early American Studies* 13 (2015), 80–110.

31. Pestana, *English Conquest*, 189, 189n11.

32. Stein and Stein, *Silver, Trade, and War*, 94–102; Jean O. McLachlan, *Trade and Peace with Old Spain, 1667–1750* (Cambridge: Cambridge University Press, 1940).

33. One example comes from Thomas Modyford's 1662 report that the Cartagena merchants who came to Jamaica in search of African captives told him that their governor was involved in their project, discussed above. Spanish American officials underwent official investigations (*residencias* or *visitas*) at the end of their terms in office as a matter of course, but a complaint could trigger an earlier investigation.

34. A parallel for English officials was their support for Dutch trade in English colonies. They sometimes argued for its necessity but seldom described their hand in its proliferation. Christian J. Koot, *Empire at the Periphery: British Colonists, Anglo-Dutch Trade, and the Development of the British Atlantic, 1621–1713* (New York: New York University Press, 2011), 87–116.

35. Zahedieh, "Merchants of Port Royal," 571–572. On the regularity of smuggling by the end of the seventeenth century, see Lance Grahn, *The Political Economy of Smuggling: Regional Informal Economies in Early Bourbon New Granada* (Boulder, Colo.: Westview Press, 1997), 1–14; Synnøve Ones, "The Politics of Government in the Audiencia of New Granada, 1681–1719" (Ph.D. diss., University of Warwick, 2000). There is a rich literature on contraband trade and other border crossing in the southern Caribbean, most of it focused on the period after the end of this study. For two recent examples, see Ernesto Bassi, *An Aqueous Territory: Sailor Geographies and New Granada's Transimperial Greater Caribbean World* (Durham, N.C.: Duke University Press, 2017), and Cromwell, *The Smugglers World.*

36. For further development of this argument, see April Lee Hatfield, "Reluctant Petitioners: English Officials and the Spanish Caribbean," in Jorge Cañizares-Esguerra, ed., *Entangled Empires: The Anglo-Iberian Atlantic, 1500–1830* (Philadelphia: University of Pennsylvania Press, 2018), 197–216.

37. Many scholars have told this story, most recently Mark Hanna in *Pirate Nests*, 102–143.

38. This analysis overlaps with but is not identical to that of Swingen in *Competing Visions of Empire.*

39. Their willingness to take commissions from Catholic French officials to pillage the Spanish testifies to the continuing power of English antagonism toward Spain and perhaps to privateers' utilitarian anti-Catholicism.

40. Originally a reference to men who hunted and grilled wild cattle on Hispaniola and Tortuga, the term *buccaneer* came into more widespread usage from the 1660s to the 1680s as the legal status of maritime predators (as either privateers manning private men-of-war or as pirates) became increasingly difficult to discern, given the proliferation of officials willing to grant commissions without a sovereign's approval, to multinational crews of questionable loyalty. English contemporaries used *buccaneer* very specifically to refer to the multinational community of men based in Hispaniola and Tortuga. For a contemporary definition of buccaneers, see the October 3, 1664, letter from Dr. Henry Stubbs to William Godolphin, CO 1/18, no. 116.

41. Kris Lane and other scholars who apply the word *pirate* broadly follow the lead of seventeenth-century Spanish sources. Lane, *Pillaging the Empire: Global Piracy on the High Seas, 1500–1750*, 2nd ed. (New York: Routledge, 2016), 2.

42. Theibert, "Making an English Caribbean," 375–390.

43. See, for example, the Jamaica Council's recommendation to Governor Thomas Modyford that he issue a privateering commission to Henry Morgan, discussed below. Although the Spanish relinquished sole claim to Caribbean waters in the 1670 Treaty of Madrid, some Spanish officials continued to arrest foreign ships on the grounds that their very presence in the Caribbean Sea was illegal. Elizabeth Mancke outlines Spanish claims of jurisdiction over the Caribbean in "Empire and State," in *The British Atlantic World, 1500–1800*, ed. David Armitage and Michael J. Braddick (New York: Palgrave Macmillan, 2002), 179–188.

44. Peter Earle, *The Sack of Panamá: Captain Morgan and the Battle for the Caribbean* (New York: Thomas Dunne Books/St. Martin's Press, 1981), 1–15. The Tortuga governor was unnamed. If Jeremie Deschamps issued the commission, it would have been out of date by the time of the invasion because Deschamps, who had governed Tortuga with commissions from

English Jamaican governor Doyley and from France, had returned to France by 1664 and ceded his right to govern the island to the French West India Company. The company's governor (Bertrand d'Ogeron) arrived the following year. C. H. Haring, *The Buccaneers in the West Indies in the XVII Century* (London: Methuen and Co., 1910), 116–117.

45. Governor Sir Thos. Modyford to Sec. Lord Arlington, June 16, 1666, Jamaica, CO 1/20, no. 100.

46. In the same letter, Modyford noted Providence/Santa Catalina's proximity to Lake Nicaragua, which shortened the overland distance across Nicaragua from the Caribbean to the Pacific, making it a potential alternative to a Panamanian overland connector. Governor Sir Thos. Modyford to Sec. Lord Arlington, June 16, 1666, Jamaica, CO 1/20, no. 100.

47. Governor Sir Thos. Modyford to Sec. Lord Arlington, June 16, 1666, Jamaica, CO 1/20, no. 100. Earle references their "Portuguese commissions issued by the French Governor of Tortuga." *The Sack of Panamá*, 4, 13.

48. Earle, *The Sack of Panamá*, 23. Kristen Block notes that Catholic pirates and privateers could "demonstrate their devotion through their raiding," citing Jean-Baptiste Labat's observation circa 1700, that French privateers "generally give a portion of their good fortune to the churches," in particular "church ornament or church linen." Block, *Ordinary Lives*, 296n52, citing Jean-Baptiste Labat, *Nouveau voyage aux isles de l'Amérique* (1742 ed.), vol. 1, ch. 9. Protestant pirates, in contrast, targeted Catholic churches and altars for destruction. Exquemelin describes Spanish horror at buccaneers' "audacity in plundering the churches." Alexander O. Exquemelin, *The Buccaneers of America*, trans. Alexis Brown (Mineola, N.Y.: Dover Publications, 1969), 123. William Crooke's 1684 edition (translated from a Spanish translation of the original Dutch) claimed that the Jamaican-born John Davis and his men, in an assault on Nicaragua, not only "pillaged" but also "prophan'd" "the Churches, and most sacred things." *Bucaniers of America* (London: William Crooke, 1684), 113.

49. Lauren Benton notes privateers' and pirates' dependence on international order and use of law in *A Search for Sovereignty: Law and Geography in European Empires, 1400–1900* (New York: Cambridge University Press, 2010), 104–161.

50. A Narrative of Sir Thomas Modyford, August 23, 1669, CO 1/24, nos. 81, 82.

51. Minutes of the Council of Jamaica, February 22, 1666, CSP. The council noted that privateering "replenishe[d] the island with coin, bullion, cocoa, logwood, hides, tallow, indigo, cochineal, and many other commodities," not mentioning captives among the "commodities" brought in, despite that reality. However, the same list of justifications for reissuing letters of marque noted that commissions had in the past and hopefully would in the future "enable many to buy slaves and settle plantations."

52. For the English use of the concept "no peace beyond the line" to justify their inability to stop English piracy, see London journalist Henry Muddiman's assertion that Jamaica pirates' attacks in Panama and Guatemala were "no breach of the peace, as being beyond the line, and but the consequence of their refusal of a free trade with us in those parts, and a retaliation of some hostilities they formerly offered in taking twice the Isle of Providence." Muddiman to Geo. Powell, February 21 1667, CSP. In 1666, the Jamaica Council argued that continuing privateering "seems to be the only means to force the Spaniards in time to a free trade, all ways of kindness producing nothing of good neighbourhood, for though all old commissions have been called in, and no new ones granted, and many of their ships restored, yet they continue all acts of hostility, taking our ships and murdering our people, making them work at their fortifications and then sending them into Spain, and very lately they denied an English fleet bound for the

Dutch colonies wood, water, or provisions." This was one of few suggestions that violence could produce more open trade. Minutes of the Council of Jamaica, February 22, 1666, CSP.

53. Earle, *The Sack of Panamá*, 23–24.

54. Earle, *The Sack of Panamá*, 23. One hundred and seventy Spanish colonists left the island. For free Black militiamen elsewhere in Spanish America, see Ben Vinson III, *Bearing Arms for His Majesty: The Free Colored Militia in Colonial Mexico* (Stanford, Calif.: Stanford University Press, 2001); Díaz, *The Virgin, the King, and the Royal Slaves.*

55. Exquemelin, *Buccaneers of America*, 122–124.

56. Abstracts of several letters from Sir James Modyford, the Duke of Albemarle, and the Lord Chancellor to Sir Thomas Modyford, Governor of Jamaica, from March 6, 1665, to February 2, 1667. Quotation is from the November 14, 1666, letter from James Modyford. Thomas Modyford also, however, noted Spanish concern that any concessions they granted to the English would create precedent and provoke similar demands from the French and the Dutch. Enclosure with A Narrative of Sir Thomas Modyford, Governor of Jamaica, August 23, 1669, CO 1/24, nos. 81, 82.

57. *Articles of Peace, Commerce, and Alliance, between the Crowns of Great Britain and Spain. Concluded in a Treaty at Madrid the 13/23 day of May 1667* (London: John Bill and Christopher Barker, Printers to the King, 1667).

58. *Articles of Peace*, Article 1. For a discussion of the European negotiations leading up to the 1667 treaty, see Theibert, "Making an English Caribbean," 258–271.

59. Information of Admiral Henry Morgan, and his officers . . . of their late expedition on the Spanish coast, September 7, 1668, CO 1/23, 59, 59i; Governor Sir Thos. Modyford to the Duke of Albemarle, October 1, 1668, CSP.

60. His emphasis on English culpability rather than on the pirates' international makeup, despite his own French evidence, made sense given his hope for redress in London. Memorial of the Spanish Ambassador to King Charles II, with enclosure, January 7/17, 1669, London, CO 1/24, nos. 1–2. (Item 1 is Molina's memorial. Item 2 is the French captain's account, in French.)

61. Abstracts of several letters from Sir James Modyford, the Duke of Albemarle, and the Lord Chancellor to Sir Thomas Modyford, Governor of Jamaica, from March 6, 1665, to February 2, 1667. Quotations are from January 13 and January 31, 1667, letters from James Modyford, enclosure with A Narrative of Sir Thomas Modyford, Governor of Jamaica, August 23, 1669, CO 1/24, nos. 81, 82.

62. Theibert, "Making an English Caribbean."

63. Commission of war by the Spaniard against the English in the West Indies, January 26, February 5, 1670, CSP.

64. Englishmen who had been imprisoned in Spanish American towns complained of fifteen-hour days of hard labor, beatings, chains, and threats of death and eternal damnation. Deposition of William Lowe before Thomas Modyford, [September 30], 1669, CSP.

65. John Style to "the Principal Secretary of State, Whitehall," January 4, 1670, CSP. For total population figures, see Dunn, *Sugar and Slaves*, 155.

66. John Style to "the Principal Secretary of State, Whitehall," January 4, 1670, CSP.

67. John Style to "the Principal Secretary of State, Whitehall," January 4, 1670, CSP; Style to Sec. Sir Wm Morrice, January 14, 1669, CSP.

68. Jamaica governor Sir Thomas Modyford to the Spanish ambassador, June 15, 1669, CO 1/24, no. 68.

69. A Narrative of Sir Thos. Modyford, August 23, 1669, CSP.

70. A Narrative of Sir Thos. Modyford, August 23, 1669, CSP. John Style believed that more planters continued to turn privateer than the other way round, selling their plantations to pay for debts incurred in drinking, then going out on "let passes" when commissions were unavailable. He claimed that the number of privateers had remained steady in Port Royal (while declining elsewhere on the island), with about eight hundred still connected to Jamaica in early 1670. Style to "the Principal Secretary of State, Whitehall," January 4, 1670, CSP.

71. Offen, "Mapping Amerindian Captivity," 37–38.

72. Governor Sir Thomas Modyford to the Duke of Albemarle, Jamaica, November 30, 1669, CSP.

73. In the seventeenth-century Caribbean, official titles did not always translate easily between languages and empires. Here Carstens referred to the "governor" of Bayamo having sent his "alcalde" to the ship. My use of "mayor" and "lieutenant" reflects my sense of the Spanish officers to whom he most likely referred. Deposition of Cornelius Carstens, Jamaica, March 21, 1670, CSP.

74. Deposition of Cornelius Carstens, Jamaica, March 21, 1670, CSP (enclosure in Gov. Sir Thos. Modyford to Sec. Lord Arlington, Jamaica, April 10/20, 1670, CSP); Extract of a letter [from Sir Jas. Modyford?] to Col. Lynch, March 18, 1670, CSP. Here the reference was simply "Bart."

75. Extract of a letter [from Sir Jas. Modyford?] to Col. Lynch, March 18, 1670, CSP. In Modyford's first report on the incident he mistakenly identified Ribeiro as the governor of Santiago (whom he also referred to as "this Biskayner.")

76. Governor Sir Thomas Modyford to Sec. Lord Arlington, March 18, 1670, CSP.

77. Extract of a letter [from Sir Jas. Modyford] to Col. Lynch, March 18, 1670, CSP.

78. Depositions of John Coxend and Peter Bursett, Jamaica, March 30, 1670, enclosure in Governor Sir Thos Modyford to Sec. Lord Arlington, April 10/20, 1670, Jamaica, CSP. Modyford reported that a privateer had taken the Spanish man-of-war, without mentioning his earlier claim to have called in all the privateering commissions.

79. Deposition of Nicholas Hicks, gent. Jamaica, March 31, 1670, enclosure in Governor Sir Thos Modyford to Sec. Lord Arlington, April 10/20, 1670, Jamaica, CSP.

80. *A treaty for the composing of differences, restraining of depredations and establishing of peace in America between the crowns of Great Britain and Spain:* concluded at Madrid the 8th/18 day of July in the year of our Lord, 1670. Printed by the Assigns of John Bill and Christopher Barker, Printers to the Kings Most Excellent Majesty, 1670, EEBO.

81. At a Council held at St. Jago Dela vega, June 29, 1670, Jamaica, BL Add. 11268, f. 66. Papers relating to Jca and Capt. Morgan's exp agst Cartagena 1670–1, ff. 8–65, in Spanish, including copy of the queen regent's cedula to Modyford via Wm [Preb] Governour of Quarera.

82. Council at St. Jago Dela vega, June 29, 1670, BL Add. 11268, f. 66. The Jamaica councilors also asserted that "diverse of the rest of the Spanish Governours have also granted Commissions," were "levying of fforces against us," and all planned to rendezvous at Santiago de Cuba, where they were amassing weapons for their combined attack on Jamaica.

83. Modyford to Morgan, July 22, 1670, BL Add. 11268, f. 68. He referred to "the Col Pedro Bayona y billa nueba Capt Genll of the Privinces of Paraguay and Govr of the Citty of St Jago de Cuba & its Province." Earle says Morgan did not receive the license until August 1. Modyford claimed that he received the king's commands for peace on August 13, the day after Morgan sailed.

Earle, *The Sack of Panamá*, 144–146. However, a Port Royal resident reported on August 11 that he had seen "a large packet from his Majesty" arrive for Modyford between August 8 and 11, suggesting that Modyford had instructions for peace before Morgan left. Rich. Browne to Williamson, August 11, 1670, CSP; Gov. Sir Thos. Modyford to Sec. Lord Arlington, August 20, 1670, CSP.

84. Thomas Modyford, Instructions for Admll Henry Morgan, July 2, 1670, BL Add. 11268, ff. 70–71.

85. For the Irish privateer Philip Fitzgerald operating under a Spanish guardacostas commission and seizing English merchants, see Petition of Thomas Jarvis, et al., to the King in Council, February 27, 1674. CSP. This entry also includes testimony by the shipmaster Matthew Fox that the governor of Havana had called him a "heretic dog" and that Habaneros bragged of having taken seventy-five English ships since the 1670 peace.

86. Modyford's interest in acquiring colonial subjects from other sovereigns coincided with growing concerns in England that colonies created a dangerous population drain on the metropole. Swingen, *Competing Visions of Empire*, 104–107.

87. Gov. Sir Thos. Modyford to Lord Ashley, July 6, 1670, CSP. Thomas Modyford, Instructions for Admll Henry Morgan, July 2, 1670, BL Add. 11268, ff. 70–71.

88. Instructions for Admll Henry Morgan, July 2, 1670, BL Add. 11268, ff. 70–71.

89. Morgan's account of his expedition, BL Add. 11268, ff. 73–78. The Spanish prisoners had come from the ships of Manoel Ribeiro Pardal, the same guardacostas that took Speirdyke. For a narrative of Morgan's attack on Panama, relying on English and Spanish sources, see Earle, *The Sack of Panamá*.

90. "Don Juan Pérez de Guzmán President of Panama, his Relation of the late Action of the English there in the West-Indies. Being a Letter intercepted by them, as it was going into Spain, and brought to Admiral Morgan. Rendred into English, out of the Spanish," in Philip Ayres, ed., *The Voyages and Adventures of Capt. Barth Sharp and others, in the South Sea . . . And Col. Beeston's Adjustment of the Peace between the Spaniards and English in the West Indies.* (London: R.H. and S.T., 1684), 145–159.

91. Pérez de Guzmán noted that after news arrived of the English landing, members of every religious order in Panama had processed through the city each day, carrying "Images of the Pure and Immaculate Conception" and of all of their patrons and saints. Moreover, the sacrament was uncovered and exposed to public view in all the churches, and masses were said "continually" for the soldiers' "happy success." Pérez de Guzmán, "Relation," 150–152. Even if this intercepted letter underwent heavy English editing, the basic religious framing, which structured the narrative, likely followed the original.

92. Pérez de Guzmán, "Relation," quotations, 149, 155. The comma makes it unclear whether he intended to identify these men as vassals of Carlos II or vassals of the asentistas. On page 152 he revised the numbers, saying that "a great part of my Men were *Negroes, Mulattos* and *Indians,* to the number of about twelve hundred, besides two hundred *Negroes* more belonging to the *Astiento [sic]*."

93. Pérez de Guzmán, "Relation," 149. Pérez de Guzmán thought more highly of these Darién Indians "than of any others," though they disappointed him.

94. At his death, Morgan's estate included 122 Black and 7 Indigenous slaves and 11 European servants. Nuala Zahedieh, "Morgan, Sir Henry," in Oxford Dictionary of National Biography (2004), https://doi-org.srv-proxy2.library.tamu.edu/10.1093/ref:odnb/19224."

95. Marcus Rediker, *Villains of All Nations: Atlantic Pirates in the Golden Age* (Boston: Beacon Press, 2004).

Chapter 2

1. Zook identifies John Reid as a slave trader to Spanish America and a Barbados factor for the Royal Adventurers in the 1660s after Modyford left for Jamaica. *The Company of Royal Adventurers*, 75. Likely he was the "Mr. Read, factor to the Royal Company," who accompanied Beeston. Lieutenant Governor Sir Thos. Lynch to Sec. Lord Arlington, August 20, 1671, CSP. William Beeston, "The Relation of Colonel Beeston, his Voyage to Carthagena, for adjusting the Peace made in Spain, for the West-Indies, &c.," in Philip Ayres, ed., *The Voyages and Adventures of Capt. Barth Sharp*, 160–172.

2. Modyford and Morgan spent two years in prison in London. Nuala Zahedieh, "Modyford, Sir Thomas, first baronet," in *Oxford Dictionary of National Biography*, 2004, https://doi-org.srv-proxy1.library.tamu.edu/10.1093/ref:odnb/18871.

3. The Spanish were angry that Morgan's sack of Panama had occurred "after certain notice of the conclusion of the Peace," which they said had been published in Cartagena on March 2, 1670 (more than four months before Morgan left Jamaica). Although it seems likely that Governor Modyford indeed knew of the peace before Morgan's departure in August, Beeston, anxious to smooth over any impediments to commerce, claimed that Jamaicans had only learned of the peace with Lynch's arrival (in early 1671). Beeston, "Voyage to Carthagena," 165–167.

4. The 1670 treaty stipulated the opposite treatment for prisoners and property: Article 6 provided that "the Prisoners on both sides, one and all, of what degree or condition soever, detained by reason of any Hostilities hitherto committed in *AMERICA* shall be forthwith set at liberty, without Ransom, or any other Price of their Freedom." Article 7 stipulated that "all . . . Losses . . . which the Nations and People of *Great Britain* and *Spain* have at any time heretofore . . . suffered by each other in *America,* shall be expunged out of remembrance, and buried in Oblivion, as if no such thing had ever past." *A treaty for the composing of differences, restraining of depredations and establishing of peace in America between the crowns of Great Britain and Spain: concluded at Madrid the 8th/18 day of July in the year of our Lord, 1670.* (Printed by the Assigns of John Bill and Christopher Barker, Printers to the Kings Most Excellent Majesty, 1670), EEBO.

5. Hatfield, "Reluctant Petitioners."

6. Beeston, "Voyage to Carthagena," 168–170.

7. Irene Aloha Wright, *The Coymans Asiento, 1685–1698* (The Hague: Martinus Nijoff, 1924); Scelle, "Slave-Trade"; Johannes Postma, *The Dutch in the Atlantic Slave Trade, 1600–1815* (New York: Cambridge University Press, 1990). For Hermans, see García-Montón, *Genoese Entrepreneurship*, 142.

8. Beeston, "Voyage to Carthagena," 171. They also disliked Hermans, then trading with the Dutch.

9. Beeston, "Voyage to Carthagena," 167–168.

10. Beeston, "Voyage to Carthagena," 171–172.

11. Lynch to Sec. Lord Arlington, August 20, 1671, CSP.

12. Minutes of the Council of Jamaica, November 28, 1671, CSP.

13. Richard Brown to Sir Jos. Williamson, Port Royal, Jamaica, January 30, 1672, CSP.

14. Sir Thomas Lynch to the Council for Trade and Plantations, March 10, 1672, CSP. Here Lynch began to substitute "pirates" for "privateers," though London officials would not join him for another ten years.

15. Lieutenant Governor Sir Thos. Lynch to Sec. Sir Joseph Williamson, November 20, 1674, CO 1/31, no. 77.

16. Nuala Zahedieh, "Morgan, Sir Henry," in Oxford Dictionary of National Biography, (2004), https://doi-org.srv-proxy2.library.tamu.edu/10.1093/ref:odnb/19224; Governor Lord Vaughan to Secretary Coventry, August 2, 1676, CO 1/37, no. 39, where du Casse appears as d Cassy.

17. Zahedieh, "Morgan."

18. Ayres, *Sharp*, 114.

19. The captured Chilean pilot Simón Calderon's description of their reception in Antigua differed considerably from those of the two anonymous English authors in Ayres. He claimed they were received without trouble. Deposition of Simon Calderon, 1682, doc. 47 in John Franklin Jameson, ed., *Privateering and Piracy in the Colonial Period: Illustrative Documents* (New York: Macmillan, 1923), 135–137.

20. One had surrendered to Morgan, who relayed to London his desire to spare the informer. Morgan regarded one of the remaining three "a bloody and Notorious villain and fitt to make an exemple of," but reported that the local judges represented the other two men as "fitt objects of mercy." Morgan claimed relief that the local court did not want to execute all three, "I much abhorring bloodshed." Sir Henry Morgan to Sir Leoline Jenkins, March 8, 1682, CO 1/48, no. 37.

21. Ayres, *Sharp*, 113–114, 133–134.

22. The trial records, dated June 10, 1682, are translated (from Latin by A. Kiralfy) and printed in Derek Howse and Norman J. W. Thrower, *A Buccaneer's Atlas: Basil Ringrose's South Sea Waggoner* (Berkeley: University of California Press, 1992), Appendix B, 283–284; Deposition of Simon Calderon, doc. 47 in Jameson, *Privateering and Piracy*, 135–137.

23. Howse and Thrower, *A Buccaneer's Atlas*, Appendix B, 284–285. Howse and Thrower argue that the mariners were pardoned because they brought back maritime charts of the Pacific that they had captured from a Spanish ship. *A Buccaneer's Atlas*, 1.

24. Two anonymous accounts of the voyage appeared in print in 1682, immediately after some of the participants reached London. Another appeared two years later, and two more were penned at about the same time but not then published. Editor Philip Ayres collected the three published narratives together with a positive reframing of Henry Morgan's Panama attack, exonerating him against Exquemelin's accusations; a translation of Juan Pérez de Guzmán's defense of his loss to Morgan; and Beeston's account of his 1671 trade overture to Cartagena. In his introduction, Ayres presented Sharpe and his men (and Morgan before him) as heroes. He also highlighted yet again just how important the Isthmus of Panama was as a conduit of wealth and therefore as the focus of confrontations that generated new definitions of border, belonging, and political economy. Together, the collection encouraged English attention to the Isthmus of Panama but left unresolved whether further English conquest, forced trade, or consensual trade represented the best route to acquiring Spanish bullion.

25. Warrant by the Governor and Council of Jamaica, May 12, 1681, CSP. Citations for Jamaica Act.

26. *The laws of Jamaica passed by the assembly, and confirmed by His majesty in council, Feb. 23. 1683: to which is added, A short account of the island and government thereof, with an exact map of the island* (London: H. Hills for Charles Harper, 1683), 46–54, EEBO; "Act for restraining and punishing privateers and pirates," July 2, 1681, CSP.

27. Richard Frohock, *Buccaneers and Privateers: The Story of the English Sea Rover, 1675–1725* (Newark: University of Delaware Press, 2012), 65–66.

28. For the two unpublished accounts, see Anonymous, "Ann acoumpt of our Intended Voyage from Jamaco with a party of shipps, departing from the afore said Island to Poartavell: Receving Letpasses to goe into the bay of Hundorus, to cutt Logwood, from his Maj'ties Reall Subject the Earle of Carlisle," BM Sloane MS 2752, fol. 29, printed in Jameson, *Privateering and Piracy*, 84–92; Anonymous, "The Journall of our Intended Voyage by the assistance of God over land into the South seas leaveing our ships att the goulden Islands, and landing on Munday Apr'll the fift, Annoque 1682," BM Sloane MS 2754, fol. 36, printed in Jameson, *Privateering and Piracy*, 92–133. According to Jameson, the author of these two accounts is the same. He avoids terms with legal definition such as *pirate* or *privateers* and instead refers to the participants as "men" and the group as "the party." Jameson describes all the extant accounts in *Privateering and Piracy*, 84n1 and 84n3.

29. Charles Howard, Earl of Carlisle, was governor from 1678 to 1681 but left the island in 1680, leaving Morgan in charge.

30. Ayres, *Sharp*, 3.

31. Ayres, *Sharp*, 4.

32. Following Ignacio Gallup-Diaz, I use the term *Tule* to refer to the Indigenous population of the isthmus that both the English and Spanish referred to in the seventeenth century as the "Darien Indians." Gallup-Diaz, *The Door of the Seas*, xi, n. 2.

33. Gallup-Diaz, *The Door of the Seas*, 26–53. In his introduction to the anonymous seamen's accounts of the voyage, the editor Ayres claimed that "the Emperour of Darien" had been seized by Spaniards, learned Spanish, and escaped, and thereafter had "never ceased making War upon them" as revenge for the harsh treatment he had suffered as a prisoner. Ayres described Darién as a distinct "Province or District" with clear borders that separated Spanish jurisdictions. It was "bounded on the South by the Kingdom of New Granada; by the Gulf of Uraba or Darien on the East; by the South Sea on the West; and on the North by the Province of Panama." He acknowledged Spanish claims to Darién in a manner that left the extent of such claims open to the reader's interpretation, stating that "so much as the Spaniards have of it" was "now annexed" to the government of Panama. Ayres, *Sharp*, iii.

34. Gallup-Diaz, *The Door of the Seas*, 26–53.

35. Deschamps's and d'Ogeron's activities in Tortuga, as well as jurisdictional struggles in Danish St. Thomas and in Spanish Cartagena, illustrate a similar lack of unity among the French, Danish, and Spanish in the region. Shannon Lee Dawdy labels such autonomy "rogue colonialism." *Building the Devil's Empire: French Colonial New Orleans* (Chicago: University of Chicago Press, 2008).

36. Such recognition that varied rulers could provide legal authority is consistent with Lauren Benton's arguments in *Law and Colonial Cultures: Legal Regimes in World History, 1400–1900* (New York: Cambridge University Press, 2002).

37. See Gallup-Diaz for Spanish references to the Native people of Darién as "rebellious." *The Door of the Seas*, ch. 5. Gallup-Diaz's analysis of the mariners' narratives rests heavily on Lionel Wafer's 1699 *A New Voyage and Description of the Isthmus of America* (London: Printed for James Knapton, 1699), because he believes it more accurately portrays the reality of Tule politics than did other accounts, making it much more useful for his analysis of the Tule. *The Door of the Seas*, 71–73. Wafer's publication explicitly defended Scottish incursions into the isthmus at the end of the century.

38. Jameson, *Privateering and Piracy*, 132.

39. Sir Thomas Lynch to Lords of Trade and Plantations, August 29, 1682, CSP.

40. Relación de servicios del Maestro de Campo don Luis Carrisoli de Alfaraz, 1699, AGI, Audiencia de Panamá, legajo 181, 811r–818r, v3. Available in the supplementary archive for Gallup-Diaz's *Door of the Seas* (www.gutenberg-e.org/gdi01/). The reference to corsarios came despite Spain's peace with England and France at the time.

41. Charles II had issued such proclamations in 1662, 1664, 1668, 1672, 1676, and 1678 (all of them available in EEBO). In 1680 the Jamaica Council requested that the king "declar[e] it felony, without benefit of clergy, for any of the King's subjects in the West Indies, to serve any foreign prince against any other foreign prince at amity with England without a licence from the Governor," and reported to London that "notwithstanding the detestable depredations of some of our nation (who pass for inhabitants of Jamaica) under colour of French commissions," trade with the Spanish was going well. Spanish confidence in the safety of that trade would grow if "these 'ravenous vermin'" could be destroyed. The council claimed that Jamaica had succeeded in curbing local support for the pirates, and when they received French protection, it "thereby strengthen[ed] them and weaken[ed] us." Also, Spaniards' "horrid butcheries" of English subjects caused any who escaped to "forget their duty to God and man, and give themselves wholly up to implacable revenge." The Council of Jamaica to the Lords of Trade and Plantations, May 20, 1680, CSP. In September the Lords of Trade and Plantations, referring to two memorials from the Spanish ambassador and the Jamaica Council's letter above regarding piracies in Jamaica, recommended that "the law therein mentioned, making it felony without benefit of clergy to serve a foreign prince, be revived." Journal of Lords of Trade and Plantations, September 18, 1680, CSP. Charles II issued such a proclamation on March 12, 1684. "By the King. A proclamation," EEBO. On March 25, 1684, a circular went to the governors of the plantations forwarding copies of Charles II's proclamation prohibiting his subjects from serving foreign princes. Sir Leoline Jenkins to the Governors of the Plantations, March 25, 1684, CSP.

42. Ayres, *Sharp*, 1–2. The *Oxford English Dictionary* dates the first use of "soldier of fortune" to 1661. Richard Frohock argues that the author did not intend his readers to take the sacralizing of greed seriously. *Buccaneers and Privateers*, 84–85.

43. Ayres, *Sharp*, 7–8.

44. Ayres, *Sharp*, 17.

45. Ayres, *Sharp*, 74.

46. These superficially contradictory claims to serve Indigenous sovereignty and assert Protestant English power over the region aided the editor Ayres's apparent goal of destroying Spanish claims to jurisdictional or commercial hegemony in the region and especially over the Panamanian isthmus.

47. Ayres, *Sharp*, 9.

48. The classic studies of the processes whereby pursuit of wealth became morally legitimate in western society are Weber, *The Protestant Ethic and the Spirit of Capitalism*, and Albert O. Hirschman, *The Passions and the Interests: Political Arguments for Capitalism Before Its Triumph* (1977; Princeton, N.J.: Princeton University Press, 2013).

49. Ayres, *Sharp*, 69.

50. Ayres, *Sharp*, 70–71.

51. Ayres, *Sharp*, 57, 85.

52. Ayres, *Sharp*, 78–79.

53. Deputy Governor Sir Henry Morgan to the Lords of Trade and Plantations, Port Royal, January 27, 1681, CSP. Croquer's license came from "the Company of Seville," likely the asentista Juan Barroso del Pozo.

54. Deputy Governor Sir Henry Morgan to the Lords of Trade and Plantations, Port Royal, January 27, 1681, CSP. Friedrich Wilhelm, Elector of Brandenburg and Duke of Prussia, sought Spanish plunder and entrée into the transatlantic slave trade during the 1680s.

55. Sir Henry Morgan to the Lords of Trade and Plantations, St. Jago de la Vega, July 14, 1681, CSP. The captain of the frigate found the Spanish fleet in Cartagena and brought to Morgan a packet that the Admiral of the Fleet sent for Charles II, which Morgan forwarded to William Blathwayt.

56. Pleitos Gobernación de Cartagena, 1682, AGI, Escribanía 589a; Juan Ignacio Croquer de los Cameros, *En la causa con el señor fiscal del Real Consejo de las Indias* [Madrid?] [1693?], Biblioteca Nacional de España.

57. Deputy Governor Sir Henry Morgan to the Lords of Trade and Plantations, Port Royal, January 27, 1681, CSP.

58. Deputy Governor Sir Henry Morgan to the Lords of Trade and Plantations, January 27, 1681, CSP.

59. Morgan had news that many of Charles II's subjects were imprisoned in Havana, Merida, and Mexico. Henry Morgan to [Sir Leoline Jenkins], March 8, 1682, CSP. The likelihood that the logwood cutters also engaged in slave trading may explain Spanish officials' reactions. Arne Bialuschewski, "Slaves of the Buccaneers: Mayas in Captivity in the Second Half of the Seventeenth Century," *Ethnohistory* 64 (2017), 41–63.

60. Lynch to the Governor of Havana, August 18, 1683; Lynch to the Governor of Carthagena, April 9/19, 1684; enclosure in Lynch to Lords of Trade and Plantations, September 29, 1682.

61. Sir Thomas Lynch to Lords of Trade and Plantations, August 29, 1682, CSP. Lynch's evidence against Clarke came from John Coxon, the original leader of the Sharpe expedition. Lynch attested that Coxon "came in and lived honestly under Lord Carlisle's or Sir Henry's Act of Oblivion" pardoning repentant privateers. Lynch to Lords of Trade and Plantations, August 29, 1682, CSP. Coxon's reform did not last: in 1686, Lieutenant Governor Molesworth wrote that after Coxon took "advantage of a clause in the Act for restraining and persuading pirates, to return to the honest life," he then "reverted to piracy." Molesworth to William Blathwayt, January 16, 1686, CSP.

62. Governor Sir Thomas Lynch to the Governor of Havana, August 18, 1683, CO 1/52, no. 62.

63. Hatfield, "Reluctant Petitioners."

64. He identified the Spanish official as the "Maestre de la Plata." Governor Sir Thomas Lynch to the Governor of Havana, August 18, 1683, CO 1/52, no. 62.

65. Governor Sir Thomas Lynch to the Governor of Havana, August 18, 1683, CO 1/52, no. 62.

66. Sir Thomas Lynch to Secretary Sir Leoline Jenkins, July 26, 1683, CO 1/52, no. 35. Lynch noted that when Dutch and French pirates (he interchanged *pirate* and *privateer*) under van Hoorn had taken Vera Cruz, they "brought away abundance of Negroes, Mulatoes and Mestizos." Lynch had issued orders "to prohibit ye sloopes from bringing any Persons in, or Goods, for as we were not ye Theyves, so wil we not be ye Receivers," despite his opinion that the "design is affirmed to be lawful" because van Hoorn held a commission from the Elector of Brandenburg and from the Governor of Tortuga, and "Warre [between Spain and a French/Brandenburg alliance] is publiquely owned & declared."

67. Governor Sir Thomas Lynch to the Governor of Havana, August 18, 1683, CO 1/52, no. 62.

68. Lynch also of course knew that many English vessels did carry illicit trade. He warned Fernandez Córdoba that his support for Corso would incite "all dissolute people" in Jamaica to resume their own plundering and pirating, and that Lynch "in spite of what I can do" would be powerless to stop them, implying that Fernandez Córdoba was responsible for preventing English seamen from turning pirate by curbing Juan Corso and his ilk. Governor Sir Thomas Lynch to the Governor of Havana, August 18, 1683, CO 1/52, no. 62.

69. Governor Sir Thomas Lynch to the Governor of Havana, August 18, 1683, CO 1/52, no. 62. The abstract in the Calendar of State Papers, Colonial, incorrectly substitutes "negroes" for "Rogues," August 18, 1683, CSP. Lynch's Spanish translation replaces "rogues" with "*semejantes*/similar peoples," simply using Corso as the measure of what was unacceptable, September 12, 1683, CSP.

Lynch repeated to his London superiors the claim he had made to Fernandez Córdoba that he could not keep Jamaicans bound to Charles II's anti-privateering laws "if other nations thus rob and insult them." But he nonetheless acknowledged them as "our people," even as he bemoaned their disobedience in the face of continued regional violence. He feared that the Jamaica "Act for Restraining and Punishing Privateers and Pirates" would backfire and, instead of securing mariners' obedience and promoting conditions conducive to increased slave trading, it would "unpeople this Island." When they could not obtain English commissions, "rogues, necessitous people and others" robbed the Spaniards under French commissions, then "dare[d] not return because of this law." Instead, they went "without concealment to other Colonies, especially to Carolina." Lynch to the Lords of Trade and Plantations, September 12, 1683, CSP.

70. Sr Thomas Lynch's answer to the Govr of Carta, April, 9/19, 1684, Jamaica, CO 1/54, no. 72.

71. Sr Thomas Lynch's answer to the Govr of Carta, April, 9/19, 1684, Jamaica, CO 1/54, no. 72.

72. Sir Thomas Lynch to Secretary Sir Leoline Jenkins, July 26, 1683, CSP.

Chapter 3

1. Much of what we know about sanctuary derives from Jane Landers's work on Spanish Florida. Landers dates the policy to November 7, 1693, when Carlos II issued a royal proclamation "giving liberty to all . . . the men as well as the women . . . so that by their example and by my liberality others may do the same." Landers, *Black Society in Spanish Florida*, 25. While the 1693 decree came in response to several groups of slaves who ran from Carolina to Florida between 1688 and 1690, it reflected at least twenty years of Caribbean practice. The practice dated to at least 1665, before the 1667 Treaty of Madrid, and persisted through periods of Anglo-Spanish peace and alliance, even though it presumed continuing enmity between Catholics and Protestants in the Atlantic world. See "Respuesta auna carta del Govérnadór de Puerto Rico (Don Juan Pérez de Guzmán) sobre aver llegado a aquella Isla un Mulato y quatro negros" (un negro y tres negras), January 18, 1665 (digitized in PARES), AGI, Santo Domingo, 873, legajo 18, 180v–181v (imágenes 360–362/1053). The Mulato man had been free when seized on the coast of Cartagena by English pirates. Three years later the governor of Cuba used this cedula, which only confirmed the Puerto Rico governor's decision about five specific shelter seekers, as a precedent for his own decision to grant freedom to ten of eleven escapees from Jamaica. Autos del gobernador de La Habana, Francisco Dávila Orejón, 1668, AGI, Pleitos del Consejo, Escribanía, 1033B, pieza 10. In Santo Domingo, officials

interpreted the policy to include even escapees from French (and so Catholic) jurisdiction. Juan José Ponce Vázquez, *Islanders and Empire: Smuggling and Political Defiance in Hispaniola, 1580–1690* (New York: Cambridge University Press, 2020), 247–248. For the importance of the category of subject, see Jane G. Landers, "*Cimarrón* and Citizen: African Ethnicity, Corporate Identity, and the Evolution of Free Black Towns in the Spanish Circum-Caribbean," in Landers and Barry M. Robinson, eds., *Slaves, Subjects, and Subversives: Blacks in Colonial Latin America* (Albuquerque: University of New Mexico Press, 2006), 111–145. Other recent work on sanctuary includes Bram Hoonhout and Thomas Mareite, "Freedom at the Fringes? Slave Flight and Empire-Building in the Early Modern Spanish Borderlands of Essequibo-Venezuela and Louisiana-Texas," *Slavery and Abolition* 40 (2019), 61–86; Linda M. Rupert, "'Seeking the Water of Baptism': Fugitive Slaves and Imperial Jurisdiction in the Early Modern Caribbean," in Lauren Benton and Richard J. Ross, eds., *Legal Pluralism and Empires, 1500–1850* (New York: New York University Press, 2013), 199–232; and Elena Schneider, guest editor, "Forum: Maritime Marronage: Archaeological, Anthropological, and Historical Perspectives," *Slavery and Abolition* 42, no. 3 (2021), esp. Fernanda Bretones Lane, "Free to Bury Their Dead: Baptism and the Meanings of Freedom in the Eighteenth-Century Caribbean," 449–465.

2. In my focus on the origins and utility of sanctuary specifically in border regions and my emphasis on it as a form of self-fashioning for Spanish officials, I do not endorse Tannenbaum's argument that we can make a broad comparison between a more benign slavery in Catholic polities and a more dehumanizing slavery in Protestant ones. Rather, legal differences mattered most at borders and during moments of contest, when people made use of them to claim belonging and other rights or privileges.

3. On the law of nations, see Richard Tuck, *The Rights of War and Peace: Political Thought and the International Order from Grotius to Kant* (Oxford: Oxford University Press, 1999), and Alexander Orakhelashvili, ed., *Research Handbook on the Theory and History of International Law* (Cheltenham, UK: Edward Elgar, 2011). There is debate about whether it is anachronistic to use the term *law of nations* in this period. I do so because merchants and officials in the early modern Caribbean did. But, like them, I refer not to one set of shared enforceable codes but to an inchoate combination of treaty agreements, legal theory, and customary shared legal practices governing trade and military engagement.

4. When the Spanish crown and the Council of the Indies were considering during the 1680s whether the asiento should go to the Dutch firm Coymans and Company or the (English-backed) Genoese merchant Nicolas Porcio, the issue of evangelism as justification for colonies was raised repeatedly. Wright, *The Coymans Asiento*, 23–62.

5. Examples of such scholarship include Landers, *Black Society in Spanish Florida*; Díaz, *The Virgin, the King, and the Royal Slaves*; Vinson, *Bearing Arms for His Majesty*; and Adrian Masters, "A Thousand Invisible Architects: Vassals, the Petition and Response System, and the Creation of Spanish Imperial Caste Legislation," *Hispanic American Historical Review* 98 (2018), 377–406.

6. Linda Rupert identifies patterns in the movement of people between Dutch Curaçao and Spanish Caracas that are similar to those I describe in this chapter. Rupert, *Creolization and Contraband*.

7. Studnicki-Gizbert, "*La Nación* among the Nations."

8. Adrian Masters, "The Two, the One, the Many, the None: Rethinking the Republics of Spaniards and Indians in the Sixteenth-Century Spanish Indies," *The Americas* 78 (2021), 3–36.

9. Landers, "*Cimarron* and Citizen," 129–130.

10. For an assessment of this separation (and its limits) in Peru, see Alcira Dueñas, "Cabildo de naturales en el ocaso colonial: Jurisdicción, posesión y defensa del espacio étnico," *Histórica* 40 (2016), 135–167.

11. Literature on race in colonial Spanish America (especially before the mid-eighteenth century) and the casta system in particular is focused on Mexico. See Martínez, *Genealogical Fictions*; Ilona Katzew, *Casta Painting: Images of Race in Eighteenth-Century Mexico* (New Haven, Conn.: Yale University Press, 2005); Ben Vinson III, *Before Mestizaje: The Frontiers of Race and Class in Colonial Mexico* (New York: Cambridge University Press, 2018); Magali M. Carrera, *Imagining Identity in New Spain: Race, Lineage, and the Colonial Body in Portraiture and Casta Paintings* (Austin: University of Texas Press, 2013); and Herman L. Bennett, *Colonial Blackness: A History of Afro-Mexico* (Bloomington: Indiana University Press, 2009). Whiteness studies include Ann Twinam, *Purchasing Whiteness: Pardos, Mulattos, and the Quest for Social Mobility in the Spanish Indies* (Stanford, Calif.: Stanford University Press, 2015); Kathleen Brown, *Good Wives, Nasty Wenches, and Anxious Patriarchs: Gender, Race, and Power in Colonial Virginia* (Chapel Hill: University of North Carolina Press, 1996); and Cecily Jones, *Engendering Whiteness: White Women and Colonialism in Barbados and North Carolina, 1627–1865* (Manchester: Manchester University Press, 2015).

12. The Spanish crown owned slaves but did not profit from systematically trading them away to foreigners. At times, Spanish royal slaveholding even served to intensify the relationship of mutual responsibility between sovereign and enslaved subjects. Díaz, *The Virgin, the King, and the Royal Slaves*.

13. In 1662, Thomas Modyford wrote from Barbados that visiting Spanish slave traders witnessed the island's Assembly prevail over the governor's and council's objections to encourage the trade of captives to foreigners without any additional local taxation. According to Modyford, the Spanish merchants said that they "did wish they had such a constitution in Spaine"—one that would allow a representative assembly to assert its own interests over those of crown-appointed officials. Modyford took advantage of that opening to boast to his visitors that, in English colonies, the assemblies "were tribunes of ye people to defend their liberties according to law." Thomas Modyford to his brother, April 30, 1662; May 26, 1662; September 13, 1662, enclosures in entry for February 26, 1663, CO 1/17, nos. 7, 8, 9. For the importance of English representative assemblies in facilitating lawmaking in the interests of slaveholders, see Edmund S. Morgan, "Slavery and Freedom: The American Paradox," *Journal of American History* 59 (1972): 5–29. For colonial assemblies' use of this power, see Edward B. Rugemer, *Slave Law and the Politics of Resistance in the Early Atlantic World* (Cambridge, Mass.: Harvard University Press, 2018); Rugemer, "The Development of Mastery and Race in the Comprehensive Slave Codes of the Greater Caribbean during the Seventeenth Century," *William and Mary Quarterly*, 3rd ser., 70, no. 3 (2013), 429–458; David Barry Gaspar, "With a Rod of Iron: Barbados Slave Laws as a Model for Jamaica, South Carolina, and Antigua, 1661–1697," in Darlene Clark Hine and Jacqueline McLeod, eds., *Crossing Boundaries: Comparative History of Black People in Diaspora* (Bloomington: Indiana University Press, 1999), 343–366.

14. Gerbner, *Christian Slavery*, 28–29.

15. Rugemer, *Slave Law and the Politics of Resistance*, 2. Rugemer stresses the importance of "slaves' indirect relationship to the law" in Barbados, which gave "the entire free community" authority to police slaves, while the same colony's laws protected servants' right to jury trial. *Slave Law and the Politics of Resistance*, 29–34. English law treated enslaved people as objects rather than subjects.

16. Rugemer notes that Barbadian lawmakers "divided their society into Christians and Africans," and that their laws made a "critical contribution to the formation of the political economy of slavery at the heart of the imperial project" that he dates to the Restoration. *Slave Law and the Politics of Resistance*, 26–27, 34. Several scholars have examined English colonists' use of Christianity to create race. Brown, *Good Wives, Nasty Wenches*; Goetz, *Baptism of Early Virginia*; Gerbner, *Christian Slavery*, Glasson, *Mastering Christianity*.

17. Gerbner, *Christian Slavery*, 104–105, cites "The Abstract of Dr. L'Jaus Papers," Rhodes House Library, SPG-J, Appendix B, no. 67.

18. In 1680, several Barbadians told the Lords of Trade and Plantations that "converted negroes" became "intractable," which lowered "their value and price." *Journal of the Lords of Trade and Plantations*, October 8, 1680, CSP. The following decade, Governor Francis Russell reported that "the keeping of Christian holy days" presented the greatest obstacle to conversion, "most of the planters thinking Sundays too much to be spared from work." Governor Russell to Lords of Trade and Plantations, March 23, 1695, CSP. For repeated legal and religious assurances that conversion did not challenge enslavement, see Travis Glasson, "'Baptism Doth Not Bestow Freedom': Missionary Anglicanism, Slavery, and the Yorke-Talbot Opinion, 1701–30," *William and Mary Quarterly*, 3rd ser., 67 (2010): 279–318.

19. Sir Richard Dutton's Speech to the Assembly of Barbados, March 30, 1681, CSP. See CSP for numerous calls to ameliorate the "ill-usage" of Christian servants during the late seventeenth and early eighteenth centuries.

20. Exquemelin, *Buccaneers of America*, 155. When Exquemelin enumerated the compensations that buccaneers provided one another for loss of limb, he did so in both pieces of eight and slaves (with each slave worth one hundred pieces of eight). *Buccaneers of America*, 172.

21. When Nikolaas van Hoorn took Vera Cruz in 1683, he put "the considerable people to ransome," threatened to burn "the prisoners," and left with one thousand "Negroes and Mulatos." "Captain Van Horn taking of la Vera Cruz. 1683," in Ayers, *Sharp*, 118–120.

22. Even if contemporaries did not always presume African descent when they read "slave," historians, who have inherited English colonial legislators' mostly binary racial categories, have often done so. Carolyn Arena shows how English discomfort with enslaving Indigenous Americans led them to erase the practice in Surinam. "Aphra Behn's 'Oronooko,' Indian Slavery, and the Anglo-Dutch Wars, 1650–1688," in L. H. Roper, ed., *The Torrid Zone: Colonization and Cultural Interaction in the Seventeenth-Century Caribbean* (Columbia: University of South Carolina Press, 2018), 31–45. Seventeenth-century Jamaica will inventories provide an exception. In those more personal and private records, owners frequently acknowledged the specific descent of individual Indigenous and mixed-race people.

23. Kristen Block and Jenny Shaw make a similar argument—that in the Caribbean the archives of one empire can often tell us things about the colonies of another empire that its own archives cannot—in "Subjects Without an Empire: The Irish in the Early Modern Caribbean," *Past and Present* 210 (2011), 33–60.

24. The following comes from Autos del gobernador de La Habana, Francisco Dávila Orejón, 1688, AGI, Pleitos de Consejo, Escribanía, 1033B.

25. Among the men, only Ignacio Hernandes, the first to testify, did not say he worked on the forts and named a master. The other four men who worked on forts seem to have belonged to the colony of Jamaica. Salvador Francisco names an owner but it is illegible and may be a title rather than a name.

26. Spanish officials in Florida used the policy to destabilize their English neighbors even during the War of the Grand Alliance, when the English and Spanish not only were not at war but were actively allied with one another against the French. Landers, *Black Society in Spanish Florida*, 23–47. Spanish willingness to risk much-needed English naval support to support the sanctuary policy suggests how difficult it was to let go of the belief that political borders correctly echoed religious boundaries.

27. Deposition of Henry Wasey, August 19, 1668, CO 1/23, no. 43.

28. Depositions of Mathew Sheares, Master of the Pellican, taken before Lord Vaughan, October 17, 1676; John Pursley and Mathew Lowe, Mathew Lowe, David de Rocque, William Green and Henry Smith, and Francisco Antonio in Spanish, October–December 1676, CSP. Lowe also said he had heard the governor of Havana say there was no peace in the Indies and that it was lawful for the Spaniards to take all they met with.

29. Memorial of Peter Dyer, July 11, 1705, CSP.

30. In Juana's telling of the story, Luis seems to have colluded with the pirates. Juana does not say whether he, too, was sold as a slave, but her story raises the possibility that pirates tricked slaves with promises of freedom, only to resell them, or bribed individuals such as Luis to betray their fellows. Exquemelin describes pirates using promises of freedom to get slaves to provide information about where wealth might be hidden. *Buccaneers of America*, 150.

31. Pingar was a *frances platero de oficio*. Autos del gobernador, AGI, Escribanía 1033B, 8.

32. She or the clerk called her Spanish mistress *ama* and her English owner *dueño*.

33. Autos del gobernador, AGI, Escribanía 1033B, 9.

34. These documents use the term *mercy* (*clemencia*) or sometimes the phrase "el abrigo de la RL Clemensia" rather than *sanctuary* to describe the king's granting of freedom.

35. For the importance of local to imperial belonging in the Spanish Atlantic, see Herzog, *Defining Nations*; Bennett, *Colonial Blackness*; and María Elena Díaz, "Conjuring Identities: Race, Nativeness, Local Citizenship, and Royal Slavery on an Imperial Frontier (Revisiting El Cobre, Cuba)," in Andrew B. Fisher and Matthew D. O'Hara, eds., *Imperial Subjects: Race and Identity in Colonial Latin America* (Durham, N.C.: Duke University Press, 2009), 197–224.

36. The practice had deep roots in Europe. Sue Peabody and Keila Grinberg, "Free Soil: The Generation and Circulation of an Atlantic Legal Principle," *Slavery and Abolition* 32 (2011), 331–339.

37. Edward Stanton to Col. Thos. Lynch, Port Royal, August 25, 1670, CSP.

38. The following comes from Piezas sobre comisos y represalias de ingleses, AGI, Contaduría 1437, Ramo 2 (Contra Manuel Fernández), 1680.

39. The Spanish clerk rendered Carlisle as *Corley*.

40. Brixida Maria de la Concepción "asistia ajembras [a hembras] en un plantaje." For literature on *casta* categories in Spanish America, see note 11 above.

41. Four years later, Jamaica governor Thomas Lynch offered a competing account of Juan Pardo. Pardo, whom Lynch referred to as Juan Brown, had been a free resident of Jamaica for twenty-two years and was the master of a sloop. In Lynch's telling, Brown/Pardo had stolen the boat from Wythywood (Carlisle) along with the sugar, cotton, indigo, and Negroes. It had been bound for Port Royal. Lynch had written to the then governor (his current addressee's predecessor) requesting the return of Brown, as a thief, and of all the goods. Sr Thomas Lynch's answer to the Govr of Carta, April 9/19, 1684, Jamaica, CO 1/54, no. 72.

42. Linda Rupert and Fernanda Bretones Lane consider the meanings of baptism to those who sought Spanish sanctuary. Rupert, "'Seeking the Water of Baptism'"; Bretones Lane, "Free

to Bury Their Dead: Baptism and the Meanings of Freedom in the Eighteenth-Century Caribbean," *Slavery and Abolition* 42 (2021), 449–465.

43. Scholarship that has helped me read these cases includes Sidney W. Mintz and Richard Price, *The Birth of African-American Culture: An Anthropological Perspective* (1976; reprint, Boston: Beacon Press, 1992); and Vincent Brown, "Social Death and Political Life in the Study of Slavery," *American Historical Review* (2009), 1231–1249.

44. Arne Bialuschewski and Linford D. Fisher, eds., "Native American Slavery in the Seventeenth Century," special issue of *Ethnohistory* 64, no. 1 (2017); Reséndez, *The Other Slavery*. For African diversity, see Linda M. Heywood and John K. Thornton, *Central Africans, Atlantic Creoles, and the Foundation of the Americas, 1585–1660* (New York: Cambridge University Press, 2007); and James Sidbury and Jorge Cañizares-Esguerra, "Mapping Ethnogenesis in the Early Modern Atlantic," *William and Mary Quarterly*, 3rd ser., 68 (2011), 181–208.

45. Gregory O'Malley also has recognized the role pirates played in bringing enslaved people into English colonies in the seventeenth century. *Final Passages*, 85–113.

46. Peter R. Galvin, *Patterns of Pillage: A Geography of Caribbean-Based Piracy in Spanish America, 1536–1718* (New York: Peter Lang, 1999).

47. This process is consistent with that described by Adrian Masters in "A Thousand Invisible Architects."

48. Governor Sir William Beeston to Council of Trade and Plantations, February 8, 1699, CSP. According to Beeston, the Cuban officials dated the royal cedula "1680 or 82." However, examples from the policy date to at least 1665. See note 1 above.

49. Governor Sir William Beeston to Council of Trade and Plantations, February 8, 1699, CSP. Jamaican complaints about the policy continued sporadically for decades. In 1718, for example, Jamaican governor Nicholas Lawes complained that pirates had "encouraged severall negroes to desart from their masters and go to the Spaniards in Cuba." By that time, despite the increasing importance of slavery in Cuba, Lawes apparently did not think Jamaican slaves' preference for Spanish Cuba required any explanation. Governor Sir N. Lawes to the Council of Trade and Plantations, September 1, 1718, CSP.

50. Governor Sir William Beeston to Council of Trade and Plantations, February 8, 1699, CSP. Beeston's admission may have resonated more as a moral failing in 1699 than it had in 1671. For heightened English ambition to convert enslaved people at the turn of the eighteenth century, see Glasson, *Mastering Christianity*, and Gerbner, *Christian Slavery*.

51. This geopolitical Caribbean context, as well as a focus on local belonging as constitutive of imperial belonging, also informed Spanish willingness to extend recognition to towns of former slaves. See Landers, "*Cimarrón* and Citizen."

52. This is a point Landers emphasizes for Florida.

53. Herbert S. Klein, "The Colored Militia of Cuba: 1568–1868," *Caribbean Studies* 6, no. 2 (1966), 17–27; Vinson, *Bearing Arms for His Majesty*.

54. For French law, see Malick Ghachem, *The Old Regime and the Haitian Revolution* (New York: Cambridge University Press, 2012).

55. Article 6 for property and Article 11 for prisoners.

56. President and Council of Nevis to Council of Trade and Plantations, February 4, 1699, CSP. Christopher Codrington and John Hamilton were the purported owners. The Nevis President and Council admitted that the slaves in question had been plunder: when they asked London for help in preventing "this growing evil," they explained that those who fled were "our French negroes."

57. Marquis D'Amblimont to Governor Norton, February 5, 1699 (enclosure in February 4, 1699, entry), CSP.

58. Memorial in Answer to the French Demands, February 1, 1699 (enclosure in February 4, 1699, entry), CSP. We can see one theoretical basis for English distinctions about prisoners of war in the practice of exchanging prisoners "either man for man and quality for quality, or all for all." Earl of Nottingham to Governor Sir B. Granville, September 14, 1703, CSP.

59. Marquis D'Amblimont and François Robert Reply to the Memorial of Col. Hamilton and Capt. Perry, February 5, 1699 (enclosure in February 4, 1699 entry), CSP. These are partial English translations in the CSP.

60. Marquis D'Amblimont and François Robert Reply to the Memorial of Col. Hamilton and Capt. Perry, February 5, 1699 (enclosure in February 4, 1699, entry), CSP.

61. Col. Codrington to Council of Trade and Plantations, June 30, 1699, CSP.

62. For a discussion of how entail encompassed enslaved people in another English colony, see Holly Brewer, "Entailing Aristocracy in Colonial Virginia: 'Ancient Feudal Restraints' and Revolutionary Reform," *William and Mary Quarterly*, 3rd ser., 54 (1997), 307–346.

63. Col. Codrington to Council of Trade and Plantations, July 10, 1699, CSP.

64. Moreover, Codrington questioned French conversions: "They baptise all their slaves (I dare not say they make them Christians)." Col. Codrington to Council of Trade and Plantations, July 10, 1699, CSP.

65. Col. Codrington to Council of Trade and Plantations, in answer to the French claim for runaway negroes, which was referred to him by the Council, July 7, 1699, CSP.

66. Glasson, *Mastering Christianity*, 141–144.

67. The petitions appear in the customary investigation (*residencia*) of Matheo Lopez de Cangas when he vacated the office of governor of Santiago de Cuba. Residencia de Matheo Lopez de Cangas, 1723, AGI, Escribanía 95B, pieza 16 (for petition and depositions) and pieza 17, 44r–45r (for decision); "Miguel negro Casta Caravali y Gaspar tambien negro Casta Moco," 5r. The testimony specified that the Africans had fled during "the war," highlighting the policy's geopolitical function.

68. Díaz, *The Virgin, the King, and the Royal Slaves*; Francisco Pérez de la Riva, "Cuban Palenques," in Richard Price, ed., *Maroon Societies: Rebel Slave Communities in the Americas*, 3rd ed. (Baltimore: Johns Hopkins University Press, 1996), 49–59. Landers, "*Cimarron* and Citizen."

69. Díaz, *The Virgin, the King, and the Royal Slaves*, 15.

70. Residencia de Matheo Lopez de Cangas, AGI, Escribanía 95a, cuaderno 5, 361–472.

Chapter 4

1. Jonathan Israel emphasizes that Dutch toleration in New Holland represented a pragmatic attempt to attract settlers rather than a principled commitment to inclusiveness. "Religious Toleration in Dutch Brazil (1624–1654)," in Jonathan Israel and Stuart B. Schwartz, *The Expansion of Tolerance: Religion in Dutch Brazil (1624–1654)* (Amsterdam: Amsterdam University Press, 2007), 13–32.

2. Natalie Zacek, "'A People So Subtle': Sephardic Jewish Pioneers of the English West Indies," in Caroline A. Williams, *Bridging the Early Modern Atlantic World: People, Products, and Practices on the Move* (Burlington, Vt.: Ashgate, 2009), 97–98. France expelled Jews from its Caribbean and American colonies as part of the Code Noir in 1685, explicitly using Christianity to limit belonging. The code required conversion of enslaved people and linked their limited rights and inclusion in the French colonial body politic to their Christianity. An English

translation by John Garrigus is available at "The 'Code Noir'" (1685), http://les.traitesnegrieres.free.fr/39_esclavage_code_noir_agl.html.

3. Mordechai Arbell, *The Portuguese Jews of Jamaica* (Kingston: Canoe Press/University of the West Indies, 2000), 8, 55.

4. Anthony D. Smith, *The Ethnic Origins of Nations* (New York: Oxford University Press, 1986); Adrian Hastings, *The Construction of Nationhood: Ethnicity, Religion, and Nationalism* (Cambridge: Cambridge University Press, 1997); Douglas Bradburn, "Nation, Nationhood, and Nationalism," in *Oxford Bibliographies* (2011), doi:10.1093/obo/9780199730414-0070.

5. J.H. Elliott, "A Europe of Composite Monarchies," *Past and Present* 137 (1992), 48–71.

6. Jonathan I. Israel, *European Jewry in the Age of Mercantilism, 1550–1750*, 2nd ed. (New York: Oxford University Press, 1989), 5–34.

7. Herzog, *Defining Nations*, 136.

8. In 1669, Jamaica, Carolina, and the Leeward Islands all vied for English Surinam's colonists, many of them Jewish, after its Dutch conquest. Memorial of "the persons concerned in Carolina" to the King, March 24, 1669, CSP. Suze Zijlstra, "Competing for European Settlers: Local Loyalties of Colonial Governments in Suriname and Jamaica, 1660–1680," *Journal of Early American History* 4 (2014), 149–166.

9. Sir Thomas Lynch to the Council for Trade and Plantations, March 10, 1672, CSP.

10. Mordechai Arbell, *The Jewish Nation of the Caribbean: The Spanish-Portuguese Jewish Settlements in the Caribbean and the Guianas* (New York: Gefen Publishing House, 2002), 228.

11. Emphasis in original. Menasseh ben Israel, *To His Highnesse the Lord Protector of the Common-wealth of England, Scotland, and Ireland the humble addresses of Menasseh ben Israel, a divine, and doctor of physick, in behalfe of the Jewish nation* (London, 1655), preface.

12. Menasseh, *To His Highnesse*, 4–9.

13. In Amsterdam, such self-governance extended beyond communal and religious matters to include long-distance trade disputes. Evelyne Oliel-Grausz, "Dispute Resolution and Kahal Kadosh Talmud Torah: Community Forum and Legal Acculturation in Eighteenth-Century Amsterdam," in Yosef Kaplan, ed., *Religious Changes and Cultural Transformations in the Early Modern Western Sephardic Communities* (Leiden: Brill, 2019), 228–257. Jonathan Schorsch notes that several congregational rulings excluded non-White people from community participation in the seventeenth century, but none came from rabbis. Indeed, he argues that "slavery and race acted together as forces that helped push Sephardim away from halakha and toward secular law and what we now call cultural Jewishness beginning in the seventeenth century." Schorsch, "Revisiting Blackness, Slavery, and Jewishness in the Early Modern Sephardic Atlantic," in Kaplan, ed., *Religious Changes and Cultural Transformations*, 534, 537.

14. Lauren Benton argues that "'layered sovereignties' emerged as one of the defining characteristics of empire." *Search for Sovereignty*, 31. Nancy Shoemaker considers imperial semi-sovereignty in *A Strange Likeness: Becoming Red and White in Eighteenth-Century North America* (New York: Oxford University Press, 2004), 83–103. For the East India Company, see Philip J. Stern, *The Company State: Corporate Sovereignty and the Early Modern Foundations of the British Empire in India* (New York: Oxford University Press, 2011). For Jamaican Maroons, see Kopytoff, "Early Political Development"; and for the Powhatan, see Dylan Ruediger, "'Neither Utterly to Reject Them, Nor Yet to Drawe Them to Come In': Tributary Subordination and Settler Colonialism in Virginia," *Early American Studies* 18 (2020), 1–31.

15. Petition of Jacob Jeosua Bueno Enriques to the King, 1661[?], CO 1/15, no. 74 (in Spanish). Shortly thereafter, another likely kinsman, Daniel Bueno Henriques, "merchant, native of

Spain, and now resident in Barbadoes," received a grant of denization (in London?), July 24, 1661, CSP. Officials' response to his subsequent petition to trade in the island reveals considerable debate about "whether it stands with his Majesty's interest and that of the colonies to admit Jews to reside and trade there." Merchants who wished to avoid competition held "that the Jews are a people so subtle in matters of trade" and so well connected in "other nations" that they would "not only ingross trade among themselves" but would "divert the benefit thereof" to the other places where they had partners and family. Planters, on the other hand, complained that without competition, English merchants, "appropriat[ed] the whole trade" and forced high prices on planters. "The admission of Jews or any other accession of free trade will tend exceedingly to the advantage of the Colonies, and consequently of his Majesty and trade." The Council of Trade and Plantations made no general recommendation but thought that Caseres and his fellow petitioners, "being recommended by the King of Denmark, and having behaved with general satisfaction many years in Barbadoes, may have a special licence to reside there or in any other Plantation," received July 24, 1661, CSP.

16. Menasseh, *To His Highnesse*, 24. Searching for uses of whiteness is of course made difficult by the word's many applications. But a search in EEBO for documents that contain both *Negro* and *White* produces few publications earlier than Menasseh's petition. The earliest are a narrative by a Dutch author and some "Newes From Brazil." All three early examples of *White* as a racial term in English language publications, then, are connected to the Dutch Atlantic. Anonymous, *A Terrible Sea-fight Related* (London: Thomas Harper, 1640), n.p. (image 5); Anonymous, *A Little true forraine newes* (London: Nathanael Butter, 1641/2), 5. Rugemer discusses the emergence of whiteness in English Caribbean law in *Slave Law and the Politics of Resistance*, 46.

17. Menasseh, *To His Highnesse*, 24. Reflecting Sephardic Jews' and conversos' long experience with Iberian concerns with *limpieza de sangre*, Menasseh opened by assuring Cromwell of Jews' "*Noblenes* and purety of blood." *To His Highnesse*, 1.

18. Zijlstra, "Competing for European Settlers," 161–162, cites "Proposalls conserning the Plantation in his Ma[jes]t[ie]s Island of Jamaica, extracted out of sr Thomas Modyford's letter," [July 18, 1664], CO 1/18 f. 85.

19. Jacob Selwood has provided a clear and detailed chronology of these events in "Left Behind: Subjecthood, Nationality, and the Status of Jews After the Loss of English Surinam," *Journal of British Studies* 54 (2015), 578–601. R. A. J. van Lier, "The Jewish Community in Surinam: A Historical Survey," in Robert Cohen, ed., *The Jewish Nation in Surinam: Historical Essays* (Amsterdam: S. Emmering, 1982), 19–24; L. L. E. Rens, "Analysis of Annals Relating to Early Jewish Settlement in Surinam," in Cohen, *The Jewish Nation in Surinam*, 29–46.

20. A contemporary English observer noted that some Jews in Surinam "trade also as merchants, they having obtained a license from the King so to do." Rens, "Analysis of Annals," 31.

21. Vincent T. Harlow, ed., *Colonising Expeditions to the West Indies and Guiana, 1623–1667* (London: Hakluyt Society, 1925), 216–218. For the English translation circulating in London (which uses "inhabitants"), see Report of the Lords Committee for Foreign Affairs to the King, [1669], CSP, CO 1/24, nos. 53–54.

22. Zijlstra, "Competing for European Settlers," 158; Rens, "Analysis of Annals," 36–38. The Dutch did, however, specify Dutch law for all, erasing the Jewish privilege of governing themselves by their own law that the English in Surinam had allowed them.

23. Extracts out of the Register of the resolutions of the High and Mighty Lords States General of the United Netherlands, The Hague, July 25/August 4 and August 11/21, 1670, CSP; Draft instructions for [Major Bannister and others], October 25, 1670, CSP. See also Draft

Commissions to Major James Bannister and others, [November 1670], CSP. According to Rens, when this 1670/71 commission offered transportation, it appears that no Jews were interested in leaving, and of the 517 people who left on February 25, 1671, likely none were Jewish. Rens, "Analysis of Annals," 36–38.

24. William Byam, Governor of Antigua, to William Lord Willoughby, Governor of Barbadoes, [1670], CSP.

25. Governor Sir Thos. Modyford to Sec. Lord Arlington, September 20, 1670, CO 1/25, 59iii.

26. Modyford argued that Scots should be especially encouraged (to prevent their going to Poland and thereby being lost to the king). He also argued that "poor indigent men," including "servants newly out of their time" and "slaves newly made free" receiving less than thirty acres, be exempt from any future fees on land grants. Modyford argued that small plantations ought to be encouraged because as "the greatest producers of provisions" they represented "the strength of the Island." Governor Sir Thomas Modyford to Secretary Lord Arlington, for forwarding to the Council of Plantations. September 20, 1670, CO 1/25, nos. 59, 59i Statement of the Revenue, ii Propositions how the Royal Revenue may be increased, iii Propositions for the speedy settling of Jamaica.

27. Lynch to Secretary Arlington December 1, 1671, Arbell, *Jewish Nation of the Caribbean*, 252, cites Stephen Alexander Fortune, *Merchants and Jews: The Struggle for British West Indian Commerce, 1650–1750* (Gainesville: University of Florida Press, 1984), 17.

28. Beeston, "Voyage to Carthagena," 162. Gomez, in partnership with Solomon Gabay, had patented over 2,500 acres in Jamaica in 1669 and 1670. The two men were naturalized at the same time in 1672. JA 1B/11/1 (Patent Books) no. 3, ff. 212, 213; no. 4, ff. 3–4, 104–105. The land was in St. Johns and St. Mary's parishes. In the Jamaica records, *Gomez* is spelled both with a *z* (Spanish variant) and with an *s* (Portuguese). Because naturalization protected land ownership, the 1672 naturalizations may have duplicated earlier patents that do not survive.

29. Minutes of the Council of Jamaica, October 21, 1671, St. Jago de la Vega, CSP.

30. Sir Thomas Lynch to the Council for Trade and Plantations, March 10, 1672, CSP.

31. Zijlstra, "Competing for European Settlers," 159.

32. J. H. Hollander, "Documents Relating to the Attempted Departure of the Jews from Surinam in 1675," *Publications of the American Jewish Historical Society* (1897), 23–24. No certain record exists of their transport to Jamaica, but of the ten Jewish men who requested to go, six identical or very similar names appear in Jamaican naturalization records in the following two decades. Each of the ten Jewish men listed as wishing to depart was listed along with the number of enslaved people he intended to take: Isaac Perera (40), Jacob Perera (40), David Perera (10), Benjamin Perera (02), Isaac de Prado (40), Isaac de Mera/Isaac de la Paxa (70), Aaron de Silva (74), Isaac Govia (25), Gabriel Antoniis (15), Moses Baruch (06). Hollander, "Documents Relating to the Attempted Departure," 17, 19. Jamaican naturalizations of individuals with the same or similar names included Isaac Pereira (1687), JA 1B/11/11, f. 104; Lopez David Pereira (1693), JA 1B/11/12, f. 173; Benjamin Pereira (1689–1697), JA 1B/11/12, f. 137; Isaac Rodriques Depardo (1682), JA 1B/11/9, f. 20; Isaac D Lapara/Isaac Paradela, February 30, 1678, JA 1B/11/7, f. 121; and Moses Baruh (1689–1697), JA 1B/11/12, f. 287.

33. For a list of Jewish and English people in Dutch Surinam, see F. E. Baron Mullert, "De bewoners van Suriname in 1675," *De Navorscher* (1917), 401–406.

34. Hollander, "Documents Relating to the Attempted Departure, 9–29.

35. Jessica Vance Roitman, "Creating Confusion in the Colonies: Jews, Citizenship, and the Dutch and British Atlantics," *Itinerario* 36 (2012), 77; Barry L. Stiefel, "Experimenting with

Acceptance, Caribbean-Style: Jews as Aliens in the Anglophone Torrid Zone," in Roper, *The Torrid Zone*, 162–175. See also Selwood, "Left Behind." All of this suggests that the 1740 Plantation Act confirmed what was already happening in the Caribbean.

36. Emphasis added. Roitman, "Creating Confusion in the Colonies," 68–69, cites Rens, "Analysis of Annals," 29–46, and Hollander, "Documents Relating to the Attempted Departure," 9.

37. Rens, "Analysis of Annals," 41. The Dutch governor's claims were perhaps disingenuous: the Dutch, like the English, defended Jewish residents of the Netherlands or its colonies in the international arena. In 1654, for example, as Jews evacuated Brazil in the wake of the Portuguese conquest, a ship carrying some to New Amsterdam was driven by weather into Spanish Jamaica. There, officials seized Jews who had been conversos, allowing those who were born Jewish to continue on. The Dutch intervened, and the Spanish released them. Roitman, "Creating Confusion in the Colonies," 68; Arnold Wiznitzer, "The Exodus from Brazil and Arrival in New Amsterdam of the Jewish Pilgrim Fathers, 1654," *Publications of the American Jewish Historical Society* 45, no. 2 (1954), 86–87.

38. An Act for Naturalization, CO 1/25, no. 60 (1670?). The act noted that "severall Aliens & Forraigners" had already come to Jamaica "in pursuance of his said Ma[jes]ties proclamacon," patented or purchased land or other real estate, and then sold it. The act protected the subsequent purchasers in their quiet possession "any former Lawe Usage or Custome to the contrary in any wise notwithstanding."

39. Warrant to the Clerk of the Signet for Abraham de Soza Mondes, July 29, 1670, CSP; Whitehall, Warrant to the Clerk of the Signet for Jacob de Tones "of Jamaica, merchant, an alien born," May 5, 1671, CSP; Warrant to the Clerk of the Signet, for Baudouin Clasen, "of Jamaica, merchant, an alien born," Windsor, June 16, 1671, CSP. Warrant to the Clerk of the Signet, for Abraham Espinosa, "of Jamaica, merchant, an alien born," Whitehall, June 22, 1671, CSP.

40. Jewish naturalizations continued beyond 1715, but Jewish land patents slowed to a trickle after 1675. Jamaica Archives Patents Index (CD) and Patent books JA 1B/11/1-16.

41. Instructions for Sir Thomas Lynch, Lieut.-Governor of Jamaica, Whitehall, December 31, 1670, CSP. Lynch, like other English colonial governors, was "in his own house and family" to profess and recommend "the Protestant religion, as it is practised by his Majesty in England." In 1672, the instructions for Barbados governor William Lord Willoughby were similar. Instructions for William Lord Willoughby, Governor of Barbadoes, April 30, 1672, CSP. But the following spring, Willoughby wrote from Barbados that even those requirements proved too stringent: he could not administer the oath of supremacy to his council members, "else [he would have] not had such a Council as directed, being obliged to continue those he found." He also noted that the leeway "pretended to tender consciences" in his instructions did not provide for all exigencies, because even without the oaths of allegiance and supremacy, judges, justices, and constables still had to take oaths specific to their offices, "which many tender consciences will refuse." As an example he noted that a Quaker judge, "as well approved as any," had "refus[ed] the oath of a judge." The council forced him to quit his position, and Willoughby would "be hard put to find a fitter" replacement. Governor Lord Willoughby to Dr. B. Worsley, Secretary to the Council for Plantations, Barbados, March 7, 1673, CSP.

42. H. S. Q. Henriques, "The Political Rights of English Jews," *Jewish Quarterly Review* 19 (1907), 298–341.

43. For his 1683 naturalization, see Baric, Benjamin Carvallo, nat., JA 1B/11/1, no. 9, f. 136.

44. The Governor of Curaçao to Governor Sir Thomas Lynch, August 29/September 8, 1683, CSP.

45. Governor of Curaçao to Governor Sir Thomas Lynch, August 29/September 8, 1683, CSP; Benjamin Baruch Carvallo to Sir Thomas Lynch, Spanish, August 29, 1683, CSP, endorsed "the Jew's letter about his cruel usage at Curaçoa by Spanish pirates."

46. Sir Thomas Lynch to Lords of Trade and Plantations, September 12, 1683, CSP.

47. For a discussion of the Plantation Act, see Stanley Mirvis, *The Jews of Eighteenth-Century Jamaica: A Testamentary History of a Diaspora in Transition* (New Haven, Conn.: Yale University Press, 2020), 69–72.

48. Sir Thomas Lynch to Lords of Trade and Plantations, September 12, 1683, CSP.

49. Sir Thomas Lynch to Lords of Trade and Plantations, September 12, 1683, CSP.

50. Sir Thomas Lynch to Lords of Trade and Plantations, September 12, 1683, CSP.

51. A Catholic priest in Brazil expressed a similar sentiment about the Dutch, calling them "mortal enemies of Christianity, directing everything into commercial business, the one idolatry they agree on . . . because" a merchant company (WIC-Zeeland) governed. Evan Haefeli, *New Netherland and the Dutch Origins of American Religious Liberty* (Philadelphia: University of Pennsylvania Press, 2012), 102; Ernst Pijning, "Idealism and Power," in Allan I. Macinnes and Arthur H. Williamson, eds., *Shaping the Stuart World, 1603–1714: The Atlantic Connection* (Leiden: Brill, 2006), 207–232.

52. Governor Sir Thomas Modyford to Secretary Lord Arlington, for forwarding to the Council of Plantations, September 20, 1670, CO 1/25, nos. 59, 59i.

53. Hollander, "Documents Relating to the Attempted Departure," 14.

54. Arbell, *Portuguese Jews of Jamaica*, 18–25.

55. Jews and Christians in Jamaica did not remain entirely separate. Hanna Azavedo, daughter of merchant Abraham Azavedo, married bricklayer Henry James sometime before 1710. JA 1B/11/1/14, f. 179. Anne Hanson, wife of St. Catherines planter John Hanson, was present at the births of Ester Mendez Gutterez and Isaac Mendez, children of Jacob and Sarah Mendez Gutterez Jr. of Spanish Town, in 1702 and 1703. JA 1B/11/1/15, f. 81.

56. Arbell, *Jewish Nation of the Caribbean*, 237.

57. Roitman stresses that Jamaican Jews "needed to persistently assert their rights and privileges to belong to these communities." "Creating Confusion in the Colonies," 77.

58. Minutes of the Council of Jamaica, October 21, 1671, St. Jago de la Vega, CSP.

59. David Armitage has shown that Declaration of Independence, including its preamble proclaiming that "all men are created equal," was a document with an international audience. Independence and legitimate sovereignty—the right to assume a place among nations—rested in part on a nation state's treatment of its citizens. David Armitage, *The Declaration of Independence: A Global History* (Cambridge, Mass.: Harvard University Press, 2007). See also Eliga H. Gould, *Among the Powers of the Earth: The American Revolution and the Making of a New World Empire* (Cambridge, Mass.: Harvard University Press, 2012).

60. In 1720, an English official used the term *sanctuary* to describe a ship captain's protection of a "fugitive Jew who was liable to the [Portuguese] Inquisition"; see Stiefel, "Experimenting with Acceptance," 174. See also Stiefel, *Jewish Sanctuary in the Atlantic World: A Social and Architectural History* (Columbia: University of South Carolina Press, 2014).

61. Rugemer, "Development of Mastery and Race," 446.

62. Petition of certain Jews of Jamaica to the Queen, August 30, 1692, CSP. Arbell names the petitioners as Isaque Fernandes Diaz, Isak Moses Barak, Isaque Nunez, Phineas Abarbine, Isaque Rodriguez de Souza, Aron Jacob Soarez, Jacob de Caseres, Jacob David de Robles, and Isaque Mendez Gutierez, all "merchants of Jamaica." Arbell, *Jewish Nation of the Caribbean*, 247–248.

63. According to Edward Long, "Jews have shewn themselves very good and useful subjects upon many occasions. When the French invaded this island during the government of Sir William Beeston, they opposed the enemy with great courage." *The History of Jamaica* (London, 1774), 2: 294–295.

64. Arbell, *Jewish Nation of the Caribbean*, 248.

65. Governor Sir William Beeston to the Council of Trade and Plantations, May 3, 1700, CSP.

66. Baron de Belmonte was also Don Manuel de Belmonte alias Isaac Nunes. Arbell, *Jewish Nation of the Caribbean*, 248. Rebecca J. Scott and Jean M. Hébrard note a similar significance of physical documents confirming status for freed people of color in Atlantic world. Scott and Hébrard, *Freedom Papers: An Atlantic Odyssey in the Age of Emancipation* (Cambridge, Mass.: Harvard University Press, 2012). While stakes were perhaps lower for Jews who remained in Jamaica (threatening their property but not their freedom), if they left, the lack of letters made them more subject to seizure and delivery to the Inquisition, where they faced torture and death.

67. Petition of Jews of Jamaica to the Queen [February 26, 1703], CSP.

68. Fortune, *Merchants and Jews*, 65.

69. Arbell, *Jewish Nation of the Caribbean*, 246, cites Samuel J. and Edith Hurwitz, "The New World Sets an Example for the Old: *The Jews in Jamaica and Political Rights 1661–1831*," *American Jewish Historical Quarterly* 55, no. 1 (1965), 42–43.

70. Arbell, *Portuguese Jews of Jamaica*, 20.

Chapter 5

1. Zahedieh, "Merchants of Port Royal," 572; Ones, "The Politics of Government in the Audiencia of New Granada"; Grahn, *The Political Economy of Smuggling*. Carolyn Nordstrom's *Global Outlaws: Crime, Money, and Power in the Contemporary World* (Berkeley: University of California Press, 2007), provides perspective on extralegal trade in the twenty-first century that has helped me to think about its normalcy in the seventeenth and eighteenth centuries. Irene Wright argues in *The Coymans Asiento* that smuggling was respectable in seventeenth-century Spanish America. During Portuguese-Spanish union from 1580 to 1640, Portuguese merchants held trading rights in Spanish America. Between 1640 and 1662 there was no organized asiento, but the Dutch carried much of Spanish America's slave trade. In 1662 the asiento went to two Genoese merchants, Grillo and Lomelin. K. G. Davies, *The Royal African Company* (London: Longmans, 1957), 13–14. In 1676 it went to Seville merchants who assigned it to the Genoese merchants Borroso and Porcio. In 1694 the asiento went to a Portuguese company, in 1701 to the French Guinea Company, and in 1713 to the British South Sea Company. Curtis Nettles, "England and the Spanish-American Trade, 1680–1715," *Journal of Modern History* 3 (1931), 2. Throughout those years smugglers carried significant portions of the slave trade.

2. For an analysis of the merchants who served this function for the South Sea Company a generation later, see Adrian Finucane, *The Temptations of Trade: Britain, Spain, and the Struggle for Empire* (Philadelphia: University of Pennsylvania Press, 2016).

3. For economic analyses of the importance of Jamaica as a conduit for Anglo-Spanish trade, see Zahedieh, "Merchants of Port Royal"; Zahedieh, "Trade, Plunder, and Economic Development"; Nélida García Fernández, "Interacciones mercantiles entre los imperios del Atlántico: El comercio directo del añil colonial Español hacia Bristol, vía Jamaica," *Caribbean Studies* 34 (2006), 47–98; Nettles, "England and the Spanish-American Trade; and O'Malley, *Final Passages*. Barbados provided some of the trade (it had the advantage of being the first port

for ships coming from Africa), but Port Royal became the primary English entrepôt because of its proximity to Cartagena, Portobelo, Vera Cruz, and Havana.

4. Wright, *The Coymans Asiento*. Barroso may have formerly worked for Coymans and Company. See C. M. Shaw, "The Overseas Spanish Empire and the Dutch Republic Before and After the Peace of Munster," *De zeventiende Eeuw*, 13 (1997), 131–139. For Porcio's (and Barroso's) Genoese identity, see Postma, *The Dutch in the Atlantic Slave Trade*, 39. Wright argues that to spread opposition to Porcio, the Dutch "bought" Cartagena governor Don Juan Pando. The president of Panama supported Porcio. Wright, *The Coymans Asiento*, 23, 41–43, cites Juan de Pando to the crown, Cartagena, November 18, 1683, August 24, 1684; Francisco Valera to the crown, Cartagena, January 8, 1685.

5. Wright, *The Coymans Asiento*, 23–25.

6. Wright, *The Coymans Asiento*, 23–30. Coymans's representatives in the Caribbean (primarily in Curaçao, but they also appeared in Cartagena) included Peter Van Belle (Pedro Bambelle) and Balthazar Beque. Wright, *The Coymans Asiento*, 25, 48.

7. Wright, 28–31, 47, cites Council for Indies to his Majesty, February 12, 1685. She refers to this one-time "condoning" as "usual procedure." Tamar Herzog describes eighteenth-century merchants' applications for belonging in the Spanish Atlantic. *Defining Nations*, 82–91. See also April Lee Hatfield, "Dutch and New Netherland Merchants in the Seventeenth-Century Chesapeake," in Peter A. Coclanis, ed., *The Atlantic Economy During the Seventeenth and Eighteenth Centuries: Organization, Operation, Practice, and Personnel* (Columbia: University of South Carolina Press, 2005), 205–228.

8. Wright, *The Coymans Asiento*, 30–42.

9. Wright, *The Coymans Asiento*, 34.

10. Wright, *The Coymans Asiento*, 35. Quotations are from Wright. She cites the Inquisition's consulta, June 7, 1686, which includes Villalobos's arguments.

11. Wright, *The Coymans Asiento*, 36.

12. Wright, *The Coymans Asiento*, 37.

13. An undated paper claimed that the Coymans asiento had "reduced the Indies to ruin" because it brought so many dry goods into American ports that Spanish merchants could not hope to compete. Dispatches ordering "intervention" reached the colonies beginning in March 1688. Wright, *The Coymans Asiento*, 41–43, 56.

14. Wright, *The Coymans Asiento*, 52–55.

15. Copy of deposition of Don Juan Santiago de Castillo, CO 1/61, no. 50, January 12–22–March 11–21, 1687, Spanish.

16. For the date of his arrival, see AGI, Escribanía 597C, pieza 25. Castillo to [Velez], October 25, 1688.

17. Castillo was not an "imperial fixer" in the way that Stephen Saunders Webb described William Blathwayt, because Castillo was less interested in empire than he was in commerce. Functioning empire (with militaries to rid the Caribbean of pirates) served commerce, but the vision of those, like Castillo, who promoted freer interimperial trade often worked at cross-purposes with a more protectionist vision of empire as viewed from London or Madrid. Webb, "William Blathwayt, Imperial Fixer: Muddling Through to Empire, 1689–1717," *William and Mary Quarterly*, 3rd ser., 26 (1968), 373–415.

18. Dn. St. Iago Dell Castillo naturalization, JA 1B/11/1, vol. 10, 137. He was naturalized again in 1693, as Sir James Castill, JA 1B/11/1, vol. 12, 144. As in the case of Jewish immigrants,

the language of Castillo's naturalization promised him the same rights and privileges as natural-born subjects. In the same year, the Jamaican Assembly reaffirmed liberty of conscience in Jamaica.

19. His will, dated March 23, 1710, is housed in the Island Record Office, Wills, vol. 13, f. 4. Besides a hundred-pound (current money) bequest to his son, he left all of his property "in ye Island of Jamaica . . . Great Britain Spain or in the Dominions belonging to the Spanish Monarchy in America" to Mary. Jamaica deed record indexes list many property transfers to Castillo, most of which are too damaged to access. Those that are accessible include over one thousand acres in Kingston and St. Thomas parishes, with a sugar mill. However, Mary's will inventory lists what appear to be the "goods and chattles Richts and Creditts" of only one estate, including twenty-seven enslaved men, women, and youths with a mixture of English, Spanish, African, and classical names, an uncertain number of enslaved children, six mares, thirteen head of cattle, the furniture from one house, silver tableware, and a significant amount of jewelry made of gold, emeralds, diamonds, amethysts, and pearls (including three crosses). JA 1B/11/17, vol. 10, 189.

20. Wright, *The Coymans Asiento*, 51. The order to arrest Castillo came as a decree in council on February 18–22, 1686. Wright, *The Coymans Asiento*, 62.

21. Wright, *The Coymans Asiento*, 47–48, citations between December 24, 1685, and May 3, 1686.

22. Porcio remained in the monastery until March 1688. (Balthazar Coymans died in Cádiz on November 8, 1686.) Wright, *The Coymans Asiento*, 50–51.

23. Records for this case are in the The National Archives, CO 1/61, no. 50 (January 12/22, 1687). They consist of fourteen pages in Spanish in two hands, copies of depositions taken in Jamaica, court proceedings in Vera Cruz, and letters written in Cuba and Jamaica.

24. Copy of deposition of Don Juan Santiago de Castillo, January 12–22–March 11–21, 1687, CO 1/61, no. 50, Spanish. Castillo also suggested that Jenes was retaliating for Jamaican officials' efforts to stop him from smuggling more than three thousand pesos worth of clothing to Vera Cruz.

25. See Antonio Lazertoza's testimony below. For examples of Jamaica governors acting (together with other judges) in their capacity as vice admirals to try pirates in the 1670s, before the Jamaica Act, see Matthew Norton, "Classification and Coercion: The Destruction of Piracy in the English Maritime System," *American Journal of Sociology* 119 (2014), 1537–1575.

26. Castillo, who referred to most men in the case by their title or occupation rather than by their name, referred to Guarín as Matheo.

27. The teniente (Juan Quixano de Palma) responded to apparent accusations that he had had a hand in illegally seizing the English sloop by insisting that he had acted according to law and committed no injustice, "much less roguery." He had not permitted the sale and distribution of the ship and goods but had "left the sea to the [guardacostas] corsairs to inhibit trade and apprehend pirates." [Copy of] Carta del Sr Then[ien]te de la Trin[ida]d Juan Quixano de Palma, part of Castillo deposition, January 12–22–March 11–21, 1687, CO 1/61, no. 50, Spanish.

28. Molesworth's declaration to the viceroy ("auto") survives in Spanish translation, so whether Molesworth's original read "resident," "denizen," or something else is uncertain. Auto de Molesworth, part of Castillo deposition, January 12–22–March 11–21, 1687, CO 1/61, no. 50, Spanish. Molesworth's "auto" is dated January 15–25, 1687, but the enclosure he refers to is dated a month later.

29. Lazertoza's deposition is dated February 25, 1687, and included in Castillo deposition, January 12–22–March 11–21, 1687, CO 1/61, no. 50, Spanish. Peter Beckford was the Royal African Company factor and Henry Egerton the secretary. The ambassador was Pedro Ronquillo.

30. Castillo to [Velez], October 25, 1688, AGI, Escribanía 597C, pieza 25.

31. Diego Evelino Hurtado de Compostela, "bishop of this island of Santiago de Cuba, Jamaica, and the Province of Florida," May 7, 1688, enclosed in Governor the Duke of Albemarle to Lords of Trade and Plantations, May 11, 1688, CO 1/64, no. 64ii.

32. Castillo to [Velez], October 25, 1688, AGI, Escribanía 597C, pieza 25.

33. Castillo to [Velez], October 25, 1688, AGI, Escribanía 579C, pieza 25.

34. Castillo to [Velez], October 25, 1688, AGI, Escribanía 579C, pieza 25. If Irene Wright is correct that the addressee was the Marques de los Velez, then Castillo was writing to Fernando Fajardo, then president of the Council of the Indies. *The Coymans Asiento*, 62.

35. For a description of Castillo's activities, see F. J. Osborne, S.J., "James Castillo--Assiento Agent," *Jamaican Historical Review* 8 (1971), 9–18.

36. Evan Haefeli, "Introduction: Anti-Catholicism, Anti-Popery, and the British-American World," in Haefeli, ed., *Against Popery: Britain, Empire, and Anti-Catholicism* (Charlottesville: University of Virginia Press, 2020), 1–22.

37. Osborne, "James Castillo," 12; Osborne, *The History of the Catholic Church in Jamaica* (1977; Chicago: Loyola University Press, 1988), 125–140.

38. He may have done so unconsciously. Indeed, he may have intended only to emphasize that James's subjects *could* be Catholic.

39. The Case of Smith Kelly, late Provost Marshal of Jamaica, and of St. Jago del Castillo stated, [May 1688], CO 1/64, no. 65.

40. The Case of Smith Kelly, late Provost Marshal of Jamaica, and of St. Jago del Castillo stated, [May 1688], CO 1/64, no. 65.

41. Castillo to [Velez], October 25, 1688, AGI, Escribanía 597, pieza 25.

42. Castillo to [Velez], October 25, 1688, AGI, Escribanía 597, pieza 25.

43. The Case of Smith Kelly, late Provost Marshal of Jamaica, and of St. Jago del Castillo stated, [May 1688], CO 1/64, no. 65. Albemarle had earlier referred to Castillo as "a Spaniard (naturalized here)." Governor the Duke of Albemarle to Lords of Trade and Plantations, May 11, 1688, CO 1/64, no. 64.

44. Copy of letter of St. Jago del Castillo to the Archbishop of Cuba, CO 1/64, no. 64i. Spanish copies of the document and letters from Castillo to the Cuban bishop are enclosed in Governor the Duke of Albemarle to the Lords of Trade and Plantations, May 11, 1688, CO 1/64, no. 64, 64i–iii. For description of its arrival in Jamaica see Castillo to [Velez], October 25, 1688, AGI, Escribanía 597C, pieza 25.

45. Copy of letter of St. Jago del Castillo to the Archbishop of Cuba, CO 1/64, no. 64i.

46. Copy of the letter from the bishop of Cuba to Santiago del Castillo, CO 1/64, no. 64ii. Spanish imperial authorities may have disagreed with the bishop's claims every bit as much as English imperial authorities did.

47. Colonial officials in Spanish and English colonies had copies of the Treaty of Madrid or instructions based on it. See CSP for references to the Treaty of Madrid in English governors' instructions and in correspondence between English and Spanish governors.

48. The Spanish crown exercised significant control over the church (including over personnel) in Spanish America. Josep M. Barnadas, "The Catholic Church in Colonial Spanish

America," in Leslie Bethell, ed., *The Cambridge History of Latin America*, vol. 1 (New York: Cambridge University Press, 1984), 512–513.

49. Copy of the letter from the bishop of Cuba (Diego Evelino Hurtado de Compostela) to Santiago del Castillo, Santiago de Cuba, April 26, 1688, CO 1/64, no. 64ii.

50. For a time line of changing oath requirements, see Charles Evans, "Oaths of Allegiance in Colonial New England," *Proceedings of the American Antiquarian Society* 34 (1924), 377–438.

51. The Case of Smith Kelly, late Provost Marshal of Jamaica, and of St. Jago del Castillo stated, [May 1688], CO 1/64, no. 65.

52. Governor the Duke of Albemarle to Lords of Trade and Plantations, May 11, 1688, CO 1/64, no.64.

53. The Case of Smith Kelly, late Provost Marshal of Jamaica, and of St. Jago del Castillo stated, [May 1688]. CO 1/64, no. 65; Minutes of Council of Jamaica, May 7, 1688, CSP. The minutes are included the "Petition of Thomas Churchill setting forth that St. Jago del Castillo had procured a manifesto for the Archbishop of Cuba prejudicial to the royal prerogative."

54. A dozen years later, the newly arrived army officer William Selwyn objected to "a Papist and a Spaniard" Castillo possessing a strategic fort during wartime and tried "to garrison, or demolish it," but his local supporters prevented the seizure. Brigadier Selwyn to the Council of Trade and Plantations, July 23, 1701, CSP.

55. In 1681 there were at least seven Anglican ministers on the island, according to Governor Sir Henry Morgan. Deputy Governor Sir Henry Morgan to Lords of Trade and Plantations, Port Royal, January 27, 1681, CSP.

56. The Case of Smith Kelly [May 1688], CO 1/64, no. 65. Castillo apparently refused to give security that he would obey King James's instructions when they arrived.

57. Castillo to [Velez], October 25, 1688, AGI, Escribanía 597C, pieza 25.

58. Castillo to [Velez], October 25, 1688, AGI, Escribanía 597C, pieza 25.

59. Michael Braddick prefers "mobilization" as more useful than "allegiance," but because my evidence contains so many cases in which professed allegiance—and symbolic allegiance—run counter to behavior (or mobilization) it is useful to retain both terms.

60. Herzog, *Defining Nations*, especially chapters 3 and 5. My evidence challenges some of Herzog's conclusions about the relationship between local and imperial identities and about the mid-seventeenth-century disappearance of their applicability to people of color in Spanish America. "War and Politics in England and Wales, 1642-1646," in Braddick, ed., *The Oxford Handbook of the English Revolution* (New York: Oxford University Press, 2015), 96–113.

61. Castillo to [Velez], October 25, 1688, AGI, Escribanía 597C, pieza 25.

62. Castillo to [Velez], October 25, 1688, AGI, Escribanía 587C, pieza 25.

63. Castillo to [Velez], October 25, 1688, AGI, Escribanía 579C, pieza 25. Castillo said that the asiento owed him owed him 34 doblones, 550 pesos, 6 reales.

64. Castillo to [Velez], October 25, 1688, AGI, Escribanía 579C, pieza 25. The governor's advisor was Colonel General Franco Manuel de Rosa.

65. Castillo to [Velez], October 25, 1688, AGI, Escribanía 579C, pieza 25.

66. Castillo to [Velez], October 25, 1688, AGI, Escribanía 597C, pieza 25.

67. Wright, *The Coymans Asiento*, 62.

68. Raising the value of pieces of eight had dissolved a proportion of Jamaican planters' debt to the company. Memorandum from the Royal African Company, July 19, 1688, CO 1/65, no. 26.

69. Answer of the Merchants and Planters of Jamaica as to the Petition of the Royal African Company, August 23, 1689, CSP.

70. Reasons Offered for Sending Colonel Hender Molesworth Governor to Jamaica, May 14, 1689, CSP.

71. Colonel Molesworth's Proposals as to the Government of Jamaica, received June 22, 1689, CSP.

72. Memorandum of Lords of Trade and Plantations, July 3, 1689, CSP.

73. A short account of the state of affairs in Jamaica, July 1689, CO 137/44, no. 12. It describes Albemarle as "threatning People in Open Court to Rule them with Rodds of Iron, to the Terrour of all the Inhabitants of the Island," a "Tyranicall & Illegall course."

74. William considered the appointment together with the Royal African Company's petition "as to the fraudulent Act of the Jamaica Assembly" (under Albemarle) for raising the value of pieces of eight. He was concerned about the company's claim that the planters of Jamaica owed it £90,000 and that the act would thereby defraud the company of one-fifth of the debt owed it. Order of King in Council, July 15, 1689, CSP. William did not appoint a governor until February 1690, when he granted the office to William O'Brien, second Earl of Inchiquin, who had no experience in Jamaica.

75. See, for example, Governor Thomas Lynch's charge that while "particular Spaniards may be in their senses . . . the Government is out of it." Sir Thomas Lynch to Lords of Trade and Plantations, February 28, 1684, CSP.

76. Address of the Council and Assembly of Jamaica to the King James II, July 12, 1689, CSP. Although Knight represented Port Royal, the Assembly as a whole favored planters, given its parish-based representation.

77. Address of the Council and Assembly of Jamaica to the King James II, July 12, 1689, CSP. Knight took particular umbrage at Coymans's asiento factors, who paid Jamaican middlemen a 35 percent commission to buy up the most sellable captives on behalf of the asiento, "and now it is feared that the Dutch have quite taken the whole trade from us."

78. Address of the Council and Assembly of Jamaica to the King James II, July 26, 1689, CSP. If Ralph Knight was son of Sir Ralph Knight (1619–1691), the two men's fathers were close, perhaps explaining Knight's defense of Albemarle. Stuart Handley, "Knight, Sir Ralph," *Oxford Dictionary of National Biography*, (2004), https://doi-org.srv-proxy2.library.tamu.edu/10.1093/ref:odnb/66325.

79. Address of the Council and Assembly of Jamaica to the King James II, July 26, 1689, CSP.

80. See also Swingen, *Competing Visions of Empire*, 124–129.

81. A Memorial of what is desired by Don Santiago Del Castillo, August 20, 1689, CO 138/6, 203–205.

82. From 1689 to 1697, Spain and England allied with one another (as well as with the Holy Roman Empire, the Netherlands, and Sweden) against France in the War of the Grand Alliance. The "Grand Alliance" of the Habsburg monarchy, England, Spain, the Dutch Republic, Portugal, and the Duchy of Savoy aimed to contain Louis XIV. Historians also know this war as the Nine Years' War, King William's War, or the War of the League of Augsburg. I have chosen to use "War of the Grand Alliance" because my focus is on one part of the alliance, that of Catholic Spain and Protestant England, which marked a shift in imperial relations that altered the context for interactions between subjects and representatives of those empires in the Caribbean.

83. A Memorial of what is desired by Don Santiago Del Castillo, CO 138/6, pp. 203–205. Castillo modeled this proposal on provisions in the asiento contracts issued by the Spanish crown to slave trading companies. The 1713 contract notes the precedent of prior asiento contracts. *The Assiento, or, Contract for Allowing the Subjects of Great Britain the Liberty of Importing*

Negroes into the Spanish America (London: John Baskett, printer to the Queen, 1713), article 13. For *jueces conservadores* see García-Montón, *Genoese Entrepreneurship*, 137–161

84. A Memorial of what is desired by Don Santiago Del Castillo, CO 138/6, 205.

85. In September the Lords of Trade and Plantations referred the questions about Castillo and the asiento the Commissioners of Custom. Journal of Lords of Trade and Plantations, September 2, 1689, CSP. By then a copy had also reached the King in Council, who referred it to the Lords of the Treasury. Order of the King in Council, Whitehall, September 3, 1689, CSP. On September 14, Blathwayt wrote to the Customs requesting a quick response. William Blathwayt to JS, September 14, 1689, CSP; JS to WB, September 16, 1689, Custom House, CSP.

86. The Attorney and Solicitor General confirmed that Castillo could furnish supplies for the asiento's ships and employees without trouble, but worried that even though unloading to careen was legal, granting asiento ships the right to do so was "dangerous" and inadvisable, as it facilitated "secret trade." Seamen routinely hid contraband trade items (textiles and other European manufactures) among their personal belongings to sell illegally in Spanish ports. Although their doing so did not directly harm English trade, Spanish officials who discovered smuggling could use it to justify seizing the entire cargo and the ship itself as prize. Protecting the asiento from liability for individual seamen's smuggling would prove difficult because of the challenges in distinguishing between actions of "owners, merchants, officers, and seamen." Journal of Lords of Trade and Plantations, August 20, 1689, CSP; Report of Attorney and Solicitor General, August 22, 1689, CO 137/2, no. 20.

87. Commissioners of Customs to Lords of the Treasury, October 14, 1689, CSP. The commissioners attached Arthur Moore's objections to Castillo's proposal.

88. Report of the Judges on the memorial of St. Jago del Castillo [November 11, 1689], CO 138/6, 284–285.

89. London officials, unlike Jamaica governors, here distinguished local denization from the full naturalization that required an act of Parliament.

90. Memorial of the Spanish Ambassador, [November] 1689, French, CSP.

91. William to Insiquin, February 12, 1690, CO 138/6, 286, referring to Ambassador Ronquillo's intervention.

92. Charles Leslie, *A New History of Jamaica* (London: J. Hodges, 1740), 252. Leslie wrote that Castillo's "good Conduct gained him universal Esteem" in Jamaica.

93. Journal of Lords of Trade and Plantations, August 20, 1689, CSP; Report of the Attorney and Solicitor General, August 22, 1689, CO 137/2, no. 20.

Chapter 6

1. Act of Parliament Constituting the Company of Scotland, Trading to Africa and the Indies (King William III, Parl. 1, Sess. 5), Edinburgh, June 26, 1695, appendix to Francis Russell Hart, *The Disaster of Darien: The Story of the Scots Settlement and the Causes of Its Failure, 1699–1701* (Boston: Houghton Mifflin, 1929), 181–191. The act referred to an earlier "Act for encouraging of Forraign Trade" that promised the king's encouragement for newly chartered companies. Hart writes that the powers of the company were confirmed twice: King William III, Parl. 1, Sess. 8–9, January 31, 1701, and Queen Anne, Parl. 1, Sess. 1, September 16, 1703.

2. *A Treaty For the Composing of Differences, Restraining of Depredations, and Establishing of Peace in America, Between the Crowns of Great Britain and Spain. Concluded at Madrid the 8th/18th Day of July . . . 1670* (London: John Bill and Christopher Barker, Printers to the Kings Most Excellent Majesty, 1670), Articles 2 and 8. "Subjects" is in Article 3.

3. Report from the Committee of the Court of Directors, Company of Scotland Trading to Africa and the Indies, 1698, MS 63, Senate House Library, University of London, 7. The directors issued this report in the same year that the Royal African Company officially lost its monopoly.

4. Report from the Committee, 8–9.

5. Report from the Committee, 21–34.

6. Report from the Committee, 24, 33–34.

7. Douglas Watt, *The Price of Scotland: Darien, Union, and the Wealth of Nations* (Edinburgh: Luath Press Limited, 2007), 33.

8. Watt, *Price of Scotland*, 28.

9. Several scholars have described these dynamics in detail, including Gallup-Diaz, *The Door of the Seas*; and Julie Orr, *Scotland, Darien and the Atlantic World, 1698–1700* (Edinburgh: Edinburgh University Press, 2018), 133–148.

10. Douglas Watt explores how the failure of New Caledonia pushed Scots to accept union. *Price of Scotland*. My interest here is the perspective of English colonial and metropolitan merchants and officials.

11. Gallup-Diaz, *The Door of the Seas*.

12. Gallup-Diaz, *The Door of the Seas*.

13. Gallup-Diaz, *The Door of the Seas*.

14. In Spanish America the term *palenque*, broadly meaning "palisade," referred to Maroon communities of escaped slaves.

15. Julie Orr provides a clear and detailed account of this international context. *Scotland, Darien and the Atlantic World*, 61.

16. Philip J. Stern discusses the implications of granting sovereign powers to joint-stock companies in his study of the East India Company. *The Company-State: Corporate Sovereignty and the Early Modern Foundations of the British Empire in India* (New York: Oxford University Press, 2011).

17. Act of Parliament Constituting the Company of Scotland, printed in Hart, *Disaster of Darien*, 186.

18. Act of Parliament Constituting the Company of Scotland, 187–188.

19. Act of Parliament Constituting the Company of Scotland, 188–189.

20. William did intercede only after the colony's defeat, on behalf of four prisoners sentenced to death in Spain. Orr, *Scotland, Darien and the Atlantic World*, 55–67, 91–92.

21. Indeed, the company pursued the possibility of negotiating with the Amsterdam-based Armenian brothers Jonas and Martin Gregory to operate a trade between India and Scotland. Watt, *Price of Scotland*, 212–213. The act gave the company a thirty-one-year monopoly among Scots to "trade or navigate" to any "Collonies, Plantations, or Possessions" the company established in Asia, Africa, or America. Other Scottish or foreign merchants would need a license or written permission from the company to trade there. The company could seize goods or ships in Asia or Africa to police its holdings. Act of Parliament Constituting the Company of Scotland, 187. It would also enjoy a twenty-one-year exception from duties.

22. Watt, *Price of Scotland*, 11. For corporate sovereignty, see Stern, *The Company-State*. For sovereignty, see Benton, *A Search for Sovereignty*; Shoemaker, *A Strange Likeness*.

23. Act of Parliament Constituting the Company of Scotland, 190.

24. Act of Parliament Constituting the Company of Scotland, 190.

25. The "Fundamental Constitutions" of New Caledonia, governing the colony once established in Darién, did contain specific benefits for Scots. After January 1, 1702, Scottish or New

Caledonian ships would pay lower duties on imports and exports than would foreign (including English) vessels. Watt, *Price of Scotland*, 131.

26. Perhaps this ability makes sense if we think of corporations as one end of a spectrum that included royal colonies at the other end and proprietary/joint-stock colonies in between.

27. Watt, *Price of Scotland*, 32–41.

28. Watt, *Price of Scotland*, 28–41.

29. Anon., *A Letter from a Member of the Parliament of Scotland to his Friend in London*, (London: John Whitlock, November 14, 1695), 13. For identification of author as MacKenzie see Watt, *Price of Scotland*, 37–38.

30. Watt, *Price of Scotland*, 39–43.

31. On November 23, William advised the English Parliament to "consider of such Laws as may be proper for the Advancement of Trade; and will have a particular Regard to that of the East Indies, lest it should be lost to the Nation." Watt, *Price of Scotland*, 39; H. Worwitx, "The East India Trade, the Politicians, and the Constitution: 1689–1702," *Journal of British Studies* 17 (1978), 7–8. When the Company of Scotland later sought investors in Amsterdam and Hamburg, it faced a similar nationalist response from Dutch East India Company merchants, and in Hamburg it faced also further English interference. Watt, *Price of Scotland*, 94–97, 101.

32. Watt, *Price of Scotland*, 38, 52, 63. Watt notes the ratio of shareholders to population was thirteen to one. *Price of Scotland*, 82–83.

33. Watt, *Price of Scotland*, 8.

34. Andrew Forrester, *The Man Who Saw the Future* (New York: Texere, 2004), 43–47.

35. While this effort also failed, Paterson made convincing enough arguments that the joint-stock Brandenburg Company tried to establish a colony or trading post at Darién, which Spain easily defeated. Watt, *Price of Scotland*, 6–7; Frank Cundall, *The Darien Venture* (New York: The Hispanic Society of America, 1926), 10.

36. Paterson, "A Proposal to Plant a colony in Darien; to protect the Indians against Spain; and to open the trade of South America to all nations" (London, 1701), in S. Bannister, ed., *The Writings of William Paterson, Founder of the Bank of England*, 3 vols. (1968), 1:158.

37. Quoted in Watt, *Price of Scotland*, 84.

38. Anonymous, *A Letter from a Gentleman in the Country to His Friend at Edinburgh: Wherein it is Clearly Proved, That the Scottish African, and Indian Company, is Exactly Calculated for the Interest of Scotland* (Edinburgh: George Mosman, 1696), 5, 8, 11; David Armitage, "Making the Empire British: Scotland in the Atlantic World, 1542–1707," *Past and Present* 155 (1997), 57.

39. Paterson, "A Proposal to Plant a Colony in Darien," 159.

40. Paterson, "A Proposal to Plant a Colony in Darien," 159. For Beeston's use of similar language, see Governor Sir William Beeston to the Council of Trade and Plantations, December 9, 1697, CSP.

41. Quoted in David Armitage, "The Scottish Vision of Empire: Intellectual Origins of the Darien Venture," in John Robertson, ed., *A Union for Empire: Political Thought and the British Union of 1707* (New York: Cambridge University Press, 1995), 97–118, 104.

42. *A Letter from a Member of the Parliament of Scotland*, 13.

43. Watt, *Price of Scotland*, 4;.

44. See "Report from the Committee of the Court of Directors of the African and Indian Company of Scotland appointed for giving the sailing orders . . . , giving their reasons for choosing the Darien site, and answering 15 objections made against the scheme, 1698," Senate House Library, University of London, MS 63.

45. Paterson, "A Proposal to Plant a Colony at Darien," 130. The Company of Scotland's project was consistent with English "independent" slave traders' arguments opposing the Royal African Company's monopoly. William A. Pettigrew, "Free to Enslave: Politics and the Escalation of Britain's Transatlantic Slave Trade, 1688–1714," *William and Mary Quarterly*, 3rd ser., 64 (2007), 3–38; and Pettigrew, *Freedom's Debt: The Royal African Company and the Politics of the Atlantic Slave Trade, 1672–1752* (Chapel Hill: University of North Carolina Press, 2013).

46. *A Poem Upon the Undertaking of the Royal Company of Scotland Trading to Africa and the Indies* (Edinburgh: James Wardlaw, 1697), n.p. (p. 14).

47. Watt, *Price of Scotland*, 2.

48. Christian Koot found Barbados merchants articulating principled defenses of free trade as early as the 1650s. *Empire at the Periphery*; Koot, "A 'Dangerous Principle': Free Trade Discourses in Barbados and the English Leeward Islands, 1650–1689," *Early American Studies* 5 (2007), 132–163. English investors responded with nationalism of their own. One English subscriber to the London offering argued against internationalizing the commercial world while at the same time doing so: he claimed he bought shares in the Company of Scotland because he thought it better "an Englishman should have the Benefit of it than a Foreigner." Watt, *Price of Scotland*, 36.

49. Philo-Britain [Walter Herries], *The Defence of the Scots Settlement at Darien, Answer'd, Paragraph by Paragraph* (London: The Booksellers of London and Westminster, 1699), 1–43. Watt, *Price of* Scotland, 7, cites Preston, *Pirate of Exquisite Mind*, 53–61.

50. Act of Parliament Constituting the Company of Scotland.

51. Gallup-Diaz, *The Door of the Seas*, 105–116.

52. Anyone could have deduced the plans by paying attention to published promotional literature such as the "lady of honour's" Darien song, or to opponents' objections. Watt, *Price of Scotland*, 9, 99.

53. Watt, *Price of Scotland*, 10.

54. Gallup-Diaz, *The Door of the Seas*, 82–89.

55. Gallup-Diaz, *The Door of the Seas*, 90–101.

56. Watt, *Price of Scotland*, 17.

57. Watt, *Price of Scotland*, 10.

58. "A True and authentick copie of the Committie of [Secreets] their letter to the Right &c the Council Caledonia," NLS Adv. MS 83.7.3, f. 7.

59. Watt, *Price of Scotland*, 18.

60. They also sent items to establish their colony: garden seeds, arms and ammunition, fishing nets and lines, carpenters' tools and nails. NLS Adv. MS 83.5.9. List of goods shipped, 1698, NLS Adv. MS 83.7.2.

61. Watt, *Price of Scotland*, 121. All London promoters, with the exception of Paterson and his associates James Smyth, Daniel Lodge, and Joseph Cohen D'Azevedo, were investors in textile manufacturing, which stood to gain from Spanish American slave trading that provided cover for smuggling cloth and clothes. Watt, *Price of Scotland*, 27.

62. Orr, *Scotland, Darien and the Atlantic World*, 51.

63. Watt, *Price of Scotland*, 151.

64. See Gallup-Diaz, *The Door of the Seas*, for the complexity of Indians' internal politics and their relations with the Spanish and other Europeans.

65. President and Council of Nevis to James Vernon, May 18, 1699, CSP.

66. The Council of the Indies to His Majesty, May 16, 1699. Communicating Message of His Britannic Majesty's Envoy and Copy of a Letter of Governor Beeston of Jamaica, AGI Audiencia de Panamá, L. 161 (2539), printed in appendix to Hart, *Disaster of Darien*.

67. The Council of the Indies to His Majesty, May 16, 1699.

68. Gallup-Diaz, *Door of the Seas*, 100–101.

69. *A Treaty For the Composing of Differences, Restraining of Depredations, and Establishing of Peace in America, Between the Crowns of Great Britain and Spain. Concluded at Madrid the 8th/18th Day of July . . . 1670* (London: Charles Bell and the Executrix of Thomas [Newcomb] Printers to the King, 1698).

70. The Scots sought trade in Dutch Curaçao in the southern Caribbean and Danish St. Thomas in the eastern Caribbean, suggesting they well understood the international nature of Caribbean trade and the region's specific economic geographies; the two islands they chose had long practiced open trade. That understanding (like company officials' earlier approach to Brandenburgers for aid) helps explain why they thought an international free port in Panama would work. Watt, *Price of Scotland*, 154.

71. Beeston to Council of Trade and Plantations, January 20, 1699, CSP.

72. For a fuller discussion of the Company of Scotland as an expression of Scottish nationalism (vis-à-vis England), see Armitage, "The Scottish Vision of Empire."

73. For the importance of contraband to Cartagena's economy, see Ones, "The Politics of Government in the Audiencia of New Granada"; and Grahn, *The Political Economy of Smuggling*.

74. Because the Company of Scotland's ships came just as Parliament dissolved the Royal African Company's monopoly, the Royal African Company faced challenges to its dominance at the end of the century more significant than the Scottish settlement at Darién.

75. Governor Sir William Beeston to Council of Trade and Plantations, February 8, 1699; John Flavell to Governor Beeston, December 24, 1698, CSP.

76. Beeston to Deonissio de Artunduaga, June 9, 1699. Beeston incorrectly identified Artunduaga as the governor of Portobelo. "Copies of Severall Letters from the Governors of the Spanish West Indies to Sir Wm. Beeston, with his answers to them, 1698–1699," Huntington Library mss BL 10, 10.

77. Orr, *Scotland, Darien and the Atlantic World*, 55.

78. Governor Sir William Beeston to the Council of Trade and Plantations, April 14, 1699, Jamaica, CSP. News of Beeston's proclamation reached Darién on May 18.

79. Opinions of the Attorney and Solicitor General as to the eligibility of Mr. Mein, a Scotchman, proposed to be of the Council of Barbados, June 27, 1698, CO 28/3, no. 66.

80. Orr, *Scotland, Darien and the Atlantic World*, 121–123; *Journals of the Assembly of Jamaica*, vol. 1, 1663–1709 (Jamaica: Alexander Aikman, 1811), 191–198.

81. Orr, *Scotland, Darien and the Atlantic World*, 52, 123. The Spanish did not capture the Scots' Jewish translator Benjamin Spencer until October (in Havana), so the ambassador's concerns likely did not stem from Spencer. Gallup-Diaz, *The Door of the Seas*, 133.

82. Copy of letter from William Murdoon to Mr. John Anderson, October 19, 1699, NAS GD 45/1/159; Orr, *Scotland, Darien and the Atlantic World*, 118–120, 160–161.

83. Governor the Earl of Bellomont to Council of Trade and Plantations, May 3, 1699, New York, CSP. Bellomont also worried that "Hyne the Pyrat's" (Hendrick van Hoven) failure to give quarter to Spaniards he captured would further provoke them.

84. Governor William Beeston to Governor the Earl of Bellomont, June 7, 1699, CSP.

85. Orr, *Scotland, Darien and the Atlantic World*, 48, 61, 104. Orr confirms that Beeston's suspicions were correct.

86. Governor William Beeston to Governor the Earl of Bellomont, June 7, 1699, CSP.

87. Governor William Beeston to Governor the Earl of Bellomont, June 7, 1699, CSP.

88. Watt, *Price of Scotland*; Armitage, "Making the Empire British"; and Armitage, "The Scottish Vision of Empire."

89. For English global anti-piracy efforts, see Robert C. Ritchie, *Captain Kidd and the War Against the Pirates* (Cambridge, Mass.: Harvard University Press, 1986).

90. Orr traces Portuguese-English diplomatic communications about New Caledonia. *Scotland, Darien and the Atlantic World*, 56–63.

91. Governor Basse to William Popple, June 9, 1699, Burlington, CSP. Andrew Hamilton, who had been governor from 1692 to 1697, was recalled because he was Scottish, but he was reinstated in 1699.

92. Governor Basse to William Popple, June 9, 1699, Burlington, CSP.

93. Governor Jeremiah Basse to Council of Trade and Plantations, June 10, 1699, Burlington, CSP, with enclosure: Proclamation by the Governor of the East and West Jersies, forbidding assistance to be given to the Scotch expedition.

94. Memorandum of Papers relating to the Scotch settlement on the Isthmus of Darien, May 22, 1699, Whitehall, CSP, with enclosures including a copy of the Memorial of the Spanish Ambassador, a copy of a Memorial on behalf of the Company of Scotland in defense of its settlement at Darien, and an extract from the Scottish Act of Parliament for establishing an East India Company in Scotland.

95. Extract of a letter from Porto Bello, October 8, 1699, CSP. For identification of author as Heathcote, see Orr, *Scotland, Darien and the Atlantic World*, 70.

96. Memorial in defence of the legality of the proceedings of the Scots Company at Darien, n.d., NAS GD 45/1/161. Undated, but this seems to be the defense that the Board of Trade refers to on May 22, 1699, hence my 1699 date.

97. Howse and Thrower, *A Buccaneers Atlas*, Appendix B, 283–285.

98. Memorial in defence of the legality of the proceedings of the Scots Company at Darien, n.d., NAS GD 45/1/161.

99. Memorandum of Report upon the Scotch Settlement at Darien, May 26, 1699, CSP.

100. Memorandum of Report upon the Scotch Settlement at Darien, May 26, 1699, CSP.

101. Memorandum of Report upon the Scotch Settlement at Darien, May 26, 1699, CSP.

102. Memorandum of Report upon the Scotch Settlement at Darien, May 26, 1699, CSP.

103. William Paterson, undaunted by the Company of Scotland's failure in Darién, in 1701 proposed to William III a new colony on the isthmus, emphasizing that the English could extract far more wealth from the region's mines than did the Spanish, because while the Spanish "employed, near 2,000 negroes," there was "room enough . . . for more than ten times as many," which the English, "who can find and afford negroes at a sixth part they usually cost the Spaniards, would be able to secure." Paterson, "A Proposal to Plant a Colony in Darien," 152. Armitage sees Paterson's willingness to turn from the Company of Scotland to William as evidence that he was a "cynical" "turncoat." Armitage, "The Scottish Vision of Empire," 113, 116. But Paterson's efforts had been less on behalf of Scotland than in service of his idea that a free port, with freedom of conscience and easy naturalization, at such an important juncture, would benefit the trading world.

104. Gallup-Diaz, *The Door of the Seas*, 117–140, quotes 127, 140.

105. Gallup-Diaz, *The Door of the Seas*, 146–148, 156, 164.

106. Watt, *Price of Scotland.*

Chapter 7

1. That fantasy was akin to the process Ernesto Bassi describes in which Cartageneros a century later imagined transferring their loyalty (and their city) to Great Britain. That they could imagine such a transfer testifies to the continued importance of Jamaica's and Cartagena's integration, which Bassi explores in detail. *An Aqueous Territory: Sailor Geographies and New Granada's Transimperial Greater Caribbean World* (Durham, N.C.: Duke University Press, 2016).

2. Consejo de Indias a V[uestra] M[a]g[esta]d, June 26, 1694, AGI, Patronato 271 R. 7 (2).

3. For an examination of the decisions of Spanish American merchants, see Aaron Alejandro Olivas, "The Global Politics of the Transatlantic Slave Trade During the War of the Spanish Succession, 1700–1715," in Francisco Eissa-Barroso and Ainara Vázquez Varela, eds., *Early Bourbon Spanish America: Politics and Society in a Forgotten Era (1700–1759)* (Leiden: Brill, 2013), 85–109.

4. Governor Sir William Beeston to Lords of Trade and Plantations. July 4, 1696, CSP.

5. In 1696 a small Spanish vessel sent express from Cuba to the president of Santo Domingo stopped at Port Royal for water. The commander of the boat told Beeston what he knew about French activities in the region, information that Beeston forwarded to London. Beeston to the Duke of Shrewsbury, September 18, 1696, CSP. See also Beeston to William Blathwayt, June 19, 1696, CSP.

6. Beeston to the Duke of Shrewsbury, July 22, 1696, CSP.

7. Governor Sir William Beeston to the Lords of Trade and Plantations, July 4, 1696, CSP.

8. Representation of George Kast to the King in Council, December 26, 1695, CSP.

9. Representation of George Kast to the King in Council, December 26, 1695, CSP.

10. Representation of George Kast to the King in Council, December 26, 1695, CSP.

11. Governor Sir William Beeston to William Blathwayt, June 19, 1696, CSP.

12. Minutes of the Council of Jamaica, June 20, 1696, CSP.

13. Minutes of the Council of Jamaica, July 20, 1696, CSP.

14. Governor Sir William Beeston to Lords of Trade and Plantations, July 22, 1696, CSP.

15. Gilbert Heathcote to James Vernon, April 15, 1696, CSP.

16. Mr. Heathcote to Council of Trade and Plantations, February 8, 1699, CSP.

17. Circular Letter from William Popple to the Governors of all the Colonies, November 30, 1697, CSP.

18. Governor Sir William Beeston to Council of Trade and Plantations, December 9, 1697, CSP.

19. Mr. Heathcote to Council of Trade and Plantations, enclosing abstract of recent advices from Jamaica, February 8, 1699, CSP.

20. Pettigrew, *Freedom's Debt*, 58.

21. Ritchie, *Captain Kidd and the War Against the Pirates.*

22. Olivas, "Loyalty and Disloyalty to the Bourbon Dynasty," 42; "Asiento con Juan Ducasse en nombre de la Compañia Real de Guinea del reino de Francia," Madrid, 1701, AGI, Contaduría 261, ff. 1239–1305, reproduction in David Marley, ed., *Reales asientos y licencias para la introducción de esclavos negros a la América Española, 1676–1789* (Windsor, Ontario: Rolston-Bain, 1985), n.p.

23. Stein and Stein, *Silver, Trade, and War*, 121. For further emphasis on the asiento as motive for the War of the Spanish Succession, see Andrea Weindl, "The *Asiento de Negros* and International Law," *Journal of the History of International Law* 10 (2008), 229–257, 242.

24. Stein and Stein, *Silver, Trade, and War*, 121; Olivas, "Loyalty and Disloyalty to the Bourbon Dynasty," 36–37; O'Malley, *Final Passages*, 168.

25. Circular Letter from the Earl of Nottingham to all the Governors, etc., in America, May 7, 1702, CSP.

26. Benbow to Vernon, May 13, 1702, CSP; Benbow to Vernon, June 1, 1702, CSP. The royal orders had been dated October 23, 1701. For Beckford's role in the RAC, see Pettigrew, *Freedom's Debt*. Sigfrido Vázquez Cienfuegos notes the arrival of the letter in Havana. "Cuba durante la Guerra de Sucesión Española: Algunos aspectos militares," in *La Guerra de Sucesión en España y América* (Madrid: Editorial Deimos, 2001), 321.

27. Benbow to Vernon, May 13, 1702, CSP; Benbow to Vernon, June 1, 1702, CSP.

28. Benbow to Vernon, May 13, 1702, CSP; Benbow to Vernon, June 1, 1702, CSP.

29. Lt.-Governor Beckford to Mr. Secretary Vernon, May 15, 1702, CSP. For evidence that Beckford was correct that instructions were coming to Bourbon Spanish America from Paris rather than from Madrid, see Olivas, "Loyalty and Disloyalty to the Bourbon Dynasty," 32–63.

30. Lt.-Governor Beckford to Mr. Secretary Vernon, May 15, 1702, CSP. Marrero emphasizes the novelty of the French asiento in allowing French merchants into the ports to trade "as subjects" more so than stressing the monopoly. Levi Marrero, *Cuba: Economía y sociedad* (Madrid: Editorial Playor, 1978), 6:14. When Spanish officials ignored English suggestions that they resist the Bourbons, Beckford believed that English Caribbean governors should obey their instructions to issue commissions, and he sent nine privateers to the Isthmus of Panama to prevent Peru's silver from reaching Spanish and French ships. Lt.-Gov. Beckford to the Earl of Nottingham, October 16, 1702, CSP.

31. In addition to the discussion that follows, see John B. Hattendorf, "Alliance, Encirclement, and Attrition: British Grand Strategy in the War of the Spanish Succession, 1702–1713," in Paul Kennedy, ed., *Grand Strategies in War and Peace* (New Haven, Conn.: Yale University Press, 1991), 11–29. The timing of the correspondence makes clear that this idea originated in the Caribbean (for the English) and was based on observing the Dutch.

32. Quary to the Council of Trade and Plantations, July 25, 1703, CSP. Col. Quary to the Council of Trade and Plantations, August 14, 1703, CSP.

33. William Penn to the Council of Trade and Plantations, April 21, 1703, CSP. Penn expressed these concerns in the course of requesting permission to construct a mint in Pennsylvania.

34. Governor Sir B. Granville to [the Earl of Nottingham], August 3, 1703, CSP. They were prohibited from trading ammunition.

35. Gilbert Heathcote to the [Council of Trade and Plantations], August 28, 1703, CSP.

36. For the intertwining over time of merchant interest and imperial interest, see John Brewer, *The Sinews of Power: War, Money, and the English State, 1688–1783* (Cambridge, Mass.: Harvard University Press, 1988). For an evocative account of wartime smuggling, see Thomas M. Truxes, *Defying Empire: Trading with the Enemy in Colonial New York* (New Haven, Conn.: Yale University Press, 2008).

37. Anon., Reasons against prohibiting trade and commerce with Spain in the West Indies to be communicated to the [Privy] Council, Received by the Board of Trade, March 18, 1703, CSP; R. Warre to William Popple, Whitehall, March 20, 1703, CSP.

38. Council of Trade and Plantations to the Queen, enclosure in Council of Trade and Plantations to the Earl of Nottingham, October 29, 1703, CSP.

39. Council of Trade and Plantations to the Earl of Nottingham, November 9, 1703, CSP.

40. Thomas Handasyd arrived to replace Beckford as Jamaica's governor in December 1702 and remained in office until 1711. Because of Jamaica's strategic location he played a major role in managing Anglo-Spanish relations during the war. Peter Beckford to [the Earl of Nottingham], Jamaica, December 8, 1702, CSP.

41. Lt.-Gov. Handasyd to the Earl of Nottingham, November 27, 1703, CSP.

42. Draught of Letter from the Earl of Nottingham to several Governors in America, as altered by the Council of Trade, enclosure in W. Popple to Richard Warr, February 16, 1704, CSP. English privateers could still seize any Dutch merchants caught trading with the French.

43. Nottingham anticipated that as soon as Charles/Carlos was "declared by the Emperor King of Spain . . . , his subjects in the West Indies" would "esteem us their best friends, who have so eminently contributed to deliver them and their countrymen in Spain from a French slavery." Earl of Nottingham to Governor Codrington, September 14, 1703, CSP.

44. Minutes of Council of Jamaica, November 25, 1703, CSP. For "pretense" see Lt. Gov. Handasyd to the Council of Trade and Plantations, November 27, 1703, CSP. To his superiors, Handasyd characterized the "settling the Crown on the House of Austria" as an effort to help Spanish Americans "defend their Laws and liberties." Lt.-Gov Handasyd to the Earl of Nottingham, November 27, 1703, CSP. Minutes of Council of Jamaica, December 7, 1703, CSP.

45. Marrero, *Cuba*, 6:73.

46. Marrero, *Cuba*, 6:73. Marrero names in particular Sargent Major Lorenzo de Prado Carvajal.

47. Marrero, *Cuba*, 6:74.

48. Handasyd to Council of Trade and Plantations, September 17, 1704, CSP. Council of Trade and Plantations to Sir Charles Hedges, May 2, 1704, CSP, includes enclosures ii and iii: original instructions to privateers, June 1, 1702, and additional instructions to privateers, May 4, 1704; Handasyd to Sir Charles Hedges, September 17, 1704, CSP. Council of Trade and Plantations to Handasyd, November 30, 1704, CSP; Secretary Hedges to Handaside [*sic*], December 7, 1704, CSP. He acknowledged receipt in Handasyd to Hedges, February 27, 1705, CSP.

49. Olivas, "Loyalty and Disloyalty to the Bourbon Dynasty," 32–63.

50. Rear Admiral Whetstone to the Secretaries of State, H.M.S. *Suffolk* at Jamaica, July 18, 1705, CSP.

51. P. Dyer to the Council of Trade and Plantations, September 1, 1705, CSP. He named as victims, in particular, the Boston privateer Isaack Hambleton and Abraham Hiams, "an English Jew." The crown responded to Dyer's petition (which begged freedom for the rest of the prisoners) by instructing Handasyd to "procure . . . the[ir] liberty" via a prisoner exchange and to threaten the Spanish with "the same severtys" if such treatment continued. Hedges to Handasyd, October 4, 1705, CSP.

52. Hedges instructed Handasyd to emphasize that English promises of assistance depended on Spanish creoles' cooperation. Mr. Secretary Hedges to Governor Handasyd, January 17, 1706, CSP; H.M. Instructions for General Handasyd, January14, 1706, CSP.

53. Mr. Secretary Hedges to Governor Handasyd, January 17, 1706, CSP; H.M. Instructions for General Handasyd, January 14, 1706, CSP.

54. Mr. Secretary Hedges to Governor Handasyd, January 17, 1706, CSP; H.M. Instructions for General Handasyd, January 14, 1706, CSP.

55. "An Account of the French monopolizing the Spanish West India Trade," 1706, enclosure in Mr. Secretary Hedges to Governor Handasyd, January 17, 1706, CSP. Secretary Hedges repeated his instructions in letters to the governors of Barbados, New York, Massachusetts, Maryland, Virginia, Jamaica, and the Leeward Islands in September 1706, instructing them to take any available opportunity to persuade Spanish officials. Mr. Secretary Hedges to Governor Sir B. Granville, September 3, 1706, CSP.

56. Weindl, "The *Asiento de Negros* and International Law," 243.

57. Vázquez Cienfuegos, "Cuba durante la Guerra de Sucesión Española," 319.

58. Marrero, *Cuba*, 6:73. The declaration of curfew was dated April 19, 1706.

59. Marrero, *Cuba*, 6:73.

60. Governor Handasyd to the Council of Trade and Plantations, January 29, 1707, CSP.

61. Governor of Carthagena to Sir J. Jennings, January 5, 1707, CSP.

62. Handasyd to Council of Trade and Plantations, January 29, 1707, CSP. Despite Handasyd's repeated requests, "we are not yet supply'd with woollens for that trade, which [he] much wonder[ed] at," given English wool merchants' interest in promoting Spanish American trade.

63. Handasyd to Earl of Sunderland, June 4, 1710, CSP; Handasyd to Board of Trade, June 4, 1710, CSP.

64. Handasyd to the Board of Trade, July 22, 1710, CSP.

65. Handasyd to the Board of Trade, October 3, 1710, CSP. The following spring, Handasyd reported that trade was dead "and like to be worse" if they could not stop the French from trading directly to Peru and the Rio de la Plata, "from whence they supply the Spaniards with negros, stores and other necessary's." Handasyd to the Board of Trade, March 20, 1711, CSP.

66. In 1694, Beeston reported a French ship landing only seven leagues from Port Royal, which made away with 370 enslaved people in addition to money and goods. Lieutenant-Governor Sir William Beeston to Lords of Trade and Plantations, February 12, 1694, CSP. In 1703, French privateers took a number of ships "laden with negroes . . . of very great value." Lt. Gov. Handasyd to the Council of Trade and Plantations, October 5, 1703, CSP. Another account said that the French had acquired 1,100 captives (from Guinea) in this seizure. Journal of Trade and Plantations, November 15, 1703, CSP. Late in the war, two Dutch privateers captured a French ship with 380 enslaved Africans on board. Handasyd to the Board of Trade, March 25, 1710, CSP.

67. Merchants trading to Barbados to the Council of Trade and Plantations, received December 8, 1703, CSP.

68. In 1703, one officer begged London for warships. If the French seized any English islands, not only would England lose customs and "the lives of so many dutifull subjects" but "the French [would] become masters of so great a number of negroes" that they could make "the French part of Hispaniola . . . a very important and formidable Settlement." Lieut. Coll [Wm] Thomas to the Council of Trade and Plantations, November 16, 1703, CSP.

69. Lt.-Gov. Handasyd to the Earl of Nottingham, November 27, 1703, CSP.

70. English sources consistently used "the people" to refer to White colonists. Lt. Governor Handasyd to the Council of Trade and Plantations, February 6, 1704, CSP. In 1707, Handasyd reduced his estimate, reporting that "the enemy" had taken no more than twenty-eight slaves during the war. Handasyd to Council of Trade and Plantations, November 7, 1707, CSP; Handasyd to Council of Trade and Plantations, October 27, 1708. In August 1703, Thomas Bryan received permission to absent himself from the Assembly because the French had "taken off several of his negroes." *Journal of Assembly of Jamaica*, August 2–4, 1703, CSP.

71. In February 1709, French privateers took thirty-two slaves and three sloops during a raid on the north side of Jamaica. Handasyd to the Council of Trade and Plantations, February 1, 1709, CSP. Privateers targeted enslaved men and women as plunder beyond the Caribbean. Virginia's acting governor Edmund Jenings reported that a recent visitor had come from Danish St. Thomas, where, because it was a neutral port, he had been able to converse with "several French privateers." They told him that "they would certainly attack Virginia this spring," where they expected "to find good booty in negros, plate and other goods." The French privateers had tried to get this unnamed mariner to pilot them into the James, York, and Rappahannock Rivers, offering him £100 besides "a full share" of the plunder. Col. Jenings to the Council of Trade and Plantations, Virginia, March 21, 1709, CSP.

72. Handasyd to Hedges, December 17, 1704, CSP.

73. Handasyd to Council of Trade and Plantations, December 31, 1704, CSP.

74. Council of Trade and Plantations to Handasyd, March 6, 1705, CSP.

75. Council of Trade and Plantations to Handasyd, July 31, 1707, CSP, and enclosure: Account of two privateers. Handasyd secured Charles Knott and Benjamin Scrivner, the two privateering captains accused of targeting Spanish Americans' canoes, but because no one brought a case against them and they brought letters from both Portobelo and Cartagena testifying to their acceptable "behaviour on the coast," he could only rescind their commissions and have "very secure persons" sign bonds worth £1,500 for each of them. Handasyd to Council of Trade and Plantations, November 9, 1707, CSP.

76. Handasyd to Council of Trade and Plantations, December 5, 1707, CSP.

77. Council of Trade and Plantations to Handasyd, August 13, 1708, CSP. Countering a narrative that metropolitan officials tried to control a lawless Caribbean of "no peace," here Caribbean officials begged for regulation from London officials, who denied it.

78. Dummer to Popple, August 2, 1708, CSP.

79. Memorial from Mr. Dummer concerning the Act for encourageing Trade to America, August 18, 1708, CSP.

80. Dummer to Popple, London, January 17, 1709, CSP; Dummer to Popple, April 1, 1709, CSP, and enclosure: W. Bignall to [Dummer], Kingston, January 17, 1708.

81. Mr. Dummer to Mr. Popple, London, April 1, 1709, CSP, and enclosure: W. William Bignall to [Dummer], Kingston, January 17, 1708.

82. Council of Trade and Plantations to Governor Handasyd, April 21, 1709, CSP.

83. Governor Handasyd to the Council of Trade and Plantations, October 20, 1709, CSP. For the higher numbers, see Dummer to Popple, January 31, 1710, CSP; and Council of Trade and Plantations to the Earl of Sunderland, May 16, 1710, CSP.

84. Dummer to Popple, January 31, 1710, CSP. Board of Trade to Governor Handasyd, April 4, 1710, CSP. Handasyd to the Board of Trade, March 25, 1710, CSP. Handasyd to the Board of Trade, June 4, 1710, CSP. Handasyd to the Board of Trade, July 22, 1710, CSP, with enclosure: "Governor Handasyd's Proclamation for pardoning certain pirates, under Capt. Michael, on the coast of Porto Bello, etc., on condition that they return to Jamaica within 60 days and take the oaths of allegiance, etc.," St. Jago de la Vega, November 19, 1709.

85. Hamilton to Board of Trade, October 10, 1712, CSP.

86. Hamilton to Board of Trade, October 10, 1712, CSP.

87. Governor Lord A. Hamilton to [the Earl of Dartmouth], October 20, 1712. CSP. The privateers had acted "against what I presume was the intent of the American Act of Parliament, tho' they seem to have evaded the letter of it."

88. Governor Lord A. Hamilton to [the Earl of Dartmouth], October 20, 1712. CSP.

89. Contemporary observers and scholars have since noted that piracy exploded after the War of the Spanish Succession ended and its privateers were decommissioned, but not that the process of turning pirate began in the midst of the war. Charles Johnson, *A General History of the Pyrates, from their First Rise and Settlement in the Island of Providence, to the Present Time* (London: T. Warner, 1724), preface; Rediker, *Villains of All Nations*, 19–37.

90. Naturalization of Francisco Angola Moso de Campo Capn Primo, Juan de Frank (or French), Lewis Angola, Antony Congo, and Antony de Leivra, signed by Inchiquin, September 26, 1690, JA 1B/11/1/12, f. 44. The nineteenth-century index to these naturalizations mistranscribed them, hiding the men's African place names.

91. Lieutenant-Governor Sir William Beeston to Lords of Trade and Plantations, February 12, 1694, CSP.

92. Governor William Beeston, Patent to Sr. James Castile to fortify his dwelling house, JA 1B/1/1A, patents vol. 12, 144v.

93. Lt.-Governor Beckford to the Council of Trade and Plantations, August 25, 1702, CSP. It was between the two wars that Beeston had complained about the frequency of enslaved Jamaicans' flights to Cuba. Governor Sir William Beeston to Council of Trade and Plantations, February 8, 1699, CSP.

94. Minutes of Council in Assembly of Jamaica, August 20, 1702, CSP.

95. Lt.-Governor Beckford to the Council of Trade and Plantations, September 22, 1702, CSP. In September 1703, the Assembly presented Capt. John King with a £100 reward for commanding "the parties against the rebellious negroes." *Journal of Assembly of Jamaica*, September 29, 1703, CSP.

96. Governor Handasyd to the Council of Trade and Plantations, July 28, 1704, CSP.

97. Handasyd to Hedges, February 27, 1705, CSP.

98. Hamilton to the Board of Trade, October 10, 1712, CSP.

99. Address of the Council and Assembly of Jamaica to Governor Lord A. Hamilton, November 8, 1712, CSP, enclosure, November 22, 1712.

100. Extracts from three memorials (by Peter Holt, etc.) relating to illegal trade carried on between Curaçoa, St. Thomas, and the British Plantations in America, enclosure in Circular letter from the Council of Trade and Plantations to the Governors and Proprietors of Plantations, January 19, 1710, CSP.

101. Merchants and Planters concerned in the Island of Jamaica to the Queen, [October] 1703, CSP.

102. Sir G. Heathcote and Sir B. Gracedieu to the Council of Trade and Plantations, July 4, 1704, CSP. Edmund Dummer wrote likewise that "from Jamaica they say the saylors are all gone to Curacoa." E. Dummer to Mr. Popple, October 12, 1703, CSP.

103. Vice-Admiral Graydon to the Earl of Nottingham, October 8, 1703, CSP.

104. At the same time, the Council and Assembly also complained that he had "permitted H.M. ships to carry negroes and other merchandize to trade," violating his instructions and threatening the "ruin of all merchant traders." Address of the Council and Assembly of Jamaica to Governor Lord A. Hamilton, November 8, 1712, CSP, enclosure November 22, 1712.

105. Patents Index 1, Jamaica Archives, Spanish Town.

106. Benton describes early modern shipping lanes as "jurisdictional corridors" in *A Search for Sovereignty*, 104–161.

107. The primary problem with the law, according to the solicitor general, was that it obliterated the crown's "prerogative in making denizens within that Island." Solicitor General to the Council of Trade and Plantations, November 11, 1703, CSP. For ships as extensions of jurisdictional space, see Lauren Benton and Adam Clulow, "Legal Encounters and the Origins of Global Law," in *The Cambridge World History*, Vol. 6, ed. Jerry H. Bentley, Sanjay Subrahmanyam, and Merry E. Wiesner-Hanks (Cambridge: Cambridge University Press, 2015), 90–91; Benton, "Legal Spaces of Empire: Piracy and the Origins of Ocean Regionalism," *Comparative Studies in Society and History* 47 (2005), 704–706.

108. Jamaica was not the only colony whose officials wished to expand the benefits of naturalization beyond what metropolitan legal experts believed permissible. The solicitor general thought the 1705 Virginia Act for Naturalization, which allowed the governor "to make Aliens and Forreigners to be upon the same foot as the naturall born subjects are," was "too great a power to be lodged in any one person," even a governor. Moreover, the act might prove "prejudiciall to our Trade and Navigacon, if the persons so naturaliz'd in Virginia" could trade as subjects, but not always act as a subjects in other matters, which "seem[s] to be contradictory to the notion of naturalizing, which is, investing them with all the rights and priviledges of any H.M. naturall free-born subject there." Sir James Mountague (Solicitor General) to the Board of Trade, November 7, 1710, CSP.

109. Handasyd to Hedges, February 27, 1705, CSP. Copy of the protection, written February 22 "to some French deserters lying concealed at Boca Toxo on the Spanish coast," is in Handasyd to Council of Trade and Plantations, February 27, 1705, CSP. He notably failed to mention their religious adherence, but their willingness to take the English oaths suggests Protestantism.

110. Handasyd to Council of Trade and Plantations, June 11, 1705, CSP.

111. Handasyd to Council of Trade and Plantations, November 1705, CSP.

112. He still had not received the news of the repeal by January 29, 1707. Handasyd to the Council of Trade and Plantations, January 29, 1707, CSP.

113. Col. Laws to Council of Trade and Plantations, August 24, 1709, CSP.

114. Council of Trade and Plantations to the Lord High Treasurer of England, August 30, 1709, CSP.

115. Lilyam Padrón Reyes, "Entre el deber y la negociación: Milicias de indios en el suroriente cubano, siglos XVII–XVIII," *Temas Americanistas* 43 (2019), 1–26, quotation 7–8. I have been unable to find clear evidence of free Black militiamen during the War of the Spanish Succession. In 1704 Governor Handasyd used an imaginary scenario of Jewish and Black militia officers (which "might tend to the utter destruction of the Island") to disparage Assembly members' attempts to exempt themselves from service. Handasyd to Sir Charles Hedges, December 17, 1704, CSP.

116. For the outline of the story that follows I have relied on Díaz's elegant *The Virgin, the King, and the Royal Slaves*, 285–298.

117. Díaz, *The Virgin, The King, and the Royal Slaves*, 287.

118. Díaz identifies the governor as Joseph Canales. His residencia names him Jose Canales Caballero. Residencias de la Gobernación de La Habana, 1710, AGI, Escribanía, 92b–c, 93b–c.

119. Díaz, *The Virgin, the King, and the Royal Slaves*, 291–292.

120. This is based on Díaz's translation and interpretation. *The Virgin, the King, and the Royal Slaves*, 292, cites Memorial of Diego de Rosas, [Madrid, ca. 1709], "Demanda," AGI, Escribanía 93a, ff. 3–5, AGI-ESC 93A.

121. Díaz, *The Virgin, the King, and the Royal Slaves*, 294–295.

122. Díaz, *The Virgin, the King, and the Royal Slaves*, 285.

Conclusion

1. Duke of Shrewsbury to Council of Trade and Plantations, November 23, 1697, CSP, with enclosures, including several letters from Admiral Nevill to "the Governor of Havana" and "the General of the Galleons."

2. Duke of Shrewsbury to Council of Trade and Plantations, November 23, 1697, CSP, with enclosures, including several letters from Admiral Nevill to "the Governor of Havana" and "the General of the Galleons."

3. Córdoba's actions may have convinced royal officials that he was the right man to reestablish imperial authority in Cartagena after the French sacked it and the former governor disappeared. Córdoba was sent from Cuba in 1702 to be president of Panama (with oversight of Cartagena), a position he held until 1712, when he joined the Council of the Indies itself. "Diego Córdoba y Lasso de la Vega," Real Academia de la Historia, n.d., https://dbe.rah.es/biografias/26099/diego-cordoba-y-lasso-de-la-vega.

4. L. C. Green and Olive P. Dickason, *The Law of Nations and the New World* (Edmonton: University of Alberta Press, 1989). Those treatises (Francisco de Vitoria, Hugo Grotius) presumed that humanity shared membership in a community that transcended multiple bodies politic whose particularities might differ. Caribbean actors and imperial officials sometimes drew on natural law theory, such as when members of Bartholomew Sharpe's crew used the Tule leader Andreas's putative sovereignty to justify their piracy against the Spanish in Panama and the Pacific. They referred to merchant law, the texts of recent treaties, and their understanding of Christianity's requirements for the treatment of fellow Christians and the particular ways these principles were shaped by the Caribbean context.

5. Jennifer Pitts, *Boundaries of the International: Law and Empire* (Cambridge, Mass.: Harvard University Press, 2018); Goetz, *Baptism of Early Virginia*; Martínez, *Genealogical Fictions*.

6. Continental European maritime law grew out of Roman civil law with adaptations developed by merchants. Beginning in the fourteenth century, in response to the specific needs of traders, English admiralty law evolved from that merchant law tradition, separate from English common law (and more closely related to continental law). Maritime and admiralty law provided for quick trials that would not interfere with voyages, and procedures that were recognized by various European mariners and courts. Thus it was intended to function in an international realm—as an "international law"—in that recognition of its legitimacy spanned imperial and national borders. Helen Crump, *Colonial Admiralty Jurisdiction in the Seventeenth Century* (London: Longmans, Green and Co., 1931).

7. Emer de Vattel's 1758 *Le droit des gens* was translated into English the following year as *The Law of Nations; or Principles of the Law of Nature: Applied to the Conduct and Affairs of Nations and Sovereigns* (London: J. Newbery, 1759). For a recent assessment of scholarship on global legal history, see Lauren Benton, "Beyond Anachronism: Histories of International Law and Global Legal Politics," *Journal of the History of International Law* 21 (2019), 7–40.

8. For the importance of such protections in interpolity law, see Lauren Benton and Adam Clulow, "Empires and Protection: Making Interpolity Law in the Early Modern World," *Journal of Global History* 12 (2017), 74–92.

9. *The Laws of Barbados Collected in One Volume* (London: William Rawlin, 1699), 160.

10. Albert O. Hirschman, *The Passions and the Interests: Political Arguments for Capitalism Before Its Triumph* (1977; Princeton, N.J.: Princeton University Press, 2013).

11. Martti Koskenniemi, "Empire and International Law: The Real Spanish Contribution," *University of Toronto Law Journal* 61 (2011), 1–36, quotations 32, 19.

12. Antony Anghie, *Imperialism, Sovereignty, and the Making of International Law* (New York: Cambridge University Press, 2005). Marilyn Lake and Henry Reynolds point to the decades surrounding the turn of the twentieth century as a period of transnational reassertion of whiteness and a "color line" as a means of drawing distinctions separating nations into different categories under international law. They presume an earlier precedent correlating national and racial categories. Lake and Reynolds, *Drawing the Global Colour Line: White Men's Countries and the International Challenge of Racial Equality* (New York: Cambridge University Press, 2008).

13. Julia Gaffield provides a helpful summary of this scholarship in "The Racialization of International Law after the Haitian Revolution: The Holy See and National Sovereignty," *American Historical Review* 125 (2020), 841–868.

14. Benton, *A Search for Sovereignty*, 149–161, quotation 157. Benton sees English-inflected law of nations as emerging especially out of Atlantic prize courts. See also Benton and Lisa Ford, *Rage for Order: The British Empire and the Origins of International Law, 1800–1850* (Cambridge, Mass.: Harvard University Press, 2016).

15. Koskenniemi, "Empire and International Law," 1.

16. Paterson, "A Proposal to Plant a Colony," 152.

17. Brown, *Good Wives, Nasty Wenches, and Anxious Patriarchs*; Goetz, *Baptism of Early Virginia*; Martínez, *Genealogical Fictions*.

18. Jennifer Pitts, "Empire and Legal Universalisms in the Eighteenth Century," *American Historical Review* 117 (2012), 92–121, quotation, 94; Gaffield, "The Racialization of International Law," 843.

19. Gaffield, "The Racialization of International Law," 843.

20. Pitts, "Empire and Legal Universalisms," 95.

21. Ntina Tzouvala, *Capitalism as Civilisation: A History of International Law* (New York: Cambridge University Press, 2020), 23–30.

22. Sir Robert Southwell to [Daniel Finch, 2nd Earl of Nottingham], March 23, 1688/9, London, William Blathwayt Papers, The Huntington Library, San Marino, California, Box 3.

23. Elena A. Schneider, *The Occupation of Havana: War, Trade, and Slavery in the Atlantic World* (Chapel Hill: University of North Carolina Press, 2018).

24. Devyn Spence Benson notes the persistence of antiracist ideology in Cuba in the nineteenth and twentieth centuries, even as she argues that antiracist language enabled and hid continued racism. *Antiracism in Cuba: The Unfinished Revolution* (Chapel Hill: University of North Carolina Press, 2016). Marixa Lasso explores how a "myth of racial harmony" became a fundamental part of Colombian nationalism during the Age of Revoluion. *Myths of Harmony: Race and Republicanism during the Age of Revolution: Colombia, 1795–1831* (Pittsburgh: University of Pittsburgh Press, 2007).

25. David Armitage makes it clear that the founders of the United States attended to the need to gain inclusion into the European-dominated international community in *The Declaration of Independence: A Global History*.

26. An Act to Establish an Uniform Rule of Naturalization (1790).

27. Gaffield, "The Racialization of International Law."

INDEX

Maps are indicated by page numbers followed by *map.*

ACKNOWLEDGMENTS

I began this book with a Barra Sabbatical Fellowship at the McNeil Center for Early American Studies. The McNeil Center's collegial and stimulating environment made it the ideal place to begin thinking about the questions I have lived with in the many years since. The History Department at Texas A&M has been generous in funding research and travel. An Internal Faculty Fellowship from the Glasscock Center for Humanities Research and a Texas A&M Faculty Development Leave each provided semester teaching releases.

I appreciate the help of librarians and archivists at the Archivo General de Indias, the British Library, the Huntington Library, the Jamaica Archives and Records Department, the National Archives of the UK, the National Library of Jamaica, the National Library of Scotland, the Senate House Library at the University of London, and Texas A&M University's Sterling Evans Library. James Robertson provided welcome and an introduction to research in Jamaica. Gabriela Iturralde Espejo read with me the first Spanish documents I brought back from Seville. Her help was crucial at that initial stage, and deciphering documents together over coffee made an otherwise often tedious process fun.

My writing group has seen this project through from beginning to end, providing repeated critiques, patience with draft after draft, support, friendship, and the occasional kick in the pants. Changing over the years as people have come and gone, it has included Julia Kirk Blackwelder, Cynthia Bouton, Kate Carté, Sylvia Hoffert, Angela Pulley Hudson, James Rosenheim, and Rebecca Hartkopf Schloss. Evan Haefeli organized a manuscript workshop funded by the Caribbean and Atlantic Studies Glasscock Center working group. The participants in that workshop—Cynthia Bouton, Bradley Dixon, Alejandro García-Montón, Evan Haefeli, Robert Olwell, James Sidbury, and Bartolomé Yun-Casalilla—improved the manuscript in ways large and small. Most importantly, they helped me see the book as a whole. During the pandemic, writing together over Zoom with Shona Jackson, Joseph Jewell, Sonia Hernandez, and Laura Oviedo provided structure, company, and a sounding board. I thank Joseph for organizing the group and the Glasscock Center for the incentive to do so.

In presenting chapter drafts at conferences and workshops, I received especially helpful criticism from Herman Bennett, Kristen Block, Alex Byrd, Jorge Cañizares-Esguerra, Max Edelson, Julie Hardwick, Josh Piker, Steve Pincus, Casey Schmitt, Nancy Shoemaker, Owen Stanwood, Alan Tully, and Molly Warsh. Marisa Fuentes and Brett Rushforth asked key questions that helped me see my sources anew, and Marcus Rediker spurred me to think carefully about what I was trying to do and why.

I have benefited enormously from the kinds of serendipitous encounters at archives and conferences that we have all missed the last two years. Such meetings led to generative conversations with Kristie Flannery, Maria Alessandra Bollettino, Holly Brewer, Alison Games, Kris Lane, Elizabeth Mancke, Carla Rahn Phillips, Daniel Richter, Jessica Chopin Roney, and Peter Wood. An anonymous reader encouraged me to widen my argument and at the same time cautioned me against overstating my claims. Natalie Zacek and Penny Livesay helped me clarify and tighten my arguments. Robert Lockhart was an attentive and generous editor, flexible through the unpredictable schedules of the last two years. All errors and misjudgments remain my own.

I apologize to everyone whose emails I did not answer. Several years ago I realized that I could not answer all the emails and also finish a book. My family has been supportive and (mostly) patient, if baffled, by the seemingly never-ending process. Ella and Coleman Maxwell have put up with this book for as long as they can remember. Their relief at its completion likely rivals mine. I could not have done it without Jon. I dedicate the book to my parents, Craig Bond Hatfield and Nancy Lee Clark Hatfield, who taught me to ask lots of questions and to accept not knowing all the answers.